Legal Self-Help Series

DIVORCE YOURSELF

THE NATIONAL NO-FAULT NO-LAWYER DIVORCE HANDBOOK

LEGALLY VALID IN ALL 50 STATES AND WASHINGTON D.C.

DANIEL SITARZ
Attorney-at-Law

Copyright 1990 Daniel Sitarz

All rights reserved. This publication may not be reproduced in whole or in part by any means without prior written consent.

Manufactured in the United States.

Library of Congress Catalog Card Number 90-32651

ISBN 0-935755-04-7

Library of Congress Cataloging-in-Publication Data
    Sitarz, Dan, 1948-
    Divorce Yourself: The National No-Fault No-Lawyer Divorce Handbook / Daniel Sitarz
    (Legal Self-Help Series) includes index; bibliographical references
    ISBN 0-935755-04-7 : $24.95
    1. No-fault divorce--United States--Popular Works. 2. Divorce--United States--Popular Works. I. Title. II. Series.
    KF535.Z9S57 1990   346.7301'66--dc20   [347.306166]   LC90-32651

This publication is designed to provide accurate and authoritative information in regard to the subject matter covered. It is sold with the understanding that the publisher and author are not engaged in rendering legal, accounting, or other professional services. If legal advice or other expert assistance is required, the services of a competent professional person should be sought.

From a Declaration of Principles jointly adopted by a Committee of the American Bar Association and a Committee of Publishers

DISCLAIMER

Because of possible unanticipated changes in governing statutes and case law relating to the application of any information contained in this book, the author, publisher, and any and all persons or entities involved in any way in the preparation, publication, sale, or distribution of this book disclaim all responsibility for the legal effects or consequences of any document prepared or action taken in reliance upon information contained in this book. No representations, either express or implied, are made or given regarding the legal consequences of the use of any information contained in this book. Purchasers and persons intending to use this book for the preparation of any legal documents are advised to check specifically on the current applicable laws in any jurisdiction in which they intend the documents to be effective. This book is not printed, published, sold, circulated, or distributed with the intention that it be used to procure or aid in the procurement of any legal effect or ruling in any jurisdiction in which such procurement or aid may be restricted by statute.

ACKNOWLEDGEMENT

This book would not have been possible without the dedicated and professional editorial assistance of Janet Harris Sitarz and Nancy Cottom. Their help is greatly appreciated.

NOVA PUBLISHING COMPANY
1103 West College Street
Carbondale, Illinois 62901

TABLE OF CONTENTS

PREFACE 5

INTRODUCTION 7

CHAPTER 1: DIVORCE AND THE LAW 9
    What is No-Fault Divorce? 10
    The Division of Marital Property 10
    Alimony and Maintenance 11
    The Changes in Child Custody 11
    The Child Support System 12
    Divorce in General 13
    The Divorce by Agreement 14
    Can You Do Your Own Divorce? 15
    How to Use This Book 17
    Mediation 18
    General Note Regarding Terminology 19

CHAPTER 2: PRELIMINARY MATTERS 21
    Preliminary Questionnaire 23
    Document Checklist 24
    Where Can You File For Your Divorce? 25
    What Will Be The Grounds For Your Divorce? 26
    Preliminary Marital Settlement Agreement Clauses 27
        Title and Introductory Clause 28
        Children Identification Clause 28
        Preliminary Explanation Clause 29
        General Agreement Clause 30
        Separation Clause 30

CHAPTER 3: DIVIDING YOUR PROPERTY AND BILLS 31
    Property Questionnaire 32
    Property Document Checklist 42
    Property Division Upon Divorce 43
        Community Property States 44
            Separate Property 44
            Community Property 46
        Equitable Distribution States 46
    Factors for Consideration in Property Divisions 49
    Note on Mississippi 49
    Considerations Regarding Specific Property 51
        The Family Home 51
        Retirement and Pension Plans 53
        Stock-option and Profit-sharing Plans 55
        Social Security Benefits 55
        Military and Federal Pensions and Benefits 55
        Cars and Other Vehicles 56
        Educational Degrees 56
    Property Division Worksheet 56
    Marital Settlement Agreement Clauses Regarding Property 61
        Property Division Clause (Property Not Listed) 61
        Property Division Clause (List Included) 62
        Division of Property (By Sale) 63
        Division of Bills (Bills Listed) 63
    Financial Statement 64

CHAPTER 4: ALIMONY, MAINTENANCE, AND SPOUSAL SUPPORT 71
    Alimony Questionnaire 72
    The Law of Alimony 74
    Factors for Consideration 75
    Marital Settlement Agreement Clauses Regarding Alimony 77
        No Alimony to Either Spouse Clause 77
        Alimony Payable in Monthly Payments Clause 78
        Alimony Payable in Lump-sum Payment Clause 79
        Life Insurance Clause 80
        Insurance Clause (Neither Spouse as Beneficiary) 80

CHAPTER 5: CHILD CUSTODY AND VISITATION 81
    Child Custody Questionnaire 82
    The Law of Child Custody and Visitation 86
        Types of Custody Arrangements 87
        Visitation 89
        Modification of Custody and Visitation Terms 90
    Factors for Consideration 91
    The Child's Bill of Rights 93

Child Custody Jurisdiction 94
Custody and Visitation Worksheet 95
Marital Settlement Agreement Clauses Regarding Child
Custody and Visitation 96
    Sole Custody and Visitation Clause (Basic Agreement)..... 97
    Sole Custody and Visitation (With Visitation Schedule) ... 97
    Child Custody and Visitation Clause (Joint Legal and
    Sole Physical Custody) 99
    Child Custody and Visitation Clause (Joint Legal and
    Physical Custody) 100

CHAPTER 6: CHILD SUPPORT 103
The Law of Child Support 104
Factors for Consideration 105
Enforcement and Modification of Child Support 107
General Child Support Guidelines 107
Child Support Worksheet 110
Minimum Child Support Guideline Chart 112
Marital Settlement Agreement Clauses Regarding
Child Support 114
    Basic Monthly Child Support Clause 114
    Life and Health Insurance Clauses 115
    Additional Child Support Clause 116

CHAPTER 7: ADDITIONAL CLAUSES AND CONSIDERATIONS 119
Tax Consequences of Divorce 119
    Property Transfers 120
    Alimony 121
    Child Support and Custody 122
Marital Settlement Agreement Taxation Clause 122
Marital Settlement Agreement Name Change Clause 123
Additional Mandatory Marital Settlement Agreement Clause . 124
Marital Settlement Agreement Signature and Notary Clause ... 125

CHAPTER 8: PREPARING YOUR MARITAL SETTLEMENT AGREEMENT . 127

CHAPTER 9: A SAMPLE MARITAL SETTLEMENT AGREEMENT 131
Marital Settlement Agreement 133

CHAPTER 10: PREPARING YOUR DIVORCE PAPERS 141
Steps in the Divorce Process 141
General Considerations 142
The Necessary Documents 144
The Petition or Complaint 147
Appearance, Consent, and Waiver 152

  Child Custody Jurisdiction form 155
  Final Judgement or Decree 159
  Certificate of Divorce or Dissolution of Marriage 163
  Instructions for Signing and Filing the Documents 164

CHAPTER 11: SAMPLE DIVORCE PAPERS 167
  Petition for Divorce 168
  Appearance, Consent, and Waiver 172
  Declaration Under the Uniform Child Custody
  Jurisdiction Act 174
  Judgement of Divorce 177

CHAPTER 12: APPEARING IN COURT 179
  General Court Appearance Rules 180
  Guide to Court Testimony 182
  Testimony Worksheet 183

CHAPTER 13: AFTER YOUR DIVORCE 189
  Final Divorce Wrap-up Checklist 190
  Post-Divorce Legal Problems 192
    Enforcement of Child Support 192
    Enforcement of Alimony 194
    Enforcement of Custody and Visitation 194
    Domestic Violence 195
    Modification of Support and Custody Provisions 195

APPENDIX: DIVORCE LAWS OF ALL 50 STATES 197

GLOSSARY OF LEGAL TERMS 303

BIBLIOGRAPHY OF DIVORCE-RELATED BOOKS 309
  Available Self-Help Divorce Books 310

INDEX 313

PREFACE

This book is part of Nova Publishing Company's continuing series on Legal Self-Help. These self-help legal guides are prepared by licensed attorneys who feel that public access to the American legal system is long overdue.

Given the proper information, the average person in today's world would easily be able to understand and apply many areas of law. However, historically, there have been concerted efforts on the part of the organized Bar and other lawyer organizations to prevent "self-help" legal information from reaching the general public. These efforts have gone hand-in-hand with an attempt to leave the law cloaked in antiquated and unnecessary legal language; language which, of course, one must pay a lawyer to translate.

Law in American society is far more pervasive than ever before. There are legal consequences to virtually every public and most private actions in today's world. Leaving knowledge of the law within the hands of only the lawyers in such a society is not only foolish, but dangerous as well. A free society depends, in large part, on an informed citizenry. This book and others in Nova's Legal-Self Help series are intended to provide the necessary information to those members of the public who wish to use and understand the law for themselves.

However, in an area as complex as divorce law, encompassing topics as diverse as child custody, property law, alimony, child support, and legal contracts, it is not always prudent to attempt to handle every legal situation which arises without the aid of a competent attorney. Although the information presented in this book will give its readers a basic understanding of the areas of law covered, it is not intended that this text entirely substitute for experienced legal assistance in all situations. Throughout this book there are references to those situations in which the aid of a lawyer is strongly recommended.

Regardless of whether or not a lawyer is ultimately retained in certain situations, the legal information in this handbook will enable the reader to understand the framework of divorce laws in this country and how they relate to their own personal situation.

To try and make that task as easy as possible, technical legal jargon has been eliminated whenever possible and plain English used instead. Naturally, plain and easily-understood English is not only perfectly proper for use in all legal documents but, in most cases, leads to far less confusion on the part of later readers. When it is necessary in this book to use a legal term which may be unfamiliar to most people, the word will be shown in *italics* and defined when first used. For reference, at the end of this book there is a glossary of other legal terms which may be encountered in divorce law contexts.

INTRODUCTION

Divorce has become a fact of life in today's society. Approximately one-half of all marriages entered into this year will end in divorce. Each year over 1.7 million people get divorced and the custody of over 1 million children is decided. The legal cost of divorce in America is well over 1 billion dollars every year.

More damaging, however, is the emotional and psychological cost of divorce. This emotional damage is directly increased as the hostility of a divorce escalates. Unfortunately, although some form of no-fault divorce is now the law in every state, the American legal system tends to cause, rather than prevent, antagonism in divorce. The U.S. legal system is an adversary system. It is designed to breed and thrive on conflict. Such a system as applied to divorce may have made sense long ago when divorce was not favored in society. However, in today's society, where divorce is fully accepted, the legal system as it is applied by most lawyers tends to add to the pain of divorce.

In many situations, the simple addition of two lawyers to the problems encountered by a couple considering divorce will merely intensify any conflict. The reason for this is rooted in the way that most lawyers approach divorce. They want to "win" a divorce and they convince their clients that "winning" is important. By doing this, the lawyers set up an enormously costly game of legal chess with the spouses and any children of a marriage as pawns in the game.

The legal maneuvering generally begins with the lawyer preparing a list of demands highly favorable to his or her own client. The client is urged to ask for everything: the house, the car, custody of the children, huge amounts of alimony and child support, the household possessions . . . This is explained to the client as a necessary step in the negotiations process. Of course, the other spouse will be outraged when confronted with such a list of demands and will immediately seek out a mercenary lawyer to draw up a list of equally outrageous counter-demands. Thus, the battle lines will have been drawn. The attempt to amicably dissolve a marriage and get on with one's life will have escalated into an economic and psychological war which will cause enormous suffering and long-term misery for the participants.

The only "winners" in a divorce that has turned into a battle will be the lawyers. The longer the divorce goes on and the more complicated and antagonistic that it gets, the more money the lawyers will make. There have actually been cases in which a divorcing couple's home has been sold as a result of the divorce and *all* of the proceeds of the sale have been used to pay the couple's legal fees in getting the divorce. In other words, if the battle rages long enough, it may be the lawyers who will get the house, the car, the jewelry . . .

There is an alternative to turning a divorce into a war waged by competing lawyers. This alternative is not for everyone, but it can be used by many people who simply wish to end a marriage as easily and as fairly as possible. The alternative is a no-fault divorce by agreement. It is obtained by the spouses sitting down and peacefully discussing how they wish to divide their property and bills and how they wish to arrange for the care of their children. It can very often be done in a civilized and amicable manner. The couple's agreements are then put in writing in the form of a Marital Settlement Agreement, which is a binding contract. This Agreement forms the basis for the ensuing divorce, which can also be routinely handled without the use of an expensive lawyer.

This book will provide all of the information necessary to obtain a divorce by agreement. Chapter 1 of this book provides a general overview of the laws relating to divorce and how the legal process works in a divorce. It also discusses the impact of the switch to a national no-fault divorce system and explains how to use this book. The second chapter goes over some of the basic preliminary considerations to divorce: Where can we obtain the divorce? What are the grounds for divorce? What steps must be taken to obtain the divorce? Preliminary clauses for a settlement agreement are also included and discussed.

The next 7 chapters deal with the actual preparation and signing of a Marital Settlement Agreement. For each important topic (property division, alimony, child custody and visitation, and child support), legal guidelines, questionnaires, worksheets, and sample clauses are provided. An actual sample Marital Settlement Agreement is provided. The final 4 chapters deal with using the Agreement to obtain a no-fault divorce in any state. Guidelines, questionnaires, and sample forms are provided, as well as instructions for court testimony and appearances.

The Appendix contains a detailed compilation of the laws relating to divorce in all 50 states and Washington D.C. A glossary of legal terms encountered in divorce contexts is included, as well as an extensive bibliography of divorce-related books for further reading.

The information in this book is intended to provide its readers with the knowledge that they need to understand the process of divorce. It is also intended to provide a framework by which a couple may achieve a fair and just agreement regarding their divorce. Even for those readers who will eventually choose to hire a lawyer, the information in this book will help in understanding the divorce process and the laws regarding divorce.

CHAPTER 1

DIVORCE AND THE LAW

There has been a sweeping revolution in divorce law in the United States during the past 20 years, and it is still under way. The changes brought about by this revolution have fundamentally altered the framework of how a divorce is obtained and how divorce affects spouses and children. These dramatic legal changes are, as yet, relatively unknown to the general public and are still not fully understood by even the lawyers and judges who administer the new laws. In order to begin the process of your divorce with realistic expectations, it is very important to understand the new framework of divorce law.

Divorce in the United States is governed by individual state law. Each state has its own particular laws to deal with all aspects of the divorce process, from residency requirements to child custody to the division of property. Until 1970, divorce was universally viewed as a social ill, to be avoided and discouraged by the laws of society. Courts in all 50 states granted divorces only on the basis of some marital fault: adultery, abandonment, physical abuse, mental cruelty, or some other form of misconduct. There was a winner (the innocent spouse) and a loser (the guilty spouse). The fruits of divorce were passed out according to the fault of the spouses. If a husband was adulterous or at fault in some other way, the wife was often awarded generous alimony, a larger portion of the marital property, custody of the couple's children, and ample child support. Alternatively, if the wife was found to be at fault, she was often denied alimony, given far less or even none of the couple's property, and could be prevented from having custody of her children. The innocent spouse was rewarded for having been faithful to the vows of marriage and the guilty spouse was punished for his or her marital misconduct.

This traditional system of divorce began to change in 1970. In that year, California passed the first no-fault divorce laws in the U.S. Since then, concluding recently when South

Dakota became the final state to embrace no-fault divorce, the sweeping changes brought about by no-fault divorce have spread across the country. No-fault divorce is now the law in all 50 of the United States and Washington D.C.

What is No-Fault Divorce?

No-fault divorce is exactly what it sounds like. There is no "fault" involved in the grounds for divorce. Neither spouse must prove that the other spouse has been guilty of misconduct. In fact, any misconduct is essentially irrelevant to obtaining the divorce. Adultery and other forms of marital misconduct are generally no longer penalized by the law of divorce. (In some states, however, misconduct may still have an effect on custody and alimony awards, but these states are gradually changing to systems in which misconduct plays no role at all in any of the divorce proceedings. Also, some states continue to retain some of the original fault-based grounds for divorce along with a no-fault method of divorce.)

The initial reasoning behind the change to no-fault divorce was to attempt to lessen the antagonism and pain of divorce. No longer would detectives need to be hired to prove adultery; no longer would a couple's "dirty laundry" need to be aired in public; no longer would a battle be waged regarding who was at fault in the marriage. A marriage could simply be terminated because the spouses no longer felt that the marriage could survive.

To some extent, no-fault divorce has succeeded. Divorce has been changed from a moral action in which a guilty spouse is punished and an innocent spouse is rewarded to, essentially, an economic action. The focus has changed from proving fault in a marriage to deciding the practical matters of dividing the couple's property and providing for child custody and care.

Along with these changes in the grounds for divorce, other equally important changes in divorce law have occurred. In many cases, divorce may now be obtained unilaterally, without the agreement of the other spouse. There is no realistic method left to prevent a divorce if one of the spouses is determined to go through with a divorce. Consent of the other spouse is no longer necessary in a majority of states. The rules regarding how a couple's property is divided, how alimony is determined, and how child custody and support are awarded have all also been radically altered in the past two decades.

The Division of Marital Property

In the area of property, the new divorce laws have brought about radical changes. Traditionally, in all but the few community-property states, the division of a couple's property upon divorce was a simple matter. The spouse whose name was on the title to the property was the owner of the property. In most cases, this was the husband. If the wife had no property of her own, she was given a share of the husband's property. Generally, however, she was awarded no more than one-third of the property. If jointly-owned prop-

CHAPTER 1: DIVORCE AND THE LAW

erty was divided, it was often done on the basis of who contributed the most money to its purchase. Again, the husband usually took the lion's share. The wife was given no credit for her non-monetary contributions to the marriage or to the purchase of property. Her home-making and child-rearing efforts counted for nothing in the traditional method of property division. A wife's own career sacrifices to put her husband through school, in order that he might better the living standards of the family, were also not taken into consideration.

Those simple and highly discriminatory rules have been universally overturned in every state except Mississippi. The property acquired during a marriage is now considered owned in equal or equitable shares by both spouses, regardless of whose name is on the title. In many states, spouses are specifically given credit for home-making duties and an effort is made to provide some level of compensation for the sacrifices of a spouse who aids another in achieving a degree in higher education. The division of property is now based on a view that marriage is an essentially equal partnership, rather than on a determination of who contributed the most actual cash to the marriage. Chapter 3 contains a comprehensive explanation of property division and related matters.

Alimony and Maintenance

Prior to the recent changes in the law, many wives were considered to be eligible for and even entitled to continued support by their ex-husbands after the marriage, often for the rest of their lives or until their subsequent remarriage. This support was provided to the wives by alimony payments.

This portion of the divorce laws has also been the subject of dramatic change. Alimony is no longer the province of the wife alone. It is now available to either spouse. A well-off wife may now be required to provide support for an indigent ex-husband. Alimony is no longer even called alimony in many jurisdictions; it is now referred to as "maintenance" or "spousal support". No longer is alimony regarded as an absolute right; no longer is alimony generally awarded on a permanent basis.

Awards of maintenance are now generally viewed as temporary in nature, designed to allow the ex-spouse adequate time to become self-sufficient; either through education, career training, or work. Awards of maintenance are now primarily based on the needs of the spouse and are not awarded for "innocence" from misconduct. Maintenance and spousal support will be dealt with in detail in Chapter 4.

The Changes in Child Custody

In the past, the law assumed that mothers were best suited to care for minor children. When a family was broken by divorce, there was a strong legal presumption that the mother, and only the mother, was to get custody. Traditionally, the only way a father could get custody was to prove that the mother was totally "unfit" to care for the child. This was a very difficult legal hurdle, given that the laws and the courts highly favored the mother having custody of any children. It required the father who desired custody to dredge up as much negative information as possible about the mother and present it in open court in as damaging a method as possible. This method of determining custody also tended to make the children pawns in the divorce negotiation, much to the detriment of the children.

This presumption in favor of the mother being granted custody of minor children is no longer the law in any state. Both parents are now presumed to be equally qualified to be granted custody, unless there is strong evidence to the contrary. The gender of the parent is irrelevant. Sole custody by one parent is also no longer considered the only proper method for child care after divorce. Most states have adopted rules allowing and even encouraging joint custody by both natural parents.

In practice, however, mothers continue to retain custody in the vast majority of the cases. Physical custody of minor children is still awarded to mothers in some 90% of all custody cases. This is simply a reflection of the fact that mothers in the U.S. are still overwhelmingly the primary care-givers to children. Divorced fathers, however, have increasingly been allowed more voice in the major decisions affecting the child through the alternative of "joint" custody.

A further major change in divorce laws as they relate to children is the adoption by all states of the Uniform Child Custody Jurisdiction Act. This act attempts to deal with the problem of child-snatching and parents taking children across state borders in the attempt to avoid adverse custody decisions. The details of custody and jurisdiction in custody cases will be explained in greater detail in Chapter 5.

The Child Support System

One of the continuing tragedies of divorce is the failure of many children of divorce to receive adequate child support. In over 50% of all child support situations, the required payments are paid late or not at all. Even in those cases where the payments are made on time, many of the child support awards are totally inadequate to provide satisfactory care for the children. Dramatic changes in the laws relating to child support have been enacted in the last decade in an effort to correct this situation.

Mandated by recent federal legislation, comprehensive new guidelines for determining the level of support required have recently been adopted in individual states. These detailed rules provide specific procedures and criteria for assuring that each child receives adequate support from both parents upon divorce.

In an effort to institute a national system to enforce the collection of delinquent child support payments, the Uniform Reciprocal Enforcement of Support Act has been adopted by all states. Numerous strict laws have also been passed in many states to aid in the collec-

CHAPTER 1: DIVORCE AND THE LAW

tion of overdue support payments. In addition, the federal government has enacted other tough national legislation in an attempt to solve this problem. The laws relating to child support are covered in Chapter 6.

Divorce in General

These major changes in all phases of divorce law have begun to incorporate the equally important changes that have taken place in society in general during the past 20 years. Economics has replaced morality as the overriding concern in many aspects of American society. Women are gradually being treated more equally and fairly under the law. They are no longer considered as the subordinate spouse in a marriage. In awarding child custody, maintenance, and property, both spouses are on a more equal footing under the new divorce laws.

These changes have been very rapid and dramatic. They have, in fact, often outpaced the ability of the legal system to cope with them. Judges and lawyers have had a somewhat difficult time putting these new laws into practice where there is no precedent to deal with potential problems which may arise. The change to no-fault divorce has made the area of divorce law the only area of law in which the traditional win/lose context of the legal system does not seem to apply. Lawyers and judges are both trained and experienced in a system of law which has antagonistic and adversarial competition as its basis, and thus, are often ill-suited to effectively deal with the no-fault basis of the new laws.

The change to no-fault divorce has somewhat reduced the potential for conflict in divorce by removing the need to prove that one of the spouses is guilty of some form of marital misconduct. However, there is still considerable room for difficulty in the decisions regarding child custody and support and in the division of property.

Simply because a divorce is obtained on a no-fault basis does not mean that it is an uncontested divorce. A true uncontested divorce is one in which the opposing spouse takes no legal part in contesting any of the decisions made regarding property, custody, maintenance, or child support. There is no necessity for an actual trial regarding aspects of a divorce in an uncontested divorce, although there is still generally a court hearing held to determine compliance with basic legal requirements. In an uncontested divorce, the opposing spouse may take no part at all, be entirely absent from the state, or may file legal documents agreeing to not contest any terms of the divorce. An uncontested divorce in which only one spouse makes the decisions on the legal matters (generally an uncontested default divorce) is not generally the most effective manner to obtain a divorce which is fair and just to both spouses. Uncontested divorces may be obtained, however, on the basis of an agreement between the spouses, as explained in the next section.

In a contested divorce, the spouses are both involved in a legal battle over some or all of these aspects of divorce. A contested divorce can be brought on no-fault grounds, yet include a bitter dispute over child custody, alimony, or property. Despite the advances made in overcoming some of the trauma of divorce by the switch to a no-fault system, contested divorces still provide an arena for lengthy and bitter hostilities.

The Divorce by Agreement

The alternative to both the uncontested default divorce (in which one spouse does not participate in the decision-making) and the contested divorce is the uncontested divorce by agreement. In this type of divorce, fault is not a factor. It is a no-fault divorce. In a divorce by agreement, both spouses play a part in all of the decisions affecting the couple and any children that they may have. In this type of divorce, fairness is the key. For this type of divorce to succeed, the agreement between the spouses must be as fair and as just as is possible under the circumstances. This type of divorce is not only accepted but is actually encouraged in virtually all states. In a modern divorce setting, a marital settlement agreement is an indispensable alternative to the traditional hostility of ending a marriage.

There are many important benefits to obtaining a divorce by agreement. Perhaps the most important is that there is far less chance that the divorce will escalate into a hostile battle. When revenge and animosity are not factors, there is a greater opportunity that the divorce settlement will accurately reflect what the spouses really desire to obtain from the divorce. If the decisions regarding the care and custody of any children are reached through rational and mature discussions, there is a greater chance that the decisions reached will be abided by without future hostility. A further benefit of a divorce settlement which is made without the assistance of attorneys is the avoidance of major legal expenses in connection with a divorce.

The divorce by agreement is the focus of this book. How to approach each of the relevant areas which require agreement will be explained in the following chapters. The actual preparation of a legally-binding Marital Settlement Agreement will be detailed. Finally, the steps necessary to obtain a no-fault divorce which incorporates the terms of the Marital Settlement Agreement will be shown.

For a divorce by agreement to be successful, both spouses must participate openly and honestly in discussing the matters to be resolved. Both spouses must be willing to compromise on major decisions and work to reach a satisfactory agreement. Both spouses must be a part of the process of preparing a settlement agreement and obtaining the divorce. It may often be very difficult to calmly discuss the issues to be covered in a divorce settlement with a spouse one no longer cares to be married to. However, the valuable benefits of a divorce by agreement are only available to those spouses who can still rationally confer on the matters to be decided.

The instructions and information which follow are designed to facilitate an amicable settlement of all of the matters which arise in the normal course of a divorce. The standards which are applied and the guidelines that are provided are based on the general modern trends of no-fault divorce laws in the United States. However, although individual state

CHAPTER 1: DIVORCE AND THE LAW

laws have moved much closer to a common ground in the area of divorce in recent years, there are still important differences in the laws of each state. For this purpose, a comprehensive Appendix has been provided at the end of this book which outlines in detail the specific individual characteristics of each state's laws relating to divorce. Throughout this book, there will often be references to this Appendix to check on the specifics of particular state laws. The introductory notes in the Appendix should be read first for an explanation of what information is presented and how to put that information to practical use.

Can You Do Your Own Divorce?

The simple answer to this question is YES. Every person has a right to represent him or herself in court without the use of an attorney. This is a well-established legal principle.

The basic minimal qualifications to prepare your own divorce settlement and obtain a divorce without using a lawyer are simply the ability to read and write basic English and understand this book. However, there are certain situations in which it is not advisable to attempt to obtain a divorce without the aid of a competent attorney. The following checklist will outline those situations. If the answers to all of the questions are YES, then this book may be confidently used to obtain a divorce.

Yes/No

_____ 1. Have you and your spouse essentially agreed that you both wish to end your marriage and go your separate ways in peace?

_____ 2. Do you feel that you and your spouse can cooperate enough to come to some form of fair agreement regarding the division of all of your property and bills?

_____ 3. If you have children, do you feel certain that you and your spouse can reach a fair and reasonable agreement regarding child custody, visitation, and child support?

_____ 4. Are you able to firmly state your wishes to your spouse and not be overly-intimidated by him or her and has your marriage been totally free of spouse or child abuse?

_____ 5. Are you or your spouse NOT in active military service?

_____ 6. Have no previous legal proceedings been instituted for a divorce, legal separation, child custody, or domestic violence between you and your spouse?

_____ 7. If you have been married for over 5 years, are you presently employed or capable of supporting yourself?

If any of the answers to the previous questions are NO, then it is advisable to seek the aid of an attorney. Competent low-cost legal aid is often available from local Legal Aid Society offices or from local legal clinics. Law schools in your area may have programs that can provide free or low-cost help with simple legal matters. State Bar Associations often have low-cost legal referral services.

If during the process of attempting to settle a divorce, you or your spouse become hostile to the point of being unable to rationally discuss the terms of a settlement, it is advisable to seek an attorney or mediator for assistance. In addition, if at any time during the process of attempting to do your own divorce, you become overwhelmed by the complications involved or become confused regarding your rights, it is advisable to seek the assistance of an attorney. Very importantly, if at any time your spouse files any legal papers for a divorce outside the context of your settlement discussions, a lawyer must be sought immediately.

The focus of the recent changes in the divorce laws is to lessen the chances for animosity to develop between the divorcing spouses. To this end, the lawyers and judges who make up the legal system should and generally do attempt to be helpful to those who wish to represent themselves in court. However, in some counties in the United States, there may continue to be very strong resistance to allowing self-help divorces. Local judges, attorneys, and even court clerks may make the legal process much more difficult than necessary in an effort to discourage self-help law. Unfortunately, if unusually strong hostility is encountered when dealing with the local legal system on a self-help basis, there may be no realistic alternative other than obtaining a lawyer. You should be able to find an attorney who will use the materials that you have already prepared and work on an hourly basis for simply filing the papers and appearing in court with you. This will still be far more economical than having a lawyer do all of the work involved.

Even if you decide that it is advisable to use an attorney, the information in this book will be useful. First, it will provide you with practical legal advice regarding the issues involved in a divorce. This will allow you to cope with the decisions that you face on an informed and intelligent basis. The discussion of the various divorce matters and the information contained in the Appendix relating to your individual state laws will provide you with an understanding of the relevant points of law that will make it much easier to talk with and understand your lawyer. In addition, the various checklists and questionnaires will enable you to complete much of the preliminary work involved in any divorce prior to seeking an attorney. If you do eventually decide to hire an attorney, the more information that you have gathered yourself in advance will mean that your attorney will not have to spend time on such preliminary matters and will be able to prepare the necessary papers much faster. This, of course, should mean that your eventual legal fees will be less. Do not, in any event, feel discouraged if you come to the conclusion that the aid of an attorney is necessary. Divorce is a major emotional and economic event and should be approached with sufficient information and assistance to allow you to feel as comfortable and at ease as is possible under the circumstances.

CHAPTER 1: DIVORCE AND THE LAW

How to Use This Book

The information that follows is set out in a step-by-step fashion. However, it is intended that the entire book first be read by both spouses before attempting to reach any final decisions on the relevant issues. This will allow you and your spouse to gain an equal understanding of all of the matters and to fully appreciate how the decisions involved in a divorce are interrelated.

Once the entire book has been read by both you and your spouse, you will be ready to confer on each issue and reach a workable decision. On each of the main areas covered (property division, alimony, and child custody and support), there is a questionnaire provided for you to assemble the necessary information and focus the issues. After each questionnaire, there follows a discussion of the law and a set of general guidelines in order to assist you in the decision-making process. After each discussion, several clauses outlining the various choices available are provided for inclusion in your marital settlement agreement. Once you have reached an agreement on each of the relevant points, a clause should be chosen which clearly states your decision.

When all of the decisions have been made and all of the appropriate clauses have been chosen, you will be instructed on how to assemble the individual clauses into a final agreement. You will then be instructed on how to sign and have the document notarized. Your settlement agreement will be a valid legal contract and will allow you and your spouse to separate legally and live under the specific terms of the agreement prior to your divorce being finalized.

Finally, you will be shown how to use your signed marital settlement agreement to obtain an actual no-fault divorce in your state. The mechanics of actually obtaining a divorce are different in every state and, in fact, may be slightly different from one county to the next in the same state. You will be shown how to obtain the general forms that you will need to prepare, how to fill in those forms, how to file those forms, and how the court process will work.

If you and your spouse are still able to work together to some extent, the steps necessary to obtain a divorce are not that difficult to follow. You will probably find that preparing your settlement agreement is far less difficult than filling out an income tax return. Understanding and controlling the phases of your own divorce will also allow you to begin the process of accepting your divorce and moving forward with your life in a positive way.

As you are working on your settlement agreement, remember that although the standards that are provided in this book are generalized to some extent, they are the basis for the decisions that are made in every divorce nationwide. As you negotiate with your spouse using the guidelines presented in this book, you will be following a general framework of what you could expect if you wind up in court. If your discussions with your spouse fail and your divorce becomes contested, these basic guidelines are still what will be used by a judge to make the important decisions in your case. In that case, however, expensive lawyers will be required, hostilities will likely erupt, and your divorce will become more and more unpleasant. You still will get a divorce, but it will cost you more money and more pain. It is much better to try to resolve your differences and reach a fair agreement without enlisting attorneys.

Mediation

If after an honest attempt to come to an agreement, you and your spouse are still unable to reach an accord, there are other methods of dispute resolution available before you seek legal help. The use of a neutral third person can often make the difference in negotiating a settlement. The third person can be a member of the clergy, a marriage or family counselor, or a professional mediator. Some states have counseling or conciliation services available for just this purpose. The use of these services is generally free and available to any who request it. Look in the yellow pages in your area, ask the clerk of your local court, or check with your local social services agencies for a referral to such counseling.

Divorce mediation is a process in which the spouses consult with a trained professional and discuss their disagreements until an understanding is reached. A professional mediator does not make the decisions. Rather, he or she is trained in conflict resolution and in methods of coaching disagreeing spouses to work out their own agreements. Submitting disputed issues to mediation is a commitment to work cooperatively.

The use of an independent mediator or counseling service should be viewed as a positive step. Often, the use of mediation services will provide all of the additional help that is needed for a couple to reach a satisfactory agreement. Mediation is an alternative method to resolve your differences on a cooperative basis. All of the issues involved in your divorce can be the subject of successful mediation: property division, child custody and visitation, child support, and alimony. Mediation can often enable a couple to reach agreement without resorting to the adversary legal process.

Most likely you and your spouse will be able to reach agreement on many of the issues that you will confront in your divorce process. In some cases, however, there may be bitter disagreement over a single problem or issue. Such disagreement may often lead to a breakdown of the entire process of negotiation. If you and your spouse run into such difficulty as you go through the process of reaching an amicable marital settlement, you should reread this section. Rather than discard all of the efforts that you have made in reaching agreement on the other points in your divorce, consider the use of mediation or counseling services to enable you get past your particular sticking point. You and your spouse will tell the mediator what it is you want to achieve. Mediation is not a marriage counseling service designed to get the two of you back together. It will be an attempt to aid you in peacefully and rationally resolving your disagreements regarding the terms of your separation and divorce.

CHAPTER 1: DIVORCE AND THE LAW

There are many organizations which may be able to provide you with information in obtaining professional mediation services. Family Services of America [11700 West Lake Park Drive, Milwaukee, WI 53224 (phone: 414-359-1040)] can provide information regarding many agencies throughout the U.S. that offer divorce counseling.

The American Arbitration Association also provides professional dispute settlement services nationwide, through its national office, [American Arbitration Association, 140 West 51st Street, New York, NY 10020 (phone: 212-484-4000)] and 25 regional offices in major cities throughout the country. In addition, State Bar Associations generally maintain lists of qualified mediators in the area of divorce and family law.

Mediation is a voluntary process and you and your spouse may choose to withdraw from mediation at any time. Mediators are not judges and have no power to force decisions on you or your spouse. Unlike a legal court proceeding, the sessions will be private and informal and will allow both you and your spouse to calmly discuss your situation and focus your disagreements. Mediators are professionally trained in the process of resolving disputes and will attempt to provide you with experienced guidance in your discussions.

General Note Regarding Terminology:

In recent years, many states have changed the terminology that applies to divorce law. Divorce may now be called "*dissolution of marriage*"; alimony may be referred to as "*spousal support*" or "*maintenance*"; child custody may be known as "*primary parental responsibility*" and a parent with custody may be referred to as a "*managing conservator*". There may be other unfamiliar legal terms used to describe common ideas. Throughout this book, the common general usage terms will be used: divorce, alimony, child custody, child support, and visitation. However, the listing in the Appendix for each state's specific laws will use the official state language for each term. In addition, most states have laws in effect which state that either terminology may be used: the familiar words or the new legal terms.

CHAPTER 2

PRELIMINARY MATTERS

The first and most important preliminary matter that you and your spouse must both confront is: Do you really want a divorce? No guidelines, questionnaires, or checklists are provided in this book for answering this basic question. However, you are urged to think very seriously about the answer to this question as you read through this entire book. Until your divorce is actually finalized by a court of law, you can attempt at any time to reconcile your differences with your spouse and continue with your marriage. None of the steps that you will take until your divorce is final are necessarily irreversible. Divorce is a very big step in your life and should not be taken lightly.

For many people, separation is the first step in the divorce process. You and your spouse may decide to separate under the terms of a separation agreement or you may wish to seek an actual legal separation from a court. A legal court-ordered separation is slightly different than a separation by agreement. Legal court-ordered separations are not provided for in all states. However, a marital separation by mutual agreement is recognized and honored in every state. Check the Appendix for the law in your state. In a legal court-ordered separation, there is actually a court order that specifies that the couple is separated. This court order may set out all of the terms of the separation, or the court order may simply validate all of the terms which the couple have already agreed to in a separation agreement. Neither a legal court-ordered separation nor a separation agreement will legally end the marriage. Only a divorce can do that.

There are some distinct benefits to a separation prior to divorce. First, the period of separation from your spouse begins to prepare you for the emotional impact of divorce. In a separation, you may enter into an agreement covering all of the issues that arise during the course of an actual divorce, and it is much easier to mutually change the terms of this agreement prior to an actual divorce. In some ways, a separation may act as a trial divorce. You can always get back together with your spouse, if you both desire. In addition, some couples who do not wish to divorce decide to live separately for religious or moral reasons.

The marital settlement agreement that you prepare using this book may be used in the same manner as a separation agreement. It will cover all of the same concerns as a separation agreement. Your marital settlement agreement addresses the issue of separation and may be used if you desire to enter into a legal court-ordered separation. However, this book is designed to show its readers how to obtain a divorce, and thus, information and instructions on how to achieve a legal court-ordered separation are not included. Your state's listing in the Appendix, however, briefly explains the law regarding legal court-ordered separations in your state.

In this chapter, you will begin the process of making the decisions necessary to prepare a marital settlement agreement. This agreement will cover all of the terms of your eventual divorce. Included in your agreement will be all of the decisions that you and your spouse make regarding how your property and bills are divided, whether either of you should get alimony, and, if you have any children, who will have custody and how their support will be provided. This agreement, when signed by you and your spouse, will become a valid legal contract that will be enforceable in a court of law if either you or your spouse violate its terms. In addition, the agreement that you prepare will be used in your actual divorce proceedings. Judges will not generally change any of the terms in a marital settlement agreement, unless they feel that the terms are obviously unfair, were obtained by force or threats, or are not in the best interests of any children.

On the next few pages you will fill out a questionnaire that covers basic personal information and details the history of your marriage. By filling in this questionnaire and the ones in the next 4 chapters, you will be able to have in front of you all of the necessary and relevant information for preparing your agreement. Following the questionnaire, there is a list of important documents that should be assembled and kept on hand for use during the process of your divorce. There will then be a discussion of some of the preliminary matters that must be understood. Finally, there are several mandatory clauses set out that must be filled in and used in every marital settlement agreement.

The method set out in this book for preparing a marital settlement agreement is essentially identical to the method used by the vast majority of lawyers who handle divorces. Upon visiting a lawyer for a divorce, you would be asked to fill out an extensive questionnaire covering all of the aspects that might arise in the course of your divorce proceeding. The lawyer would then determine what you want to achieve in your divorce; what property you wish to retain, which parent you wish to have custody, and whether child support or alimony is desired. Your lawyer and your spouse's lawyer would then attempt to negotiate the various issues, and if possible, put them in the form of a marital settlement. The lawyers would use legal texts that contain clauses very similar to the ones that follow to prepare your agreement. The only difference is that the language in the agreement that most lawyers would prepare would be unintelligible to most people.

CHAPTER 2: PRELIMINARY MATTERS

You and your spouse, however, are the two people who know the most about your current relationship. You both are the two most qualified people to understand what each wants out of the marriage. If you can both cooperate enough to agree to the terms of your marital settlement agreement, your subsequent divorce should be achieved with far less difficulty and expense than if you use the services of lawyers. If you can't agree to the terms of your agreement without lawyers, it is not likely that you will be able to agree once you both have hired lawyers. If you can't come to an agreement, even with the assistance of lawyers, a judge who knows very little about you and your spouse will make the important decisions that you were unable to make.

With these points in mind, try to make an honest and mature effort to reach an agreement with your spouse that will be fair and workable for both of you. An agreement that is one-sided, unfair, or made in haste just to get it over with is worse than no agreement at all. To use this book correctly will take some time. It is time that you would normally be paying for a lawyer to complete the same tasks. In effect, you and your spouse will be saving two times a lawyer's normal hourly fees (about $100 per hour X two) for every hour that you both spend doing the work yourselves. In addition, the time that you spend achieving an agreement that is fair to both of you will be repaid many times over in the ease with which you will both make the transition from married to single life.

PRELIMINARY QUESTIONNAIRE

Wife's Full Name:_____

Wife's Former or Maiden Name:_____

Does Wife Desire to Use Her Former Name?_____

Wife's Social Security #:_____

Wife's Date of Birth:_____

Wife's Present Address:_____

_____

Wife's Future Address (if known):_____

_____

Date Future Address Valid:_____

Wife's Present Phone #:_____

Wife's Present Occupation:_____

Wife's Present Place of Employment:_____

_____

Wife's General Health:_____

Was Wife Previously Married?_____

DIVORCE YOURSELF

If YES, how was marriage terminated? (divorce, death, etc.):
_____

Husband's Full Name:_____
Husband's Social Security #:_____
Husband's Date of Birth:_____
Husband's Present Address:_____
_____

Husband's Future Address (if known):_____
_____

Date Future Address Valid:_____
Husband's Present Phone #:_____
Husband's Present Occupation:_____
Husband's Present Place of Employment:_____
_____

Was Husband Previously Married?_____
If YES, how was marriage terminated? (divorce, death, etc.):
_____

Full Address(es) Where Husband and Wife Have Lived During the Past 12 Months:_____
_____
_____

Date of Marriage:_____
Place of Marriage:_____
Have you and your spouse separated?_____
If YES, on what date did you separate?_____
Have you previously separated at any time?_____
If YES, on what dates and for how long?_____
Names and Birth Dates of any Children of this Marriage: (born or adopted)
_____
_____
_____
_____

DOCUMENT CHECKLIST

The following is a listing of various documents that may be necessary during your divorce. The list is as comprehensive as possible and many of the documents may not apply to your

CHAPTER 2: PRELIMINARY MATTERS

individual situation. Certain documents are mandatory and a copy of these must generally be included with the papers that you file for your divorce or in your possession when you go to court. The mandatory documents are noted. If you have the documents listed in your possession, assemble them into one place and make a note of that fact on this list. If your spouse has the documents, request that he or she do the same. If you know that the document exists, but do not have access to it, make a note to that effect on this list.

Wife's Birth Certificate: (Mandatory) _____

Husband's Birth Certificate: (Mandatory) _____

Immigration and Naturalization Documents: (Mandatory if applicable) _____

Marriage License: (Mandatory) _____

Birth Certificates of any Children: (Mandatory) _____

Any Written Agreements between Wife and Husband: (Mandatory) _____

Social Security Cards: _____

Personal Financial Statements: (See Chapter 3) _____

Documents relating to any prior marriage: (Settlement Agreements, Divorce documents, Death Certificate, etc.) _____

All documents relating to income, expenses, and property: (See Chapter 3)_____

After you have filled in this first questionnaire and assembled the necessary documents, you are ready to begin the process of preparing your marital settlement agreement and obtaining your divorce. Based on what you have put on your questionnaire, you must make certain preliminary decisions. First, you must decide in which state and county (or parish) you will be allowed to file for your divorce. Following that decision, you must determine what the specific grounds for your divorce will be.

Where Can You File For Your Divorce?

Before you begin to prepare your actual divorce papers, you need to know exactly where you will be filing for your divorce. Three legal considerations enter into this decision. The first is *residency*. All states have some type of residency requirement regarding filing for divorce. You may only file for your divorce in the state in which you or your spouse reside. Residency is also referred to in some states as *domicile*. Both terms refer to the place where you permanently live; the place where you return to after any temporary absence. In general, you must have been a resident of the state in which you wish to file for divorce for some length of time in order for the court to hear your case.

Each state has differing residency requirements and these are shown in the Appendix. Some states require that you be a resident for 1 year in the state before you will be allowed to file for divorce. A few states merely require that you actually be a bona-fide resident; there is no time limit specified. In general, you will be allowed to file for divorce in the state in which you were married if you have lived there since marriage or in the state in which you currently reside if you have met the residency requirements as shown in the Appendix. It is not a good idea to move about frequently when you are contemplating divorce, as this may delay your ability to file for divorce in the state and county that you wish.

The other two considerations for determining where to file are technical legal ones: *jurisdiction* and *venue*. Jurisdiction refers to the authority of the court to make binding orders regarding the subject matter of the case (in this instance, divorce) and regarding the people involved in the case. In some states, residency is a jurisdictional requirement. In others, it is not. Notification of the opposing party in a lawsuit also generally provides the court with jurisdiction over the person. Jurisdictional considerations are also important in determining which actual court within the state is the proper one for divorce proceedings. Venue refers to the legal selection of which county (or parish) should be the actual site of the trial. Both venue and jurisdiction decisions are based on the actual statutes in your particular state. Some states may require the divorce proceedings to be instituted in the county where the spouse the divorce is filed against lives. Other states may require that the lawsuit be in the county where the spouse filing for divorce lives. Still other states may allow the divorce action in any county where either spouse resides. Check with the Appendix to determine the rules in effect in your state.

It is recommended that, until your divorce is completed, you and your spouse remain in the same state. It will also make compliance with these technical legal requirements easier if you both remain in the same county. Of course, that may not always be possible. If you and your spouse have lived in the same county and the same state for one year, you can be assured that it is in that state and county that you will be allowed to file for your divorce. If you have moved around frequently or if you have separated and live in different states, it may be somewhat more difficult to determine which state and county is proper. Some states will allow a spouse in a divorce suit to waive any venue or jurisdiction difficulties. Other states take the position that a person can not waive such legal formalities. If you can not easily determine which state and county to properly file for your divorce by using the Appendix in this book, you will need to consult a lawyer on this decision. You should still be able to prepare and file your own divorce papers once you have ascertained where exactly they should be filed.

The state which you choose for filing for your divorce should be the state whose Appendix you refer to for the rest of this book. The county which you have determined is correct will be the county in which you file your actual divorce papers as explained in Chapter 10. The name of the particular court within the county is also noted in the Appendix.

What Will Be the Grounds for Your Divorce?

Your divorce will be based on the particular no-fault basis which is allowed in your own state. Some states have more than one basis for filing. In general, however, there are 4

CHAPTER 2: PRELIMINARY MATTERS

basic types of no-fault grounds: (1) irretrievable breakdown of the marriage; (2) irreconcilable differences; (3) incompatibility; and (4) living separate and apart for a certain time period. The grounds for filing for a no-fault divorce in your state are listed in the Appendix. Most states have only 1 available ground for a no-fault divorce and it is this one that you will use. However, a few states have available a choice of no-fault grounds. You must choose the grounds that most closely fits your particular circumstances.

In states which have "irretrievable breakdown of the marriage", "irreconcilable differences", or "incompatibility" as grounds, it is generally easy to satisfy the grounds. If either spouse decides that the marriage should be ended, it is very difficult for the other spouse to prevent the divorce. If both spouses agree on the no-fault grounds or if the other spouse does not deny that the marriage is broken, the grounds are generally satisfied. There may be a court-enforced mediation attempt or a counseling session required if the other spouse does deny that the marriage is irretrievably broken or that there are irreconcilable differences. Any such denial of the breakdown of the marriage will only delay the divorce for a specific period of time while an attempt at reconciliation is made. The divorce will proceed after the mediation period is over, usually after about 30-90 days. A few states have certain specific ways to prove that the marriage is irretrievably broken. Two states only allow a no-fault divorce if there is a written agreement reached between the spouses. One state (Texas) uses a unique ground which is very similar to the other general no-fault grounds. The different state's requirements are listed in the Appendix. In any states with these type of no-fault grounds, the couple may separate prior to the actual divorce. During the time of separation, the spouses can live under the terms of the marital separation agreement that may be prepared by using this book.

The fourth type of grounds for obtaining a divorce is "living separately and apart" for a specific length of time. This type of grounds is able to be shown by objective evidence, and is proven merely by showing that the spouses did not live together, nor sleep together, for the required time limit. There is no requirement that either spouse be at fault for the separation. The necessary time limit for living apart ranges from 6 months to 3 years. During the time of separation, the spouses can live under the terms of the marital separation agreement that may be prepared using this book. Please refer to the Appendix to see if your state requires this type of ground.

As noted, a few states will show two or more no-fault grounds. Generally, if there is more than one no-fault ground for divorce, there is a general marital breakdown ground and a separation-based ground. Which ground that you and your spouse choose will depend on your individual circumstances and an agreement between you and your spouse.

Preliminary Marital Settlement Agreement Clauses

You are now ready to begin choosing and preparing the first clauses in your agreement. These clauses will lay the legal groundwork that identify you, your spouse, and any children; and will satisfy the basic minimum legal requirements for a valid contract. You will use these clauses in Chapter 8 when you actually assemble and sign your settlement agreement. For now, simply read through the clauses, choose those that apply to your circumstances, and fill in the appropriate blanks.

Title And Introductory Clause:

This introductory clause specifies the effective date of the agreement and identifies the spouses, their places of residence, and the date and place of their marriage. Fill in the appropriate information. This information is important and is mandatory in all agreements.

MARITAL SETTLEMENT AGREEMENT

This agreement is made on the _____ day of _____, 19 ___, between _____ [Wife's full name], the Wife, who lives at _____ _____ [Wife's street address], in the _____ [Town, City, or Village] of _____, _____ [County or Parish] of _____, State of _____ and _____ [Husband's full name], the Husband, who lives at _____, in the _____ [Town, City, or Village] of _____, _____ [County or Parish] of _____, State of _____.

We were married on the _____ day of _____, 19 ___, in the _____ [Town, City, or Village] of _____, _____ [County or Parish] of _____, State of _____.

Children Identification Clause:

Chose the clause that applies to your particular circumstances. This clause identifies whether or not any children will be involved in the terms of the agreement. Fill in the names and birth dates of any children. One of these clauses is mandatory. If the wife is currently pregnant and there are already children, use both appropriate clauses.

There were no children born or adopted into our marriage, and none are expected.

The Wife is currently pregnant and the expected birth date is _____, 19 ___.

CHAPTER 2: PRELIMINARY MATTERS

> The following children were born *[or adopted]* into our marriage:
>
> Child's name   Child's Birth date   Child's Sex
>
> Child's name   Child's Birth date   Child's Sex
>
> Child's name   Child's Birth date   Child's Sex
>
> Child's name   Child's Birth date   Child's Sex

Preliminary Explanation Clause:

Chose one of the following clauses that most closely fits the divorce grounds that you have chosen in your state and your particular circumstances. Refer to your state's listing in the Appendix to determine the grounds that you will use for your divorce. One of these clauses is mandatory for your agreement.

> As a result of disputes and serious differences, we sincerely believe that our marriage is irretrievably broken and that there is no possible chance for reconciliation.

> As a result of disputes and serious difficulties, we sincerely believe that there are irreconcilable differences between us and that there is no possible chance for reconciliation.

> As a result of disputes and serious differences, we sincerely believe that there is a complete incompatibility of temperament between us and that there is no possible chance for reconciliation.

DIVORCE YOURSELF

> As a result of disputes and serious differences, we have separated and are now living apart and intend to continue to remain permanently apart.

General Agreement Clause:

This clause outlines the basic desire to reach an agreement. This clause is mandatory in all agreements. Use the phrase relating to children if any children are to be covered in the agreement. If there are no children, delete this phrase.

> We both desire to settle by agreement all of our marital affairs, including the division of all of our property and bills, and spousal support or maintenance *[and all issues relating to our child(ren), including custody, visitation, and child support]*.
>
> THEREFORE, in consideration of our mutual promises, and other good and valuable consideration, we agree as follows:

Separation Clause:

This clause relates that the spouses desire to live apart as if they were single. This clause should be used in all situations in which the spouses have already separated or in which they desire to separate as soon as an agreement is reached. In the vast majority of cases, you will use this clause. The small box to the left of the clause will be shown for all of the remaining clauses in this book. It provides a place for the numbering of each consecutive clause that you and your spouse choose for inclusion in you agreement. This clause is numbered #1. After you have selected all of the clauses which you will use, Chapter 8 provides instructions for the proper numbering of the clauses. For now, leave all of the small number boxes blank. All of the clauses which you and your spouse have chosen in this chapter will be used when you prepare your marital settlement agreement in Chapter 8. Please refer back to this chapter at that time.

> **1.** We both desire and agree to permanently live separate and apart from each other, as if we were single, according to the terms of this agreement. We each agree not to annoy, harass, or interfere with the other in any manner.

CHAPTER 3

DIVIDING YOUR PROPERTY AND BILLS

In the course of your attempts to reach a marital settlement agreement with your spouse, the division of your property is one of most likely areas in which arguments may arise. As the change to no-fault divorce has essentially removed the relevance of marital misconduct from consideration, many spouses are unable to vent their hostilities regarding the faults of their spouse during the course of a modern divorce proceeding. Thus, there may often be a tendency to attempt to bring anger and animosity to bear on the other areas left to resolve in a divorce settlement. This, however, is not a productive manner in which to approach the division of you and your spouse's property. As much as is possible, you should attempt to keep the discussion of the division of your property on an amicable level. The division of your marital property may be the most important economic event of your lives, and should be dealt with in a mature and businesslike manner.

Prior to actually making the important decisions regarding the division of your property, it is important to have before you a complete inventory of all of your property. Even if you feel that you have no property to divide, in order to make sure that your marital settlement agreement covers all of your property, you should fill out the following questionnaire. It is very easy to overlook certain types of property. In order to try to list every possible type of property, this questionnaire is very comprehensive. Many of the listings may not apply to your particular situation. Fill in only those areas which apply. Each spouse should fully answer as many of the questions that he or she is able to. You should include on this questionnaire *everything* that you and your spouse own or owe money on. This is a big task but it is crucial in understanding and properly dividing your possessions and obligations in a fair manner.

Following the questionnaire is a property document checklist for assembling those documents necessary for valuing and dividing your property. If after filling out the questionnaire, you decide that you actually do not have any significant property to divide, you may skip to the section on settlement agreement clauses and select the first clause listed (which deals with minimal property).

After the questionnaire and document list, there is a discussion of property laws in the individual states and various other matters which are relevant to the division of your property. Next, there is a property division worksheet on which you will list the property that each spouse will retain. Following this are optional property division clauses for selection and inclusion in your marital settlement agreement. Finally, at the end of this chapter there is a Financial Statement that details you and your spouse's employment, monthly income, expenses, assets, and liabilities. Both of you will need to prepare one of these forms for attachment to your completed marital settlement agreement.

PROPERTY QUESTIONNAIRE

Real Estate:

Family Home:

Do you lease a home or apartment? _____

If (YES): How much time is left on the lease? _____

Do you own your own home? _____

If (YES): What is the address? _____

When was it purchased? _____

    (Was this before or during the marriage?) _____

Whose money was used for down payment? _____

Whose name(s) is on the deed? _____

How much was the down payment? ....$ _____

What was the original purchase price? ....$ _____

What is the present market value? ....$ _____

How much is left unpaid on the mortgage? ....$ _____

What is the equity (market value minus mortgage balance)? ....$ _____

How much is the monthly mortgage payment? ....$ _____

How much are the taxes? ....$ _____

How much is the homeowner's insurance? ....$ _____

Have there been any major improvements made since its purchase? _____

(If YES): When were the improvements made? _____

    How much did they cost? ....$ _____

CHAPTER 3: DIVIDING YOUR PROPERTY AND BILLS

Whose money was used? _____

Here list the actual legal description of the home (taken directly off the deed or mortgage): _____

_____

_____

_____

Other Real Estate #1:

What is the address? _____

When was it purchased? _____

(Was this before or during the marriage?) _____

Whose money was used for down payment? _____

Whose name(s) on the deed? _____

How much was the down payment? ....$ _____

What was the original purchase price? ....$ _____

What is the present market value? ....$ _____

How much is left unpaid on the mortgage? ....$ _____

What is the equity (market value minus mortgage balance)? ....$ _____

How much is the monthly mortgage payment? ....$ _____

How much are the taxes? ....$ _____

How much is the insurance? ....$ _____

Is there any rental income? ....$ _____

Have there been any major improvements made since its purchase? _____

If (YES): When were the improvements made? _____

How much did they cost? ....$ _____

Whose money was used? _____

Here list the actual legal description of the property (taken directly off the deed or mortgage): _____

_____

_____

_____

Other Real Estate #2:

What is the address? _____

When was it purchased? _____

(Was this before or during the marriage?) _____

Whose money was used for down payment? _____

Whose name(s) on the deed? _____
How much was the down payment? ....$ _____
What was the original purchase price? ....$ _____
What is the present market value? ....$ _____
How much is left unpaid on the mortgage? ....$ _____
What is the equity (market value minus mortgage balance)? ....$ _____
How much is the monthly mortgage payment? ....$ _____
How much are the taxes? ....$ _____
How much is the insurance? ....$ _____
Is there any rental income? ....$ _____
Have there been any major improvements made since its purchase? _____
(If YES): When were the improvements made? _____
    How much did they cost? ....$ _____
    Whose money was used? _____
Here list the actual legal description of the property (taken directly off the deed or mortgage): _____
_____
_____
_____

(If there is any more real estate, answer the same questions for each property.)

Personal Property: (The term "owner" refers to the person in whose name the account, stock, bond, etc. is held. If jointly held, write "joint".)

Bank Accounts:
  Savings:
    Bank_____
    Owner _____ Amount $ _____

    Bank_____
    Owner _____ Amount $ _____

  Checking:
    Bank _____
    Owner _____ Amount $ _____

    Bank_____
    Owner _____ Amount $ _____

CHAPTER 3: DIVIDING YOUR PROPERTY AND BILLS

Certificates of Deposit:
    Bank _____
    Owner _____ Amount $ _____

    Bank _____
    Owner _____ Amount $ _____

Money Market Accounts:
    Bank _____
    Owner _____ Amount $ _____

    Bank _____
    Owner _____ Amount $ _____

Stocks:
    Company _____
        Owner _____ # Shares _____
        Dividend $ _____ Value $ _____

    Company _____
        Owner _____ # Shares _____
        Dividend $ _____ Value $ _____

    Company _____
        Owner _____ # Shares _____
        Dividend $ _____ Value $ _____

    Company _____
        Owner _____ # Shares _____
        Dividend $ _____ Value $ _____

Bonds:
    Company _____
        Owner _____ # Shares _____
        Interest $ _____ Value $ _____

Company _____
    Owner _____ # Shares _____
    Interest $ _____ Value $ _____

Company _____
    Owner _____ # Shares _____
    Interest $ _____ Value $ _____

Company _____
    Owner _____ # Shares _____
    Interest $ _____ Value $ _____

Names and addresses of you and your spouse's stockbrokers:

_____
_____
_____
_____

Income Tax:
    Did you file a joint return for the last tax year? _____
    Is there a tax or refund due? _____
        How much State? .... $ _____
        How much Federal? .... $ _____
        How much Local? .... $ _____

Other personal property:
    Car #1: Year _____ Make and model _____
    Who has possession? _____
    Whose name on title? _____
    License plate # and state: _____ Payment $_____
    Amount of car loan unpaid $_____ Value $_____

    Car #2: Year _____ Make and model _____
    Who has possession? _____
    Whose name on title? _____
    License plate # and state: _____ Payment $_____
    Amount of car loan unpaid $_____ Value $_____

CHAPTER 3: DIVIDING YOUR PROPERTY AND BILLS

Other vehicles (boats, campers, motorcycles, etc): describe _____
Who has possession? _____ Value $_____

Stereo: describe _____
Who has possession? _____ Value $_____

Jewelry: describe _____
Who has possession? _____ Value $_____

Tools: describe _____
Who has possession? _____ Value $_____

Sporting Goods: describe _____
Who has possession? _____ Value $_____

Furniture: describe _____
Who has possession? _____ Value $_____

Appliances: describe _____
Who has possession? _____ Value $_____

Other property: describe _____
Who has possession? _____ Value $_____

Other property: describe _____
Who has possession? _____ Value $_____

Business Assets: (Corporations, Partnerships, Proprietorships)
   Description: _____
   Location: _____
   Who has ownership? _____ Value $_____

   Description: _____
   Location: _____
   Who has ownership? _____ Value $_____

DIVORCE YOURSELF

Description: _____
Location: _____
Who has ownership? _____ Value $ _____

Retirement/Pension/Profit-sharing/Stock Option Plans:

IRA Accounts:

    Bank or broker_____
    Owner _____ Amount $ _____

    Bank or broker_____
    Owner _____ Amount $ _____

    Bank or broker_____
    Owner _____ Amount $ _____

Retirement Funds:

    Company _____
    Whose fund? _____ Value $ _____

Profit-sharing Plan:

    Company _____
    Whose fund? _____ Value $ _____

Stock Option Plan:

    Company _____
    Whose fund? _____ Value $ _____

Pension Plan:

    Company _____
    Whose fund? _____ Value $ _____

Insurance:

    Life Insurance:

        Company: _____
        On whose life: _____ Beneficiary: _____
        Premium: $ _____ Cash Value $ _____

CHAPTER 3: DIVIDING YOUR PROPERTY AND BILLS

    Company: _____

    On whose life: _____ Beneficiary: _____

    Premium: $ _____ Cash Value $ _____

    (On children) Company: _____

    On whose life: _____ Beneficiary: _____

    Premium: $ _____ Cash Value $ _____

Medical Insurance:

    Company: _____

    On whom: _____ Premium: $ _____

    Company: _____

    On whom: _____ Premium: $ _____

    (On children) Company: _____

    On whom: _____ Premium: $ _____

Disability Insurance:

    Company: _____

    On whom: _____ Premium: $ _____

    Company: _____

    On whom: _____ Premium: $ _____

Auto Insurance:

    Company: _____

    Which car?: _____ Premium: $ _____

    Company: _____

    Which car?: _____ Premium: $ _____

Homeowner' Insurance:

    Company: _____

    Property address _____

    _____ Premium: $_____

Other Insurance:
    Company: _____
    What purpose? _____ Premium: $_____

Separate Property: (The term "separate property" generally refers to the property that each spouse held individually prior to the marriage and any property acquired individually by each spouse by gift or inheritance. Please see pages 44-49).

Was the amount of separate personal property that you or your spouse owned at the time of your marriage valued at over $1,000? _____

If (YES): List all specific property owned prior to marriage that is still owned (note who owns each item and its value). List property here even if listed previously.

    Description _____
    Owner_____ Value $ _____

    Description _____
    Owner_____ Value $ _____

    Description _____
    Owner_____ Value $ _____

    Description _____
    Owner_____ Value $ _____

    Description _____
    Owner_____ Value $ _____

Was any of you or your spouse's property received by gift or inheritance? _____

If (YES): List all specific property received by gift or inheritance that is still owned (note who owns each item and its value). List property here even if listed previously.

    Description _____
    Owner_____ Value $ _____

    Description _____
    Owner_____ Value $ _____

CHAPTER 3: DIVIDING YOUR PROPERTY AND BILLS

Description _____
Owner_____ Value $ _____

Description _____
Owner_____ Value $ _____

Description _____
Owner_____ Value $ _____

Bills and Debts:

Credit Cards:

Name of Company: _____
Reason for debt: _____
In whose name: _____
Monthly payment: $_____ Balance due $_____

Name of Company: _____
Reason for debt: _____
In whose name: _____
Monthly payment: $_____ Balance due $_____

Name of Company: _____
Reason for debt: _____
In whose name: _____
Monthly payment: $_____ Balance due $_____

Name of Company: _____
Reason for debt: _____
In whose name: _____
Monthly payment: $_____ Balance due $_____

Other debts:

Name of Company: _____
Reason for debt: _____
In whose name: _____
Monthly payment: $_____ Balance due $_____

DIVORCE YOURSELF

Name of Company: _____
Reason for debt: _____
In whose name: _____
Monthly payment: $_____ Balance due $_____

Name of Company: _____
Reason for debt: _____
In whose name: _____
Monthly payment: $_____ Balance due $_____

Name of Company: _____
Reason for debt: _____
In whose name: _____
Monthly payment: $_____ Balance due $_____

Property Document Checklist

The following documents should be assembled for use in understanding and arranging for the distribution of your property. This list is comprehensive and not all of the documents listed will apply to your particular circumstances. It is, however, important for you and your spouse to assemble all of the documents that do relate to your situation in order that you will both be fully aware of the details and nature of all of your property. Next to each document, note who has the document and where it is currently located. If your spouse refuses to supply you with any of the important property documents, you may need to seek the aid of an attorney in order to protect any rights that you may have to property or assets that your spouse may be attempting to conceal.

Federal, state, and local income tax returns _____
Payroll stubs and W-2 Forms _____
Records regarding any other income_____
Records regarding monthly living expenses _____
Pension and retirement plan policies and records _____
Stock option and profit-sharing plans and records _____
Business tax returns (Corporate, partnership, or sole
proprietorship) _____
Business financial statements _____
Deeds to any real estate _____
Mortgages or deeds of trust for any real estate _____
Copies of any leases _____

CHAPTER 3: DIVIDING YOUR PROPERTY AND BILLS

Checking account statements _____
Savings account statements and passbooks _____
Certificates of Deposit _____
Stock certificates and bonds _____
Securities stockbroker account statements_____
Titles to cars, boats, motorcycles, etc._____
Any outstanding loan documents_____
Credit card records _____
Records of any other debts _____
Life insurance policies _____
Health insurance policies _____
Auto insurance policies _____
Homeowner's insurance policy _____
Other insurance policies _____
Inventory of contents of safety deposit boxes _____
Appraisals of any property _____
Records of any gifts or inheritances _____

Property Division Upon Divorce

As noted earlier, there have been many recent changes in the way that the law deals with each spouse's property upon divorce. Under prior law in most states, the property generally belonged to the person whose name was on the title. This lead, in many instances, to the wife being left with little or no property upon divorce, since it was usually the husband whose name was used to title property.

Today, there are two general sets of rules that apply to the division of property upon divorce in the United States. There are nine "community property" states which essentially view all of the property obtained during a marriage as being owned equally by the spouses. The community property states are: Arizona, California, Idaho, Louisiana, Nevada, New Mexico, Texas, Washington, and Wisconsin. All of the other states (except Mississippi: please see Note on Mississippi later in this chapter) are known as "equitable distribution" states. In these states, upon divorce a couple's property is subject to being divided on a more or less fair or "equitable" basis. The Appendix will explain which laws apply to your state and will also give some detail as to which property is subject to being shared with your spouse upon divorce.

Bear in mind that these methods of property distribution are what a judge will use if you and your spouse can not come to an agreement regarding the division in your situation.

However, these rules are only guidelines. You and your spouse may legally divide your property in any manner that you choose and can mutually agree on. The only qualification is that the division must be relatively fair. If the division of property by your marital settlement agreement appears inherently unfair to one of the spouses, the judge in most states has the authority and power to change the division upon your ultimate divorce.

What follows is a general discussion of the method by which property is divided in "community property" states and "equitable distribution" states. Check the Appendix to see which method of property division applies to your state and then read that section carefully. The property division rules provided here are general in nature and reflect the modern trends in property division law. However, specific legal rights to particular pieces of property may not always be clear. By following the general rules and applying a sense of fairness in your attempts to reach a settlement, you should be able to reach an equitable agreement. The laws relating to property and property division, however, can get extremely complicated. If you or your spouse have a great deal of property, or your property is owned in complex manners, or you are confused about your rights, it may be wise to seek professional assistance. A lawyer, accountant, or real estate broker may be able to provide enough information for you to understand your property and continue with preparing your own settlement agreement. If you are hesitant about losing any property or feel that you and your spouse can not agree to a fair division, you should seek the aid of a competent attorney or mediator.

Community Property States

The law in "community property" states generally stems from French or Spanish civil law. Under this type of law, it was felt that all property which a couple obtained while they were married should be shared equally by the spouses. Marriage was viewed essentially as an equal business partnership. Property owned by spouses in these states is divided into two distinct classes: separate property and community property.

Separate Property

Separate property is generally described as consisting of three types of property:

- Property that each spouse owned individually prior to their marriage;

- Property that each spouse acquired by individual gift, either before or during the marriage (Gifts given to both spouses together or gifts given by one spouse to the other are generally considered community property); and

- Property that each spouse acquired by inheritance (legally referred to as "by bequest, descent, or devise"), either before or during the marriage.

CHAPTER 3: DIVIDING YOUR PROPERTY AND BILLS

Each spouse's separate property is treated as their own sole property and is not generally subject to being divided upon divorce. Typically, community property states also provide that if a spouse's particular separate property is exchanged for another piece of property, the new property continues to be separate property. Similarly, in most cases if separate property is sold and the proceeds are used to purchase different property, this new property is also considered separate property. In order for a piece of property to remain classified as "separate property", however, the property must generally be actually kept separate from any jointly-owned property. It must not be mixed at all with community property: for example, in a joint savings account or in a joint investment. Generally, you must be able to clearly trace the whereabouts of the separate property and show that it has remained separate in order to claim it as separate. In addition, interest or profits earned by separate property and any increases in value of the separate property during the marriage are also generally considered to be separate property. Some states, however, do not classify increase in value or exchanges as separate property. Check the Appendix for your state's specific rules.

Bills and obligations which either spouse incurred prior to their marriage are also considered separate property. The spouse who incurred the debt prior to getting married is solely liable for the payment of the unpaid balance. In addition, you may agree that any debts that either of you incur after your separation are to be considered separate. Be aware, however, that even though you may have a valid legal agreement with your spouse that you will each only be responsible for your own debts, such an agreement does not bind any third party. In other words, even if you have a settlement agreement, if your spouse runs up substantial debts prior to your divorce, you may still be liable for payment on these debts. You will, however, generally be able to sue your spouse for reimbursement under the terms of your settlement agreement.

As a rule, if you have a clear record or understanding with your spouse that certain property is your personal separate property, then that property is not to be included in your division of community property. List each of your individual pieces of separate property on the Property Division Worksheet that follows. That property is yours to keep regardless of the division of your community property. Be aware, however, that some community property states do allow a spouse's separate property to be subject to division by a judge under certain circumstances. If there is a very lop-sided amount of separate property owned by one of the spouses and it is felt that an equal division of the community property is not at all fair to the other spouse, some states will allow a court to invade a spouse's separate property to provide for a more equitable division. Remember, though, that you and your spouse can agree to divide your own property in any manner that you both agree is fair. Please check the Appendix to see how your state deals with this situation. If the Appendix does not contain enough specific information for you to classify a particular piece of property, you may have to consult an attorney for that determination.

Community property

All marital property that is not separate property is referred to as "community property". This includes anything that either spouse earned or acquired at any time during the marriage that is not separate property. The property acquired during the marriage is considered community property regardless of whose name may be on the title to the property, and regardless of who actually paid for the property (unless it was paid for entirely with one spouse's separate property funds and remains separate). All of a couple's bills and obligations that are incurred during a marriage are also considered community property and are to be divided equally upon divorce. (A few states, however, consider educational loans for one spouse to be a separate debt and not to be shared by the other spouse upon divorce).

Unless there is an agreement otherwise, and unless separate property can be clearly shown, all property that the spouses own at the time of their divorce is generally presumed to be community property. If there is no separation or settlement agreement stating otherwise, this may include any property acquired even after the couple has separated.

Most "community property" states require an equal division of all community property or start with a presumption that an *equal* division is the fairest method, although even these states will allow some leeway from an exact 50-50 division depending on the facts of the case. The remaining "community property" states provide for an *equitable* division of the community property. In this situation, equitable is defined to mean fair and just. An exact equal division is not necessarily required. However, in practice, judges generally begin their distribution deliberations from a 50-50 division point, adjusting the balance as the particular circumstances of the case may dictate. To deviate from an equal division of the property, judges are commonly guided by a set of statutory guidelines or factors that are to be considered. A few states, however, have no statutory guidelines to follow. The guidelines available in "community property" states are, in most cases, similar to those available in "equitable distribution" states and are discussed later in this chapter under "**Factors for Consideration in Property Division**".

Finally, in California and a few other states, there is a class of property that is referred to as "quasi-community" property. It is simply property that the spouses may have acquired before they moved to the particular state which would have been "community" property if they had lived in the state when they acquired it. This type of property may generally be treated as "community" property.

Equitable Distribution States

There are 40 states that abide by what is known as an "equitable distribution" method of property division. This is a relatively new property law concept which is still evolving. It has distinct similarities to the "community property" system, and yet is different in many

CHAPTER 3: DIVIDING YOUR PROPERTY AND BILLS

respects. There are several versions of this system of property law in effect in various states. Check the Appendix to determine which specific method is used in your state.

In "equitable distribution" jurisdictions, certain marital property is subject to division by the judge upon divorce. Which property is subject to division varies somewhat from state to state but generally follows three basic patterns:

1. The most common method of classifying property in "equitable distribution" states closely parallels the method used in "community property" states. Property is divided into two basic classes: *separate* or *non-marital* property and *marital* property. What constitutes property in each class is very similar to the definitions in "community property" states.

   Separate or *non-marital* property typically consists of property which either spouse brought to the marriage, property acquired by individual gift, and property which was obtained by inheritance (legally known as "bequest, devise, and descent"). Each spouse's separate non-marital property is treated as their own sole property and is not generally subject to being divided upon divorce. Typically, states which use this method of property division also provide that if a spouse's particular separate non-marital property is exchanged for another piece of property, the new property continues to be separate non-marital property. Similarly, in most cases if separate non-marital property is sold and the proceeds used to purchase different property, this new property is also considered separate non-marital property. In order for a piece of property to remain classified as "separate non-marital property", however, the property must generally be actually kept separate from any jointly-owned property. It must not be mixed at all with marital property: for example, in a joint savings account or in a joint investment. Generally, you must be able to clearly trace the whereabouts of the separate non-marital property and show that it has remained separate in order to claim that it should not be subject to division. In addition, interest or profits earned by separate non-marital property and any increases in value of the such property during the marriage are also generally considered to be separate non-marital property. Some states, however, do not classify increase in value or exchanges as separate non-marital property. Check the Appendix for your state's particular rules.

   Similarly to community property states, *marital* property consists of all other property; essentially all property which the spouses acquired, either jointly or individually, at any time during the marriage, regardless of whose name is on the title and regardless of who actually paid for the property (unless it was paid for entirely with one spouse's separate non-marital property funds and remains separate). All of a couple's bills and obligations that are incurred during a marriage are also generally considered marital property and are to be divided equally upon divorce. Unless there is an agreement otherwise, and unless separate non-marital property can be clearly shown, all property that the spouses own at the time of their divorce is generally presumed to be marital property. If there is no separation or settlement agreement stating otherwise, this may include any property acquired even after the couple has separated.

2. The second method for distribution which is used in several states is to make ALL of a couple's property subject to division upon divorce. Regardless of whether it was obtained by gift, by inheritance, or was brought into the marriage, and regardless of whose name is on the title or deed, the property may be apportioned to either spouse depending upon the decision of the judge. There is no differentiation between marital, non-marital, or separate property. The property is still divided on a basis which attempts to achieve a general fairness, but all of a couple's property is available for such distribution.

3. The third method for distribution is basically a hybrid of the above two methods. In several states, specific property is exempted from distribution. For example, in some states all property except gifts may be subject to division upon divorce. In other states, only inheritances may be exempted from division. In still others, marital property may consist of all property owned by the spouses except that brought to the marriage by either spouse and kept separate. The rules for these states are outlined in the Appendix.

You will need to carefully read the Appendix that applies to your state to determine which property is subject to division and distribution in your state. Keep in mind, however, that regardless of what your state law dictates, you and your spouse may divide your property in any manner that you can agree on. If you both feel that it is fair to share in a particular gift, or divide the proceeds of an inheritance, you may accomplish this by use of your marital settlement agreement. If it seems fair for one spouse to use his or her separate funds to purchase another's share of a particular piece of jointly-held property, this may also be accomplished. The state laws and guidelines are only a starting point for discussions and negotiations.

Bills and obligations which either spouse incurred prior to their marriage are also considered separate or non-marital property (except in the few states which make all property subject to division). The spouse who incurred the debt prior to getting married is solely liable for the payment of the unpaid balance. In addition, you may agree that any debts that either of you incur after your separation are to be considered separate non-marital debts. Be aware, however, that even though you may have a valid legal agreement with your spouse that you will each only be responsible for your own debts, such an agreement does not bind any third party. In other words, even if you have a settlement agreement, if your spouse runs up substantial debts prior to your actual divorce, you may still be liable for payment on these debts. You will, however, generally be able to sue your spouse for reimbursement under the terms of your settlement agreement.

Generally, in "equitable distribution" states, you will decide which property is you or your spouse's separate non-marital property and which is marital property. In those few states that allow any property to be subject to division, this step will not be necessary. Once you have determined which of your property is subject to being divided, you must then decide how exactly you will accomplish this task. As in many community property states, a 50-50 division of property is most often the starting point for property division decisions made by courts in equitable distribution jurisdictions. Please note, however, the individual differences in your state's property division laws as shown in the Appendix.

> Note on Mississippi: Mississippi is the only state remaining that has not enacted either the equitable division or community property systems of property division. Mississippi law is based on former English common law principles that hold that the owner of property is the spouse whose name is on the title. This system has had harsh results in the past by denying the wife in a marriage a fair share of the property accumulated during a marriage, even if it was substantially the wife's efforts that provided the largest contribution. Recently, however, Mississippi judges have softened the strict application of this property division system by allowing for ample lump-sum alimony awards to take the place of an equitable distribution of property. With these differences in mind, you may wish apply the general modern trends in property law to divisions of your property in Mississippi. Please refer to the Appendix for more detail.

Factors for Consideration in Property Divisions

In most states, there is a list of factors provided in the statutes for the judge to use in making any property distribution decisions. These factors are present in both "community property" and "equitable distribution" states. Each state is free to allow its judges to consider what has been determined to be relevant factors in dividing the property.

Each factor carries no specific weight in the decisions to be made. In no state is a particular preference given to each factor. Rather, the list of factors is to be used as a guideline to balance the contributions of each spouse and attempt to arrive at a fair division of the couple's property.

Recently, there have been some substantial changes in what factors are considered relevant in dividing a couple's property. Marital fault is no longer a factor for consideration in most states. Adultery, desertion, cruelty and other marital faults have no bearing on property decisions in a majority of states. However, in many states (even those which do not consider marital fault) economic misconduct continues to be a factor. Economic misconduct is generally viewed as one spouse attempting to hide any property from the other spouse, dissipating joint assets, cleaning out joint bank accounts and keeping the money, running up major joint bills in anticipation of divorce, or other such vengeful acts.

It is wise to close all of your joint bank accounts and cancel all joint credit cards upon your separation. This, however, should be a joint decision. The obligations and proceeds of these joint accounts will then be dealt with in your settlement agreement. If you do not trust your spouse enough to discuss the closing of a joint account, or if you fear that your spouse may attempt to clean out your accounts, you will probably not be able to cooperate enough to reach a marital settlement agreement without the aid of a lawyer or mediator. Do not try to hide or conceal any of the assets that belong to both you and your spouse. If your divorce ends up contested and before a judge, you will be required to account for these assets. Such economic misconduct may influence your right to property and support.

In order to attempt to equalize the treatment of homemakers and spouses who give primary care to a couple's children, the efforts of a spouse in caring for children and homemaking are now specifically being considered as a relevant factor in a majority of states. The career and economic sacrifices that one spouse has made to put the other through school is also increasingly being considered as a factor in property divisions.

The trend is for the consideration of any relevant factors which have accounted for the economic contributions to the marriage, whether such contributions are tangible (wages, salary, etc.) or intangible (homemaking, child care, career sacrifices, etc.). The tax consequences of your property division may also be an important factor and this is discussed later in Chapter 7.

Other relevant factors which may be considered in the division of property:

- The contribution of each spouse to the acquisition of the marital property, including the contribution of each spouse as homemaker;
- The length of the marriage;
- The age and health of each spouse;
- The value of each spouse's separate property;
- Any increase or decrease in the value of the separate property of each spouse during the marriage;
- Any depletion of a spouse's separate property for marital purposes;
- The economic circumstances of each spouse at the time the division of property is to become effective;
- The amount of alimony that either spouse may be awarded;
- The occupation and vocational skills of each spouse;
- The income and liabilities of each spouse;
- The employability of each spouse;
- The opportunity of each spouse for further acquisition of capital assets and income;
- The time necessary for either spouse to acquire sufficient education to enable the spouse to find appropriate employment;
- The present and potential earning capacity of each spouse;

CHAPTER 3: DIVIDING YOUR PROPERTY AND BILLS

- The presence of any retirement benefits, including social security, civil service, military and railroad retirement benefits;
- Any child care or child support burdens;
- The standard of living of both spouses during the marriage;
- The tax consequences of the property division;
- How and by whom the property was acquired;
- The economic needs of each spouse; and
- Any other relevant factor.

As you can see from the above list, the division of property is generally considered to be interrelated to any provisions for alimony and child support. As you work through your agreement with your spouse, realize that all of the provisions that you discuss relate to each other. For your agreement to be a success in eliminating discord from your divorce, it must be a careful balance of all factors and considerations. In short, it must be fair to both you and your spouse.

How each of these factors should be taken into account is up to you and your spouse. What is important to understand is that these detailed factors for consideration were developed in an effort to somewhat quantify the process of property distribution for judges who knew little or nothing about a couple's actual circumstances. They are used as an outline for the presentation of evidence to courts in an effort to show that certain elements of a couple's life together should have a bearing on how their property is divided on divorce.

If the property settlement discussions can be kept on a rational and mature level, you and your spouse are in a far better position to determine how these factors should affect your agreement on the division of property. Please carefully read the factors listed in your state's Appendix. If your state does not have any statutory factors listed, the general factors listed here may be used.

Considerations Regarding Specific Property

Regardless of what type of property division system your state uses, certain types of property require individual consideration. These specific types of property will be discussed below.

The Family Home

For most people, a home is, by far, their most important possession. Any attempt to divide a single home between two divorcing spouses will be difficult. Many different factors will influence your ultimate decision on how to account for your home.

The first thing you will need to know is the current market value of the home. You can determine this by the use of a professional real estate appraisal. If you have not owned the home for very long, local real estate brokers may be able to give you a good indication of its current market value. Once you know the market value, you must subtract how much is still owed on the mortgage or trust deed (including any amounts owed on second mortgages or home-equity loans) in order to determine the "equity" in the home.

For example, if your home is appraised at $50,000 and your mortgage balance is $35,000, then the "equity" in your home is $15,000. It is the equity value of any property that you will be dividing with your spouse.

By using the above example, we can examine the various ways to deal with the division of a house. In general, there are two main methods by which to deal with a family home.

First, the simplest method of dealing with the division of the home is to sell it and divide the net proceeds. In the example above, a couple might sell the $50,000 home, pay off the mortgage, and have a gross profit of $15,000. Out of this would come any real estate commission, usually about 7% or $3,500. This would leave a net profit of $11,500. Divided equally, each spouse would receive $5,750 from the sale and division of their home. There will also usually be tax consequences to the sale of your home and any tax liabilities should be considered and shared in an equal manner. A marital settlement agreement clause defining the sale of property and the division of the proceeds is included later in this chapter.

Next, you may wish for one spouse to keep the home. If there are minor children who have lived in the home, serious consideration should be given to finding a method of division which will allow the spouse who retains physical custody of the children to remain in the family home. This is highly favored by most judges and is generally considered to be in the best interests of the children. In addition, it lessens the severe economic burdens that may be placed on the spouse with custody. Although it may seem one-sided for one spouse to have custody of the children and to have possession of the family home, in reality in nearly every divorce situation involving children, it is the spouse without custody who fares better economically.

Whether there are children or not, you may decide that one of the spouses will retain possession of the house. To accomplish this, there are several standard methods. First, title to the home may be transferred to the spouse who wishes to retain possession. When there are children, this will normally be the spouse with physical custody. This transfer is generally made in a trade or exchange for something worth the one-half value of the equity of the home. Again, using the example above, if the equity of the home is $15,000, and the home is to be transferred to one spouse, the other spouse should receive a trade-off of cash or property worth $7,500. This trade can be accomplished in a number of ways. If there is sufficient cash or property available, it is a relatively simple matter.

CHAPTER 3: DIVIDING YOUR PROPERTY AND BILLS

Two other methods may be: (1) for the spouse retaining possession to take out a second mortgage and pay off the other spouse from the proceeds; and (2) for the spouse retaining possession to give the other spouse a note for payment of the one-half equity interest and either defer payment until the house is sold, make payments directly to the other spouse, or agree to pay off the note when the children are grown. Marital settlement agreement clauses relating to these rather complex methods are not included in this book. A real estate professional or an attorney should be consulted for assistance in structuring these particular deals. However, clauses regarding a trade-off or exchange of a property are provided later in this chapter.

Another less common method would be for both spouses to retain shared ownership of the home as tenants-in-common, with the spouse with the children retaining possession. An agreement allowing possession until the children are grown and an agreement on when the home will be sold should be reached if this method is chosen. Because of the continuing joint ownership under this method, it is more likely to cause later problems and is therefore less favored and no settlement agreement clauses for use in this situation are included.

To transfer the ownership of the home to one spouse, a deed (usually a quitclaim deed) will be necessary. To transfer the title from joint marital ownership (usually referred to on the deed as "joint tenancy with right of survivorship" or "tenancy-by-the-entireties") to a third party upon a sale of the home will generally require a warranty deed. If there is to be a note taken back by one spouse (where one spouse agrees to pay the other for his or her share of the home), this should be secured by a Deed of Trust or Mortgage. Any deeds or mortgages must be recorded in the office of your county recorder. For assistance in transferring real estate, you may wish to use a real estate broker, title or escrow company, attorney, or bank. In Chapter 7, a general mandatory marital settlement agreement clause is included which obligates both you and your spouse to cooperate in signing any necessary documents to implement any of the provisions under the terms of your agreement.

Retirement and Pension Plans

A majority of states now consider the value of benefits in retirement and pension plans which were accumulated during a marriage to specifically be subject to division by the court upon divorce. Realistically, if the benefits were earned during the course of the marriage, there is no reason why such benefits should not be considered as part of a spouse's income or assets which should be shared with the other spouse. The most difficult aspect of attempting to divide the value of a pension or retirement plan is actually determining what the actual present value is. There are many different types of pension plans and each may have a slightly different method for determining what benefits are available and when they are due.

Some common retirement arrangements are:

- Individual Retirement Accounts (IRA's);
- Self-Employed Person's Individual Retirement Account (SEP-IRA's);
- HR-10 Retirement Plans (KEOGH's);
- IRS 401(K) Retirement Plans;
- Tax Sheltered Annuities (TSA's);
- Employee Stock Option Plans (ESOP's);

In order to determine a plan's value for division, an estimate of the current value of benefits that accrued during your marriage is necessary. The assistance of the administrators of the plan will probably be necessary to determine how much money was contributed and when the contributions were made. You may also ask them to give you an estimate of the current value of the plan or tell you how much would be due if the plan was immediately terminated. For an actual detailed valuation, a professional actuary skilled in pensions, an accountant, CPA, or an attorney may be necessary.

If you have not been married for very long, the value of the retirement plan may be very little and a rough estimate of its value may be used for purposes of division. If, however, you have been married for a considerable time and you or your spouse have substantial contributions to retirement funds or pension plans, you should get expert assistance in valuing these funds. For many older Americans, the value of pension or retirement funds may be the largest single asset that they own.

If you feel that the value of your share of your spouse's pension or retirement plan may be significant or you are unable to accurately value the benefits, you may wish to consult an attorney to be certain that you do not lose any rights to this benefit. If the value of the plan can be ascertained, division of the benefits can be accomplished by trade-off. Since a retirement plan is very difficult to divide without actually terminating it and cashing it in, the easiest method for division is for the spouse who owns it to retain the full interest in the plan. If there is a family home, the spouse retaining the home may trade his or her share of the pension plan for the other spouse's share of the home. If there are other assets available, these also may be used in a trade-off.

An example of a trade-off of retirement benefits would be as follows: Spouse A has benefits in a retirement plan which are valued at $5,000, and all of the benefits were earned while the couple was married. Spouse B has no retirement benefits. The only other property that the couple owns is a car worth $3,000 and which is fully paid off. They also have $2,000 in a joint bank account. The couple's joint marital property, thus, is valued at $10,000 ($5,000 retirement benefits + $3,000 car + $2,000 cash = $10,000). Using an equal 50/50 division, each spouse should get $5,000 worth of their marital assets on divorce. Spouse A may retain his or her entire interest in the retirement fund by trading off his or her interests in the bank account and car. Spouse A would then retain the entire retirement fund ($5,000) and spouse B would keep the car and cash ($2,000 + $3,000 = $5,000).

CHAPTER 3: DIVIDING YOUR PROPERTY AND BILLS

Stock-option or Profit-sharing Plans

Like pension and retirement funds, these assets are a clear benefit accrued as a result of a spouse's employment. If you or your spouse were participants in such a plan during your marriage, the benefits that were earned during the marriage should be considered as property to be shared and divided. Again, the most difficult problem may be in determining the value of such benefits. With most of these type of plans, however, the value should be easier to ascertain than with pension plans. Check with the employer or administrator of the plan for assistance in determining the value of the benefits that accrued to the spouse during the time of the marriage. The value of any such plans should then be included in the total amount of marital property which is available for division.

Social Security Benefits

Social Security benefits are not community or marital property and are not subject to division by a court upon divorce. They are federal benefits and are not governed by state law. You will need to contact your local Social Security office to determine your rights to benefits after divorce. If you have been married for 10 years or more, you will have a right to Social Security benefits that accrued during your marriage even though you become divorced. You will also generally be eligible for Social Security survivor benefits if you and your spouse have been married for at least 10 years. If you are approaching being married for 10 years, be aware that divorce from your spouse before you reach the 10-year deadline may cost you significant Social Security benefits.

In addition, even though Social Security benefits are not subject to division in a divorce, the value of such benefits may be taken into account in any considerations regarding the amount of alimony or property to be allocated to a spouse.

Military and Federal Pensions and Benefits

Although military retirement pensions and federal civil service annuity benefits are also federally administered, they are subject, in most cases, to division upon divorce. Military *disability* pay is not, however, subject to division upon divorce. For military retirement benefits, there is a requirement that your marriage has lasted 10 years in order to share in the benefits which have accrued to your spouse. In addition, certain other benefits (such as PX and commissary rights) will be retained on divorce if your marriage lasted through 20 years of military service.

If you or your spouse are currently in military service, you will probably need to seek legal advice in order to obtain a divorce. Many states have specific legal requirements that must be met in order to obtain a divorce from a person on active military service. If you or your spouse are no longer in the service, but have military benefits that accrued while you were both married, you will need to determine the value of these benefits in much the same manner as outlined above in the section on pension and retirement plans. You will need to contact the agency or service branch which administers the plan or benefits.

As with standard retirement benefits, an actual division of military and federal benefits will generally be difficult. A trade-off for something of equivalent value is typically the most effective method for dealing with such benefits.

Cars and Other Vehicles

The division of cars may be accomplished by selling the vehicle and dividing the proceeds, or by a trade-off of one spouse's share of the car's value. For the trade-off method, first determine the equity value of the car. This is determined by subtracting the amount owed on the car from its current market value. You can check with a car dealer or bank to find approximate (Blue Book) values of cars or trucks. The equity value should then be divided between the spouses. If you or your spouse desire to keep the car, a trade of something of a value equal to the other spouse's share must be made. Transfer of title and registration (license plates) should then be made to the spouse who will retain the vehicle.

Educational Degrees

Many states now consider the value of a professional educational degree which was earned during the marriage to be part of the marital or community property and subject to division. The rationale behind this is that, in many cases, the spouse who did not earn the degree has sacrificed important career or educational opportunities of his or her own in order to assist the other spouse in earning the degree. The intention of most couples in such a situation was that the spouse who earned the degree would then be in a better position to bring income into the family. Upon divorce and in order to equalize the potential earning power of the degree-holder with that of the spouse who made the sacrifices for the attainment of the other's degree, a value is placed on the degree and it is considered as property to be divided. It is, however, very difficult to place a specific value on the future earning potential value which is directly traceable to a particular professional degree. If you feel that the value of a professional degree is an important factor in your particular situation, it may be prudent to seek professional assistance from either a qualified accountant or attorney.

Property Division Worksheet

With the various differences between state laws in mind, you must make certain decisions regarding the division of your property. You and your spouse should use the information that you previously filled in on the Property Questionnaire to examine your total property

CHAPTER 3: DIVIDING YOUR PROPERTY AND BILLS

holdings. By using the following Worksheet, you will be able to clearly and fairly decide who will get which pieces of property.

The first step in filling in your Worksheet should be to list the property that you both agree is the *separate* property of each. For this worksheet, we will use the term *separate* to mean that property that you and your spouse agree is not to be subject to division, either because of your state's law on the matter or simply because of your agreement as such. Generally, this is property that either of you owned prior to your marriage and any property that either of you acquired by gift or inheritance. If you are unclear on this, refer to the specific discussion of your state's laws in the Appendix.

The next step will be to list, in the general areas provided, the type and value of all of your *marital* property. For the purpose of this worksheet, the term *marital* property will be used to refer to all property that you and your spouse agree should be subject to division. This should include all of your property that is not listed in the *separate* property section. Be aware that various states may refer to such property by differing terms, such as "community" property. At this same time, you should make a general listing of all of the bills that you and your spouse have accumulated. These, too, will need to be divided.

The next step will generally be the most difficult. You will need to divide all of the listed marital property and bills into two equal or equitable shares. The joint bills of each of you will be used as an off-set against any property. As a general rule, you should begin with an equal division of the marital property and bills. Most "community property" states require an equal division of property and many "equitable division" states also tend to use an equal division. An equal division is perhaps the easiest and most fair method of division to apply in most cases. Courts have found that the equal division method eliminates much of the confusion which may result from trying to value many of the intangible items that are relevant to the decision, such as the value of home-making, child-rearing, and career sacrifices. If an exact equal division is not possible, attempt to reach agreement on a division that is as close to equal as is reasonably possible. On a piece-by-piece basis, divide and list the property to that spouse who wishes to retain it.

Certain pieces of property will not be easily subject to division. For those, there are various ways to reach a fair settlement. If one spouse truly desires the property, other property or cash may be traded for the property sought in order to essentially equalize the division. If an agreement can not be reached on a particular piece of property, the property can be sold and the proceeds simply divided in half. If a specific value can not be readily attached to a particular piece of property, it is wise to have an independent appraisal made of the property.

Certain mediators have used a method of equal division to assure that each spouse is satisfied with the conclusion. Simply attempt to reach a division of property settlement in which either spouse would be satisfied with either share of the marital property. If you or your spouse would be content with either share of the divided property, you can be relatively assured that a generally fair division has been achieved.

Here is an example of a couple's property division: The couple had the following assets: Spouse A had cash from an inheritance of $3,000. Spouse B had a boat that he owned prior to the marriage worth $2,000. They bought a $5,000 car during the marriage (which is now worth $3,000) and still owe $1,000 on it. They have furniture worth $1,000, a $500 stereo and $2,500 in a joint checking account. Their joint bills (mostly credit card balances) amount to $1,000.

Spouse A's separate property would be the $3,000 inheritance funds. Spouse B's separate property would be the $2,000 boat. Their marital property would consist of the equity of $2,000 in the car, the furniture and stereo worth $1,500 the $2,500 cash in the bank for a sub-total of $6,000. From this would be subtracted the $1,000 in bills for a total of $5,000. Each would be entitled to about a $2,500 share of the total marital property.

Their agreement is that Spouse A would keep the car and stereo for his or her share ($2,000 car equity + $500 stereo = $2,500). Spouse A would also be liable to pay off the remaining balance due on the car loan. Spouse B would keep the furniture and the cash in the bank and pay off the credit card bills ($1,000 furniture + $2,500 cash - $1,000 bills = $2,500). Any number of other agreements could have been reached to divide the property but the method is essentially the same in any instance.

The method to follow is to first determine what property you both have. Next, take out the separate property that you will each keep and which will not be subject to your marital property division. Then, determine the total value of all of your marital property that remains. Finally, agree on a method that apportions approximately one-half of the value of the remaining marital property and bills to each party.

If at this point you are not clear about what property you own or your rights to that property or are unable to reach a fair agreement with your spouse regarding the division of your property, it may be wise to consider consulting a mediator or an attorney. Once you are clear on your position, you may still be able to proceed with preparing your own settlement agreement.

Property Division Worksheet

Separate Property of Spouse #1 (Name) _____

    Description _____ Value $ _____

    Description _____ Value $ _____

    Description _____ Value $ _____

    Description _____ Value $ _____

    Description _____ Value $ _____

    Description _____ Value $ _____

CHAPTER 3: DIVIDING YOUR PROPERTY AND BILLS

    Description _____ Value $ _____
    Description _____ Value $ _____
    Description _____ Value $ _____
    Description _____ Value $ _____
    Description _____ Value $ _____

    Total Of Separate Property (Spouse #1): $ _____

Separate Property of Spouse #2 (Name)_____

    Description _____ Value $ _____
    Description _____ Value $ _____
    Description _____ Value $ _____
    Description _____ Value $ _____
    Description _____ Value $ _____
    Description _____ Value $ _____
    Description _____ Value $ _____
    Description _____ Value $ _____
    Description _____ Value $ _____
    Description _____ Value $ _____
    Description _____ Value $ _____

    Total Of Separate Property (Spouse #1): $ _____

Marital Property of Both Spouses:

    Real estate:_____ Value $ _____
    Auto: _____ Value $ _____
    Furniture: _____ Value $ _____
    Cash: _____ Value $ _____
    Auto: _____ Value $ _____
    Jewelry: _____ Value $ _____
    Tools: _____ Value $ _____
    Other: _____ Value $ _____
    Stocks: _____ Value $ _____
    Bonds: _____ Value $ _____

    A.   Total Amount Of Marital Property: $ _____

Marital Bills and Obligations:

Creditor: _____ Balance $ _____
Creditor: _____ Balance $ _____
Creditor: _____ Balance $ _____
Creditor: _____ Balance $ _____
Creditor: _____ Balance $ _____
Creditor: _____ Balance $ _____
Creditor: _____ Balance $ _____
Creditor: _____ Balance $ _____

B. Total Amount Of Marital Bills: $ _____

Value Of Marital Property To Be Divided:

Total Amount Of Marital Property (A): $ _____
Minus (-)
Total Amount Of Marital Bills (B): $ _____
Equals (=)
Total Value To Be Divided (C) (A - B = C): $ _____

Approximate Value To Each (1/2 or C/2): $ _____

Agreed Share of Marital Property and Bills for Each Spouse:

Spouse #1: _____
Description: _____ Value: $ _____
Description: _____ Value: $ _____
Description: _____ Value: $ _____
Description: _____ Value: $ _____
Description: _____ Value: $ _____
Description: _____ Value: $ _____
Description: _____ Value: $ _____
Description: _____ Value: $ _____
Description: _____ Value: $ _____
Description: _____ Value: $ _____
Description: _____ Value: $ _____

TOTAL MARITAL PROPERTY Spouse #1: $ _____

CHAPTER 3: DIVIDING YOUR PROPERTY AND BILLS

Spouse #2: _____

Description:_____ Value: $_____

Description:_____ Value: $_____

Description:_____ Value: $_____

Description:_____ Value: $_____

Description:_____ Value: $_____

Description:_____ Value: $_____

Description:_____ Value: $_____

Description:_____ Value: $_____

Description:_____ Value: $_____

Description:_____ Value: $_____

Description:_____ Value: $_____

TOTAL MARITAL PROPERTY Spouse #2: $_____

Marital Settlement Agreement Clauses Regarding Property

Once you have reached an agreement on the division of your property and bills that you are both satisfied with, you are ready to select the appropriate clauses for your settlement agreement. The following clauses cover the most common methods for dividing your property. Choose the clause that most nearly describes your agreement with your spouse. The small box to the left of each clause will be used in Chapter 8 for numbering the individual clauses that you have chosen.

Property Division Clause (Property Not Listed)

This clause should be used for cases where there is very little or even no property and there are no significant bills to divide. It simply allows each spouse to keep the property currently in his or her possession. It also provides that any bills have already been divided and taken care of by you and your spouse. If you have significant property (car, furniture, appliances, etc.) or bills owed or if you have property that you have not yet divided, you should use a different clause. Also, if you or your spouse have a pension or retirement plan that will be divided, you must use a different clause so that such a plan may be listed and identified specifically. You may use this clause, however, if you have no property or bills or all of your property and bills have actually been divided.

DIVORCE YOURSELF

☐ We both agree that our property and bills are minimal, and that we have already divided all of our property and bills to our mutual satisfaction. We each transfer and quitclaim to the other any interest that we may have in the property of the other. We both agree that all of the property that the other now possesses is the sole and separate property of the other. We also agree not to incur any further debts or obligations for which the other may be liable.

Property Division Clause (List Included)

This clause should be used if you and your spouse have agreed to a division of property and you are able to specifically list the property that each of you will retain. This clause provides that both of you have transferred the property mentioned and quitclaimed it to the other spouse. It should be used if you have relatively significant property (home, car, appliances, major furniture items, etc.), and if your method of division is in the form of a trade-off or off-set. If this clause is chosen, you will also need to choose a further clause listed later that describes the division of your bills. For each item of property, provide a complete description. For real estate, list the legal description as shown on the deed to the property. For other property, list the serial number, if available, or a clear description. If either of you has a pension plan or retirement plan, list that plan under the appropriate spouse and describe it fully.

☐ We agree that the following property shall be the sole and separate property of the Wife, and the Husband transfers and quit-claims any interest that he may have in this property to the Wife: *[Here list Wife's property]*.

_____
_____
_____
_____
_____

We also agree that the following property shall be the sole and separate property of the Husband, and the Wife transfers and quit-claims any interest that she may have in this property to the Husband: *[Here list Husband's property]*.

_____
_____
_____
_____
_____

CHAPTER 3: DIVIDING YOUR PROPERTY AND BILLS

Division of Property (By Sale)

This clause should be used if there is marital property that is to be sold and the proceeds of the sale divided between you and your spouse. It may be used for the disposition of anything from items to be sold at a yard sale to the sale of your home. An exact description of the property to be sold should be included. If the property is real estate, the description should be the legal description as shown on the deed to the property. This clause provides for an equal division of the proceeds of the sale after any expenses of the sale are deducted. In the case of the sale of a home, this would allow for any appraisal expenses and real estate broker fees to be deducted from the proceeds of the sale before dividing the profits. This clause may be used in conjunction with the previous clause.

> ☐ We agree that the following property will be sold as soon as possible and any proceeds from the sale of this property, after the deduction of any expenses of the sale, will be divided equally between us: *[Here list a description of the property to be sold]*. _____
> _____
> _____
> _____
> _____
> _____

Division Of Bills (Bills Listed)

This clause is used to specifically divide your bills. It should be used if you have relatively significant bills (outstanding loans, unpaid credit card balances, etc.). It provides that you will each individually assume and pay the bills listed after your name and not hold the other liable for the debts (hold harmless and indemnify). It also provides that neither of you will incur any more debts that the other spouse would be liable for. For each bill, list to whom the bill is owed and the amount to be paid. If you have used the first clause listed in this chapter for dividing your property and bills [**Property Division Clause (Property Not Listed)**], do not use this clause.

☐ We agree that the Wife shall pay and indemnify and hold the Husband harmless from the following debts: *[Here list debts that Wife will pay].*
_____
_____
_____
_____

We agree that the Husband shall pay and indemnify and hold the Wife harmless from the following debts: *[Here list debts that Husband will pay].*
_____
_____
_____
_____

We also agree not to incur any further debts or obligations for which the other may be liable.

All of the above clauses which you and your spouse have chosen will be used when you prepare your marital settlement agreement in Chapter 8. Please refer back to this chapter at that time.

Financial Statement

The following Financial Statement will be your record of the disclosures that you and your spouse have made to each other regarding your joint and individual economic situations. It details both your monthly income and expenses and your overall net worth (assets and liabilities). The information which you include on this form should be current and should be based upon your economic situation immediately *after* your settlement agreement takes effect. The monthly income that you list should be based on your current job and sources of income, but should not include any income derived from child support payments or alimony from your current spouse. The expenses that you include on this statement should be based on your estimated or actual expenses while you are living separate from your spouse. If you have physical custody of any children, any expenses related to their care should also be included. The assets and liabilities listed should be your separate and marital property and bills as you and your spouse have agreed to in your marital settlement agreement. Fill in only those items that apply to your circumstances.

The Financial Statement of each of you will become a permanent part of your marital settlement agreement and will also become a part of your final divorce papers. Both you and your spouse will need to prepare an individual copy of this statement. This Financial Statement is mandatory for you to fill out and is required, in some form, in most states. Some states have similar mandatory Financial Statement forms and you should use such

CHAPTER 3: DIVIDING YOUR PROPERTY AND BILLS

forms. Check the Appendix. This form assures that both you and your spouse are fully aware of each others economic circumstances and that you have made your decisions and agreements based on full knowledge of all of the facts relating to your property and income.

The method for preparation is as follows:

1. Make 2 photo-copies of the entire blank Financial Statement.

2. Each spouse should then take a copy of the Financial Statement and fill in all of the items that apply to their personal situation. Use information that will apply on the day that you sign your marital settlement agreement. In other words, describe your employment, ownership of property, and debts, as of the day that you and your spouse sign your agreement.

3. Each filled-in financial statement should then be neatly typed double-spaced on one side of white 8 1/2" X 11" paper. You should then make two photo-copies of each of the completed, but unsigned, original Financial Statements. (References to "originals" in this book refer to any unsigned documents, even if they are photo-copies. "Copies" refer to photo-copies of *signed* documents).

4. You and your spouse will then sign all three original copies of your own individual Financial Statement in front of a notary and have the final Financial Statements notarized at the same time that you sign your final Marital Settlement Agreement as explained in Chapter 8. (You may even decide to sign all of your settlement and divorce forms at the same time as explained in Chapter 10).

```
FINANCIAL STATEMENT OF _____ [Full name]


EMPLOYMENT:
    Occupation: _____
    Employed by: _____
    Address of Employer: _____
    Pay period: _____
    Next pay day: _____
    Rate of pay: $ _____

[Continued on next page]
```

[Continued from previous page]

AVERAGE MONTHLY INCOME
    Gross monthly salary or wages .... $_____
        minus Social Security .... $_____
        minus income tax .... $_____
    Other deductions from paycheck on monthly basis
        Insurance .... $_____
        Credit Union .... $_____
        Union dues .... $_____
        Other .... $_____
    Net monthly salary, wages .... $_____

    Monthly income from other sources
        Commissions, bonuses, etc. .... $_____
        Unemployment, welfare, etc. .... $_____
        Dividends, interest, etc. .... $_____
        Business income .... $_____
        Rents, royalties .... $_____
        Other monthly income .... $_____

    TOTAL AVERAGE MONTHLY INCOME: .... $_____

AVERAGE MONTHLY EXPENSES
    Mortgage or rental payment .... $_____
    Property taxes .... $_____
    Homeowner's insurance .... $_____
    Electricity .... $_____
    Water, garbage, sewer .... $_____
    Cable television .... $_____
    Telephone .... $_____
    Fuel oil and natural gas .... $_____
    Cleaning and laundry .... $_____
    Repairs and maintenance .... $_____
    Pest control .... $_____
    Housewares .... $_____

[Continued on next page]

CHAPTER 3: DIVIDING YOUR PROPERTY AND BILLS

[Continued from previous page]

    Food and grocery items .... $ _____
    Meals outside home .... $ _____
    Clothing .... $ _____
    Medical, dental, prescriptions .... $ _____
    Education .... $ _____
    Day care/baby sitter .... $ _____
    Entertainment .... $ _____
    Gifts or donations .... $ _____
    Vacation expenses .... $ _____
    Public transportation .... $ _____
    Automobile:
        Gasoline and oil .... $ _____
        Repairs .... $ _____
        License .... $ _____
        Insurance .... $ _____
        Payments .... $ _____
    Insurance:
        Health .... $ _____
        Disability .... $ _____
        Life .... $ _____
        Other .... $ _____
    Any other expenses .... $ _____
        .... $ _____
        .... $ _____
        .... $ _____
        .... $ _____

    Fixed debts on a monthly basis:
    Creditor _____   Monthly payment $ _____
    Creditor _____   Monthly payment $ _____
    Creditor _____   Monthly payment $ _____
    Creditor _____   Monthly payment $ _____
    Creditor _____   Monthly payment $ _____
    Creditor _____   Monthly payment $ _____

[Continued on next page]

[Continued from previous page]

Any other debts:
Creditor _____ Monthly payment $_____
Creditor _____ Monthly payment $_____
Creditor _____ Monthly payment $_____
Creditor _____ Monthly payment $_____

TOTAL AVERAGE MONTHLY EXPENSES: ....$_____

ASSETS:
   Cash: ....$_____
   Stocks: ....$_____
   Bonds: ....$_____
   Real estate: ....$_____
   Automobiles: ....$_____
   Contents of home or apartment: ....$_____
   Jewelry: ....$_____
   Other: (list) ....$_____
   ....$_____
   ....$_____

   TOTAL ASSETS: ....$_____

LIABILITIES:
   Creditor _____ Balance due: $_____
   Creditor _____ Balance due: $_____
   Creditor _____ Balance due: $_____
   Creditor _____ Balance due: $_____
   Creditor _____ Balance due: $_____
   Creditor _____ Balance due: $_____
   Creditor _____ Balance due: $_____
   Creditor _____ Balance due: $_____
   Creditor _____ Balance due: $_____

   TOTAL LIABILITIES: ....$_____

[Continued on next page]

[Continued from previous page]

SUMMARY OF INCOME AND EXPENSES:
    Average Monthly Income: .... $_____
    Average Monthly Expenses: .... $_____

SUMMARY OF ASSETS AND LIABILITIES:
    Total Assets: .... $_____
    Total Liabilities .... $_____

Dated this _____ day of _____, 19 ___.

_____
[Full name and signature of spouse signing form]
Address: _____
_____
Phone: _____

State of _____)
) SS.
County *[or Parish]* of _____)

On this day, before me, the undersigned authority, in and for and residing in the above county *[or parish]* and state, personally appeared *[Full name of spouse]* _____, who is personally known to me to be the same person whose name is subscribed to the foregoing document, and, being duly sworn, _____ *[he or she]* verified that the information contained in the foregoing document is true and correct on personal knowledge and acknowledged that said document was signed as a free and voluntary act.

Subscribed and sworn to before me this _____ day of _____, 19 ___.

_____
Title *[and Signature]*
Notary Seal *[if required]*
                                       My commission expires: _____

CHAPTER 4

ALIMONY, MAINTENANCE, AND SPOUSAL SUPPORT

Alimony has been a subject of both fear and confusion for many people considering divorce. For some, there is an unfounded fear that they will be forced to make exorbitant alimony payments to their former spouse for the rest of his or her life. For others approaching divorce, there is a fear that they will be left stranded without any income, job skills, or support. For most people, confusion is the likely response to questions regarding alimony. The best way to approach a consideration of alimony is to try and forget all of your preconceived notions about alimony. The laws regarding alimony have changed drastically in the last few years and the common understandings regarding alimony no longer apply. The modern trends in the awarding of alimony will be discussed below.

Before the general discussion of alimony, however, there follows a questionnaire regarding the desirability and need for alimony in your divorce situation. Two copies of this form should be made and a copy should be filled out by each spouse. The comparison of the answers on the two forms will form the basis for the beginning of your discussions regarding alimony. The responses to the questions should be openly and honestly discussed by both spouses during the conversations relating to alimony. The purpose of this questionnaire is to isolate and present the facts relating to your circumstances that are relevant to alimony. This will give both you and your spouse the information necessary to reach a rational decision on this difficult subject.

DIVORCE YOURSELF

ALIMONY QUESTIONNAIRE

Please note that all of the information that is listed on both the Property Questionnaire and the Financial Statement in the previous chapter is relevant to any discussion of alimony and may be necessary for filling in this questionnaire. Please refer to those forms when necessary.

How long have you been married? _____

Are you presently employed? _____

    If YES, where? _____

    _____

        For how long? _____

        What rate of pay? $_____

        What education necessary? _____

Prior to that what was your former job? _____

    Where? _____

    _____

        For how long? _____

        What rate of pay $_____

        What education necessary? _____

Prior to that what was your former job? _____

    Where? _____

    _____

        For how long? _____

        What rate of pay $_____

        What education necessary? _____

Prior to that what was your former job? _____

    Where? _____

    _____

        For how long? _____

        What rate of pay $_____

        What education necessary? _____

If you are not now employed when was your last job? _____

    Where? _____

    For how long? _____

    What rate of pay $_____

    What education necessary? _____

CHAPTER 4: ALIMONY, MAINTENANCE, AND SPOUSAL SUPPORT

Were you employed at the time of your marriage?
   Where?_____
   _____
   For how long? _____
   What rate of pay $_____
   What education necessary? _____
What was the level of education that you had attained at the time of your marriage?
_____

What level of education have you attained now? _____
What job skills, training, or experience did you have at the time of your marriage?
_____

What job skills, training, or experience do you now have? _____
_____

What is your usual occupation? _____
What will be your monthly income at the time of your separation? $___
What will be your monthly expenses at the time of your separation? $___
What will be the value of your property at the time of your separation? $___
How long would it take you to achieve the education or skills necessary to be able to individually attain the standard of living that you enjoyed during your marriage? _____
_____

At any time during your marriage, did your spouse attend college or a special or professional training course? _____
Did you sacrifice any career opportunities in order to allow your spouse to attend school or achieve success in his or her occupation?_____
Do you feel that you will be able to be self-sufficient after your divorce?_____
_____

Do you anticipate any unusual expenses or circumstances in the near future which may affect your ability to become self-supporting?_____
Do you and your spouse have any type of written pre-marital agreement?_____
   (If YES, what are the details that relate to alimony?) _____
   _____

Do you feel that you deserve alimony? _____
   If YES, how much? $_____
   Should it be paid in a lump-sum? _____
   Should it be paid in monthly payments? _____
      If YES, how long should the payments continue? _____

73

The Law of Alimony

The laws relating to alimony have undergone enormous changes in recent years. Most of these changes have been in response to the phenomenal changes in our society in the last few decades. Much of prior alimony law was based on the stereotypical subservient role of the wife in a marriage. This traditional role pattern has been irrevocably altered. As more women are seeking and finding employment outside of the home during a marriage the role of alimony in a divorce has shifted.

In the past, alimony was paid almost exclusively to the wife and was used, in many cases, to enable the wife to continue to live in the lifestyle to which she had become accustomed to during the marriage. Alimony has evolved from this traditional pattern to a modern method by which to enable the spouse in the least secure economic position to become self-supporting. The right to alimony in a modern divorce setting is no longer the sole province of the wife. Both spouses are considered to be equally eligible to receive alimony under the laws in all states. Although it is still far more common for a husband to provide alimony to the wife, husbands have been awarded alimony in some cases. In situations where the wife is the sole support of the family or the husband is incapable of self-support, the law ignores the sex of each spouse and awards alimony on the basis of need.

Alimony awards are not commonly awarded to either spouse, however. Such awards are only made in approximately 15% of all divorces. Thus, in only about one out of every seven divorces is alimony even considered necessary. Spousal support after marriage is definitely not common, and you should approach your discussion of alimony with this fact firmly in mind. In certain situations, however, alimony is an important and valuable right.

The length of time during which alimony payments are typically paid after a divorce has also been decreasing in recent years. The average duration of alimony payments is now approximately 2 to 5 years. This is because the emphasis for economic support has been shifting away from providing periodic alimony payments toward awarding the non-working spouse a larger share of the marital assets. By providing a larger lump-sum share of marital assets as a form of alimony rather than periodic payments, the continued involvement between the spouses is terminated much sooner.

Misconduct by either spouse during the marriage is also no longer an important factor in alimony awards. It is the economic and not the moral aspects of the divorce situation which have attained prominence in the legal process. Although most states no longer consider marital fault relevant to the awarding of alimony, some few states continue to allow misconduct to play a role in alimony decisions. Please check the Appendix to determine how the laws of your state approach this aspect of alimony.

Alimony is not generally favored when the marriage has been of short duration. If you have not been married for at least 2 years, it is very unlikely that a court would award any alimony. Where there are no children and both spouses are healthy and have the ability to be self-sufficient, there is also far less chance that a court will order either spouse to pro-

CHAPTER 4: ALIMONY, MAINTENANCE, AND SPOUSAL SUPPORT

vide alimony to the other. If the marriage has been of long duration (at least 10 years), however, and one spouse is essentially without the ability to become self-sufficient in a reasonable length of time, alimony of long duration may be necessary to prevent injustice.

If one spouse has been a homemaker or has provided full-time child care for the couple's children, there is a likelihood that he or she will have difficulty in making the transition from a position as a supported married person to that of a self-sufficient single person. The difficulty can stem from lack of formal education, lack of necessary job skills, the age of the spouse, and any number of other factors. In such situations, alimony is a necessary aspect of the divorce. Neither spouse should be forced to accept a dramatically lower standard of living upon divorce than he or she was accustomed to during the marriage. There is, however, generally no realistic way that one spouse's income can continue to support two households at the same level of comfort and in the same manner which was established during the marriage. The additional expenses of providing for the utilities, maintenance, and cost of two separate living spaces when spouses separate will automatically increase the total cost of living for the spouses.

Somewhat related to alimony is the problem of a divorced spouse obtaining health insurance protection. For those spouses who were formerly covered by the other spouse's employer-sponsored group health insurance, obtaining sufficient health insurance coverage at a reasonable rate may be a serious problem. This is particularly true if the spouse who will lose the coverage is not presently employed in a job which provides health insurance. In an effort to alleviate this problem, recent federal legislation now requires that employer-sponsored group health plans must offer divorced spouses of employees with coverage continued health insurance coverage at group rates for up to three years after divorce. If you are in this situation, contact the office of the insurance company which provides the group coverage for your spouse.

Generally, in modern divorce law, an award of alimony is made in an effort to allow a spouse the time and education or training to become self-supporting. However, for those spouses who have dedicated a large portion their lives to caring for their home and families, alimony will continue to provide important compensation and allow them to lead a secure life after divorce.

Factors for Consideration

The approach that most courts have taken to making decisions about alimony has been to review a list of factors that are relevant to support of a spouse. Other than these lists of factors, there have generally been no set guidelines provided for use in determining the actual amount of alimony to award. This decision is difficult to quantify and must be made on a case-by-case basis. Whether alimony is required and, if so, how much alimony is necessary and for how long it should be provided are decisions that you and your spouse will have to work out between yourselves.

The general factors that a court will consider are listed below. No set weight is given to any particular factor and how much importance each item should be afforded depends on the particular circumstances of your situation. The Appendix regarding your state contains a review of its particular law on alimony and should be referred to for guidance. Some states, however, do not provide any list of factors for consideration. In those states, you may use this general list for a basis of discussion. Remember that these factors are only a general outline for a judge's deliberations and that any relevant factor may be considered. Recall also that you and your spouse may reach any decision regarding alimony that you both feel is fair and satisfactory to both of you.

The general factors that a judge would use when considering an award of alimony are:

- The time necessary for a spouse to acquire sufficient education and training to enable the spouse to find appropriate employment;
- Both spouse's future earning capacities;
- The standard of living established during the marriage;
- Whether the spouse seeking support is the custodian of a child;
- Whether the spouse with child custody should be required to seek outside employment;
- The duration of the marriage;
- The financial ability of the spouse from whom alimony is sought to meet his or her needs while meeting those of the spouse seeking alimony;
- The financial resources of the spouse seeking alimony, including any marital (or community) property apportioned to the spouse and the spouse's ability to meet his or her own needs independently;
- The comparative financial resources of the spouses, including their comparative earning abilities in the labor market;
- The contribution of each spouse to the marriage, including services rendered in homemaking, child care, education, and career building of the other spouse;
- The educational level of each spouse at the time of the marriage and at the time the alimony is requested;
- The tax consequences of alimony payments to each spouse;
- The age of both spouses;
- The physical and emotional conditions of both spouses;
- The usual occupation of the spouses during the marriage;
- The vocational skills and employability of the spouse seeking alimony;
- The probable duration of the need for alimony.

Each of these factors which are relevant to your situation should be considered in arriving at a fair agreement regarding alimony. If you and your spouse can not reach an agreement regarding alimony you may need to seek legal assistance in order to protect your rights to

CHAPTER 4: ALIMONY, MAINTENANCE, AND SPOUSAL SUPPORT

sufficient future alimony. In cases where you decide that alimony is not necessary or in situations where you and your spouse are able to decide upon the amount and duration of the alimony payments, a lawyer is generally not needed.

If your marriage has been of long duration and one of you will be reasonably incapable of self-support in the future, it is recommended that you seek the assistance of a competent attorney. In such cases, alimony may be the most important economic factor in the divorce and may be the only method by which a non-self-sufficient spouse will be able to achieve a secure life. In cases where alimony will be a major factor and constitute the primary economic support for one spouse, many other factors (for example: cost-of-living adjustments and long-term tax consequences) become important. The advice of a lawyer is generally necessary in such situations.

Finally, the general tax consequences of alimony payments for both spouses are discussed in Chapter 7.

Marital Settlement Agreement Clauses Regarding Alimony

One or more of the following clauses should be selected for inclusion in every marital settlement agreement. There are clauses for use if: (1) neither spouse is to receive alimony; (2) one spouse is to receive monthly alimony payments for a set period of time; or (3) one spouse is to receive a one-time lump-sum payment of alimony. Finally, there are two clauses that relate to life insurance coverage. Choose the clause or clauses that most nearly fits your particular situation.

No Alimony to Either Spouse Clause

This clause should only be used if, after careful consideration, both you and your spouse agree that neither of you should be required to pay any alimony to the other. By using this clause, you will be giving up forever any rights that you may have to alimony. However, if this is what you have both decided is fair, then you should use this clause.

> ☐ After careful consideration of our circumstances and all of the other terms of this agreement, we both agree to waive any rights or claims that we may have now or in the future to receive alimony, maintenance, or spousal support from the other. We both fully understand that we are forever giving up any rights that we may have to alimony, maintenance, or spousal support.

Alimony Payable in Monthly Payments Clause

This clause should be used if you and your spouse have agreed that one of you should receive and one of you should pay alimony to the other in the form of periodic monthly payments. You will need to decide the amount of each payment, the day of the month that each payment will be due, and the date on which the payments should begin.

You will also need to decide when the payments are to end. You may wish the payments to end on remarriage, on death, or on a particular date. Or you may decide that the alimony payments should end on the first happening of any one of these events. If you decide that the payments are to end on the death of either spouse and the duration of the payments is for a long period, you may wish to consider the use of life insurance coverage to protect the support of the receiving spouse. Please see the clauses relating to insurance coverages later in this chapter.

In addition, in this clause you will need to decide if you wish for your decisions to be modifiable by a court in the future. If you decide that your alimony provisions may not be modified by a court, then a court will only modify this clause if it can be shown that there was fraud, coercion, or threats made in reaching the agreement or if the agreement is obviously and grossly unfair to one spouse. If you agree that this clause may be subject to court modification, please refer to Chapter 13 regarding what you may do after your divorce becomes final. In order to allow for a modification due to changed circumstances in the lives of either spouse, it is recommended that you allow for a future court modification of this clause.

Finally, through the use of this clause you will need to choose a method by which the payments should be made. Some states have enacted legislation which allows or requires any support payments to be made through the court or through certain state agencies and then be passed on to the spouse who is to receive the payment. This indirect method of payment, although generally slower, has the benefit of allowing for immediate action to be taken if any payments are missed. There is a clear record of payment in the hands of the appropriate state authorities. In fact, some states automatically take direct action against any spouse who is late with a payment, which may include garnishing wages, requiring a bond or deposit, or actually seizing a delinquent spouse's property. However, in virtually all states that allow this indirect method of payment, there are provisions that allow the spouses to opt out of the state requirement. If you and your spouse agree that the payments may be made directly to the spouse who is to receive them, you must make this decision in the clause below. If you do make the decision to allow payments to be made directly to a spouse and not through a court or state agency, it is extremely advisable to make this clause modifiable by a court at a later date. By making the clause subject to court modification, the spouse receiving the payments will retain the right to have the payments made through the court or state at a later date should any problems in late or delinquent payments arise.

CHAPTER 4: ALIMONY, MAINTENANCE, AND SPOUSAL SUPPORT

☐ | We both agree that, as alimony and maintenance, the _____ [Husband or Wife] shall pay to the _____ [Husband or Wife] the sum of $_____ per month, payable on the _____ day of each month. The first payment will be due on the _____ day of _____, 19___ and the payments shall continue until the first of the following occurrences: _____ [Select two or more of the following phrases: (1) the date that either of us dies; (2) the date that the spouse receiving alimony remarries; or (3) any specific date that you both agree upon (for example: May 5, 1995)]. We both intend that the amount and the duration of the payments _____ [may or may not] be modified by a court in the future. We also both agree that these payments should be made directly to the spouse to whom they are due. [Choose if appropriate: However, in the event of divorce or dissolution of marriage, we agree that the payments should be made through the appropriate court or state agency for payment to the spouse by such court or state agency].

Alimony Payable in a Lump-Sum Payment Clause

This clause should be used if you and your spouse agree that the fairest method of dealing with the payment of alimony is for one spouse to pay the other a one-time lump-sum payment. The funds may then be used by the spouse who receives the payment to obtain education, job skills, or training to become self-supporting. This lump-sum payment is separate from and in addition to any shift in funds or property under the terms of your property settlement. To be fair, this alimony lump-sum payment should be taken out of a spouse's share of separate and marital property after all of their property has been equally or equitably divided.

This method of spousal support has the benefit of lessening the future ties between you and your spouse and, thus, lessening the opportunities for problems to develop. It also has the benefit of not leaving one spouse subject to over-due payments from the other spouse. This method, however, is not workable if the spouse who is to pay the lump-sum payment does not currently have the assets by which to pay.

☐ | We both agree that in full payment of any claims or rights to alimony, spousal support, or maintenance, the _____ [Husband or Wife] shall pay to the _____ [Husband or Wife] the sum of $_____, which shall be paid on the _____ day of _____, 19___.

DIVORCE YOURSELF

Life Insurance Clause

This clause should be used if you and your spouse have agreed that one of you will remain as a beneficiary on a life insurance policy of the other. Retaining a position as beneficiary on the other's life insurance is generally a good idea if there are continuing support payments to be paid. The spouse who pays the alimony will be the spouse who maintains the insurance. The spouse who receives the alimony will be the spouse who is designated as beneficiary. In the event of the supporting spouse's death, this allows the spouse who is due the support to collect the benefits of any insurance and apply it to the continuing maintenance or child support obligations.

The use of this clause may be wise in any situation where there are support obligations. It is, however, highly recommended in the following circumstances:

- If you have decided that alimony should be payable in monthly payments; and
- The duration of the payments is for a long period; and
- The payments are to end on the death of either spouse.

In a situation of this nature, it is prudent to have the spouse who is to receive the payments be the beneficiary of a life insurance policy on the life of the spouse who is to make the payments. In this manner, the one receiving payments will not be left destitute on the death of a long-time ex-spouse.

> ☐ The _____ [Husband's or Wife's] life is currently insured by _____ [Name of insurance company] in the amount of $_____, and ____ [He or she] agrees to keep this policy in full force until death. We agree that the _____ [Husband or Wife] shall be designated as irrevocable sole beneficiary of this policy. The spouse obligated to provide such insurance will provide the other spouse with annual proof of such coverage.

Insurance Clause (Neither Spouse to Remain as Beneficiary)

If you or your spouse currently have insurance policies, but agree that neither of you will be retained as beneficiaries on the other's policy, use this clause. If you used the clause providing for one of you to be retained as beneficiary, do not use this clause.

> ☐ We both agree that neither of us shall remain as the beneficiary on any insurance policy carried by the other.

CHAPTER 5

CHILD CUSTODY AND VISITATION

Each year, over 1 million children experience the divorce of their parents. Too often, when children are part of a divorcing family, a devastating legal battle is waged over the right to retain custody. The emotional and psychological scars that children receive in these fierce custody wars are perhaps the most tragic results of divorce. Unfortunately, in too many instances, children become pawns in a destructive game of revenge and vindictiveness between their divorcing parents.

If you and your spouse have children, the decisions that you will face regarding their custody and visitation will perhaps be the most difficult of the entire divorce process. But in many respects, they may also be the most important. Your children's future well-being will depend directly on your ability to come to a reasonable agreement with your spouse regarding custody and visitation. If you have children, you must understand that your divorce will not end the relationship between you and your spouse. You will still both continue to be parents, even though you will no longer be wife and husband. Because of the necessity for this on-going relationship, it is very important to keep your settlement discussions regarding your children on a calm and peaceful level.

In many cases there is a temptation to allow personal animosity toward your spouse to enter into the discussions regarding your children. If you personally no longer wish to live with your spouse, you may feel that you don't want your children to live with him or her either. There may also be a tendency to attempt to vent your frustration at the prospect of divorce through a battle over custody. For your children's sake, you must make every effort to keep your discussions about custody on a reasonable and mature basis. Your children will have to live the rest of their lives with the results of you and your spouse's custody decisions.

DIVORCE YOURSELF

On the following pages, you will find a Child Custody Questionnaire. This form is designed to assist you in understanding what factors are pertinent to your discussions regarding custody and visitation. Two copies of this questionnaire should be made and both you and your spouse should honestly and completely answer the questions. Although the questions relate to one "child", if you have more than one child please include answers relating to each child on the form. Many of the questions relate to which parent, in general, currently provides the primary care for the children. Your answers will be the basis for your custody discussions with your spouse and will allow both of you to focus on the relevant issues.

Following the questionnaire, there is a general discussion of the law relating to custody, an examination of various types of custody arrangements, and information regarding how courts are guided in their decisions in this difficult area. Finally, there are various marital settlement agreement clauses describing custody and visitation alternatives.

CHILD CUSTODY QUESTIONNAIRE

What is your child's full name? _____

What is your child's birth date? _____

In what city and state was your child born? _____

Have there *ever* been any previous court proceedings regarding custody of your child? ____

    (If YES, describe in full; indicating dates, city, state, name of court, and outcome). __

_____

_____

Where does your child currently live? _____

    With whom? _____

    For how long? _____

What is your educational level? _____

    Your spouse's? _____

Do you or your spouse have any children by a previous marriage? _____

    If YES, list names, ages, and whereabouts. _____

_____

Do you have any specific physical or emotional health problems? (if YES, please
    describe). _____

    Your spouse? _____

    Your child? _____

Does your child have any special medical needs? (If YES, please describe). _____

    Is any special treatment required? _____

    Any special medication? _____

CHAPTER 5: CHILD CUSTODY AND VISITATION

Who is your child's doctor? _____

Who is your child's dentist? _____

Who takes the child to the doctor/dentist? _____

Does you child have any special educational needs? (If YES, please describe). _____
_____

What school or day care does your child currently attend? _____

    For how long? _____

    Who is your child's teacher? _____

    Who takes your child to school or day care? _____

    Who helps with homework? _____

    Who attends parent/teacher conferences? _____

Who prepares the child's meals? _____

    What is your child's favorite food? _____

    Who does the grocery shopping? _____

    Who does the dishes? _____

Do you read to your child? _____

    What is your child's favorite story? _____

Is your child involved in any sports activities? If YES, please describe). _____

    Who goes to the games? _____

    Who is the coach or teacher? _____

Is your child involved in any music, crafts, or art activities? (If YES, please describe). ____

    Who takes your child or participates? _____

    Who is the teacher? _____

What is your religious affiliation? _____

    Your spouse's? _____

    Your child's? _____

    Does your child attend church? _____

When was the last time that you or your spouse took your child to the following? (Indicate when, which parent or both).

    Library _____ Museum _____

    Zoo _____ Movie _____

    Ballgame _____ Playground _____

    Your work _____ Bike ride/hike _____

For the following questions, please answer and explain in detail in your own words regarding both you and your spouse:

Which of you is more likely to allow the child frequent and continuing contact with the other parent?
    You: _____
    Your spouse: _____

Describe the love, affection, and other emotional ties which exist between each of you and your child:
    You: _____
    Your spouse: _____

Describe the ability of each of you to provide for your child's basic needs (food, clothing, shelter, medical care):
    You: _____
    Your spouse: _____

How long has your child lived with you in a stable environment?
    You: _____
    Your spouse: _____

In your opinion, in which home will your child receive better ethical, moral, and spiritual guidance?
    You: _____
    Your spouse: _____

In your opinion, in which home will your child find the most love and affection?
    You: _____
    Your spouse: _____

CHAPTER 5: CHILD CUSTODY AND VISITATION

In your opinion, in which home will your child have the most educational enrichment and opportunities?

You: _____

Your spouse: _____

In your opinion, in which home is the child most familiar with the schools, neighborhood, and community?

You: _____

Your spouse: _____

Describe each of your efforts at the discipline of your child:

You: _____

Your spouse: _____

Has there ever been any evidence of spouse or child abuse?

You: _____

Your spouse: _____

Describe the physical, mental, and moral fitness of both you and your spouse:

You: _____

Your spouse: _____

If your child is of sufficient intelligence and understanding to form an opinion, do you feel that your child has a preference regarding who should retain custody?

You: _____

Your spouse: _____

Which of you has been the parent who has provided the primary day-to-day care for the child?

You: _____

Your spouse: _____

DIVORCE YOURSELF

Do you feel that you should have custody of your child? _____

Do you feel that you and your spouse would be able to effectively and peacefully share in making the major decisions regarding your child in the future? (For example: which school to attend, which doctor to visit, etc.)._____

What visitation should be allowed the parent who does not have physical custody of your child? (Include times and dates).

    Contact during the week? _____

    Contact on weekends? _____

    Contact on school holidays? _____

        Which holidays? _____
        _____
        _____

    Contact on winter vacation? _____

    Contact on spring vacation? _____

    Contact on summer vacation? _____

The Law of Child Custody and Visitation

Determining which parent is to have custody of a minor child is one of the most difficult decisions that you will encounter in your divorce. Judges and legislators have also grappled extensively with the difficulty of this decision. In recent years, certain legal trends have emerged regarding how an impartial judge might decide which parent is to be awarded custody of a minor child. These relatively new legal doctrines are a clear break with many of the traditional methods which were previously used to determine custody.

In the past, there were several legal doctrines which governed child custody decisions. Most notably, there was a very strong presumption that a mother should be awarded custody of any child. This presumption stemmed directly from the traditional, though not universal, role of the mother as homemaker in our society at that time. The younger the child was, the stronger the presumption that custody be given to the mother. This doctrine was known as the "tender years doctrine", and carried very considerable weight in legal custody decisions. If the child in question was a girl, the presumption that custody be awarded to the mother was almost insurmountable.

Effectively, the only method by which a father could get custody of a minor child was to prove in open court that the mother was totally unfit to care for the child. This required, in most instances, that the father and his attorney attempt to paint as negative a picture as possible of the mother for the court. Innocent past actions and harmless present circumstances were often distorted and misrepresented to the court in attempts to have a mother declared unfit. This type of custody battle provided a forum for some of the most psycho-

CHAPTER 5: CHILD CUSTODY AND VISITATION

logically and emotionally damaging court proceedings in our society's history. The traumatic effects on the children involved in these proceedings were particularly tragic.

In an attempt to overcome the type of proceeding which encouraged the dredging up of irrelevant details of each parent's private life, a doctrine known as the "best interests of the child" was developed. Under this legal theory, the mental, physical, and emotional well-being of the child was considered paramount in any legal proceeding regarding custody. Theoretically, a parent's actions were pertinent only to the extent that they had an impact on the child. In practice, however, much irrelevant testimony and evidence was still allowed in custody battles. Detailed lists of factors were also developed to guide a court in determining what actually was important in making decisions regarding the custody of a child. Most states continue to provide these guidelines for custody decisions and these factors for consideration are discussed below.

In the 1970's, extensive legal battles were waged in attempts to overturn the "tender years" doctrine and allow fathers an equal footing in custody disputes. For the most part, they were successful. Fathers now do have an equal legal ability to obtain custody of any minor children. However, despite the changes in the law that provide that both parents have an equal right to custody, mothers are still overwhelmingly the parent who retains custody. In over 90% of all custody cases, it is the mother who is awarded custody of the children.

There is an unhappy consequence of the legal changes which make it easier for fathers to request custody. Some fathers and their attorneys have unscrupulously used this right as a weapon to pressure the mother into trading her property, alimony, or child support rights for uncontested custody of a child. Fathers who have no desire at all to actually have custody have used this manipulative tactic to prey upon the maternal fear of losing a child. In order to be certain that they do not lose custody of their child, many mothers have given up their rights to substantial property and support. Any attempts to engage in this tactic are highly disfavored by courts. If you feel that this tactic is being used in your situation, you should consult an attorney for legal guidance.

Another legal doctrine has emerged recently, however, which allows both parents much greater flexibility in sharing parental responsibility. Joint or shared custody has been developed in an effort to allow a child reasonable access to both parents while growing up. Some confusion has resulted from the use of this phrase and it is important to understand exactly what joint custody is and is not. Some definitions are offered here in an attempt to clear up this confusion. Unfortunately, some people (lawyers and judges included) will use some of these terms interchangeably or incorrectly. Be certain in your discussions regarding custody that you both agree exactly what you are taking about.

Types of Custody Arrangements

In the past, *sole* custody by one parent was the standard form of custody. Under sole custody, one parent was awarded both the *physical* custody of the child (the right to have the child live with the custodial parent) and the *legal* custody (the right to make all of the major decisions relating to the up-bringing of the child). Decisions regarding which school the child should attend, whether the child should have medical attention, what religion the child should be taught, and all decisions regarding the child's activities, conduct, and well-being are the responsibility of the parent with sole custody. In most sole custody arrangements, the non-custodial parent is afforded some type of reasonable visitation rights unless there is a danger of harm to the child. This form of custody arrangement, with sole custody to one parent and liberal visitation for the other parent, is still the predominant method used in the majority of divorce situations involving children.

Joint or *shared* custody, on the other hand, is an attempt to allow both parents a voice in the major decisions involved in the raising of a child. Joint custody is generally divided into two separate rights: joint *physical* custody (actual custody of the child); and joint *legal* custody (rights to share in important decisions regarding the child). While both parents may be awarded joint physical custody of a child, one parent is generally still awarded sole physical custody of the child, with the other parent being allowed reasonable visitation privileges. However, both parents are awarded joint legal custody of the child. This rather confusing terminology simply means that both parents will continue to share the rights and responsibilities that come with parenthood. They will both have a right to jointly make the major decisions that will affect the child's life: religious, educational, medical, and social decisions. Naturally, the parent with actual physical custody for the majority of the time is allowed individual control over the minor day-to-day decisions that must be made. In many joint custody situations, the actual physical custody time a child spends with each parent mirrors sole custody situations. It is the decision-making process affecting the child that is the responsibility shared by the parents.

Divided or *alternating* custody is another form of custody (in some areas this is referred to as *split* custody; in others, this is referred to a joint *physical* custody). Under this form of custody, each parent is awarded actual physical and legal custody for alternating periods of time. A child may be awarded to each parent for 6 months out of a year, or for alternating months or weeks. This type of custody arrangement is not generally favored by either the courts or child psychologists. It is seen as emotionally difficult for a child to be continually shifted back and forth between each parent, without a sense of where their "home" is truly located. In some situations, however, it may be appropriate.

Another alternative, which has also proved to be difficult for the children involved is also known as *split* custody. This type of custody has been used in the past to attempt to achieve a technical fairness when there is more than one child by giving each parent physical custody of one or more of the children. For the children involved, however, this constitutes not only a splitting up of one's parents but also a forced separation from one's siblings. Arrangements of this type are not favored by courts.

Currently, there seems to be a general national trend towards approval of joint custody arrangements. The encouragement of frequent and continuing contact with both parents is clearly preferable to fostering single-parent childhoods for children of divorce. These type of arrangements work well and are a benefit to the child, however, only if both parents can maturely cooperate in the necessary decision-making. For joint custody to be successful, both parents must be willing to compromise for the sake of the child, and both parents must be willing to consider the well-being of the child as the most important factor. In situations where there is genuine hostility between the parents, however, one parent should generally be granted sole physical and legal custody. This is often the clearest and most definite method to establish which parent has the necessary authority to make the major decisions.

Some states have established a legal preference for joint custody, while others clearly state that there is no preference for one particular type of custody. Most states specifically allow for joint custody, while others have no particular statutory authorization for any type of shared custody. In all states, however, there is legal precedent to allow custody arrangements which are most beneficial to the children involved.

The most recent trend in custody legislation and court decisions provides one of the most common-sense approaches to the problem. Increasingly, courts are looking at a child's day-to-day circumstances in an effort to determine which parent has been the primary care-giver of the child. The parent who has provided most of the day-to-day care for the child during the marriage is then considered to be the most likely candidate to continue on as the primary custodian of the child after the divorce. The preference is given to the parent which has actively participated in caring for the child and performed the majority of the parenting activities: preparing meals, readying the child for sleep, sharing in their playtime, dealing with medical problems, participating in their education, etc.

This method does not presuppose that either parent has an entitlement to being awarded custody, but rather is based on an examination of the reality of the burdens of parenthood. The decision is based on the practical considerations of which parent has provided the most time, care, and guidance to the child prior to the actual divorce. It allows each parent an equal right to *earn* the custody of a child by providing care for the child before the divorce proceeding begins. This method of selection of the parent to have physical custody places the greatest emphasis on which has been providing the most parental care for the child prior to the divorce. Selection of the primary care-giver as continuing custodian generally fosters a home life of stability and continuity for the child. In the family upheaval caused by divorce, this factor deserves considerable attention.

Visitation

In any custody arrangement, and in all states, the parent who is not awarded actual physical custody of a child has a legal right to reasonable and frequent visitation with the child. Unless there is a genuine and substantiated fear of emotional or physical harm to the child, such visitation is generally allowed on an unsupervised basis and in the non-custodial parent's home. A court does have the authority to completely deny any visitation to a parent who has abused a child. In most cases, however, reasonable visitation is standard.

When, where and how long such visitation should be is one of the major decisions that you and your spouse will have to work out as you discuss your children's future.

Visitation should be structured to allow frequent contact between the non-custodial parent and the child and should attempt to fit into the child's normal schedule. The schedule should be firm enough to allow for a degree of long-term planning, but flexible enough to allow for reasonable changes. Remember that any visitation schedule is only a starting point. Reasonable adjustments can be made as you and your spouse become more comfortable in your roles as divorced parents. Visitation is as much the child's right as it is the parents.

As you approach the decisions on visitation, you should remember certain points. You should remember and keep in mind that:

- Visitation with the other parent is necessary and helpful for your child's normal development and future welfare.
- Visitation should be a pleasant and positive experience for both the parents and for the child.
- Visitation is a time for the parent and child to be with each other and enjoy each other's company and should be maintained on a clear schedule and without interference.
- Visitation exchanges may be the only time that you see your spouse after the divorce. Both of you should show mutual respect for the other while in the child's presence.

As you and your spouse discuss specific visitation terms, you should make every effort to insure that both of you are treated fairly regarding visitation. As you discuss the amount of visitation, put yourself in the other's place. Imagine that your only contact with your child will be the visitation which is agreed upon. You would want it to be as liberal and as frequent as possible. An agreement which is fair and reasonable for both parents will generally be the best for your child.

Modification of Custody and Visitation Terms

Finally, in all states, any custody and visitation agreements which are reached between parents remain subject to court modification. Of all the terms of your marital settlement agreement, the terms which relate to the care and custody of your children will receive the closest scrutiny by a court. The court has total authority in this area and has the power to totally disregard any agreement that is felt to be harmful to the children. In many states, in fact, the court has the authority to appoint a lawyer who will represent the interests of the child in a contested custody situation. This court-appointed legal guardian of a child's legal rights is referred to generally as a *guardian ad litem*.

CHAPTER 5: CHILD CUSTODY AND VISITATION

In the vast majority of cases, however, a court will accept reasonable custody and visitation provisions contained in marital settlement agreements, particularly if it appears that such agreements were obtained through thoughtful and mature negotiation. Most judges, however, are conservative when it comes to the rights of children and will not favor any unusual custody arrangements that fall outside of the traditional boundaries. Recognize also that although the court which handles your divorce will have the right to modify your custody agreement at any time in the future, it is much more difficult to have such modifications made after your divorce is finalized. For the sake of promoting a sense of stability in a child's life, courts are somewhat reluctant to make changes in settled custody arrangements. For this reason, you and your spouse should work diligently to attempt to initially fashion a fair agreement for custody and visitation.

As you examine your own lives and consider the realities of custody and visitation, keep these legal trends in mind. They are what guide most courts in their deliberations of custody disputes. You should also refer to the Appendix for the details of your state's particular laws regarding child custody. Decisions on custody and visitation, however, are best made by both parents in a cooperative manner without the involvement of courts and lawyers. Cooperating parents can adopt any practical arrangement that provides a reasonable resolution to the difficult problems of dividing a child's time between two parents who no longer desire to live together.

Both parents deserve an opportunity to interact with their child during childhood. More importantly, your child deserves to have both of you available for love, affection, and guidance as he or she grows up. You should make every possible attempt to work out a reasonable child custody arrangement that is satisfactory to both of you and your child. However, if you and your spouse are unable to reach an agreement, the use of an impartial mediator may be useful. Please refer back to Chapter 1 for a discussion of mediation. In child custody disputes, mediation is the preferred first alternative for providing a solution. If personal negotiation and mediation both fail to help you achieve an agreement, a resort to the legal process may be necessary. However, keep in mind the tremendous psychological and emotional toll that a bitter court battle over custody can have on both you and your child . If your spouse hires a lawyer to engage in a custody battle, you should, however, seek legal assistance immediately.

Factors For Consideration

In most states, judges are provided with a specific list of items which have been determined to be relevant to custody decisions. The factors are provided only as guidelines and there are generally no mandatory requirements that each factor be considered. They are used as a framework by which to approach the complex set of circumstances that influence the decision of which parent should be awarded custody of a child.

The wishes of the parents and of the child are almost universally considered to be relevant, particularly if the child is old enough to have a mature and intelligent choice. Marital mis-

DIVORCE YOURSELF

conduct is not considered at all in many states to be relevant, unless the misconduct has a direct bearing on the parent's relationship with the child.

The following is a list of the most important factors that are in use in courts throughout the United States. A few states do not list specific factors in their statutes. For those states, this general list of factors may be used. Please check the Appendix for the laws regarding custody in your particular state.

- The age and sex of the child;
- The physical, emotional, mental, religious, and social needs of the child;
- Which parent provides the primary care for the child;
- The capability and desire of each parent to meet the child's needs;
- The preference of the child, if the child is of sufficient age and capacity to form a meaningful opinion;
- The love and affection existing between the child and each parent;
- The length of time the child has lived in a stable, satisfactory environment and the desirability of maintaining continuity;
- The desire and ability of each parent to allow an open, loving, and frequent relationship between the child and the other parent;
- The wishes of the parents;
- The child's adjustment to his or her home, school, and community;
- The mental and physical health of all individuals involved;
- The relationship of the child with parents, siblings, and other significant family members;
- The material needs of the child;
- The stability of the home environment likely to be offered by each parent;
- The education of the child;
- The advantages of keeping the child in the community where the child resides;
- The optional time for the child to spend with each parent;
- Any findings or recommendations of a neutral mediator;
- A history of violence between the parents or a history of child abuse; and
- A need to promote continuity and stability in the life of the child.

In addition, there are other factors that a court will take into consideration when joint or shared custody is an issue. These factors relate to the ability of the parents to cooperate and to the practical aspects of allowing joint custody. These factors are as follows:

- The ability of the parents to cooperate and make decisions jointly;
- The ability of the parents to encourage the sharing of love, affection, and contact between the child and the other parent;

CHAPTER 5: CHILD CUSTODY AND VISITATION

- Whether the past pattern of involvement of the parents with the child reflects a system of values and mutual support which indicates the parent's ability as joint custodians to provide a positive and nourishing relationship with the child;
- The physical proximity of the parents to each other as this relates to the practical considerations of where the child will reside;
- Whether an award of joint custody will promote more frequent or continuing contact between the child and each of the parents;
- The permanence, as a family unit, of the existing or proposed custodial home;
- The nature of the physical and emotional environment in the home of each of the persons awarded joint custody;
- The willingness and ability of the persons awarded joint custody to communicate and cooperate in advancing the child's welfare;
- Whether the child has established a close and beneficial relationship with both of the persons awarded joint custody;
- Whether both parents have actively cared for the child before and since the separation;
- Whether one or both parents agree to, or are opposed to, joint custody.

The tax aspects of child custody and visitation may be an important factor in your particular situation and are discussed in Chapter 7.

As you examine your particular situation, use the above factors to attempt to realistically assess what type of child custody and visitation arrangements would be best suited to your family. Remember that you and your spouse are in the best position to clearly understand the particular circumstances that influence your lives and the life of your child. Although a judge will use a list of factors similar to those presented here to make custody decisions in contested cases, a court decision will never be as meaningful to a child as one which his or her parents have worked out in an amicable and loving manner.

The Child's Bill of Rights

In addition to the various factors that courts consider, an outline of the rights of children was developed from Wisconsin Supreme Court decisions and is now used throughout the United States. Delaware recently enacted legislation that makes it a requirement that parents sign an affidavit that they have read and understand these rights. This Child's Bill of Rights is useful in reminding parents involved in a divorce that there are certain important rights that their children are entitled to have considered during any discussions relating to custody and visitation. A review of these rights can help each of the parents to better view the effects of their divorce through the eyes of their child. Of all of the factors that you and your spouse will consider in your discussions on child custody and visitation, these are the most important.

The Child's Bill of Rights is as follows:

1. The right to a continuing relationship with both parents;

2. The right to be treated as an important human being, with unique feelings, ideas, and desires;

3. The right to continuing care and guidance from both parents;

4. The right to know and appreciate what is good in each parent without one parent degrading the other;

5. The right to express love, affection, and respect for each parent without having to stifle that love because of disapproval of the other parent;

6. The right to know that a parent's decision to divorce was not the responsibility of the child;

7. The right not to be a source of argument between the parents;

8. The right to honest answers about the changing family relationships;

9. The right to be able to experience regular and consistent contact with both parents and the right to know the reason for any cancellation of time or change of plans;

10. The right to have a relaxed, secure relationship with both parents without being placed in a position to manipulate one parent against the other.

Child Custody Jurisdiction

Related to the actual custody decisions is the issue of which specific state has the proper authority and jurisdiction to hear a child custody case. All 50 states have now enacted a uniform law relating to jurisdiction in custody matters: The Uniform Child Custody Jurisdiction Act. This legislation was passed in an effort to create a uniform nationwide system for determining which individual state should be the proper forum for custody decisions in every situation. It is an attempt to deal with the problems of child-snatching by parents who are dissatisfied with a particular state's custody decision.

In the past, some parents who have lost custody battles have taken their children across state lines in an attempt to have another state's court award custody to them. This new uniform legislation provides a set of standardized guidelines to determine which single state should have the sole power and authority to decide the custody of a child in all situations. The decision as to which state will have jurisdiction is based on a variety of factors,

CHAPTER 5: CHILD CUSTODY AND VISITATION

such as: the length of time the child has resided in the state, whether there has been any previous court proceedings concerning the child's custody; the residency of both parents, etc.

If you and your spouse: (1) have never before been involved in any child custody proceedings concerning your children; and (2) are both able to agree upon the arrangements regarding your child's care; and (3) both live in the same state; then, you may assume that the state that you both live in presently is the state with the proper jurisdiction to decide your child's custody. Later, in Chapter 10, you will fill out a short legal form relating to child custody jurisdiction for inclusion with your divorce papers. If, however, you or your spouse or child have previously been involved in child custody litigation in another state, you will need to consult a lawyer for advice relating to the court with proper jurisdiction in your particular situation.

Custody and Visitation Worksheet

With all of the various factors which influence the decisions regarding child custody firmly in mind, you and your spouse should be ready to approach the actual mechanics of custody and visitation arrangements. The following is a worksheet which sets out the most common questions which arise in custody situations. Following the worksheet, various clauses are listed outlining custody and visitation arrangements. Several are provided, ranging from very simple statements of general rights to detailed provisions regarding times and dates. You and your spouse may not wish to make as detailed an arrangement as this worksheet provides. In such case, you may choose to use the simplified version of the custody and visitation clause.

Which parent will have actual primary physical custody of the child? (In other words, with whom will the child generally live?) _____

Will both parents share in the major decisions regarding the child? _____

    If YES, do you desire a joint custody arrangement? _____

    If YES, on what decisions will you both jointly confer?

        Education/school choice _____

        Medical care _____

        Dental care _____

        Religious training _____

        Vacation dates _____

    If YES, does the non-custodial parent have the right to be notified in advance of any up-coming decisions? _____

    If YES, does either parent have veto power over the decisions of the other? _____

Will the custodial parent have the right to move out of the state with the children without the other parent's consent? _____

Will both parent's have the right to be informed of any change of address or telephone number of the other? _____

On what dates and times will the non-custodial parent have visitation?:

Weekends: _____

Weekdays: _____

Holidays: _____

(New Year's Day, Martin Luther King Jr's Birthday, Valentine's Day, Easter, Mother's Day, Memorial Day, Father's Day, 4th of July, Labor Day, Halloween, Thanksgiving, Christmas/Hanukkah, the child's birthday, any other special days)

Vacations: _____

(Winter, Spring break, Summer)

Will the non-custodial parent be allowed to see the child at any other times if reasonable notice is provided? _____

Will the non-custodial parent have the right to be informed about the child's activities, illnesses, school, etc.? _____

Will the non-custodial parent have the right to obtain the child's school, medical, or dental records? _____

Will there be any visitation privileges for grandparents? _____

What last name will the child use? _____

Marital Settlement Agreement Clauses Regarding Child Custody and Visitation

There are many possible arrangements that may be made for custody and visitation. They can range from very brief to extremely complex and lengthy statements. Below are listed four separate child custody and visitation clauses. The first is a very simplified clause, the second a moderately-detailed clause, and the third and fourth are very comprehensive clauses. According to your particular situation, you and your spouse should read through each of these clauses and choose the one that you feel most comfortable with. In each of the two more detailed clauses, you will be given various choices regarding specific provisions of your arrangements. You may wish to add other specific provisions to these clauses that you both agree are important. You may do so if you use simple straight-forward language that you both agree clearly states your agreements. When you prepare your marital settlement agreement in Chapter 8, please delete those portions of the clause that you choose which are in *italics*.

CHAPTER 5: CHILD CUSTODY AND VISITATION

Sole Custody and Visitation Clause (Basic Agreement)

The following clause is a very simplified and straight-forward agreement relating to your child's custody arrangements. It provides for sole custody to be given to one parent. It should only be used if both you and your spouse are cooperative and amicable in your relationship and it is likely that you will remain that way in the future. This approach allows a wide range of flexibility in setting up visitation and vacation arrangements. Such arrangements are not spelled out at all in this clause, but are left for you and your spouse to structure as they arise.

The very flexibility of this approach has some inherent dangers, however. Since there are no definite details or dates and times of visitation provided, there is a danger that arguments may erupt regarding interpretation of this clause. This clause should, therefore, only be used if you both: (1) feel that you have a clear understanding of each other's views and feelings regarding custody and visitation; and (2) have complete faith that you and your spouse will be able to agree on the details of visitation in the future. Even if you and your spouse are currently on friendly terms, it may be wise to use a clause with a more detailed schedule of visitation terms. Then, you can always mutually agree after the divorce to allow different visitation, but you will at least have a written base of minimum terms. If you wish to provide for joint custody, you will need to use one of the more detailed clauses later in this chapter.

> We both agree that it is in the best interests of our child*[ren]* that the _____ *[Wife or Husband]* have sole physical and legal custody of our child*[ren]*. We also agree that the other parent has the right to be with our child*[ren]* on a frequent and liberal basis through reasonable visitation, at such times as we and the child*[ren]* can agree upon. We agree that we will share as equally as possible the right to be with our child*[ren]* on holidays, birthdays, and during the child*[ren]*'s school vacations. We agree that our child*[ren]*'s time with either of us should not interfere with their attendance at school. We also agree that the parent with custody should have the right to make the major decisions regarding the care and up-bringing of the child*[ren]*, but that the other parent has the right to be notified of any major decisions.

Sole Custody and Visitation Clause (with Visitation Schedule)

This clause is somewhat more detailed than the above clause. In particular, it allows for provisions to be made for specific times and dates for visitation with the non-custodial parent. This detailed schedule has the advantage of putting your agreements as to how to deal with visitation in writing. This will generally lessen the opportunity for future dis-

DIVORCE YOURSELF

agreements to arise over what was actually agreed upon during your discussions. This clause also provides for sole physical and legal custody to be given to one parent with reasonable visitation rights for the non-custodial parent. If you and your spouse have agreed that joint custody is preferable, you should use one of the more detailed clauses that follow later in this chapter.

☐ We both agree that it is in the best interests of our child*[ren]* that the _____ *[Wife or Husband]* have sole physical and legal custody of our child*[ren]*. We also agree that the other parent has the right to be with our child*[ren]* on a frequent and liberal basis through reasonable visitation, at such times as we and the child*[ren]* can agree upon. If in the future we are unable to agree upon visitation, the _____ *[Husband or Wife]* will have the right to be with our child*[ren]* as follows:

(A). On the following holidays during even-numbered years: _____
_____
_____

(B). On the following holidays during odd-numbered years: _____
_____
_____

(C). On the following dates and times each *[or every other]* weekend: ____
_____
_____

(D). On the following dates and times during each *[or every other]* _____ week]. _____
_____
_____

(E). For the following vacation periods each year: _____
_____
_____

We agree that our child*[ren]*'s time with either of us should not interfere with attendance at school. We also agree that the parent with custody should have the right to make the major decisions regarding the care and up-bringing of our child*[ren]*, but that the other parent should have the right to be notified of any major decisions.

CHAPTER 5: CHILD CUSTODY AND VISITATION

Custody and Visitation Clause (Joint Legal and Sole Physical Custody)

The following clause provides a very detailed and comprehensive agreement for joint custody. It should be used in all situations in which both you and your spouse have decided that joint decision-making but sole physical custody with one parent is the best alternative. In some states, a detailed agreement of this nature is a requirement for both parents being awarded joint or shared custody. This agreement provides for both parents to share in the major decisions and lists the general categories of such decisions. It provides that the home of one parent shall be the primary residence of the child, but that the other parent be allowed frequent and liberal visitation and contact with the child. Specific visitation provisions are also included. In addition, various other rights and responsibilities of the parents are spelled out in detail in this clause.

☐ We both agree that it is in the best interests of our child*[ren]* that we both have joint legal custody of our child*[ren]*. We also agree that it is in the best interests of our child*[ren]* that the _____ *[Wife or Husband]* have sole physical custody of our child*[ren]*. We acknowledge that our child*[ren]* presently live*[s]* with the _____ *[Wife or Husband]* and that the actual physical residence of our child*[ren]* may be changed at any time as we may mutually agree.

All decisions pertaining to the education, discipline, health, extracurricular and summer activities, religious training, medical and dental care, and welfare of our child*[ren]* will be decided by both of us after reasonable and adequate discussion. We also agree that the parent with physical custody shall have control over the minor day-to-day decisions affecting the child, including any medical or dental emergencies. We agree that if, after reasonable attempts, we are unable to reach an agreement on any of the decisions affecting our child*[ren]*, we will jointly seek professional mediation to resolve our differences.

We also agree that each of us has the right to know of any circumstances or decisions that affect our child*[ren]* and that each of us has the right to any medical, dental, or school records of our child*[ren]*. Neither of us will do anything to hamper or interfere with the natural and continuing relationship between our child*[ren]* and the other parent.

[Continued on next page]

> *[Continued from previous page]*
>
> We both realize that the well-being of our child*[ren]* is of paramount importance and, therefore, we agree that our child*[ren]* should have as much contact as possible with the parent that does not have physical custody and that our child*[ren]* may visit that parent as often as may be agreed upon. Although visitation may be scheduled more often, the parent that does not have physical custody will have the right to be with our child*[ren]* at least as follows:
>
> (A). On the following holidays during even-numbered years: _____
> _____
> _____
> _____
>
> (B). On the following holidays during odd-numbered years: _____
> _____
> _____
> _____
>
> (C). On the following dates and times each *[or every other]* weekend: ____
> _____
> _____
> _____
>
> (D). On the following dates and times during each *[or every other]* week._
> _____
> _____
> _____
>
> (E). For the following vacation periods each year: _____
> _____
> _____
> _____
>
> We additionally agree to use our very best efforts to insure that our child*[ren]* receive the most care, love, and affection possible from both parents throughout their entire childhood.

Custody and Visitation Clause (Joint Legal and Physical Custody)

This clause is the most detailed and comprehensive provided. This does not necessarily mean that this is the most appropriate clause in all situations. The following clause provides for both parents to share the physical and legal custody of their child. As you can see, this clause still designates one parent's home as the primary residence of the child and provides for visitation with the other parent. Most of the other terms of this clause are identical to the preceding clause. For practical purposes, the day-to-day lives of parents

CHAPTER 5: CHILD CUSTODY AND VISITATION

and children under this clause would be very similar to their lives under the terms of the preceding clause. Legally, however, there are slight differences between these clauses. Under this clause, both parents actually have the right to retain the actual physical custody of the child. For this reason, there is an agreement included in this clause regarding taking the child out of the state in which you both live. In addition, there is a provision relating to the name by which the child is to be known. Where there is a genuine and honest joint effort and agreement to cooperate in raising a child, this clause may provide the most even and equal division of the rights to the upbringing and custody of the child.

> We both agree that it is in the best interests of our child*[ren]* that we both have joint legal and physical custody of our child*[ren]*. We also agree that it is in the best interests of our child*[ren]* that the home of the _____ *[Wife or Husband]* be the primary residence of the child*[ren]*. We acknowledge that our child*[ren]* presently live*[s]* with the _____ *[Wife or Husband]* and that the actual physical residence of our child*[ren]* may be changed at any time as we may mutually agree.
>
> All decisions pertaining to the place of residence, discipline, education, health, extracurricular and summer activities, vacations, religious training, medical and dental care, and welfare of our child*[ren]* will be decided by both of us after reasonable and adequate discussion. We also agree that the parent with physical custody shall have control over the minor day-to-day decisions affecting the child, including any medical or dental emergencies. We agree that if, after reasonable attempts, we are unable to reach an agreement on any of the decisions affecting our child*[ren]*, we will jointly seek professional mediation to resolve our differences.
>
> We also agree that each of us has the right to know of any circumstances or decisions that affect our child*[ren]* and that each of us has the right to any medical, dental, or school records of our child*[ren]*. Neither of us will do anything to hamper or interfere with the natural and continuing relationship between our child*[ren]* and the other parent.
>
> We both agree that our child*[ren]* will be known by the last name of _____.
>
> We both agree that frequent and continuing contact with both parents is vital to our child*[ren]*, and therefore we both agree that neither of us will permanently remove our child*[ren]* from this state without the express written permission of the other parent.
>
> *[Continued on next page]*

> *[Continued from previous page]*
>
> We both realize that the well-being of our child*[ren]* is of paramount importance and, therefore, we agree that our child*[ren]* should have as much contact as possible with the parent that does not have physical custody and that our child*[ren]* may visit that parent as often as may be agreed upon. Although contact may be scheduled more often, the parent that does not live in the primary physical residence of the child*[ren]* will have the right to be with our child*[ren]* at least as follows:
>
> (A). On the following holidays during even-numbered years: _____
> _____
> _____
> _____
>
> (B). On the following holidays during odd-numbered years: _____
> _____
> _____
> _____
>
> (C). On the following dates and times each *[or every other]* weekend:____
> _____
> _____
> _____
>
> (D). On the following dates and times during each *[or every other]* week.__
> _____
> _____
> _____
>
> (E). For the following vacation periods each year: _____
> _____
> _____
> _____
>
> We additionally agree to use our very best efforts to insure that our child*[ren]* receive the most care, love, and affection possible from both parents throughout their entire childhood.

The particular child custody and visitation clause that you have chosen will be used when you prepare your actual marital settlement agreement in Chapter 8. Please refer back to this chapter at that time.

CHAPTER 6

CHILD SUPPORT

Closely related to the decisions that must be made regarding child custody are those decisions relating to the support of a child. In most instances, the parent who does not have physical custody of a child must provide child support to the parent who has custody. Child support agreements are essentially financial in nature. Much of the information that you and your spouse have already provided each other in the financial questionnaire and financial statements in Chapter 2 will be used in determining the proper support amounts. However, a child support worksheet will be provided later in this chapter to allow you to gather the necessary information for these decisions.

Before you and your spouse consider the legal aspects of child support, you should both understand that child support terms are the provisions of marital settlement agreements and divorce orders that are most often defaulted upon or ignored. Tragically, this has resulted in the creation of a new class of poverty-level individuals: children of divorced parents. The majority of court-ordered child support payments are neither paid in full nor on time. Nearly one-third of the children entitled to child support receive no support at all. The reasons for this tragedy are many, but perhaps the most important stems from the frustration of the non-custodial parent having to pay for the support for children that he or she does not live with or raise. If you and your spouse can come to a reasonable and workable agreement regarding the custody and visitation arrangements for your child, there will be a far greater chance that your child support agreement will also be seen as reasonable. As you approach your child support discussions, please keep these tragic statistics firmly in mind.

The Law of Child Support

Both natural parents of a minor child have a legal obligation to provide adequate support for the child until the child reaches 18 years of age (21 in some states). This legal duty includes providing food, clothing, shelter, medical care, and education for a child. This is the law in every state. Parents of adopted children also have this same obligation. Child support, however, is not merely the delivery of a monthly support payment. It is a legal, moral, and ethical obligation to provide full care and support for your offspring.

Divorce does not end this legal obligation for support. It merely complicates the duty. Both parents have an equal duty to support their children. In the vast majority of divorces which involve children, however, the mother is awarded physical custody of those children. Also, in the majority of family situations, it is the mother who earns a disproportionately lower income than the father. Thus, in most divorce situations involving children, there will be an immediate and definite need for considerable child support to be provided by the father. Regardless of which parent has physical custody and even when the incomes of both parents are equal, both parents still need to provide their fair share of support for the child. A child should not be forced to suffer economically because of the divorce of his or her parents.

When a single family unit is divided into two households upon divorce, the total living costs will naturally escalate. Two homes must be maintained instead of one. Two sets of furniture, appliances, and housewares must be provided. Two cars, two televisions, two of almost every household item will need to be purchased and maintained. Unfortunately, the income of the divorced family will not increase. In many cases, in fact, it may actually decrease as the parent with custody may find it more difficult to maintain a full-time job. Because both parents are no longer able to share their time with the child as easily, child care costs may also increase.

The goals of child support laws are to achieve a fair division of the income of both parents in order to provide for the satisfactory support of the children of a marriage. As much as is possible, a child should be entitled to share in the income of both parents, despite their divorce.

Recent federal legislation (the Family Support Act of 1988) requires each state to provide some type of formula or guidelines for the determination of child support awards. In the attempt to provide specific financial guidelines for child support provisions, many states have adopted detailed legislation and rules regarding how to arrive at a fair support amount. Some states have provided only simple formulas. Later in this chapter, a general set of guidelines for determining child support will be presented.

In recent years, these child support guidelines have tended to become more detailed, specific, and mathematic. The newest versions of child support legislation are full of various charts and financial formulas for determining the correct amount of support. These detailed guidelines are an attempt to take the mystery out of the manner in which a court

CHAPTER 6: CHILD SUPPORT

determines how much child support to award. In most states which have such guidelines, however, the rules are only to be used to provide a structure for determining a minimum amount of child support. A court has the authority to order more or less child support if necessary.

While each state's guidelines may be somewhat different, they all generally require that if the non-custodial parent has sufficient income, he or she must provide a specific level of monthly support to the parent who has custody of the child. Increasingly, states are adopting legislation that goes beyond simply providing a monthly payment for child support. Some of these recent laws may require various non-monetary forms of support: that a parent provide health insurance, dental insurance, life insurance for the parent with the child as sole beneficiary, or that the family home not be sold for a particular period of time. All of these provisions are an attempt to provide sufficient security for a child of divorce to prevent the child from requiring welfare or other social service support from the state. Please check the Appendix for information on your state's specific statutory child support guidelines.

Factors for Consideration

In addition to any specific detailed statutory child support guidelines, most states also provide a list of factors which are considered relevant in child support cases. A judge will determine how much weight to give each factor depending on the unique circumstances of each case. You and your spouse should use this general list of factors to focus your discussions regarding child support. Please check the Appendix for the factors in use in your state. Some states do not provide a list of factors in their statutes. Residents of those states may use this list as a general guideline for their negotiations regarding child support.

The factors that are considered pertinent in most states revolve around two specific areas: (1) the needs of the child; and (2) the ability of the parents to pay support. Each of these basic factors has many sub-factors, which are outlined below. Aspects of the first main factor, the needs of the child, are generally used to determine the minimum amount of child support that is necessary to provide the child with the basic comforts of life. Considerations regarding the second major factor, the ability of the parents to pay, are then often used to establish the maximum amount which the supporting parent should pay. The standard of living of both parents is considered in this decision.

The general factors which are considered pertinent to decisions relating to child support are as follows:

- The financial resources of the child;
- The age and health of the parents;
- The standard of living the child would have enjoyed if the marriage had not been dissolved;

- The physical and emotional conditions and educational needs of the child;
- The financial resources, needs, and obligations of both the non-custodial and the custodial parent;
- Any excessive expenditures, destruction, or concealment of assets;
- The occupation of each parent;
- The earning capacity of each parent;
- The amount and sources of income of each parent;
- The vocational skills and employability of each parent;
- The age and health of the child;
- The child's occupation (if old enough to work);
- The vocational skills of the child (if old enough to work);
- The employability of the child (if old enough to work);
- The needs of the child;
- The standard of living and circumstances of each parent;
- The relative financial means of the parents;
- The need and capacity of the child for education, including higher education;
- The responsibility of the parents for the support of others;
- The value of services contributed by the custodial parent;
- The desirability of the parent having either sole custody or physical care of the child remaining in the home as a full-time parent;
- The cost of day care to the parent having custody or physical care of the child if that parent works outside the home, or the value of the child care services performed by that parent if the parent remains in the home;
- The tax consequences of child support to each parent.

A very important factor which is not listed here, but that you and your spouse must take into consideration, is that the court always has absolute authority over child support decisions. This power is retained regardless of any agreement that you may reach. The obligation for child support can not be bargained away in your negotiations. Courts are very protective of the rights of a child to be supported by both parents and will not accept the terms of any settlement agreement that does not provide for reasonable levels of support. Although courts will often accept the child support terms that parents agree to in settlement negotiations, they can and will ignore any agreements they find unreasonable. Ultimately, it is the court which has final authority to issue support orders for dependent children and they take that power very seriously. Much as you can not trade away the custody of your child for monetary rewards, you can not bargain away your child's rights to support. The marital settlement agreement that you and your spouse sign will bind the two of you, but will not bind your children. Their rights to reasonable support may be enforced by a court if necessary, despite you and your spouse's agreement.

CHAPTER 6: CHILD SUPPORT

The income tax aspects of child support may be an important factor in your considerations. Please refer to Chapter 7 for a detailed discussion of all of the tax aspects of your divorce.

Enforcement and Modification of Child Support

Of all the provisions of a final divorce, child support obligations are, unfortunately, the ones which are most often ignored. Over one-half of court-ordered child support payments are not paid in full or on time. Nearly one-third of qualifying children receive no child support at all. Recent studies have shown that the income level of the divorced parents has no bearing on whether a child will receive adequate child support. Unfortunately, wealthy parents are just as likely to default on child support payments as poor parents.

There is now a concerted national effort to collect and enforce overdue child support payments. This effort is backed by very comprehensive and powerful laws which are beginning to turn the tide of non-payment of child support. In recent years, all 50 states have enacted legislation to deal with this problem: the Uniform Reciprocal Enforcement of Support Act. Many states have also enacted other strict laws dealing with methods to enforce child support obligations. In addition, the federal government has enacted very tough child support enforcement legislation. These laws will be discussed further in Chapter 13.

Child support provisions in a marital settlement agreement or final divorce order are always subject to modification, regardless of any attempt to limit such future modification. The courts always have authority to increase or decrease the amount of the support. However, modifying a child support order in the future involves a showing of changed circumstances and an often lengthy lawsuit and court hearing. It is far easier to attempt to anticipate any lifestyle and income changes in advance than to resort to the courts to keep changing the amount of child support. Modification of child support terms after the divorce is also discussed in Chapter 13.

General Child Support Guidelines

The guidelines provided here are just that: guidelines. They are not intended to be an ultimate method for determining support payments in all cases. They should be reviewed and used while considering all of the other relevant factors in your particular situation. The determination of the proper amount of child support in each case will always be difficult. A careful balance must be obtained between providing an adequate level of support and overburdening the parent who must pay the support. If the support payments are set at a level which becomes a tremendous financial burden to the paying parent, there will be a tendency and temptation to default on the payments. On the other hand, if the payments are too low, the child will suffer the consequences. Both parents must work together carefully to actually determine a fair and reasonable amount of support. Care must be taken to keep the negotiations on a mature and rational basis. Discussions involving child support have the very real potential of deteriorating into hostile arguments. Of all of the aspects of divorce, child support obligations have spawned more post-divorce lawsuits than any other.

Many different methods of determining the amount of child support payments have been utilized around the country. A mathematical formula method of determining child support has been adopted recently in many states. Generally, this method consists of (1) determining the actual monthly needs of the child based on the particular circumstances of the family; and (2) determining the ability of the parents to pay. Other methods rely upon charts of child support amounts. The method of determining the proper amount of child support which is provided in this book was adapted from the guidelines used in many different states and is a combination of the most common methods in use. It attempts to take both parents' economic situations into account. Your particular state may use a similar method or a variation. You should refer to the Appendix for information regarding your state's specific requirements. In addition, you may wish to check with the clerk of the court in the county where you live to see if there are any local child support guidelines or rules in effect. In addition, many states have specific child support worksheets which are to be used. Check the Appendix and with your court clerk.

To determine the figures necessary for these calculations, please refer back to the Financial Statement that you and your spouse prepared in Chapter 3, when you negotiated the division of your property. These guidelines are provided as an example of how various states have decided to calculate minimum child support amounts. For your situation, you should use the *highest* amount provided by the calculations as a starting point for your discussions. Other factors, in addition to income and deductions, may then be used to adjust the amount accordingly.

This type of child support guideline uses a chart of minimum child support amounts. To use this method, you must first determine the monthly net income of each parent. To obtain this figure, combine all of the income of each parent from any source. Then, subtract the mandatory deductions from this income as shown on the following worksheet. This will give you the monthly net income of each parent for child support purposes. If there are seasonal or monthly fluctuations in the parent's income or deductions, you may wish to determine the income and deductions on an annual basis and then divide that amount by 12 for the net monthly income.

Next, combine the two monthly net income amounts for a total net family income. Using this combined net monthly family income, consult the child support chart to determine the total minimum amount of child support which is necessary. Always go to the next higher level if your combined monthly income falls in between the amounts shown. As with all decisions concerning children, the courts will always favor the decision which benefits the children the most. Remember, the amount shown is only the general minimum amount necessary and the actual amount of support required may be higher (or even lower) than this amount, depending on the particular circumstances of your situation. Federal law

CHAPTER 6: CHILD SUPPORT

requires that if a judge decides to award less child support than is warranted by a state's guidelines, the specific reasons must be stated. Also remember that your particular state may have a slightly different set of guidelines or various other charts for determining support. Note also that the amount shown on the chart is the amount of support required by both parents together. The amount of the non-custodial parent's individual share is determined as explained in the next paragraph.

After the amount on the chart is determined, the non-custodial parent's share must be determined. Divide the net monthly income of the parent without custody by the total net monthly family income to determine the fractional or percentage share of the total child support. This figure multiplied times the figure from the support guideline chart will be the minimum monthly support required. To this amount should then be added any child care costs which are required to enable the parent with custody to obtain employment.

For example, Parent A has an income of $1,350 per month, with allowable deductions of $350 per month, for a net individual monthly income of $1,000 per month. Parent B has an income of $2,700 per month, with allowable deductions totalling $700, for a net individual monthly income of $2,000 per month. The combined net family income would be $3,000 per month. They have two children, so the total child support amount shown on the chart is $972. Parent A incurs $168 per month child care expenses in order to hold a job. Thus, the total minimum amount of family child support would be $1,140 per month.

Parent A has custody of the children. Because Parent B contributes two-thirds of the total family income ($2,000/$3,000 or 2/3), Parent B's share of this total amount will be 2/3 of the total amount of family support or $760 ($1,140 X 2/3 = $760). Only the parent without physical custody of the child (in this example: Parent B) will be required to make the child support payment to the parent with custody (Parent A). Parent A's share of the support amount is assumed to be used to provide the household in which the child lives.

This final figure is only a determination of the general minimum amount of child support necessary. The actual amount of the monthly payments may be more or less. This final general minimum figure should be adjusted up or down based on the following factors and any other relevant information:

- Any extraordinary medical, dental, or health expenses;
- Any independent income of the child;
- Any seasonal variations in a parent's income;
- The age of the child, taking into consideration the greater needs of older children;
- Any special needs that have previously been met by the family budget;
- The total assets available to the parents and the child;
- The custody arrangements for the child. In situations where there is joint physical custody, the actual amount of time the child spends with each parent may be particularly relevant.

DIVORCE YOURSELF

The amount of the actual payment as calculated using this method depends upon the income, deductions, and child care expenses of both parents. If the income of the parent with custody is very low, the non-custodial parent will be required to pay all or the bulk of the amount of child support shown on the chart. On the other hand, if the income of the parent with custody is very high and that of the non-custodial parent is low, the required child support payment may be very low.

Child Support Worksheet

Net Monthly Income of Parent with Custody:

Gross Monthly Income

Wages, salary, bonuses .... $ _____

Interest, dividends .... $ _____

Business income .... $ _____

Unemployment/Social Security .... $ _____

Income from other sources .... $ _____

Total Gross Monthly Income .... $ _____

Monthly Deductions

Income taxes withheld .... $ _____

Social Security withheld .... $ _____

Union dues withheld .... $ _____

Children's health insurance premiums .... $ _____

Mandatory retirement withheld .... $ _____

Total Monthly Deductions .... $ _____

Total Net Monthly Income of Parent With Custody

Total Gross Monthly Income .... $ _____

Minus (-)

Total Monthly Deductions .... $ _____

Equals (=)

Total Net Monthly Income (A) .... $ _____

CHAPTER 6: CHILD SUPPORT

Net Monthly Income of Parent without Custody:

Gross Monthly Income

Wages, salary, bonuses .... $ _____

Interest, dividends .... $ _____

Business income .... $ _____

Unemployment/Social Security .... $ _____

Income from other sources .... $ _____

Total Gross Monthly Income .... $ _____

Monthly Deductions

Income taxes withheld .... $ _____

Social Security withheld .... $ _____

Union dues withheld .... $ _____

Mandatory retirement withheld .... $ _____

Children's health insurance premiums .... $ _____

Total Monthly Deductions .... $ _____

Total Net Monthly Income of Parent Without Custody

Total Gross Monthly Income .... $ _____
Minus (−)
Total Monthly Deductions .... $ _____
Equals (=)
Total Net Monthly Income (B) .... $ _____

Total Combined Net Monthly Family Income:

Net Monthly Income of Parent With Custody (A) .... $ _____
Plus (+)
Net Monthly Income of Parent Without Custody (B) $ _____
Equals (=)
Combined Net Monthly Family Income (C) .... $ _____

Use the Combined Net Monthly Family Income figure (C) to find the total minimum amount of child support required on the following chart. If this figure is over $4,200, please use the percentages listed following this chart. To this amount is added any child care expenses that are required in order that the parent with custody may obtain employment.

Minimum Child Support from Both Parents .... $ _____
Plus (+)
Required Monthly Child Care Expenses .... $ _____
Equals (=)
Minimum Total Child Support .... $ _____

Using this figure (Minimum Total Child Support), determine the minimum child support necessary from the parent without custody as follows:

Monthly Net Income of Parent Without Custody (B) $ _____
Divided by
Combined Net Monthly Family Income .... $ _____
Equals (=)
Non-Custodial Parent's percentage share .... _____%
Times (X)
Minimum Total Child Support from Both Parents ... $ _____
Equals (=)
Monthly Minimum Child Support to be paid .... $ _____

Remember that this final figure is a general *minimum* amount and is subject to adjustment based on the other factors in your particular situation.

Minimum Child Support Guideline Chart

This chart is similar to charts used in various states throughout the country. In general, it tends to be slightly higher than those in use in most states. However in nearly all cases, if the figures in this chart are used for your calculations, your child support decisions will be accepted by the court.

Combined Monthly Income	One Child	Two Children	Three Children	Four Children	Five Children	Six Children
500	48	48	49	49	50	50
750	177	274	279	282	285	288
1000	231	359	450	507	520	525
1100	251	390	489	551	600	620
1200	271	421	528	595	648	693
1300	291	452	566	638	695	744
1400	311	483	605	682	742	794
1500	332	516	645	728	792	847
1600	353	548	686	773	842	901
1700	374	580	726	819	892	954
1800	395	612	767	865	942	1007

CHAPTER 6: CHILD SUPPORT

Combined Monthly Income	One Child	Two Children	Three Children	Four Children	Five Children	Six Children
1900	416	645	807	910	992	1060
2000	437	677	847	956	1042	1113
2100	457	709	887	1000	1091	1166
2200	476	739	924	1042	1136	1215
2300	495	768	961	1084	1182	1264
2400	514	798	999	1126	1228	1313
2500	532	828	1036	1167	1274	1362
2600	551	857	1073	1209	1319	1411
2700	570	887	1110	1251	1365	1460
2800	589	917	1147	1292	1411	1509
2900	607	945	1176	1332	1453	1554
3000	624	972	1209	1370	1495	1598
3100	642	999	1243	1408	1536	1643
3200	659	1026	1276	1446	1578	1687
3300	677	1052	1310	1484	1619	1731
3400	694	1079	1343	1521	1660	1775
3500	712	1106	1377	1559	1702	1819
3600	729	1133	1410	1597	1743	1863
3700	747	1160	1444	1635	1785	1907
3800	764	1187	1477	1673	1826	1951
3900	778	1208	1510	1704	1859	1986
4000	791	1227	1534	1731	1889	2018
4100	804	1246	1559	1758	1919	2050
4200	817	1265	1583	1785	1949	2082

For combined net monthly income amounts over $4200, use the following percentages to determine the minimum child support payments:

- 1 Child: 20% of the net monthly combined income
- 2 Children: 30 % of the net monthly combined income
- 3 Children: 38 % of the net monthly combined income
- 4 Children: 43 % of the net monthly combined income
- 5 Children: 47 % of the net monthly combined income
- 6 + Children: 50 % of the net monthly combined income

Marital Settlement Agreement Clauses Regarding Child Support

Once you have determined the specific amount that the monthly child support payments should be, it is a relatively simple matter to include that provision in a clause for your marital settlement agreement. A standard clause for this purpose is set out below. However, in addition to selecting the amount of the payment, several other child support issues must be addressed.

First, a decision must be reached on how the payment is to be made. In response to the enormous rate of default on child support payments, in recent years and in response to federal legislation, all states have adopted various methods to attempt to insure that the payments will continue to be paid and paid on time. These methods range from automatic wage assignments and withholding of wages to having the support payments made through the clerk of the court or some other government agency. The various child support enforcement techniques are explained in Chapter 13.

The most common arrangement is for the paying parent to be required to make the payments directly to the clerk of the court. Once the payment is received, the clerk then pays the parent who is due the payment. There are several benefits to having the payments made in this indirect way. By having the payment made through an official government body instead of directly to the other parent, there is an official documented record of the amount and date the payment is made. Further, many states have programs to collect past due payments that will automatically go into effect when a payment is missed. This takes much of the burden of enforcement off the parent who is to be paid the support.

Basic Monthly Child Support Clause

The basic child support clause provided in this book offers two alternatives for this situation. The first is for the payments, in the event of a divorce, to be made to an official state agency or court official for disbursement to the other parent. The other alternative is for the payments to be made directly to the other parent. Most courts will allow a couple to waive any requirement that the payments be made through the state if the agreement to make the child support payments directly to the parent is in the form of a marital settlement agreement. To allow the payments to be made directly to the parent, there must be valid reason why the parents wish to avoid the indirect payment method. Good reasons might be that the parent who is to make the payments is very reliable or has established a clear record of making the payments on time while the parents were separated. However, if there is any doubt as to whether the payments may be paid late or not at all after a divorce, you should to choose the alternative that requires the payments to be made through an official state agency or court official. The clause that provides for direct payment to the other spouse also allows the payments to be switched to collection by the court or state if problems arise in the future. Remember that there is a definite tendency for child support payments to be paid late or not at all in the majority of cases.

CHAPTER 6: CHILD SUPPORT

☐ We both agree that the _____ *[Wife or Husband]* will pay to the _____ *[Wife or Husband]*, for child support, the amount of $_____ per child per month, for a total monthly payment of $_____. The payments will begin on the _____ day of _____, 19___ and will continue for each child until that child has reached the age of majority, died, become self-supporting, or married. We both agree that this obligation is subject to modification by a court at any time.

We both further agree that should the parent obligated to pay the support receive a salary or income increase in the future, the amount of child support due per child per month shall be increased proportionately. The parent obligated to pay support agrees to notify the other parent immediately of any salary or income increase.

[Choose one: Either:] We agree that the required child support payments should be made directly to the parent to whom they are due. However, in the event of a divorce or dissolution of marriage, we agree that the required child support payments are to be paid directly to the court or state official or agency so designated by the laws of this state to receive and disburse such payments. We both further agree that, in the event of a divorce or dissolution of marriage, we will cooperate in obtaining any necessary income withholding orders or income assignments if required to guarantee this obligation.

[Or:] We agree that the required child support payments should be made directly to the parent to whom they are due and should not be required to be paid through any court or state agency or official. The parent receiving the payments, however, does not waive the right to request, at any time and in his or her sole discretion, that such payments be made directly through a court or state agency or official in the future. We both further agree that, in the event of a divorce or dissolution of marriage, we will cooperate in obtaining any necessary income withholding orders or income assignments if required to guarantee this obligation.

Life and Health Insurance Clauses

Two provisions regarding insurance as additional child support are provided here. These require that, as additional child support, the parent who is to pay the support must: (1) maintain a life insurance policy naming the children as beneficiaries; and (2) maintain health insurance coverage for the children.

These provisions are highly recommended and are required in some states. Federal law requires that states require a parent responsible for child support to include any children under a health and dental insurance plan if such a plan is available to the parent through their place of employment or otherwise at a relatively low cost. The life insurance provision provides some measure of security and insurance protection for the children in the event of death of the paying parent. The health insurance protection provides the child with protection in case of illness or injury.

☐ As additional child support, we both agree that as long as support payments are due the _____ [Wife or Husband] will carry and maintain life insurance in the amount of $ _____, naming our child[ren] as sole irrevocable beneficiary[ies]. The parent obligated to provide such insurance will provide the other parent with annual proof of such coverage.

☐ As additional child support, we both agree that as long as support payments are due the _____ [Wife or Husband] will carry and maintain adequate health, dental, and hospitalization insurance for the child[ren]'s benefit, pay any required deductible amount, and pay for any necessary medical or dental expenses of the child[ren] that are not covered by such insurance. The parent obligated to provide such insurance will provide the other parent with annual proof of such coverage.

Additional Child Support Clause

Finally, a general clause is provided for those parents who wish to provide a written agreement on any other provisions regarding the support of their children. This clause may be used, for example, to indicate that the non-custodial parent will contribute additional amounts for the college education of the child. Generally, a parent's legal support obligation ends when the child reaches the age of majority (usually 18 years old). However, parents may legally agree to provide support beyond this minimum cut-off date.

You and your spouse may also desire to use this clause to provide additional sums for other needs of your children, such as summer camp fees, special educational costs, or religious training. For any such additional support provisions, use clear explanatory language to define the obligations that you have agreed upon.

CHAPTER 6: CHILD SUPPORT

☐ As additional child support, we both agree that the _____ *[Wife or Husband]* will provide *[here include the terms of the agreed upon provision (for example: one-half of the amount necessary for the child's college education)]*:

_____
_____
_____

The various child support clauses that you have chosen will be used when you compile and prepare your marital settlement agreement in Chapter 8. Please refer back to this chapter at that time.

CHAPTER 7

ADDITIONAL CLAUSES AND CONSIDERATIONS

Various additional matters must be considered as you prepare your marital settlement agreement. Among these are the tax consequences of your divorce and any necessary name changes (for example: from married name back to maiden name). These matters and the clauses that relate to them are discussed in this chapter. In addition, two other clauses are included at the end of this chapter. The first is a mandatory agreement clause relating to various technical and legal requirements. The second is the required signature and notary clause that you will need to complete your marital settlement agreement.

The Tax Consequences of Divorce

There are various tax consequences to your divorce that must be considered as you prepare your marital settlement agreement. Among these are:

- Whether you will file joint or separate returns for the current tax year;
- Who will be liable for any taxes due for the current year;
- Who will have a right to any refund due for the current tax year;
- Who will receive the tax exemption for any dependent children.

The full details regarding the potential tax aspects of divorce are beyond the scope of this book. Tax laws are among the most complex and rapidly changing laws in existence. Detailed information regarding current federal income tax laws may be found in IRS Publication #504: *Tax Information for Divorce or Separated Individuals*. For information on your individual state's treatment of divorce for tax purposes, please consult the instructions or regulations available from your state's department of taxation or revenue. For further information, you should consult a competent accountant, attorney, or other qualified tax professional.

There are, however, some general taxation guidelines that may assist you in determining your personal income tax situation before and after your divorce.

Property Transfers

The most important rule regarding federal income taxes relating to property is that any transfers of property between you and your spouse that are related to your divorce or separation are not taxable. There will be no recognition of any gain or loss on the transfer of any property, regardless of who actually owned the property. The transfer of property related to a divorce is considered a gift from one spouse to the other for tax purposes as long as the property is actually transferred within one year after the date of the actual final divorce. The spouse who receives the property is not required to report any gain or income as the result of the receipt of any such property.

However, there may be future tax consequences to a spouse who receives property which has increased in value while it was held during the marriage. In general, the spouse who receives such property in a divorce settlement and later sells the property will be liable for any taxes due on any gain in the value of the property.

For example, as a result of their divorce negotiations, Spouse A agrees to sign a deed transferring full ownership of their jointly-owned home to Spouse B. The original equity in the home at the time of original purchase was $10,000 (their down payment). Therefore, the value of Spouse A's one-half share at purchase was $5,000. The equity value of the home is now $40,000. The current market value of Spouse A's share of the equity value of the home is $20,000. Upon transfer of Spouse A's share to Spouse B, Spouse B is not required to report any gain or income related to the transfer. However, if Spouse B later sells the home, the $15,000 gain in value which is attributable to Spouse A's share ($20,000 - $5,000 = $15,000) will be considered as taxable gain to Spouse B. Spouse B's own share of the equity will also be taxable as gain on the sale of the home.

Additionally, there are some relatively complex tax regulations that relate to the treatment of community property in the 9 community property states (Arizona, California, Idaho, Louisiana, Nevada, New Mexico, Texas, Washington, and Wisconsin). In general, the IRS may choose to disregard community property rules in certain specific tax situations. Although these situations seldom arise under normal circumstances, IRS Publication #504: *Tax Information for Divorce or Separated Individuals* should be referred to for more information on this aspect of taxation.

CHAPTER 7: ADDITIONAL CLAUSES AND CONSIDERATIONS

Alimony

In general, alimony payments are treated as income to the spouse who receives them. Conversely, the spouse who actually pays the alimony may deduct such payments as an expense. The spouse paying alimony can (at the present time) deduct the alimony payments from income for tax purposes whether or not deductions are itemized on the federal tax forms.

In order for alimony payments to qualify for this tax treatment for federal income tax purposes, there are certain conditions. For payments based on agreements made after 1984, the following requirements must be met:

- The alimony payment must be the result of a written settlement agreement or a divorce decree or judgement;
- The payment must be by cash, check or money order;
- The spouses do not live together when the payment is made;
- The payment is not child support; and
- The agreement must not allow the payments to continue after death.

The terms of the marital settlement agreement clauses included in this book relating to alimony would qualify under current federal tax law as long as: (1) the payments are terminated on the death of the recipient; (2) they are not a one-time lump-sum payment; and (3) all of the other above conditions are met. A one-time lump-sum alimony payment is treated as a simple transfer of funds from one spouse to the other. Such a lump-sum alimony payment is neither taxable to the spouse receiving it nor deductible by the spouse paying it.

Life insurance premium payments that are made by an ex-spouse for a policy that names the other ex-spouse as sole irrevocable beneficiary are also considered to be alimony, as long as the payments also meet the above qulifications. Any other voluntary payments in excess of the amount required under the marital settlement agreement or divorce decree, however, will not qualify as alimony and may not be deducted as alimony expenses for tax purposes.

For example, under the terms of their marital settlement agreement, Spouse A has agreed to pay Spouse B $500 per month for 3 years or until Spouse B's death, whichever occurs first. The spouses currently have separated and live apart. Spouse A makes the required payments for a full year. For income tax purposes, Spouse A may deduct the full $6,000 from his income, even if other deductions are not itemized. Spouse B must report the entire $6,000 as income for federal income tax purposes.

Child Support and Custody

For federal income tax purposes child support payments are treated differently from alimony payments. In general, any amount which is fixed in your marital settlement agreement or in your final divorce decree as child support will not be treated as income to the parent who receives it. In addition, unlike alimony payments, the parent who makes such child support payments can not deduct this payment as an expense for federal income tax purposes.

For example, Parent A has custody of one child and Parent B has agreed to pay $400 per month in child support. The payments are made on time for a full year. Parent B may not deduct any of the amount of the child support payments from income and Parent A is not required to report any of the payments as income for tax purposes.

Which parent receives the benefit of the tax exemption for a dependent child is also subject to IRS regulations. In general, the parent with physical custody of the child for over one-half of the year will have the right to the exemption if the following qualifications are also met:

- You are divorced, separated, or live apart for at least the last 6 months of the current tax year;
- You and your spouse *together* provided over one-half of the total support for the child (as opposed to support being provided by a non-parent);
- You and your spouse had custody of the child, either alone or together for over one-half of the current year (as opposed to a non-parent having custody); and
- You have not agreed in writing that your spouse should have the right to claim the dependency exemption and filed a written IRS waiver form *[IRS Form 8332: Release of Claim to Exemption for Child of Divorced or Separated Parents]*.

In the settlement agreement tax clause which follows, you and your spouse have an opportunity to choose which of you will receive $1,000 dependency exemption. Generally, the parent with custody should receive the exemption. This is true even if the non-custodial parent provides over one-half of the actual monetary support for the child. If the non-custodial parent is given the right to claim the exemption, IRS Form 8332 must be signed by the custodial parent and filed with the non-custodial parent's tax return in order to officially waive the right to the exemption.

Marital Settlement Agreement Taxation Clause

The following clause may be used to define your various decisions regarding the tax consequences of your divorce. If you are living apart under the terms of your marital settlement agreement or under the terms of a separation decree but your divorce is not final by the

CHAPTER 7: ADDITIONAL CLAUSES AND CONSIDERATIONS

end of the year, you may choose to file: (1) a joint tax return with your spouse; (2) a separate return; or (3) you may be considered unmarried and file a "head of household" return. You may choose to file a joint income tax return with your spouse for the current tax year only if your divorce has not been made final before the end of the year. If your divorce is final by the end of the year, you must file either an individual return or a "head of household" return. In addition, if your divorce is finalized prior to the end of the current tax year, you may not claim your spouse as an exemption, even if you have provided all of the support for your spouse for the year.

> We both agree that we will cooperate in the filing of any necessary tax returns. We also agree that any tax refunds for the current year will be the property of the _____ [Wife or Husband] and that any taxes due for the current tax year will be paid by the _____ [Wife or Husband].
>
> [Use if necessary:] We both agree to file a joint income tax return for the current year.
>
> [Use if you have children:] We also agree that the _____ [Wife or Husband] may claim the federal dependency tax exemption for our child[ren].

Marital Settlement Agreement Name Change Clause

Most states have specific laws which allow a person to request that his or her former name be restored upon divorce. Although many of these laws are now written to make no reference to the sex of the person requesting this type of change, it is generally a wife who desires to use either her maiden name or her former name (if her former name was a previous married name). The restoration of this name may be accomplished by a simple request in the divorce papers and a provision in the divorce decree or judgement. This will be covered in detail in Chapter 10. You may use this clause also to state the last name that the children of your marriage will be known by, if you did not use a clause that contained a provision for children's names in Chapter 5.

It is useful to have your spouse's agreement to such a name change request, and such an agreement is contained in the following clause.

DIVORCE YOURSELF

> We both agree that, in the event of divorce or dissolution of marriage, the Wife desires to and shall have the right to be known by the name of _____ *[Desired name]*.
>
> We both also agree that, in the event of divorce or dissolution of marriage, our child*[ren]* will be known by the last name of _____ *[Desired name]*.

Additional Mandatory Marital Settlement Agreement Clause

There are various other marital settlement agreement issues which must be included in order for your agreement to have the necessary legal force. This will always be the last numbered clause in your marital settlement agreement. These standard legal phrases are important and should not be altered. They cover the following points:

- That you both want the terms of your marital settlement agreement to be the basis for your a court order in the event of a divorce;
- That you both have prepared complete and honest Financial Statements and they are attached to your agreement;
- That you both know that you have the right to see your own lawyers and that you both understand your legal rights;
- That you both will sign any necessary documents;
- That you both intend that your agreement is the full statement of your rights and responsibilities; and
- That your agreement will be binding on any future representatives of yours.

> We both desire that, in the event of our divorce or dissolution of marriage, this marital settlement agreement be approved and merged and incorporated into any subsequent decree or judgement for divorce or dissolution of marriage and that, by the terms of the judgement or decree, we both be ordered to comply with the terms of this agreement, but that this agreement survive.
>
> We have prepared this agreement cooperatively and each of us has fully and honestly disclosed to the other the extent of our assets, income, and financial situation. We have each completed Financial Statements which are attached and incorporated by reference.
>
> *[Continued on next page]*

CHAPTER 7: ADDITIONAL CLAUSES AND CONSIDERATIONS

> *[Continued from previous page]*
>
> We each understand that we have the right to representation by independent counsel. We each fully understand our rights and we each consider the terms of this agreement to be fair and reasonable. Both of us agree to execute and deliver any documents, make any endorsements, and do any and all acts that may be necessary or convenient to carry out all of the terms of this agreement.
>
> We agree that this document is intended to be the full and entire settlement and agreement between us regarding our marital rights and obligations and that this agreement should be interpreted and governed by the laws of the State of _____ *[Name of state]*.
>
> We also agree that every provision of this agreement is expressly made binding upon the heirs, assigns, executors, administrators, successors in interest, and representatives of each of us.

Marital Settlement Agreement Signature and Notary Clause

The following signature, witness, and Notary clause is mandatory and must be used with all marital settlement agreements. This will always be the last clause used in the preparation of your agreement. This clause should not be numbered.

> Signed and dated this _____ day of _____ , 19 ___.
>
> _____ _____
> Witness for Wife   Wife *[Type full name]*
>
> _____
> Witness for Wife
>
> _____ _____
> Witness for Husband   Husband *[Type full name]*
>
> _____
> Witness for Husband
>
> *[Continued on next page]*

[Continued from previous page]

State of _____)
) SS.
County *[or Parish]* of _____)

On this day, before me, the undersigned authority, in and for and residing in the above county *[or parish]* and state, personally appeared *[Full name of wife]* _____, who is personally known to me to be the same person whose name is subscribed to the foregoing document, and, being duly sworn, _____ *[he or she]* acknowledged that the foregoing document was signed as a free and voluntary act for the purposes stated.

Subscribed and sworn to this _____ day of _____, 19 ___.

Notary Seal *[if required]*

Title *[and Signature]* _____

My commission expires: _____

State of _____)
) SS.
County *[or Parish]* of _____)

On this day, before me, the undersigned authority, in and for and residing in the above county *[or parish]* and state, personally appeared *[Full name of husband]* _____, who is personally known to me to be the same person whose name is subscribed to the foregoing document, and, being duly sworn, _____ *[he or she]* acknowledged that the foregoing document was signed as a free and voluntary act for the purposes stated.

Subscribed and sworn to this _____ day of _____, 19 ___.

Notary Seal *[if required]*

Title *[and Signature]* _____

My commission expires: _____

CHAPTER 8

PREPARING YOUR MARITAL SETTLEMENT AGREEMENT

After you and your spouse have reached all of the necessary decisions, have chosen the appropriate clauses in the preceding chapters, and have filled in all of the required information in the blanks, you are ready to assemble your marital settlement agreement. After it is assembled, you will be given instructions on signing and having your agreement notarized.

Once you have reached this step in your divorce process, you may relax somewhat with the knowledge that the most difficult decisions in your divorce are behind you. You and your spouse have essentially worked out all of the matters relating to your marriage that require agreement. The divorce procedure now becomes the rather routine matter of preparing and processing the necessary paperwork.

Before you begin to actually assemble your agreement, you should both carefully review each clause that you and your spouse have chosen and be certain that it embodies your complete agreement. If you are both satisfied that your choices are complete, you are ready to complete and finalize the agreement. The actual preparation of your marital settlement agreement will be accomplished in 4 easy steps. These steps are as follows:

1. Make a photo-copy of each page of this book which contains a clause which you and your spouse have chosen for inclusion in your marital settlement agreement. Don't forget the preliminary clauses in Chapter 2 or the mandatory ending clause in Chapter 7. If you don't have children, you will have

clauses from Chapters 2, 3, 4, and 7. If you have children, you will have clauses from Chapters 2 through 7.

2. Beginning with the "separation" clause from Chapter 2, number each clause consecutively in the small boxes provided to the left of each of your chosen clauses. The "separation" clause is already numbered #1; one of the property division clauses from Chapter 3 will be numbered #2; and so on. Do not number the final signature/witness/notary clause.

3. Using a typewriter (or hiring a typist), carefully and consecutively type (or have typed) each provision of the Marital Settlement Agreement double-spaced on one side of clean white 8 1/2" X 11" paper. With your filled-in and numbered photo-copies of the clauses before you, this should be a relatively simple task. Each page of the agreement should be numbered on the bottom as follows: Page 1 of X pages, Page 2 of X pages, etc. Do not type any portions of a clause which are shown in *italics* in this book. In addition, the only blank lines that should appear on your original should be the spaces for the signatures on the final page. You may refer to the sample completed Marital Settlement Agreement which is contained in Chapter 9 for reference. Both you and your spouse should then carefully proofread your entire Marital Settlement Agreement when it is completed. If any corrections are necessary, type the entire page over. When you are satisfied that the Agreement is complete, make 2 photo-copies of the unsigned original, so that you will have 3 original unsigned copies. Attach a complete unsigned original copy of each of your Financial Statements that you prepared in Chapter 3. Staple the upper left hand corner of all of the pages of each original copy together. (References to "originals" in this book refer to any unsigned documents, even if they are photo-copies. "Copies" refer to photo-copies of *signed* documents).

You should now have 3 identical unsigned "original" documents. Each document will consist of a complete Marital Settlement Agreement, a Financial Statement completed by you, and a Financial Statement completed by your spouse.

4. Take all 3 original copies of your Agreement document along with two witnesses to the office of a local notary public or other similar authority for signing. The witnesses that you and your spouse use may be the same. They may be family or friends, as long as they are over 18 years old. There may be acceptable people to use as witnesses available at the office of the notary. Call in advance and check. In front of the notary, both you and your spouse should sign the all 3 copies of your Marital Settlement Agreement where indicated on the last page and all 3 copies of your own individual Financial Statement where indicated. Your witnesses should then also sign both copies of the Marital Settlement Agreement where indicated. Finally, the notary will need to sign all 3 agreements and each copy of each Financial Statement. The

CHAPTER 8: PREPARING YOUR MARITAL SETTLEMENT AGREEMENT

notary will also need to fill in the appropriate information, and affix a notary seal if required. There may be a small notary fee.

The notary will be signing his or her signature in 4 places on each of the 3 full documents for a total of 12 notary signatures [(twice on the Marital Settlement Agreement and once each on each Financial Statement) X 3]. You and your spouse will be signing in 2 places each on each of the 3 original documents, for a total of 6 signatures each [(once on the Marital Settlement Agreement and once on the Financial Statement) X 3].

You should each retain one of the complete signed original copies of your agreement. The third original signed copy will be filed with your divorce papers. You will also need to make at least 3 photo-copies of the original for use later when you file for your divorce. Place the original and the photo-copies in a safe place.

In order to save time and trouble, you may wish to prepare all of the necessary divorce papers as shown in the next few chapters and sign all of those documents at the same time that you sign your Marital Settlement Agreement.

The final signed and notarized Marital Settlement Agreement (with its attached Financial Statements) will be a valid legal contract between you and your spouse which is enforceable in a court of law if either of you break your promises in the agreement. Under the terms of your agreement, you may proceed to fulfill the promises that you made to each other. You may begin to live separately. You may divide your property and sell any that you have agreed to sell. Any necessary papers for transferring property may be signed (for example: car titles, quitclaim deeds, etc.). The custody and visitation provisions of your agreement should go into effect and you may begin to make and receive any alimony or child support payments. Essentially, under the terms of your marital settlement agreement, you may begin to live your life as a single person again. However, you are not yet free to remarry and you can not yet legally have sexual relations with other people. You are not yet divorced. In Chapters 10-13, the legal procedures for using your Marital Settlement Agreement to obtain a divorce are explained.

CHAPTER 9

A SAMPLE MARITAL SETTLEMENT AGREEMENT

In this chapter, a complete sample marital settlement agreement is presented. It has been assembled using clauses from Chapters 2 through 7 of this book. By reviewing this sample agreement, you will be able to see what a final completed settlement agreement should look like and how the various parts are put together.

For the purposes of preparing this sample agreement, a fictional family was used. Mrs. Mary Ellen Smith is the wife and Mr. John William Smith is the husband. They were married on January 1, 1985 and have two minor children: Alice Mary Smith and James John Smith, ages 2 and 4.

They own the following property:

> A home valued at $50,000, with an outstanding mortgage balance of $40,000.
>
> A Chevrolet car valued at $7,500, with an outstanding loan balance of $1,000.
>
> Furniture and household furnishings worth $3,000.
>
> Tools worth $2,000.
>
> Cash in a checking account in the amount of $2,000.
>
> Jewelry which Mrs. Smith inherited from her mother valued at $1,500.
>
> A boat valued at $2,000 which Mr. Smith owned prior to the marriage.

DIVORCE YOURSELF

They jointly owe the following debts (other than mortgage and car payments):

    Visa Credit Card: Balance of $1,500.

    Jones Furniture Store: Balance of $1,000.

The value of their separate or non-marital property is as follows:

    Mrs. Smith: Jewelry valued at $1,500.

    Mr. Smith: Boat valued at $2,000.

The value of their marital or community property is as follows:

Tools:	$ 2,000
Car: equity value	$ 6,500
Furniture and furnishings	$ 3,000
Home: equity value	$10,000
Cash:	$ 2,000
Sub-total	$23,500
Minus (-)	
Visa Credit balance	($1,500)
Jones Furniture Credit balance	($1,000)
Equals (=)	
Total value of marital property	$21,000

Mr. Smith has a life insurance policy on his life for $100,000 and health insurance through his place of employment which covers both of their children. Mr. Smith works full-time, while Mrs. Smith works only part-time and cares for both children at home. She is, however, educated and capable of full-time employment.

They have agreed to the following terms:

- Mrs. Smith will keep the home and Mr. Smith will transfer (by quitclaim deed) his share of the home to her. She also will keep two-thirds of the home furnishings. None of the cash in the bank account will be hers. She agrees to pay off the Visa bill. The value of her share of the marital or community property is $10,500 ($10,000 (home equity) + $2,000 (furnishings) - $1,500 (Visa bill) = $10,500).

- Mr. Smith will keep the tools, the car, and the one-third of the home furnishings. All of the cash in the bank will be his to keep. He agrees to pay off the Jones Furniture bill. His share of the marital or community property is also $10,500 ($1,000 (furnishings) + $6,500 (car equity) + $2,000 (tools) + $2,000 (cash) - $1,000 (furniture bill) = $10,500). They have separated their furnishings, closed their joint

CHAPTER 9: A SAMPLE MARITAL SETTLEMENT AGREEMENT

bank account, and opened individual accounts. In addition to signing this Marital Settlement Agreement and their Financial Statements, they will need to prepare a quit-claim deed for their home and have the title to their car transferred.

- They have also agreed that Mrs. Smith will have sole physical custody of the children, that they will share joint legal custody, and that liberal visitation will be provided. Mr. Smith agrees to pay $650/month in child support. He also agrees to pay Mrs. Smith $400/month alimony for three years or approximately until both children are in elementary school.

Various other minor decisions that they have made are shown in the appropriate sections of the clauses in their Agreement. Although not shown here, each spouse will also need to have prepared a Financial Statement as explained in Chapter 3. The Marital Settlement Agreement which embodies all of their agreements and which will be used in their later divorce is as follows:

MARITAL SETTLEMENT AGREEMENT

This agreement is made on the 1st day of May, 1991, between Mary Ellen Smith, the Wife, who lives at 150 Emerald Lane in the Town of Centerville, County of Washington, State of Superior, and John William Smith, the Husband, who lives at 2000 Main Street, Apartment #2, in the Town of Centerville, County of Washington, State of Superior.

We were married on the 1st day of January 1985, in the City of Columbia, County of Lincoln, State of Superior.

The following children were born into our marriage:

Alice Mary Smith	April 21, 1989	Girl
Child's name	Child's Birth date	Child's Sex
James John Smith	October 26, 1986	Boy
Child's name	Child's Birth date	Child's Sex

As a result of disputes and serious differences, we sincerely believe that our marriage is irretrievably broken and that there is no possible chance for reconciliation.

We both desire to settle by agreement all of our marital affairs, including the division of all of our property and bills, spousal support or maintenance, and all issues relating to our children, including custody, visitation, and child support.

Page 1 of 7 Pages

THEREFORE, in consideration of our mutual promises, and other good and valuable consideration, we agree as follows:

1. We both desire and agree to permanently live separate and apart from each other, as if we were single, according to the terms of this agreement. We each agree not to annoy, harass, or interfere with the other in any manner.

2. We agree that the following property shall be the sole and separate property of the Wife, and the Husband transfers and quitclaims any interest that he may have in this property to the Wife:

> Diamond Ring and Bracelet valued at $1,500
> All of the furnishings currently in the family home
> The family home located at 150 Emerald Lane, Centerville, Superior, with the legal description as follows:
>> Lot 5 of Centerville Subdivision as shown on Plat 3 on Page 65 of Book 200 in the Records of Washington County, Superior.

We also agree that the following property shall be the sole and separate property of the Husband, and the Wife transfers and quitclaims any interest that she may have in this property to the Husband:

> Woodworking Tools valued at $2,000
> 1988 Chevrolet, serial #123456, Superior License #ABC 789, valued at $6,500
> $2,000 cash currently in the Centerville Bank in his individual account
> Household furnishings currently located at 2000 Main Street, Apartment #2, Centerville, Superior

3. We agree that the Wife shall pay and indemnify and hold the Husband harmless from the following debts:

> Visa Credit Card Account # 987654
> Home mortgage currently held by the Centerville National Bank on the family home located at 150 Emerald Lane, Centerville, Superior, with the legal description as follows:
>> Lot 5 of Centerville Subdivision as shown on Plat 3 on Page 65 of Book 200 in the Records of Washington County, Superior.

We agree that the Husband shall pay and indemnify and hold the Wife harmless from the following debts:

> Jones Furniture Store Account #321
> Auto loan currently held with the GMAC Finance Company on the 1988 Chevrolet, serial #123456, Superior License #ABC 789

We also agree not to incur any further debts or obligations for which the other may be liable.

4. We both agree that, as alimony and maintenance, the Husband shall pay to the Wife the sum of $400 per month, payable on the 1st day of each month. The first payment will be due on the 1st day of June, 1991, and the payments shall continue until the first of the following occurrences: (1) the date that either of us dies; (2) the date that the spouse receiving alimony remarries; or (3) June 1, 1994. We both intend that the amount and the duration of the payments may be modified by a court in the future. We also both agree that these payments should be made directly to the spouse to whom they are due.

5. We both agree that neither of us shall remain as the beneficiary on any life insurance policy carried by the other.

6. We both agree that it is in the best interests of our children that we both have joint legal custody of our children. We also agree that it is in the best interests of our children that the Wife have sole physical custody of our children. We acknowledge that our children presently live with the Wife and that the actual physical residence of our children may be changed at any time as we may mutually agree.

All decisions pertaining to the education, discipline, health, extracurricular and summer activities, religious training, medical and dental care, and welfare of our children will be decided by both of us after reasonable and adequate discussion. We also agree that the parent with physical custody shall have control over the minor day-to-day decisions affecting the child, including any medical or dental emergencies. We agree that if, after reasonable attempts, we are unable to reach an agreement on any of the decisions affecting our children, we will jointly seek professional mediation to resolve our differences.

We also agree that each of us has the right to know of any circumstances or decisions that affect our children and that each of us has the right to any medical, dental, or school records of our children. Neither of us will do anything to hamper or interfere with the natural and continuing relationship between our children and the other parent.

We both realize that the well-being of our children is of paramount importance and, therefore, we agree that our children should have as much contact as possible with the parent that does not have physical custody and that our children may visit that parent as often as may be agreed upon. Although visitation may be scheduled more often, the parent that does not have physical custody will have the right to be with our children at least as follows:

(A). On the following holidays during even-numbered years: Martin Luther King Jr.'s Birthday, Easter, Fourth of July, Halloween, and Christmas.

(B). On the following holidays during odd-numbered years: New Year's Day, Valentine's Day, Memorial Day, Labor Day, and Thanksgiving.

(C). On the following dates and times every other weekend: From 5:00 PM on Friday evening until 5:00 PM on Sunday evening.

(D). On the following dates and times during every other opposite week: On Tuesday and Thursday evenings from 5:00 PM until the children's bedtime.

(E). For the following vacation periods each year: For one week during either the children's winter or spring school vacation and for three consecutive weeks during the children's summer school vacation.

We additionally agree to use our very best efforts to insure that our children receive the most care, love, and affection possible from both parents throughout their entire childhood.

7. We both agree that the Husband will pay to the Wife, as child support, the amount of $325 per child per month, for a total monthly payment of $650. The payments will begin on the 1st day of June, 1991, and will continue for each child until that child has reached the age of majority, died, become self-supporting, or married. We both agree that this obligation is subject to modification by a court at any time.

We both further agree that should the parent obligated to pay the support receive a salary or income increase in the future, the amount of child support due per child per month shall be increased proportionately. The parent obligated to pay support agrees to notify the other parent immediately of any salary or income increase.

CHAPTER 9: A SAMPLE MARITAL SETTLEMENT AGREEMENT

We agree that the required child support payments should be made directly to the parent to whom they are due. However, in the event of divorce or dissolution of marriage, the required child support payments are to be paid directly to the court official or state agency so designated by the laws of this state to receive and disburse such payments. We both further agree that, in the event of divorce or dissolution of marriage, we will cooperate in obtaining any necessary income withholding orders or income assignments if required to guarantee this obligation.

8. As additional child support, we both agree that as long as support payments are due the Husband will carry and maintain life insurance in the amount of $100,000 naming our children as sole irrevocable beneficiaries. The parent obligated to provide such insurance will provide the other parent with annual proof of such coverage.

9. As additional child support, we both agree that as long as support payments are due the Husband will carry and maintain health, dental, and hospitalization insurance for the children's benefit, pay any required deductible amount, and pay for any necessary medical or dental expenses of the children that are not covered by such insurance. The parent obligated to provide such insurance will provide the other parent with annual proof of such coverage.

10. We both agree that we will cooperate in the filing of any necessary tax returns. We also agree that any tax refunds for the current year will be the property of the Husband and that any taxes due for the current tax year will be paid by the Husband.

    We also agree that the Wife may claim the dependency tax exemption for the children.

11. We both agree that, in the event of divorce or dissolution of marriage, the Wife desires to and shall have the right to be known by the name of Mary Ellen Carter. We also agree that, in the event of divorce or dissolution of marriage, the children shall continue to use the names shown on their birth certificates.

12. We both desire that, in the event of our divorce or dissolution of marriage, this marital settlement agreement be approved and merged and incorporated into any subsequent decree or judgement for divorce or dissolution of marriage and that, by the terms of the judgement or decree, we both be ordered to comply with the terms of this agreement, but that this agreement shall survive.

We have prepared this agreement cooperatively and each of us has fully and honestly disclosed to the other the extent of our assets, income, and financial situation. We have each completed Financial Statements which are attached and incorporated by reference.

We each understand that we have the right to representation by independent counsel. We each fully understand our rights and we each consider the terms of this agreement to be fair and reasonable. Both of us agree to execute and deliver any documents, make any endorsements, and do any and all acts that may be necessary or convenient to carry out all of the terms of this agreement.

We agree that this document is intended to be the full and entire settlement and agreement between us regarding our marital rights and obligations and that this agreement should be interpreted and governed by the laws of the State of Superior.

We also agree that every provision of this agreement is expressly made binding upon the heirs, assigns, executors, administrators, successors in interest, and representatives of each of us.

Signed and dated this 1st day of May, 1991.

_____   _____
Witness for Wife   Mary Ellen Smith, Wife

_____
Witness for Wife

_____   _____
Witness for Husband   John William Smith, Husband

_____
Witness for Husband

CHAPTER 9: A SAMPLE MARITAL SETTLEMENT AGREEMENT

State of Superior)
) SS.
County of Washington)

On this day, before me, the undersigned authority, in and for and residing in the above county and state, personally appeared Mary Ellen Smith, who is personally known to me to be the same person whose name is subscribed to the foregoing document, and, being duly sworn, she acknowledged that the foregoing document was signed as a free and voluntary act for the purposes stated.

Subscribed and sworn to this 1st day of May, 1991.

_____
Title *[and Signature]*

Notary Seal *[if required]*

My commission expires: _____

State of Superior)
) SS.
County of Washington)

On this day, before me, the undersigned authority, in and for and residing in the above county and state, personally appeared John William Smith, who is personally known to me to be the same person whose name is subscribed to the foregoing document, and, being duly sworn, he acknowledged that the foregoing document was signed as a free and voluntary act for the purposes stated.

Subscribed and sworn to this 1st day of May, 1991.

_____
Title *[and Signature]*

Notary Seal *[if required]*

My commission expires: _____

Page 7 of 7 pages

Once your marital settlement agreement is typed double-spaced on one side of clean white 8 1/2" X 11" paper in the same format as the preceding sample agreement and both you and your spouse have carefully checked the final copy to be certain that it is correct, you are ready to sign the document and have it notarized as explained in Chapter 8. Before you sign the document, it may be a good idea to read the final completed agreement aloud to each other to be certain that it is correct and that you both fully understand the terms of your settlement.

CHAPTER 10

PREPARING YOUR DIVORCE PAPERS

Once you and your spouse have completed and signed your Marital Settlement Agreement and your individual Financial Statements, you are ready to begin preparation of your actual divorce documents. This chapter will take you through the process and steps necessary to complete this portion of the divorce procedure.

As stated previously, divorce is governed by individual state law. Even individual counties within a single state may have certain local legal rules which will govern your divorce process. Although the basic general pattern followed in divorce proceedings is similar throughout all 50 states, there are significant minor differences between the particular documents that you will be required to submit to a court and the specific procedures to follow in each state or county. The information given in this chapter will instruct you on how to prepare documents that will satisfy the legal requirements in the vast majority of all states and counties. Please refer to the listing for your individual state in the Appendix for the specific requirements in your state.

Steps in the Divorce Process

The process of divorce is similar in all jurisdictions. Although the legal terminology and procedure may be difficult to understand at times, the process itself is not complicated. If you understand the process, you will be able to approach your divorce with much less fear and concern about the outcome.

DIVORCE YOURSELF

In general, by filing for a divorce you will be asking a court to formally declare that your marriage is over. In order to make this legal request and have it granted, you must prepare certain legal documents and follow certain court procedures. There are, generally, five basic steps that must be followed in order to obtain a divorce:

1. Prepare all of the necessary legal documents. You have already prepared your Marital Settlement Agreement and Financial Statements. Preparation of the other necessary documents will be explained later in this chapter.

2. File a first set of divorce documents with the clerk of the court which has the proper authority to decide on your case.

3. File a second set of divorce documents with the clerk of the same court. Which documents this includes will be explained later.

4. Schedule and attend a short court hearing on your divorce. This aspect of your divorce will be explained in Chapter 12.

5. Have the judge sign the final court document which declares your marriage over. The preparation of this document will be explained in this chapter and the procedure to follow in court will be discussed in Chapter 12.

Courts handle over 1.7 million divorce cases every year. It is the most common legal proceeding in the nation. Because of this enormous volume of cases, the procedures and process for uncontested divorces have become relatively routine. Although it will be an entirely new experience for you and your spouse, the judges and clerks with whom you will be dealing have handled, literally, thousands of divorce cases. The divorce papers prepared using the instructions in this book are very basic and routine and should be processed without difficulty.

General Considerations

There are certain general instructions that will apply to the preparation and use of all of the legal documents that you will file with the court. By following these instructions, your legal documents will look like and be treated like every other legal document that a court examines.

For all of the legal forms that you prepare using this book, you should follow these instructions:

1. Each form should be neatly typed double-spaced on one side of a clean white piece of typing paper. For every document that is over one page long, each page should be numbered in the following manner: Page 1 of X pages, Page 2 of X pages, Page 3 of X pages, etc. Most courts now use 8 1/2" X 11" paper for court records. However,

CHAPTER 10: PREPARING YOUR DIVORCE PAPERS

some courts still use 8 1/2" X 14" (legal size) paper for court documents. Check with the clerk of the court where you will file your divorce to determine which size paper is standard in your area. Some courts may require various other localized practices such as having holes punched in the papers, or attaching your documents to blue paper backing sheets. Check with the court clerk.

2. Keep all of your papers neat, clean, orderly, and in one place. Each document that you file that has more than one page should be stapled together in the upper left hand corner of the pages.

3. Each of the documents that you prepare must be signed and notarized (if necessary) according to the instructions at the end of this chapter.

4. The original of each document (with the actual signatures) will be filed with the court. You should, however, make at least 2 copies of each document that you prepare: one copy for you and one copy for your spouse. Your complete file of all documents should be brought with you at the time of your court appearance. (See Chapter 12).

The Appendix also contains information that you will need to prepare the court documents in the proper format. Each state and often each county may have a slightly differing form for court papers that they will use. The top portion of the first page of each court document will consist of specific information which the courts have standardized to some extent to aid in the filing and referencing of court records. This is known as the *caption* of the document. Each document must have this information present or the court clerk will not accept the document for filing. This information is: (1) the name of the court; (2) the name of the parties involved; (3) the case number assigned to the case by the clerk; and (4) the title of the document. Below is a sample of this caption portion of a typical court document. The Appendix will contain the data that you need to prepare your own document caption. If you have obtained court records for a divorce in your county (as explained in the next section), you should prepare the caption of your documents exactly as shown on the official court records.

In the District Court for Washington County, State of Superior

In re: The Marriage of)
)
Mary Ellen Smith, Petitioner)
and) Case #: ABC123
John William Smith, Respondent)
)

TITLE OF DOCUMENT

DIVORCE YOURSELF

The documents that you will prepare will be legal court documents and will generally be acceptable in all courts. Most judges are glad to see situations in which a potential legal battle has been settled outside of court. Many judges will provide considerable guidance as you negotiate your way through the legal process. Be aware, however, that in certain areas of the country and in certain courts, there may still be strong resistance to allowing self-help divorces to take place. Some judges may be very strict in the interpretation of laws and may allow no deviation at all in the precise legal wording of court documents. If you encounter resistance of this nature, try to understand what the problem is and make every attempt to correct it. If you can not successfully correct the difficulty, you will need to see a lawyer for assistance.

The Necessary Documents

In addition to your Marital Settlement Agreement and Financial Statements, there are four or five relatively short legal documents that you will need to prepare for submission to the court. These documents, in general, are:

- Petition or Complaint
- Appearance, Consent, and Waiver form
- Child Custody Jurisdiction form (if children are involved)
- proposed Final Judgement or Decree
- Certificate of Divorce or Dissolution of Marriage

Some states or counties may require one or more other routine forms. For example, some California counties require couples to submit a short form that indicates that they desire or have declined marriage counseling services. Other states may require forms which outline child support calculations or other information relating to child support. The most common type of other form required will relate to the payment of child support payments. If you and your spouse have agreed to have any child support payments paid through a court or government agency or official, there will be certain required forms which will need to be filled out. In addition, many states have procedures and forms available for use if there will be an automatic wage withholding order or assignment of wages when there are child support payments involved. Any of these type of forms should be available from the office of the clerk of the court where you will file your divorce papers.

Although the legal method that is outlined in this book does not require the use of a *summons* or *citation*, some states may still require that a summons or citation be used as a formality. A summons/citation is a document that is officially delivered to a person against whom a lawsuit has been filed. The initial court papers which are filed in a lawsuit are also delivered with the summons/citation. The summons/citation notifies the person that the suit has been filed and specifies a time limit in which the person must respond to the lawsuit. Since you and your spouse are cooperating in the filing of your divorce, your spouse will file an *Appearance, Consent, and Waiver* form which takes the place of the

CHAPTER 10: PREPARING YOUR DIVORCE PAPERS

summons/citation in the vast majority of states. When you file your actual divorce papers, you should, however, ask the clerk of the court if a summons/citation will be required if your spouse files the written waiver of service of process. The *Appearance, Consent, and Waiver* form will be explained later in this chapter.

In order for the judge to properly handle your case, you must file all of the documents which are required in your jurisdiction. Refer back to the decision that you made in Chapter 2 regarding where to file for your divorce. It is the specific forms and procedure for that state and county (or parish) that you will need to adhere to. There are three steps that you should take initially to determine exactly what documents must be filed:

1. First, you should carefully read through the Appendix regarding your state's laws to see if any specific additional forms are mentioned. Some states have specific mandatory fill-in-the-blank type forms for use in filing for your divorce. Michigan and California are examples of states that use this method. Florida has provisions for the use of mandatory forms in certain situations. Other states are noted in the Appendix. If your state has mandatory official forms, you *must* use them. They are generally available directly from the clerk of the court where you will file for your divorce. If there are mandatory forms, they will usually contain their own instructions and these should be followed carefully. The information that you have compiled in your questionnaires and in your Marital Settlement Agreement and Financial Statements should be all that you will need to easily prepare most forms of this nature.

    Some areas have optional or unofficial blank legal forms for use in divorce proceedings. These are normally available through legal forms distributors or through stationery or office supply stores. If the use of these forms is customary in your locale (check with the court clerk), you should use the locally-available pre-printed forms. The instructions for filling in these type of forms will be the same as for the forms contained in this book. Simply follow the instructions for preparing and signing the divorce forms as explained in this chapter.

2. Second, you should ask the clerk of the court where you intend to file your divorce papers if any other forms are required, beyond the basic forms listed earlier. Some courts may have specific state or local forms in use which may be required. You can easily do this by phone or you may do so in person. Most court clerks are very helpful and will be glad to assist you. Remember to be courteous and respectful when you deal with the clerk. Court clerks, however, are not attorneys and are not allowed to provide any legal advice. They can and often will assist you in being certain that the forms that you file are the correct ones, but do not ask them for answers to specific legal questions. They are not authorized to offer legal assistance. You may also wish to inquire with the court clerk at this time about the general procedure that is followed in divorce cases. The clerk should be able to inform you regarding any time limits, waiting periods, filing requirements, the customary order in which the documents are filed, how much the filing fees are, and other technical information

DIVORCE YOURSELF

regarding your case. You should write down any information that you receive from the court clerk. If you run into a particular clerk that is less than helpful, be polite and try to determine if there is a problem. If you can't correct the problem, try later with a different clerk.

3. Finally, you should request and obtain from the court clerk a copy of another couple's divorce papers that were filed recently in an uncontested divorce in the county where you intend to file for your divorce. Legal documents filed with the court clerk are public records and are generally available to the public for a small copying fee. A few states, however, seal divorce records. In most jurisdictions, you have a right to obtain a copy of the court file for any other divorce which has been filed. You will have to make your request and pick up the copies in person. The documents in these other court records can be very useful in your preparation of your own divorce papers. They will show you the exact format which is in use in your particular county. Copies of any other required forms will also be included in any such records. They will provide you with a basic outline of the set of documents which are necessary in your particular county to obtain a divorce. To obtain such court records, ask the clerk of the court for "a copy of the court file of any uncontested divorce which was made final within the last six months". They should easily be able to fill this request. There will usually be a small per-page charge for copying the documents in the file. Lawyers often obtain court records for exactly this same purpose.

The clerk may require that you provide the specific names of the people involved in another case in order to find a proper court file. In that case, you should consult your local newspaper to determine the names of couples who were recently divorced. Most newspapers will list such names in a legal listing or notice section. Once you have located the names of several recently divorced couples, simply present the list of names to the court clerk and request a copy of that couple's file that obtained an uncontested divorce. You will then need to pay the necessary fee. If you are unable to obtain the names of recently divorce couples from a newspaper, you may be able to consult the daily or weekly docket sheets in the courthouse. On these calendar sheets the daily schedules for each judge or court room are shown. By locating a final hearing for divorce on such schedule, you should be able to determine the name and case number of appropriate records.

By using the above methods, you should be able to determine the exact documents that are required for your divorce. A simple list of the necessary documents that are necessary in your county should be compiled. The preparation of these documents is explained next. A complete sample set of prepared divorce papers is contained in Chapter 11 for reference as you prepare your own documents.

CHAPTER 10: PREPARING YOUR DIVORCE PAPERS

The Petition or Complaint

The main document that you will file with the court may be titled a *petition* or a *complaint* (A few states may refer to this document as an *action, application, bill of complaint,* or *declaration*: check the Appendix). The names of the two spouses on this and the other court documents will be either the *petitioner* and *respondent* (for petitions) or the *plaintiff* and *defendant* (for complaints). The Appendix listing for your state will give you the proper titles to use. (A few states allow the filing of a Joint Petition for Divorce or Dissolution of Marriage. In these cases, the spouses are both referred to as *co-petitioners*). The petition/complaint will contain your formal request to the court that your marriage be terminated. It will also include your request that the terms of your marital settlement agreement be used as the terms of your divorce. It will contain all of the basic information that a court will need to decide your case. The information that you have compiled in the various questionnaires throughout this book should be used when completing this form. Your questionnaire answers should contain all of the necessary facts for your petition/complaint. For preparing your petition/complaint you will need the following specific information:

You and your spouse's full names _____

The length of time that you have resided in the county and state where you have decided to file for divorce _____

You and your spouse's Social Security #'s _____

The date and place of your marriage _____

The date of your separation _____

The age, occupation, and place of employment of you and your spouse _____

The names and birth dates of any children born or adopted during your marriage _____

The grounds for your divorce that you have chosen from those listed for your state in the Appendix _____

You will now need to decide which of you will be the petitioner/plaintiff in your case and which of you will be the respondent/defendant. The spouse who will be the respondent/defendant will have no duties other than signing documents. The spouse who is the petitioner/plaintiff will sign documents, file the papers with the court, and attend the court hearing, if one is necessary. Legally, it will make no difference which of you serves as petitioner/plaintiff and which of you serves as respondent/defendant. Your particular state procedures relating to which county (or parish) to file your divorce papers in may have bearing on which spouse is chosen as petitioner/plaintiff. You may decide to allow either spouse to be petitioner/plaintiff if it will result in the court proceedings being held in the most convenient county (or parish) for you and your spouse.

The following is a sample of a typical petition/complaint form. For preparing your own, you should use either the title/caption information that is contained in the Appendix for

DIVORCE YOURSELF

your state or follow the format as shown on the divorce record files that you have obtained from the clerk of the court. Once you have determined the exact information for the caption, you will use the same caption for each court document.

This document or a close variation of it, as prepared below, should be generally acceptable in every jurisdiction in the United States. However, you should consult your local court clerk in advance to determine any local rules which may result in slight differences in this form. At most, you may be required to add a sentence or two of further information to this form or change the wording slightly. You should always substitute the official legal terminology which is in use in your state wherever appropriate as shown in the Appendix. You may, for example, need to substitute *dissolution of marriage* for *divorce*; or *maintenance* for *alimony*, etc. Of course, if mandatory official forms are in use in your state or county, you must use them instead.

Fill in the appropriate information on this form and then re-type (or have re-typed) the document onto clean white typing paper, making sure to double space every line. Do not make any alterations in the wording of this form unless it is to comply with wording in an actual sample that you have obtained from the court or to information contained in the Appendix of this book. Instructions for signing this document and the rest of the documents in this chapter and filing them with the court clerk are included at the end of this chapter.

In the _____ Court for _____ County, State of _____
[Use court title as shown in Appendix]

In re: The Marriage of:)
)
  [Name of spouse],   )
  Petitioner [or Plaintiff]   )
  and   )   Case #: [Obtain from clerk upon filing]
  [Name of other spouse],   )
  Respondent [or Defendant]   )
)
[Use only if there are children]:)
And in the interest of:)
)
  [Name of minor children,   )
  if any]   )

TITLE OF DOCUMENT [as shown in Appendix]

[Continued on next page]

CHAPTER 10: PREPARING YOUR DIVORCE PAPERS

[Continued from previous page]

This action is brought by _____, *[Petitioner or Plaintiff]* _____, age _____, who resides at _____ _____, whose Social Security # is _____, and who is employed as a _____ at _____ _____.

The *[Respondent or Defendant]* _____ is _____, age _____, who resides at _____ _____, whose Social Security # is _____, and who is employed as a _____ at _____ _____.

The undersigned *[Petitioner or Plaintiff]* _____ states, under oath, the following:

1. RESIDENCY. *[Petitioner or Plaintiff]* _____ has been a resident of and domiciled in the State of _____ for the preceding _____ and the County *[or Parish]* of _____ for the preceding _____. *[Length of time for residency as shown in the Appendix. If no time limit is required, state actual time of residency]*.

2. SERVICE OF PROCESS. The *[Respondent or Defendant]* _____ has agreed to file a Waiver of Service of Process in this cause and, therefore, no service of process is necessary at this time.

3. JURISDICTION. The court has proper jurisdiction to hear this cause. The *[Respondent or Defendant]* _____ has agreed to file an Appearance in this cause. Neither party has ever been involved in any other domestic relations proceeding involving the other party in this or any other jurisdiction. Neither party is currently an active member of any branch of the Armed Forces of the United States.

4. MARRIAGE. The *[Petitioner or Plaintiff]* _____ and *[Respondent or Defendant]* _____ were married on the _____ day of _____, 19 ___, in the State of _____ and lived together as husband and wife until on or about the _____ day of _____, 19 ___, at which time they separated and ceased to live together and they have lived separate and apart without cohabitation ever since.

5. CHILDREN. *[Use one of the following:* No children were born or adopted to the marriage and the *[Petitioner or Plaintiff]* or *[Respondent or Defendant]* _____ is not now pregnant.

[Continued on next page]

149

[Continued from previous page]

[Or]: There were _____ children born *[or adopted]* to the marriage and their names and dates of birth are as follows: _____
_____
and the *[Petitioner or Plaintiff]* or *[Respondent or Defendant]* _____ is not now pregnant.

6. GROUNDS. *[In a complete sentence, state the grounds which apply to your situation and which you have chosen from the Appendix]*. _____
_____

7. AGREEMENT. This proceeding is uncontested. The *[Petitioner or Plaintiff]* _____ and *[Respondent or Defendant]* _____ have both signed a Marital Settlement Agreement, dated the _____ day of _____, 19___, which is attached and incorporated by reference. By the terms of this Marital Settlement Agreement they have settled all of the issues relating to their marriage, including the division of all of their property, the disposition of all of their bills and obligations, the need for any alimony, maintenance or spousal support, *[(use if there are children involved:) and the custody, visitation, care, and support of their children]*. A Financial Statement has been prepared by each of the parties listing their respective income, expenses, assets, and liabilities and the individual Financial Statements are attached and incorporated by reference. The Marital Settlement Agreement and Financial Statements were signed under no duress or force and without collusion.

8. CONSENT. The *[Respondent or Defendant]* _____ has agreed to file a Consent to the incorporation and merger of said Marital Settlement Agreement into a Final *[Judgement or Decree of Divorce or Dissolution of Marriage (check in Appendix)]* _____ in this cause.

9. WAIVER. The *[Petitioner or Plaintiff]* _____ hereby waives any rights to findings of fact and conclusions of law, a record of testimony, motion for a new trial, notice of entry of final judgement or decree, and the right to appeal, but does not waive any rights to the future modification of any judgement or decree in this cause.

The *[Petitioner or Plaintiff]* _____ respectfully requests and prays:

1. That a *[Divorce or Dissolution of Marriage (check in Appendix)]* _____ be granted by the court dissolving and terminating forever the marriage between the parties.

[Continued on next page]

CHAPTER 10: PREPARING YOUR DIVORCE PAPERS

[Continued from previous page]

2. That all of the terms and conditions of the party's Marital Settlement Agreement, which is attached, be approved and be incorporated, merged into, and made part of a Final *[Judgement or Decree of Divorce or Dissolution of Marriage (check in Appendix)]* _____, and that the parties be ordered to comply with all terms and conditions of the Marital Settlement Agreement, but that the Marital Settlement Agreement survive.

3. That the court award the parties any other further relief as may be just and equitable.

Dated this _____ day of _____, 19 ___.

_____
[Full Name of Petitioner or Plaintiff]
Address: _____

_____
Phone: _____

State of _____)
) SS.
County *[or Parish]* of _____)

On this day, before me, the undersigned authority, in and for and residing in the above county *[or parish]* and state, personally appeared *[Full Name of Petitioner or Plaintiff]* _____, who is personally known to me to be the same person whose name is subscribed to the foregoing document, and, being duly sworn, _____ *[he or she]* verified that the information contained in the foregoing document is true and correct on personal knowledge and acknowledged that said document was signed as a free and voluntary act.

Subscribed and sworn to this ____ day of _____, 19 ___.

                                                     _____
                                                     Title *[and Signature]*
Notary Seal *[if required]*
                                                    My commission expires: _____

[Continued on next page]

DIVORCE YOURSELF

[Continued from previous page]

_____
[Full Name of Respondent or Defendant]
Address: _____
_____
Phone: _____

State of _____)
) SS.
County [or Parish] of _____)

On this day, before me, the undersigned authority, in and for and residing in the above county [or parish] and state, personally appeared [Full Name of Respondent or Defendant] _____, who is personally known to me to be the same person whose name is subscribed to the foregoing document, and, being duly sworn, _____ [he or she] verified that the information contained in the foregoing document is true and correct on personal knowledge and acknowledged that said document was signed as a free and voluntary act.

Subscribed and sworn to this _____ day of _____, 19 ___.

_____
Title [and Signature]
Notary Seal [if required]
My commission expires: _____

Appearance, Consent, and Waiver

This form will need to be filed in all cases, except those in which a state allows a petition for divorce or dissolution of marriage to be filed jointly. It serves several functions. First, through its use the requirement for a formal serving of the divorce papers on one of you is made unnecessary. The delivery of the divorce papers is formally known as *service of process*. Filing this form effectively waives the right to have papers served formally by a sheriff or some other process server. Since you have both cooperated in the preparation and signing of all of the documents to be filed with the court, there is no need for this formal step in the process.

CHAPTER 10: PREPARING YOUR DIVORCE PAPERS

By this document, the spouse who is *not* designated as the petitioner/plaintiff officially makes a legal appearance and consents to the jurisdiction and venue of the court. This means that he or she agrees that the court in which your divorce is filed has the proper authority to grant your divorce. This other spouse (officially the respondent/defendant) also offers his or her consent to the adoption of the Marital Settlement Agreement into the final divorce order. The other spouse also waives his or her right to findings of fact, conclusions of law, a record of testimony, motion for a new trial, notice of entry of final judgement or decree, and right to appeal. These rights were also waived by you in the petition/complaint in an effort to eliminate any unnecessary and extraneous legal proceedings and technicalities. The purpose of the entire document is to streamline and speed up the legal process when you have both agreed to the results desired. It is a formality that is required in states that require that only one spouse file the petition or complaint for divorce. This form is basically an agreement by the other spouse to join in the effort to obtain a divorce. Filing this form generally eliminates much paperwork and often considerable expense from the process of obtaining a divorce. Once the spouse who will act as respondent/defendant has signed this form, no further action by that spouse should be necessary for the remainder of the divorce process.

The title to this document will normally always be *Appearance, Consent, and Waiver*. The rest of the caption portion of this document should be identical to that used in your petition/complaint. Fill in this form now and prepare the final version for signing as described at the end of this chapter.

In the _____ Court for _____ County, State of _____
[Use court title as shown in Appendix]

In re: The Marriage of:)
)
   [Name of spouse],   )
   Petitioner [or Plaintiff]   )
   and   )   Case #: [Obtain from clerk upon filing]
   [Name of other spouse],   )
   Respondent [or Defendant]   )
)
[Use only if there are children]:)
And in the interest of:)
)
   [Name of minor children,   )
   if any]   )

APPEARANCE, CONSENT, AND WAIVER

[Continued on next page]

[Continued from previous page]

The undersigned *[Respondent or Defendant]* _____, _____, states on oath, that:

1. RESIDENCY. I have been a resident of and domiciled in the State of _____ for the preceding _____ and the County *[or Parish]* of _____ for the preceding _____. *[Length of time for residency as shown in the Appendix. If no time limit is required, state actual time of residency]*.

2. ADMISSION. I have received a copy of the *[Petition or Complaint]* _____ which was filed in this cause and I have read and understand it and admit all of the allegations contained in it.

3. APPEARANCE AND WAIVER. I waive all objections to venue and the issuance, service, and return of process in this cause and voluntarily enter my general appearance in this cause and submit personally to the jurisdiction of the court. I have never been involved in any other domestic relations proceeding involving the other party in this or any other jurisdiction. I am not currently an active member of any branch of the Armed Forces of the United States.

4. AGREEMENT. I have freely and voluntarily entered into a Marital Settlement Agreement, dated the _____ day of _____, 19 ___, and a Financial Statement which are attached to and incorporated into the original *[Petition or Complaint]* _____. The Marital Settlement Agreement and Financial Statements were signed under no duress or force and without collusion.

5. CONSENT. I consent to said Marital Settlement Agreement and Financial Statements being approved and incorporated, merged into, and made part of a Final *[Judgement or Decree of Divorce or Dissolution of Marriage]*, and that the parties be ordered to comply with all terms and conditions of the Marital Settlement Agreement, but that the Marital Settlement Agreement survive.

6. ADDITIONAL CONSENT. I agree that this proceeding is uncontested. I further consent that this cause be heard on any day convenient to the court without further notice to me and that the court enter an Order granting the relief prayed for in the *[Petition or Complaint]* _____.

7. ADDITIONAL WAIVER. I further waive my rights to notice of trial, findings of fact and conclusions of law, a record of testimony, motion for a new trial, notice of entry of final judgement or decree, and right to appeal, but do not waive any rights to the future modification of any judgement or decree in this cause.

[Continued on next page]

CHAPTER 10: PREPARING YOUR DIVORCE PAPERS

[Continued from previous page]

_____
[Full Name of Respondent or Defendant]
Address: _____
_____

State of _____)
) SS.
County *[or Parish]* of _____)

On this day, before me, the undersigned authority, in and for and residing in the above county *[or parish]* and state, personally appeared *[Full Name of Respondent or Defendant]* _____, who is personally known to me to be the same person whose name is subscribed to the foregoing document, and, being duly sworn, _____ *[he or she]* verified that the information contained in the foregoing document is true and correct on personal knowledge and acknowledged that said document was signed as a free and voluntary act and that a copy of the *[Petition or Complaint]* _____ has been received.

Subscribed and sworn to this _____ day of _____, 19 ___.

                                                           _____
                                                           Title *[and Signature]*
Notary Seal *[if required]*
                                                           My commission expires: _____

Child Custody Jurisdiction form

This particular form should only be used if there are minor children who were born or adopted during the marriage. If there are no children involved in your divorce, skip this section. If there are children, fill in the appropriate information on this form where indicated. The purpose of this form is to provide the court with information relevant to the jurisdiction of the court to issue orders concerning the children. If you have minor children, the information on this form is mandatory under the Uniform Child Custody Jurisdiction Act in all states. You and your spouse will be making an official delclaration under oath to the court regarding the following matters:

- The number of children that you have that are subject to a custody order in your upcoming divorce;
- The names, sex, social security numbers, dates and places of birth, and dates and places each child has lived for the past 5 years;
- That the child has not been involved in any previous custody lawsuits;
- That neither of you have any knowledge of other current custody lawsuits; and
- That neither of you is aware of any other person with or claiming a right to custody of any of your children.

This form and the law on which it is based is an attempt to be certain that only one court will exercise jurisdiction over the issue of child custody for a particular child. If you or your spouse have been involved in prior custody proceedings involving any of your children or if you are aware of any current proceedings or persons claiming custody, you should consult a competent lawyer. You may still be able to file your own divorce, but a lawyer's assistance will generally be essential.

In the _____ Court for _____ County, State of _____
[Use court title as shown in Appendix]

In re: The Marriage of:)
)
[Name of spouse],)
Petitioner *[or Plaintiff]*)
and)
) Case #: *[Obtain from clerk upon filing]*
)
[Name of other spouse],)
Respondent *[or Defendant]*)
)
And in the interest of:)
)
[Name of any minor children]

DECLARATION UNDER THE UNIFORM CHILD CUSTODY JURISDICTION ACT

We, the undersigned, _____ and _____, are both parties to this proceeding to determine the custody of a minor child, and upon oath state:

1. There ____ *[is/are]* _____ *[number of children]* minor child*[ren]* subject to this proceeding. For each child, the name, sex, Social Security number, date and place of birth, and time and place of residence and name and relationship of person child lived with for the past 5 years, is as follows:

[Continued on next page]

CHAPTER 10: PREPARING YOUR DIVORCE PAPERS

[Continued from previous page]

A. Child's Name: _____ Sex of Child: _____
Place of Birth: _____ Date of Birth: _____
Child's Social Security Number: _____

Present residence: _____
Person child lives with: _____ Relationship: _____
Dates of Residence: From: _____ To: Present

Previous residence: _____
Person child lived with: _____ Relationship: _____
Dates of Residence: From: _____ To: _____

Previous residence: _____
Person child lived with: _____ Relationship: _____
Dates of Residence: From: _____ To: _____

B. Child's Name: _____ Sex of Child: _____
Place of Birth: _____ Date of Birth: _____
Child's Social Security Number: _____

Present residence: _____
Person child lives with: _____ Relationship: _____
Dates of Residence: From: _____ To: Present

Previous residence: _____
Person child lived with: _____ Relationship: _____
Dates of Residence: From: _____ To: _____

Previous residence: _____
Person child lived with: _____ Relationship: _____
Dates of Residence: From: _____ To: _____

2. Neither of us have participated as a party or a witness or in any other capacity in any other litigation or custody proceeding in this state or elsewhere, concerning the custody of a child subject to this proceeding.

3. Neither of us have any information concerning any other litigation or custody proceeding in this state or elsewhere, concerning the custody of a child subject to this proceeding.

[Continued on next page]

[Continued from previous page]

4. Neither of us knows of any other person who is not a party to this proceeding who has physical custody or claims to have custody or visitation rights of any child subject to this proceeding.

Dated this _____ day of _____, 19 ___.

_____
[Full Name of Petitioner or Plaintiff]
Address: _____

Phone: _____

State of _____)
) SS.
County *[or Parish]* of _____)

On this day, before me, the undersigned authority, in and for and residing in the above county *[or parish]* and state, personally appeared *[Full Name of Petitioner or Plaintiff]* _____, who is personally known to me to be the same person whose name is subscribed to the foregoing document, and, being duly sworn, _____ *[he or she]* verified that the information contained in the foregoing document is true and correct on personal knowledge and acknowledged that said document was signed as a free and voluntary act.

Subscribed and sworn to this ____ day of _____, 19 ___.

                                       _____
                                       Title *[and Signature]*
Notary Seal *[if required]*
                                       My commission expires: _____

_____
[Full Name of Respondent or Defendant]
Address: _____

Phone: _____

[Continued on next page]

[Continued from previous page]

State of _____)
) SS.
County *[or Parish]* of _____)

On this day, before me, the undersigned authority, in and for and residing in the above county *[or parish]* and state, personally appeared *[Full Name of Respondent or Defendant]* _____, who is personally known to me to be the same person whose name is subscribed to the foregoing document, and, being duly sworn, _____ *[he or she]* verified that the information contained in the foregoing document is true and correct on personal knowledge and acknowledged that said document was signed as a free and voluntary act.

Subscribed and sworn to this ____ day of _____, 19 ___.

_____
Title *[and Signature]*

Notary Seal *[if required]*

My commission expires: _____

Final Judgement or Decree

This particular document is actually the ultimate goal your are seeking in your divorce. It is the legal court order that declares that your marriage is officially over. It will also include the formal court order regarding all of the other terms of your divorce. This final court order may be called a Judgement of Divorce, Judgement of Dissolution of Marriage, Decree of Divorce, Decree of Dissolution of Marriage, or some other similar title. Check the Appendix and with the clerk of the court to determine the title in your jurisdiction.

As you prepare this document, be very careful and take your time. It must be prepared to reflect exactly what you and your spouse have agreed upon in your Marital Settlement Agreement. It should also parallel exactly what you have requested in the last section of your petition/complaint. You should substitute the official legal terminology which is in use in your state wherever appropriate as shown in the Appendix. You may, for example, need to substitute *dissolution of marriage* for *divorce*; or *maintenance* for *alimony*, etc. Most judges will allow some deviation from strict technical application of legal terminology if it is clear what is intended by the particular language used. However, some judges are very strict in this regard. To be safe, you should try and comply as closely as possible to the particular legal language used in your locale.

Judges in some localities may require that the actual judgement or decree contain all of the terms of the court's order. In other words, these judges want to have all of the various terms and conditions which are in your Marital Settlement Agreement actually typed into the judgement/decree form. There should be no problem with this, other than a little more work typing this form. If your particular area has this requirement, simply delete those portions of the judgement/decree form that state that your property, custody, child support, alimony, and name change will be according to or as set forth in the Marital Settlement Agreement. Then actually type into the judgement/decree the relevant portions of your Marital Settlement Agreement which apply.

Although this document will not be signed by the judge until the end of your divorce hearing, it should be prepared in advance. In an uncontested divorce proceeding which is based on a written and signed marital settlement agreement (as yours will be), a pre-prepared final judgement/decree is common. In the vast majority of cases, the judge will sign this document at the close of your court hearing. Although it is unlikely, there is a slight possibility that the judge may make some changes in the final version of the decision. For example, the amount of child support may be increased or decreased by the judge. If this happens, the judge will orally inform you of such a change during your hearing. Any such changes must be noted carefully at the time of your hearing. Your judgement/decree must then be retyped and resubmitted to the court clerk for the judge's signature. Please see Chapter 12 for information on your court appearance.

In the _____ Court for _____ County, State of _____
[Use court title as shown in Appendix]

In re: The Marriage of:)
)
   [Name of spouse],   )
   Petitioner [or Plaintiff]   )
)
and   )   Case #: [Obtain from clerk upon filing]
)
   [Name of other spouse],   )
   Respondent [or Defendant]   )
)
)
And in the interest of:)
)
   [Name of any minor children)

TITLE OF DOCUMENT [as shown in Appendix]

[Continued on next page]

CHAPTER 10: PREPARING YOUR DIVORCE PAPERS

[Continued from previous page]

On the _____ day of _____, 19 ___, a final hearing was held in this cause.

The *[Petitioner or Plaintiff]* _____ was present, in person.

The *[Respondent or Defendant]* _____ waived issuance, service, and return of process and appeared generally by an Appearance, Consent and Waiver duly filed and did not otherwise appear.

The Court, having examined the verified pleadings and heard the evidence and being fully advised finds:

1. That all necessary residency requirements and prerequisites of law have been legally satisfied;

2. That this Court has personal jurisdiction of the parties and of the subject matter;

3. That all of the material allegations contained in the *[Petition or Complaint]* _____ are true; and

4. That the parties have voluntarily waived findings of fact, conclusions of law, a record of testimony, motion for a new trial, notice of entry of final Judgement, and right to appeal, but have not waived their rights to future modification of this Judgement.

THE COURT ORDERS, ADJUDGES, AND DECREES:

1. That the marriage of the *[Petitioner or Plaintiff]* _____ and the *[Respondent or Defendant]* _____ is hereby dissolved and that they are hereby divorced;

2. That all of the terms and provisions of the Marital Settlement Agreement between the parties and dated the _____ day of _____, 19 ___, which is attached and incorporated by reference, are hereby approved and incorporated, merged into, and made part of this court order, and the parties are ordered to comply with all terms and conditions of said Marital Settlement Agreement, but that it shall survive this order;

3. That the party's property and obligations shall be distributed and apportioned according to the terms and conditions of said Marital Settlement Agreement;

[Continued on next page]

[Continued from previous page]

4. That alimony and maintenance shall be as set forth in said Marital Settlement Agreement;

5. *[Include if appropriate]*: That the custody, visitation, care, and support of the parties children shall be as set forth in said Marital Settlement Agreement;

6. *[Include if appropriate]*: That the *[Petitioner's or Plaintiff's]* _____ or *[Respondent's or Defendant's]* _____ name be restored to _____ as set forth in said Marital Settlement Agreement.

Signed and Entered this _____ day of _____, 19 ___.

_____
Presiding Judge

Approved as to form and content:

_____
[Full Name of Petitioner or Plaintiff]
Address: _____

Phone: _____

Approved as to form and content:

_____
[Full Name of Respondent or Defendant]
Address: _____

Phone: _____

CHAPTER 10: PREPARING YOUR DIVORCE PAPERS

Certificate of Divorce or Dissolution of Marriage

Most states require that a certificate be filed upon the granting of the final divorce. This certificate is similar to a birth certificate and will generally be filed with the state's Bureau of Vital Statistics or some similar agency. It is prepared on a official form and is, generally, very simple to fill out. The official forms for this purpose should be available from the clerk of the court where you file for your divorce. A sample form is shown here for illustration purposes only. Do *not* use this form. You must use the official forms for your state. This form should be filled out and taken with you to the court hearing in your case.

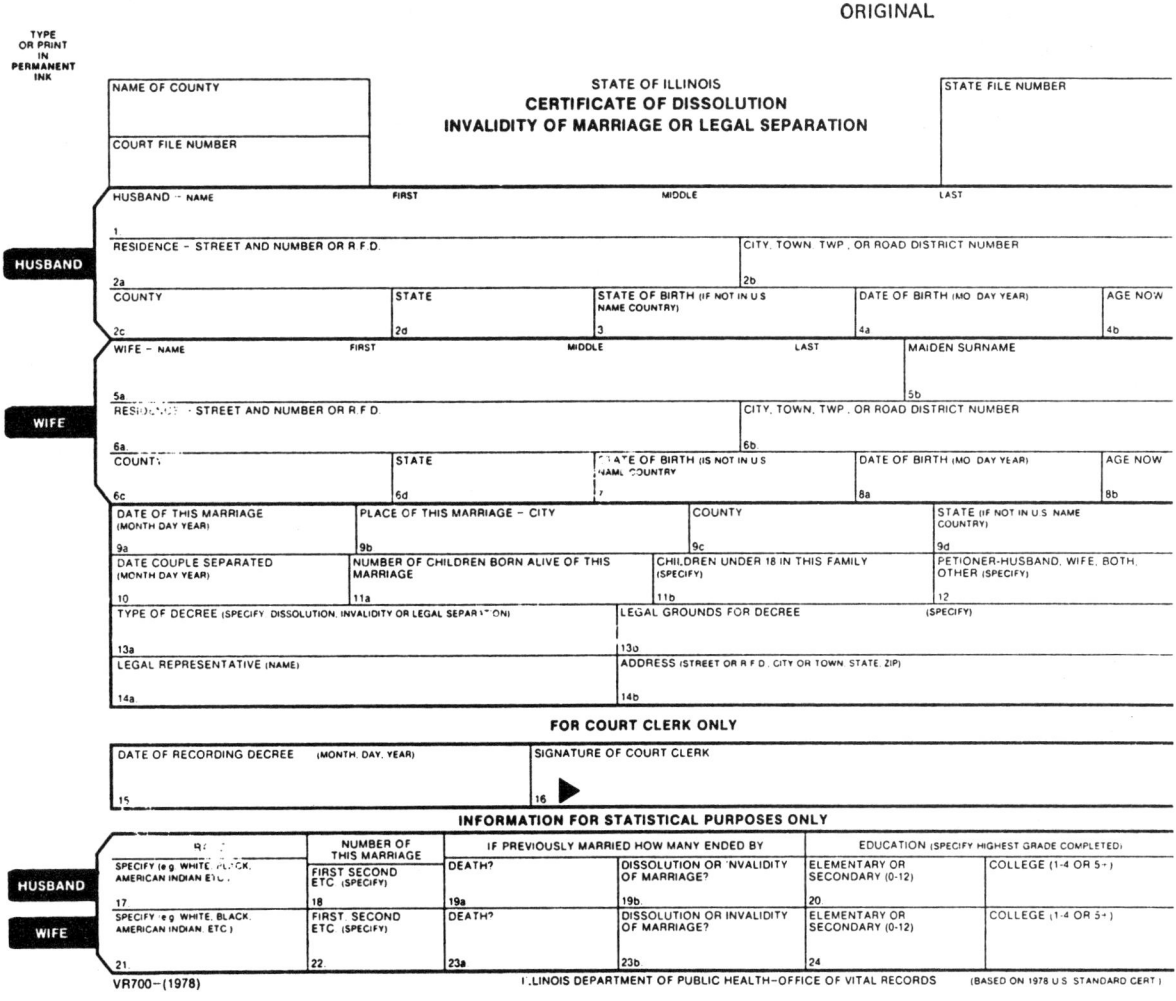

Instructions for Signing and Filing the Documents

Once you have properly filled in all of the blank spaces on the preceding forms, you will need to recheck your list of documents to be certain that you have all of the necessary papers on hand. If you have previously determined that there are other documents required in your jurisdiction, you will need to check those documents and fill in the appropriate information on them. Most additional documents are self-explanatory and should be easy to complete. In general, there are four easy steps necessary to complete and file the forms:

1. You should make a photo-copy of all of the filled-in pages of the forms that you have. From these photo-copies, all of the various court documents that you need should now be neatly typed double-spaced on one side of clean white typing paper. The paper should be the size which is used in your locale (either 8 1/2" X 11" or 8 1/2" X 14"). Every document that is over 1 page should have the pages numbered at the bottom in this manner: Page 1 of X pages; Page 2 of X pages; etc. When typing, any portion of the forms shown in italics in this book should be omitted. After typing, 2 photo-copies should be made of each document. Each original document and the photo-copies should then be individually stapled together if there is more than one page. Do not, however, staple any of the documents to any other documents.

    You will now have before you 3 original copies of each of at least 3 different documents: your Petition/Complaint; your Appearance, Consent, Waiver form; and your final Judgement/Decree form. You may, of course, also have various other forms depending on your circumstances and any local or state requirements: a Child Custody Jurisdiction form; a Certificate of Divorce or Dissolution of Marriage; a Withholding of Wages Order; an Assignment of Wages; etc. (Recall that references to "originals" or "original copies" in this book refer to any unsigned documents, even if they are photo-copies. "Copies" refer to photo-copies of signed documents).

2. All of the various documents should now be taken to a notary public or similar official for signing. Although some states do not specifically require that all of these forms be signed before a notary, it is a good idea to do so. The Judgment/Decree form does not require a notary. Any statistical Certificate of Divorce or Dissolution of Marriage will also not generally require notarization. In addition, unlike the Marital Settlement Agreement, none of these forms will require the use of witnesses.

    In front of the notary, you and your spouse should each sign all 3 original copies of each of the necessary documents, except the Appearance, Consent, and Waiver. (The Appearance, Consent, and Waiver form will be signed later). You should then have the notary sign all original copies of the forms (except the Judgement/Decree and Certificate) where indicated and fill in the appropriate date and information regarding his or her authority. The notary should affix a seal to each original copy if required in your state.

CHAPTER 10: PREPARING YOUR DIVORCE PAPERS

3. To each of the 3 original copies of the Petition/Complaint you should now staple one original copy of the signed and notarized Marital Settlement Agreement and one original copy of each of your signed and notarized Financial Statements. You will now have 3 complete original signed and notarized copies of a rather large main document, consisting of the Petition/Complaint, the Marital Settlement Agreement, and two versions of the individual Financial Statement. One original copy of this master document will be for you and one original copy should be given to your spouse. The third original copy will be the one that you will file with the court. Assemble all of the other original documents and give one original copy of each to your spouse, keep one original copy for yourself, and set aside one original copy for filing with the clerk of the court.

4. The complete third original copy of the signed notarized main document (consisting of the Petition/Complaint, the Marital Settlement Agreement, and two versions of the individual Financial Statement) should now be brought to the office of the clerk of the appropriate court. This will be the only document that you file with the clerk at this time. At the clerk's office, you should tell the clerk that you wish to file the Petition/Complaint and ask that a case number be assigned to your divorce case. There will be a filing fee which must be paid at this time. The clerk will assign a case number to your case. Make careful note of the number and write it in ink on all copies of your other court documents. You may also request at this time that a final hearing be scheduled on the court calendar. If this is the practice in your area, the clerk will assign you a court date and time. In some jurisdictions, there will be a waiting period before a court date is actually scheduled. Make note of the waiting period and contact the clerk of the court at the appropriate time to schedule a hearing. If there is any difficulty in filing the forms, or if the clerk tells you that other forms should be filed, try to determine exactly what is necessary and make every effort to comply.

5. Your spouse must now return to the notary and sign the 3 original copies of the Appearance, Consent, and Waiver form. Once this form is completed and notarized, you are ready to file all of your other forms with the clerk of the court. Assemble one complete signed and notarized original copy of each document. (A notary may not be necessary on all of your additional documents). You may also need to file a certified copy of your Marriage Certificate with the clerk at this time. (Check with the clerk in advance). Take all of these documents to the clerk of the court and request that they be filed with your case records. You will need to tell the clerk the Case number that was assigned to your case. The clerk may not accept your unsigned (by the judge) Final Judgement/Decree form for filing or your incomplete Certificate of Divorce/Dissolution of Marriage form. Don't worry. Some jurisdictions do not file incomplete, unsigned forms. Just be sure to take these forms with you to your court hearing. You will use them at that time.

Once you have completed these 5 steps, you will have completed all of the paperwork necessary for your divorce. You are ready for the final step in your divorce: your brief court appearance. Instructions on how to **conduct yourself** during your court appearance are contained in the next chapter.

CHAPTER 11

SAMPLE DIVORCE PAPERS

In this chapter you will find a complete set of sample divorce documents similar to those which you will prepare for filing with a court. These forms are provided only as examples of how the actual completed court documents should look when they have been properly prepared according to the instructions in the previous chapter. The titles, captions, and actual contents of these sample forms will not be appropriate for your particular jurisdiction. They should *not* be used other than as an example. You should prepare your own forms according the instructions in the previous chapter and the information as shown in the Appendix. However, as you prepare and type your own documents, you may wish to consult these forms for reference regarding the form and style of typical divorce documents.

The fictional Smith family that was used in Chapter 8 for preparing the sample Marital Settlement Agreement is again used. The actual forms required in your particular state and county may differ from the forms contained here. The sample forms which are included in this chapter are:

- Petition for Divorce
- Appearance, Consent, and Waiver
- Declaration Under the Uniform Child Custody Jurisdiction Act
- Judgement of Divorce

DIVORCE YOURSELF

In the Circuit Court for Washington County, State of Superior

In re: The Marriage of:

    Mary Ellen Smith,
    Petitioner
    and
    John William Smith,
    Respondent

And in the interest of:

    Alice Mary Smith and
    James John Smith

Case #: ABC123

PETITION FOR DIVORCE

This action is brought by Mary Ellen Smith, Petitioner, age 30, who resides at 150 Emerald Lane, Centerville, Superior, whose Social Security # is 333-33-3333, and who is employed as a homemaker at 150 Emerald Lane, Centerville, Superior.

The Respondent is John William Smith, age 32, who resides at 2000 Main Street, Apartment #2, Centerville, Superior, whose Social Security # is 444-44-4444, and who is employed as a mechanic at Town Garage, 14 Broadway, Centerville, Superior.

The undersigned Petitioner states, under oath, the following:

1. RESIDENCY. Petitioner has been a resident of and domiciled in the State of Superior for the preceding 12 months and the County of Washington for the preceding 6 months.

2.   SERVICE OF PROCESS. The Respondent has agreed to file a Waiver of Service of Process in this cause and, therefore, no service of process is necessary at this time.

3.   JURISDICTION. The court has proper jurisdiction to hear this cause. The Respondent has agreed to file an Appearance in this cause. Neither party has ever been involved in any other domestic relations proceedings involving the other party in this or any other jurisdiction. Neither party is currently an active member of any branch of the Armed Forces of the United States.

Page 1 of 4 Pages

CHAPTER 11: SAMPLE DIVORCE PAPERS

4. MARRIAGE. The Petitioner and Respondent were married on the 1st day of January, 1985, in the State of Superior, and lived together as husband and wife until on or about the 1st day of May, 1991, at which time they separated and ceased to live together and have lived separate and apart without cohabitation ever since.

5. CHILDREN. There were 2 children born to the marriage and their names and dates of birth are as follows:

Alice Mary Smith, born April 21, 1989;
James John Smith, born October 26, 1986;

and the Petitioner is not now pregnant.

6. GROUNDS. The marriage between the Petitioner and Respondent is irretrievably broken and there is no possible chance for reconciliation.

7. AGREEMENT. This proceeding is uncontested. The Petitioner and Respondent have both signed a Marital Settlement Agreement, dated the 1st day of May, 1991, which is attached and incorporated by reference. By the terms of this Marital Settlement Agreement they have settled all of the issues relating to their marriage, including the division of all of their property, the disposition of all of their bills and obligations, the need for any alimony, maintenance or spousal support, and the custody, visitation, care, and support of their children. A Financial Statement has been prepared by each of the parties listing their respective income, expenses, assets, and liabilities and the individual Financial Statements are attached and incorporated by reference. The Marital Settlement Agreement and Financial Statements were signed under no duress or force and without collusion.

8. CONSENT. The Respondent has agreed to file a Consent to the incorporation and merger of said Marital Settlement Agreement into a Final Judgement of Divorce in this cause.

9. WAIVER. The Petitioner hereby waives any rights to findings of fact and conclusions of law, a record of testimony, motion for a new trial, notice of entry of final judgement, and the right to appeal, but does not waive any rights to the future modification of any judgement in this cause.

The Petitioner respectfully requests and prays:

1. That a Divorce be granted by the court dissolving and terminating forever the marriage between the parties.

2. That all of the terms of the party's Marital Settlement Agreement, which is attached, be approved and incorporated, merged into, and made part of a Final Judgement of Divorce and that the parties be ordered to comply with all terms and conditions of the Marital Settlement Agreement, but that said Marital Settlement Agreement survive.

3. That the court award the parties any other further relief as may be just and equitable.

Dated this 4th day of June, 1991

_____
Mary Ellen Smith, Petitioner

Address: 150 Emerald Lane
Centerville, Superior
Phone: (555)555-5555

State of Superior   )
)   SS.
County of Washington   )

On this day, before me, the undersigned authority, in and for and residing in the above county and state, personally appeared Mary Ellen Smith, who is personally known to me to be the same person whose name is subscribed to the foregoing document, and, being duly sworn, she verified that the information contained in the foregoing document is true and correct on personal knowledge and acknowledged that said document was signed as a free and voluntary act.

Subscribed and sworn to this 4th day of June, 1991

_____
Notary Public

Notary Seal

My commission expires: January 1, 1992

_____
John William Smith

Address: 2000 Main Street, Apt. #2
Centerville, Superior
Phone: (555)555-4444

State of Superior	)
	) SS.
County of Washington	)

On this day, before me, the undersigned authority, in and for and residing in the above county and state, personally appeared John William Smith, who is personally known to me to be the same person whose name is subscribed to the foregoing document, and, being duly sworn, he verified that the information contained in the foregoing document is true and correct on personal knowledge and acknowledged that said document was signed as a free and voluntary act.

Subscribed and sworn to this 4th day of June,1991

_____
Notary Public

Notary Seal

My commission expires: January 1, 1992

In the Circuit Court for Washington County, State of Superior

In re: The Marriage of:

    Mary Ellen Smith,
    Petitioner
    and
    John William Smith,
    Respondent

Case #: ABC123

And in the interest of:
    Alice Mary Smith and
    James John Smith

APPEARANCE, CONSENT, AND WAIVER

The undersigned Respondent, John William Smith, states on oath, that:

1.   RESIDENCY. I have been a resident of and domiciled in the State of Superior for the preceding 12 months and the County of Washington for the preceding 6 months.

2.   ADMISSION. I have received a copy of the Petition which was filed in this cause and I have read and understand it and admit all of the allegations contained in it.

3.   APPEARANCE AND WAIVER. I waive all objections to venue and I further waive the issuance, service, and return of process in this cause and voluntarily enter my general appearance in this cause and submit personally to the jurisdiction of the court. I have never been involved in any other domestic relations proceeding involving the other party in this or any other jurisdiction. I an not currently an active member of any branch of the Armed Forces of the United States.

4.   AGREEMENT. I have freely and voluntarily entered into a Marital Settlement Agreement, dated the 1st day of May, 1991, and a Financial Statement, which are attached to and incorporated into the Original Petition. The Marital Settlement Agreement and Financial Statements were signed under no duress or force and without collusion.

5.   CONSENT. I consent to said Marital Settlement Agreement and Financial Statements being approved and incorporated, merged into, and made part of a Final Judgement of Divorce, and that the parties be ordered to comply with all terms and conditions of the Marital Settlement Agreement, but that the Marital Settlement Agreement survive.

CHAPTER 11: SAMPLE DIVORCE PAPERS

6. ADDITIONAL CONSENT. I agree that this proceeding is uncontested. I further consent that this cause be heard on any day convenient to the court without further notice to me and that the court enter an Order granting the relief prayed for in the Petition.

7. ADDITIONAL WAIVER. I further waive my rights to notice of trial, findings of fact and conclusions of law, a record of testimony, motion for a new trial, notice of entry of final judgement, and right to appeal, but do not waive any rights to the future modification of any judgement in this cause.

_____
John William Smith
Address: 2000 Main Street, Apt. #2
Centerville, Superior
Phone: (555)555-4444

State of Superior   )
)   SS.
County Washington   )

On this day, before me, the undersigned authority, in and for and residing in the above county and state, personally appeared John William Smith, who is personally known to me to be the same person whose name is subscribed to the foregoing document, and, being duly sworn, he verified that the information contained in the foregoing document is true and correct on personal knowledge and acknowledged that said document was signed as a free and voluntary act and that a copy of the Petition has been received.

Subscribed and sworn to this 5th day of June, 1991

_____
Notary Public

Notary Seal

My commission expires: January 1, 1992

Page 2 of 2 Pages

DIVORCE YOURSELF

In the Circuit Court for Washington County, State of Superior

In re: The Marriage of:

   Mary Ellen Smith,
   Petitioner
   and
   John William Smith,
   Respondent

And in the interest of:

   Alice Mary Smith and
   James John Smith

Case #: ABC123

DECLARATION UNDER THE UNIFORM CHILD CUSTODY JURISDICTION ACT

We, the undersigned, Mary Ellen Smith and John William Smith, are both parties to this proceeding to determine the custody of a minor child, and upon oath state:

1. There are 2 minor children subject to this proceeding. For each child, the name, sex, Social Security number, date and place of birth, and time and place of residence, name and relationship of person child lived with for the past 5 years is as follows:

A. Child's Name: Alice Mary Smith   Sex of Child: Girl
Place of Birth: Centerville, Superior   Date of Birth: April 21, 1989
Child's Social Security Number: 555-44-3333

Present residence: 150 Emerald Lane, Centerville, Superior
Person child lives with: Mary Ellen Smith   Relationship: Mother
Dates of Residence: From: April 21, 1989   To: Present.

Previous residence: None

B. Child's Name: James John Smith   Sex of Child: Boy
Place of Birth: Centerville, Superior   Date of Birth: October 26, 1986
Child's Social Security Number: 333-44-5555

Present residence: 150 Emerald Lane, Centerville, Superior
Person child lives with: Mary Ellen Smith   Relationship: Mother
Dates of Residence: From: April 1, 1989   To: Present

Previous residence: 101 Center Ave., Centerville, Superior
Persons child lived with: Mary Ellen Smith   Relationship: Mother and Father
                 and John William Smith
Dates of Residence: From: October 26, 1986 To: April 1, 1989

Previous residence: None

2. Neither of us have participated as a party or a witness or in any other capacity in any other litigation or custody proceeding in this state or elsewhere, concerning the custody of a child subject to this proceeding.

3. Neither of us has any information concerning any other litigation or custody proceeding in this state or elsewhere, concerning the custody of a child subject to this proceeding.

4. Neither of us knows of any other person who is not a party to this proceeding who has physical custody or claims to have custody or visitation rights of any child subject to this proceeding.

Subscribed and sworn to this 4th day of June, 1991

_____
Mary Ellen Smith, Petitioner

Address: 150 Emerald Lane
Centerville, Superior
Phone: (555)555-5555

State of Superior	)	
	)	SS.
County of Washington	)	

On this day, before me, the undersigned authority, in and for and residing in the above county and state, personally appeared Mary Ellen Smith, who is personally known to me to be the same person whose name is subscribed to the foregoing document, and, being duly sworn, she verified that the information contained in the foregoing document is true and correct on personal knowledge and acknowledged that said document was signed as a free and voluntary act.

Subscribed and sworn to this 4th day of June, 1991

Notary Seal

_____
Notary Public

My commission expires: January 1, 1992

_____
John William Smith

Address: 2000 Main Street, Apt. #2
Centerville, Superior
Phone: (555)555-4444

State of Superior   )
)   SS.
County of Washington   )

On this day, before me, the undersigned authority, in and for and residing in the above county and state, personally appeared John William Smith, who is personally known to me to be the same person whose name is subscribed to the foregoing document, and, being duly sworn, he verified that the information contained in the foregoing document is true and correct on personal knowledge and acknowledged that said document was signed as a free and voluntary act.

Dated this 4th day of June,1991

Notary Seal

_____
Notary Public

My commission expires: January 1, 1992

CHAPTER 11: SAMPLE DIVORCE PAPERS

In the Circuit Court for Washington County, State of Superior

In re: The Marriage of:

    Mary Ellen Smith,
    Petitioner
    and
    John William Smith,
    Respondent

And in the interest of:
    Alice Mary Smith and
    James John Smith

Case #: ABC123

JUDGEMENT OF DIVORCE

On the 6th day of July, 1991, a final hearing was held in this cause.

The Petitioner, Mary Ellen Smith, was present, in person.

The Respondent, John William Smith, waived issuance, service, and return of process and appeared generally by an Appearance, Consent and Waiver duly filed and did not otherwise appear.

The Court, having examined the verified pleadings and heard the evidence and being fully advised in the premises finds:

1. That all necessary residency requirements and prerequisites of law have been legally satisfied;

2. That this Court has personal jurisdiction of the parties and of the subject matter;

3. That all of the material allegations contained in the Petition are true; and

4. That the parties have voluntarily waived findings of fact, conclusions of law, a record of testimony, motion for a new trial, notice of entry of final Judgement, and right to appeal, but have not waived their rights to future modification of this Judgement.

THE COURT ORDERS, ADJUDGES, AND DECREES:

1. That the marriage of the Petitioner Mary Ellen Smith and the John William Smith is hereby dissolved and that they are hereby divorced;

2. That all of the terms and provisions of the Marital Settlement Agreement between the parties, dated the 1st day of May, 1991, which is attached and incorporated by reference, are hereby approved and incorporated, merged into, and made part of this court order, and the parties are ordered to comply with all terms and conditions of said Marital Settlement Agreement, but that it shall survive this order;

3. That the party's property and obligations shall be distributed according to the terms of said Marital Settlement Agreement;

4. That alimony and maintenance shall be as set forth in said Marital Settlement Agreement;

5. That the custody, visitation, care, and support of the parties children shall be as set forth in said Marital Settlement Agreement;

6. That the Petitioner's name be restored to Mary Ellen Carter as set forth in said Marital Settlement Agreement.

Signed and Entered this 6th day of July, 1991

_____
Presiding Judge

Approved as to form and content:

_____
Mary Ellen Smith, Petitioner

Address: 150 Emerald Lane
Centerville, Superior
Phone: (555)555-5555

Approved as to form and content:

_____
John William Smith

Address: 2000 Main Street, Apt. #2
Centerville, Superior
Phone: (555)555-4444

CHAPTER 12

APPEARING IN COURT

The court appearance is the part of the divorce procedure which usually produces the most fear and uneasiness. There are many reasons for this: fear of the unknown; the general lack of understanding of the often arcane courtroom procedures; the unfamiliar surroundings of a courtroom atmosphere. As no-fault divorce has swept the country, the judicial system has made some attempts to deal with the increased case load that has resulted. In most states, there are procedures in place that allow for the required court appearance to be short and straight-forward. Some states allow the court appearance to be held in a judge's office (or chambers). Other states have entirely eliminated court appearances in certain uncontested no-fault divorce cases. Still other states have procedures for your hearing to be held informally before a *master* or lesser court official. In some states, there are different rules for each county. Some counties may require a short 5 minute hearing in uncontested cases, while others may require no hearing at all. Generally, there has been an attempt to streamline and modernize the court proceedings relating to divorce in many jurisdictions.

The actual procedure for the court hearing (if one is required) may also be somewhat different in different locales. Some courts will only require that you state under oath that the information in your petition/complaint is true and correct. Judges in other courts may ask a few simple questions to verify the information. Some counties or states will require that you bring a witness to court with you to testify that you have been a resident of the state for the required time and, perhaps, to answer a few other simple questions. A few courts may insist that both you and your spouse attend the court hearing. (The Appearance, Consent, and Waiver form that you filed should eliminate the necessity that both of you attend, however.) In general, however, in most states and in most counties, only the spouse who is the plaintiff/petitioner will be required to attend. The actual time of the court hearing may range from a few minutes to an hour. The average time for a hearing in a uncontested divorce which is based on a marital settlement agreement is, perhaps, fifteen minutes. You will need to check with the clerk of the court in your particular county (or parish) to determine the local procedure for uncontested divorce court hearings.

General Court Appearance Rules

Although each county and state may have slightly differing procedures and slightly different rules, there are certain basic guidelines that apply generally to all courtroom situations.

1. Once you have filed all of the proper papers with the court (your Petition/Complaint; Appearance, Consent, and Waiver form; Marriage Certificate; etc.) you should ask the court clerk to schedule a date and time for a hearing for your case. In some states, there is a mandatory waiting period before the hearing is scheduled. Check the Appendix or ask the clerk of the court. If no hearing is necessary, they will inform you. They will also generally know how much time will be required for the hearing, based on previous cases which are similar to yours. The clerk will note your particular hearing time on the court calendar or court docket. The daily court calendar or docket sheet should be posted in the court house or the court clerk's office. Make a note of the courtroom number and time of the hearing.

    In addition, you should ask the court clerk if a witness is normally required. If there is any doubt or question as to whether a witness will be required, you should arrange for a witness to accompany you to the court hearing. Your witness should be an adult who has known you and your spouse for at least as long as the required residency time in your particular state. The witness should also be able to testify truthfully regarding the few questions noted under #15 in the **Testimony Worksheet** later in this chapter.

2. Well before the time of the hearing, you should assemble all of your documents. You should bring with you to the court all of the documents that were noted as *Mandatory* in the document checklist in Chapter 2, as well as any important documents relating to property (deeds, titles, etc.). These documents should be neatly placed in a file folder in a manner that allows you to find them immediately, if necessary. You should also assemble your original copies of all of the documents that were filed with the court. Unless it is already filed with the clerk, be certain that you have an original and several copies of your judgement/decree of divorce/dissolution with you when you arrive in court. This is the document that the judge will sign to finalize your divorce.

3. You should review the testimony guidelines and your actual testimony that you have prepared using the instructions later in this chapter. It is highly recommended that, a few days before your own hearing is scheduled, you attend a hearing for another

CHAPTER 12: APPEARING IN COURT

uncontested divorce being held before the same judge as yours. This will greatly aid you in understanding what will be required for your own hearing. It will allow you to see how the hearing is handled, what questions are likely, and what documents are generally necessary. You will see that the hearing is relatively straight-forward and not frightening. If the hearings are customarily held in a judge's office (or chambers), you may not be allowed to attend. That's okay, because if the hearing is held in the judge's office it will generally be less formal and, thus, less intimidating.

4. You should arrive early on the day of your scheduled hearing to determine the location of the courtroom and find your place. Many courts prefer that you check in with the court clerk in advance of the hearing. Some will require you to pick up your own official case file from the clerk before going to the courtroom. Again, you will need to ask the court clerk for instructions *before* the day of your hearing.

5. In every court in the land, the judge will require that all participants show respect for the court. The courtroom judge has extremely wide powers inside a courtroom. In the extreme, a disrespectful and disruptive person can, potentially, be immediately removed from the courtroom and imprisoned for contempt of court. Since you and your spouse are attempting to obtain a divorce with as little hostility as possible, you should make certain that your courtroom behavior is courteous and respectful. You should dress appropriately in a business-like manner. The judge should always be referred to as "Your Honor". You should be patient, speak firmly and directly, and try to remain relaxed and calm.

6. Once in the courtroom, you should be seated and wait patiently until your name is called. The amount of time that you wait will most likely be longer than your actual hearing. When your name or the name of your case is called, state "Ready, Your Honor" to the judge and take your documents and your case file with you to the place where the clerk or judge directs. You may take a seat in a witness stand; you may be directed to sit at a table; or you may be asked to stand before the judge. You will normally be sworn in. Take a deep breath and relax.

7. As your hearing begins, you may be asked direct questions by the judge relating to the information that is in your petition/complaint. The judge will not try to confuse you or embarrass you. He or she just wants the facts of your situation. Answer any questions concisely and truthfully. In most locales, the judge will want you to present your case in the manner outlined later in this chapter under **Guide to Court Testimony**. You should have with you a written or typed copy of the testimony guidelines. You shouldn't take a copy of this book to court with you, however.

In all cases where there is a court hearing, the intent is to be certain that the statements that you and your spouse made in your court papers are true and correct and that you understand the proceedings. If you have gotten this far in the divorce procedure, you should be confident that you understand the laws relating to divorce much better than most people. You should be as brief and as clear as possible in

DIVORCE YOURSELF

your answers. If the judge wants more information, he or she will ask for it. Your testimony or questions/answers will generally follow the outline of your petition/complaint. You do not need to elaborate on any of the information--unless the judge specifically asks for it.

8. When you have finished your own testimony and if a witness is required to testify regarding your residency, etc., you should tell the judge: "Your Honor, I would now like to call _____ *[name of witness]* to testify". If no witness is required, your case is finished and the judge will generally announce his or her decision immediately. Carefully read through your judgement/decree to be certain that it exactly follows what the judge states as his or her decision. If the judge's decision is exactly what is contained in your prepared judgement/decree, this final document will generally be signed immediately by the judge. If there are differences between what the judge states and your document, you will need to take the judgement/decree home with you and type a new version which exactly states the judge's decision. Once the judgement/decree is correct, bring it back to the courthouse and the judge will sign it. Some states may have a waiting period before your divorce becomes effective. The judge or court clerk will inform you if this is the case.

9. Unless your state has a short waiting period, as soon as the judge signs the judgement/decree in your case, you are officially divorced. You should now refer to the items listed in the next chapter to determine the important final steps that you must take to tie up all the loose ends of your divorce.

Guide to Court Testimony

The following is a general guide to the testimony that is most often required in uncontested divorce hearings. As you can see, the information required is merely a restatement of the information that is contained in your various court documents. When you have filled in this information, you should write or type up a copy of this testimony and have it with you when you attend your hearing. Although the judge may ask you direct questions instead of allowing you to present your testimony, this testimony worksheet will provide you with an outline which will aid you in any hearing setting. Lawyers commonly use prepared testimony sheets similar to the one you will prepare. If the judge does not begin by asking you direct questions, you should begin your case by stating the following information as contained on your prepared testimony sheets. Speak directly to the judge, go carefully, and don't skip anything. If the judge interrupts you, answer his or her questions and then ask if you should continue. In the vast majority of situations, the hearing will be over in a few minutes.

In certain instances, however, you may encounter problems. If you become confused, ask the judge to explain. If the judge feels that your paperwork is not in order, ask the judge exactly what is necessary to correct the problem. Take very careful notes regarding what the judge tells you. If you feel that the hearing is going very badly or you simply do not

CHAPTER 12: APPEARING IN COURT

understand what the difficulty is, you have an escape route. Simply state to the judge: "Your Honor, I would like a continuance to seek advice and to further prepare my case. I would like this hearing to be rescheduled, please." This will allow you time to seek out advice from an attorney or other legal professional as to the difficulty. In most cases, the problem relates to some legal formality for your locale that has not been satisfied. When you return, start at the beginning of your testimony and proceed.

Testimony Worksheet

You will need to tailor the testimony shown on this worksheet to fit your case exactly. Check the Appendix relating to your state carefully to determine if there are any specific requirements in your state. Also carefully check the details of residency and grounds for divorce. The residency and grounds testimony that you use on your personal Testimony Worksheet must match the information stated in the petition/complaint exactly.

After you have filled in the appropriate blanks in this testimony outline, you should neatly type or write all of these statements on clean sheets of paper. You will bring these testimony sheets with you when you appear for your court hearing as explained earlier in this chapter. It may be a good idea to practice reading your testimony a few times before you appear in court.

1. "Your Honor, my name is _____, and I am the *[Petitioner or Plaintiff]* _____ in this case."

2. "All of the facts stated in my verified *[Petition or Complaint]* _____ are true and correct."

3. "Immediately prior to filing the *[Petition or Complaint]* _____, I had continually been a resident of and domiciled in this state for more than *[required residency time limit]* _____, and this *[county or parish]* _____ for more than *[required time limit]* _____."

4. "I am now married to _____, who is the *[Respondent or Defendant]* _____ in this case. We were married on _____, 19 ___, in the State of _____ and a copy of our marriage certificate has been filed with the court. *[Here hold up the Marriage Certificate]*. I am familiar with the Marriage Certificate and recognize it as the Certificate of my marriage to the *[Respondent or Defendant]* _____. We separated on _____, 19 ___, and have lived separate and apart without cohabitation since that time."

DIVORCE YOURSELF

5. "I seek a *[divorce or dissolution of marriage]* _____ on the grounds that:"*[here state the grounds that apply in your state in an affirmative manner]. For example:* "there are irreconcilable differences between us and there is no possible chance for reconciliation." *Or:* We have lived separate and apart without interruption and without cohabitation for over 12 months." *[These are only examples. Your statement must conform exactly to the particular grounds that are applicable in your state and which you have selected from the Appendix for inclusion in your petition/complaint].*

    At this point, the judge may ask you to elaborate on the reasons for your divorce. Simply and **briefly** *explain why your marriage can't continue. Describe conflicts, arguments, fights, neglect, etc. But don't emphasize fault. Respond directly to any questions that the judge asks but don't volunteer information.*

6. "Your Honor, my spouse and I have signed a written Marital Settlement Agreement resolving all of our differences. Attached to and incorporated into this Agreement are two individual Financial Statements that my spouse and I have signed and verified. The information contained in my Financial Statement is true and correct. The original of this Agreement and the Financial Statements were attached to and incorporated into the *[petition/complaint]* _____ which was filed. *[Here hold up the Marital Settlement Agreement and Financial Statements]*. I am familiar with the signature of my spouse on both of those documents and can state that it is genuine. I request that the Marital Settlement Agreement and attached Financial Statements be admitted into evidence and approved by this court."

7. "My spouse, the *[Respondent or Defendant]* _____, has also signed an Appearance, Consent, and Waiver which was filed in this case. *[Here hold up the Appearance, Consent, and Waiver form]*. I am familiar with the signature of my spouse and can state that it is genuine. By the terms of this Appearance, Consent, and Waiver, my spouse admitted all of the allegations as contained in the *[petition/complaint]* _____, waived all objections to venue, waived issuance, return, and service of process, entered a general appearance, and consented to the entry of judgement in this case."

8. "Your Honor, I have prepared and submitted a *[Judgement or Decree]* _____ which prays for a *[divorce/dissolution of marriage]* _____ and that our Marital Settlement Agreement be approved, incorporated, and merged into the *[Judgement or Decree]* _____ and that we both be ordered to comply with all terms and conditions. The *[Judgement or Decree]* _____ has been approved by my spouse, whose signature is on the last page. *[Here hold up the proposed Judgement or Decree]*. I am familiar with the signature of my spouse and can state that it is genuine."

CHAPTER 12: APPEARING IN COURT

9. "My spouse and I have agreed to the division of all of our property and debts under the terms of our Marital Settlement Agreement which I have submitted."

10. *Select the statement which applies:* "My spouse and I have agreed that neither of us should receive any alimony or maintenance from the other and we have forever waived our claims to such support. We have both agreed to this in our Marital Settlement Agreement, which I have submitted." *Or:* "My spouse and I have agreed in our Marital Settlement Agreement that *[I or he/she]* _____ should receive the following alimony and maintenance: *[Here state the terms exactly as contained in your Marital Settlement Agreement]*."

11. *Select the statement which applies:* "Your Honor, my spouse and I have no minor children and none are expected." *Or:* "Your Honor, my spouse and I are the parents of _____ child(*ren*). Their names, ages, birthdates, and birthplaces are as follows: *[State the information]*.

12. *If you have children, also state:* "Apart from personal possessions, no property is owned by the child(*ren*). My spouse and I have both signed a Declaration regarding Child Custody Jurisdiction which is true and correct and which was filed in this case. *[Here hold up the Declaration regarding Child Custody Jurisdiction]*. I am familiar with the signature of my spouse and can state that it is genuine. I request that this Declaration be admitted into evidence."

"Your Honor, my spouse and I have agreed on all issues concerning the care, custody, and support of our children and our agreement is contained in our Marital Settlement Agreement, which was submitted. It would be in the best interests of our children that: *[Here state the terms regarding custody and child support as contained in your Marital Settlement Agreement]*".

The provisions that you and your spouse have made regarding your children will be the most likely area in which the judge will question you carefully. Be prepared to answer questions relating to how your custody and visitation provisions will actually be instituted and how the child support payments may be guaranteed. The judge may insist that the payments be made though the clerk of the court or other state agency. If so, ask the judge what additional forms will be necessary. The judge may also inquire into your health insurance coverage. Be prepared to answer as to how the child will be covered. The judge may also insist that automatic wage withholding or some other method to guarantee the child support payments be used. If so, ask the judge what forms will be necessary. Take careful notes and later ask the court clerk for any of the necessary forms.

13. *If desired, state:* "Your Honor, I request that the *[Petitioner's or Plaintiff's or Respondent's or Defendant's]* _____ name be restored as set forth in the Marital Settlement Agreement and *[Judgement/Decree]* _____."

14. "I respectfully request that our marriage be dissolved and that the relief prayed for in the *[judgement or decree]* _____ be granted. *If no witness will be required, state:* "That concludes my testimony, your Honor."

15. *If a witness is required in your situation, state:* "Your Honor, I would now like to call _____ *[name of witness]* to testify." *Have your witness come forward and be sworn in. Then ask the following questions:*

    a. "What is your name, please?"

    b. "Where do you live and how long have you lived there?"

    c. "Are you personally familiar with the *[Petitioner or Plaintiff]* _____ in this case?"

    d. "How long have you known *[him or her]* _____?"

    e. "Where does the *[Petitioner or Plaintiff]* _____ live?"

    f. "To your own knowledge, how long has *[Petitioner or Plaintiff]* _____ lived in this State and in this County (or Parish)?"

    g. "Are you personally familiar with the *[Respondent or Defendant]* _____ in this case?"

    h. "How long have you known *[him or her]* _____?"

    i. "Where does the *[Respondent or Defendant]* _____ live?"

    j. "To your own knowledge, how long has *[Respondent or Defendant]* _____ lived in this State and in this County (or Parish)?"

    k. "Are you familiar with the marital status of the *[Petitioner or Plaintiff]* _____ and the *[Respondent or Defendant]* _____?"

    l. "To your own knowledge, what is their marital status?"

CHAPTER 12: APPEARING IN COURT

> m. *[If the grounds for your divorce are based on separation for a specific period of time, ask the following 2 questions]*: "To your knowledge, do the *[Petitioner or Plaintiff]* _____ and the *[Respondent or Defendant]* _____ currently live together?"
>
> n. "On your own knowledge, how long have they not lived together?"
>
> o. *[In all cases, state:]* "Thank you very much, you are excused."

16. *In those few jurisdictions in which the testimony of both spouses is necessary, your spouse should prepare a testimony sheet substantially the same as yours. It should, of course, be altered to be read from the point of view of your spouse. After you have concluded your testimony, your spouse should stand, ask the court when to begin, and then begin his or her own testimony. At the end of his or her testimony, he or she should state:* "Your Honor, that concludes my testimony." *Then be seated and wait for the judge's decision.*

CHAPTER 13

AFTER YOUR DIVORCE

Once your divorce decree or judgement has been officially entered, you are legally a single person again. A few states have a short waiting period before you may remarry. Check with the court clerk in your county if this is an immediate consideration in your situation. Although you are both now single, there are some very important steps that you and your ex-spouse must take to complete the divorce process. Essentially, you must do all of the things that you agreed to do in your Marital Settlement Agreement and you must begin to satisfy those parts of the Agreement that are ongoing obligations. These final steps are required to actually complete the total separation of you and your ex-spouse's affairs and to transfer any property that has not yet been properly transferred.

This final chapter will provide you with a basic checklist of items that you should consider as you wrap up the last loose ends of your divorce. There may be a tendency to put off dealing with these concluding steps. It is important that you attend to these final considerations as promptly as possible. Go through the checklist item by item until you and your ex-spouse are both satisfied that all of the appropriate final steps have been accomplished. Take care that no important detail is overlooked.

Following the final checklist, there are some basic legal guidelines that apply to various post-divorce situations. An overview is provided of methods available for the: (1) enforcement child support or alimony orders; (2) modification of support orders; (3) enforcement of visitation provisions; (4) modification of custody rights; and (5) issuance of domestic violence protective orders.

Final Divorce Wrap-up Checklist

1. From the court clerk, you should order several certified copies of your final Judgement or Decree for each of you. You and your ex-spouse may need these documents for any transfers of property, bank accounts, loan releases, etc.

2. Be certain that you have filed a Certificate of Divorce or Dissolution of Marriage with the clerk of the court or your state's department of vital statistics. This is required in most states. Check with the court clerk in your jurisdiction.

3. If there is any personal or household property that has not yet been exchanged, you should do so at this time. Arrange for delivery or pick-up of any items that you and your ex-spouse have agreed are to be the property of the other: furnishings, jewelry, tools, appliances, stereos, etc.

4. If you have not yet closed all of your personal joint bank accounts, you should do so at this time. Verify the balance in any joint accounts and then divide any proceeds of the accounts according to the terms of your Marital Settlement Agreement.

5. If you have any joint credit accounts that still remain open, these should also now be closed. The payment of the remaining outstanding bills should be arranged according to the terms you and your ex-spouse have set out in your Agreement. You should determine the exact balance as of the date of your final decree. If there are utility or other bills that you must split, determine the pro-rated amount for each ex-spouse. Change any addresses as necessary to be sure that future bills are delivered to the proper person. For joint credit card accounts, you should destroy the cards or surrender them back to the company. You should advise all of your joint creditors of your divorce and that, from now on, you will only be liable for your own debts. You and your ex-spouse should furnish each other with any necessary account records regarding your joint debts.

6. If you and your ex-spouse have any outstanding joint loans, you should notify the lending institution of your divorce. You may need to supply them with a certified copy of your divorce Judgement/Decree or of your Marital Settlement Agreement if it contains a hold-harmless and indemnification agreement from your ex-spouse. If possible, the ex-spouse whose duty to pay is being taken over by the other ex-spouse should try to obtain a *Release* from the lending institution relieving him or her of liability for the debt. Be sure to notify the lender of any address or billing changes.

7. If you have cars or other property for which the ownership is determined by a title, you should make any appropriate transfers of title. Be sure to also change the registration and license plates to the appropriate ex-spouse at this time, if necessary. Recall that you each agreed take any necessary steps and to sign any documents required to complete all of the terms of your Marital Settlement Agreement.

CHAPTER 13: AFTER YOUR DIVORCE

8. If you have real estate that will need to be transferred between the two of you, you will need to complete any necessary deeds to accomplish this task. You may need to contact a real estate professional or attorney for assistance in preparing the required paperwork. If there is a mortgage on the property, you should contact the lending institution regarding any changes required in the mortgage documents. Again, you may need to supply them with a certified copy of your divorce Judgement/Decree or of your Marital Settlement Agreement if it contains a hold-harmless and indemnification agreement from your ex-spouse. If possible, the ex-spouse whose duty to pay is being taken over by the other ex-spouse should try to obtain a *Release* from the lending institution relieving him or her of liability for the mortgage. Any documents relating to real estate will need to be recorded in the appropriate office (usually the county recorder) in the county or parish where the real estate is located.

9. If any of your jointly-owned property is to be sold and the proceeds divided, you and your ex-spouse will now need to arrange for this. If the property is real estate, you will need to contact a broker or list the property for sale yourselves. Keep a record of any expenses that are required to complete the sale (for example: appraisal fees, surveys, advertising charges, brokerage fees, etc.). These expenses will be deducted from the gross proceeds of the sale to determine the profits to be divided. Again, any documents relating to real estate will need to be recorded in the appropriate office (usually the county recorder) in the county or parish where the real estate is located.

10. Each of your insurance policies should be reviewed. Any beneficiary changes should be directed to the insurance company or agent who handles your policy. The policies that should be reviewed include: any life insurance policies; any health or hospitalization policies; any homeowner or personal property policies; auto insurance policies; and any insurance policies pertaining to children. If you or your ex-spouse are required to maintain life or health insurance as part of your agreement or decree, you should furnish the other ex-spouse with proof of the policy. If you are converting from group to individual coverage under a group health insurance plan, you must generally do so quickly. There may be a time limit for doing this (often 30 days).

11. Be certain that both you and your ex-spouse understand how your income tax situation is to be handled. If you have agreed to file a final joint return, arrange to do so. (Remember, that to file a joint return you need to have still been legally married on the last day of the year for which you will file). If you have agreed on who will actually pay the tax or on who will receive any tax refund, you should go over these terms with your ex-spouse. If you will file separate returns, you should supply each other with any tax information that will be necessary for completing the returns. Each of you should keep copies of all of the tax returns that you filed while you were married. You should discuss and clarify the tax status of any required property settlement, alimony, or child support payments.

12. Finally, if you or your ex-spouse have a will, it will need to be revised to conform with your new legal status as a single person. Individual states deal with the effect of divorce on a will in various manners. Some states consider any provisions for an ex-spouse in a will as automatically revoked by the divorce. Other states do not. Some states have provisions that declare the entire will of either ex-spouse to be revoked upon divorce. To be absolutely safe, a new will should be prepared which takes into account you and your ex-spouse's new legal relationship. If you have children, preparing a will which contains adequate provisions for their future is especially important. If you don't presently have a will, you should consider preparing one. Compared with obtaining your own divorce, preparing a will is a very easy legal task. Nova Publishing Company's Legal Self-Help Series contains an excellent reference on this topic: *"Prepare Your Own Last Will and Testament-Without a Lawyer"*.

Post-Divorce Legal Problems

Various legal problems relating to your divorce can confront you and your ex-spouse well after your divorce has become final. These legal difficulties fall into two general categories: (1) enforcement of provisions in your divorce decree or judgement; or (2) modification of provisions in your divorce decree or judgement.

The need for legal action in either of these situations is much more likely to occur to a divorced couple who have minor children. Divorced couples without children typically go their own separate ways and begin to lead fully independent lives with little or no interaction with an ex-spouse. The situation is different if children are involved. There will necessarily be continued contact with an ex-spouse who is also a parent of a child due to the continuing obligations of child support and the ongoing responsibilities of custody.

Enforcement of Child Support

The most common legal difficulty encountered after a divorce is the need to collect overdue child support payments. The delinquency of child support payments is a massive problem and a national disgrace. In the last few years, both federal and state governments have taken major steps in an effort to correct this problem. All states have passed the Uniform Reciprocal Enforcement of Support Act which coordinates state efforts at enforcement. The recent passage of the latest federal legislation in this area has been a large step in the efforts to correct this problem. The federal Family Support Act of 1988 mandates that each state must establish a formula for child support award amounts. Earlier federal legislation, most notably the 1984 Child Support Enforcement amendments to Title IV-D of the Social Security Act, established guidelines and requirements for states to follow in the area of child support collection and enforcement.

There is a wide range of weapons now available to states in the battle to collect child support. The use of these techniques has been simplified and, in most cases, can be arranged

CHAPTER 13: AFTER YOUR DIVORCE

without the aid of a lawyer. Court clerks and child support enforcement agency personnel should be able to provide assistance in obtaining and filing the proper forms. Many of the necessary forms for the enforcement of child support obligations are now simplified and pre-printed for easy use without a lawyer.

States may use *wage or payroll deductions* or *wage withholding orders*. This type of court order will require that an employer must take a direct withholding out of a delinquent employee's wages and that the employer must then make the child support payments to either the custodial parent, a court clerk, or the local support agency. Every state now has laws in effect which grant similar powers to the local support enforcement agencies or courts. Some states refer to this method as a *wage* or *income assignment*, in which a portion of the future wages or income of the parent ordered to pay is actually legally transferred to the parent entitled to receive the support. "Wages" are generally defined broadly to include income from pensions, retirement funds, annuities, Social Security, unemployment compensation, and other benefits.

Under current federal law, employers are now required to withhold wages from parents of children receiving Aid to Families with Dependent Children. Beginning in 1994, income withholding will become mandatory for all parents required to pay child support, *unless* the non-custodial parent who receives the support formally waives the protection of withholding. In addition, under the federal Child Support Enforcement Amendments of 1984, child support offenders can be tracked across state lines with powerful government computer networks.

Another very powerful method of collection of unpaid support payments is the *tax refund intercept*. This legal device allows the delinquent support payments to be taken directly out an ex-spouse's federal or state income tax refund, before the refund is ever sent out. The ability to collect overdue payments from an ex-spouse in any state is a particularly attractive aspect of this legal weapon. In addition, if all other means of collection of overdue child support payments have failed, the IRS may also use all of its tax-collecting powers to collect the delinquency, including seizing property and money from the parent.

Other weapons in the support enforcement arsenal include: (1) *attachments*: this amounts to a claim or *lien* which is legally "attached" to a specific piece of property. If the property is sold, the claim for overdue support is paid off first. Variations of this legal device can be used to impound funds in bank accounts; (2) *garnishment of wages*: similar to a wage withholding order, this method is available for any money-based legal judgment; (3) *security or bond*: this method requires a parent to post bond to guarantee the future payments; (4) *no discharge in bankruptcy*: a defaulting parent can not be relieved of a child support obligation by filing for bankruptcy; (5) *no retroactive judicial reduction of child support obligations;* a defaulting parent can not convince a court that the past-due payments were too high and have them reduced; (6) *civil contempt of court*: this method can result in imprisonment of an ex-spouse for failure to obey a court order which requires child support payments; and (7) *criminal prosecution*: many states make it a crime to fail to provide child support, punishable by fines and/or imprisonment.

If you need immediate assistance regarding collection of child support, check your phone book for the nearest office of the federal Child Support Enforcement Administration or your state's own child support enforcement agency. They will be able to provide assistance with enforcement and collection of your overdue payments. There is a also national organization which may be able to provide you with assistance in this area: Organization for the Enforcement of Child Support, 119 Nicodemus Road, Reistertown, MD 21136.

Enforcement of Alimony

In the past, when alimony awards of long duration were more common, alimony payments were more likely to be overdue or totally delinquent. The trend to providing alimony on a short-term basis and often solely for the education or training of an ex-spouse has, to some extent, lessened the problems of collecting alimony payments over long periods of time.

Many of the same weapons available in child support enforcement situations are also available for the collection of overdue alimony payments. If the alimony and child support payments are lumped together into a single payment, all of the enforcement techniques mentioned above are available. If the alimony is a separate payment, tax intercepts are not available. However, wage withholding, income assignments, attachments, liens, garnishment of wages, and contempt of court orders are all generally available to aid in the collection of delinquent alimony payments.

Enforcement of Custody and Visitation

Visitation and custody can often create legal difficulties between ex-spouses. One parent may deny visitation on the grounds of overdue child support payments. Another parent may intentionally withhold support payment because of interference with visitation rights. A parent with custody may wish to move across the country with the child, effectively denying the other parent the right to reasonable visitation.

Courts and legislatures have been struggling with these problems and have yet to resolve them in a uniform manner. Each state may view the denial of visitation somewhat differently. In most states, however, you may seek various court relief from failure to abide by the court-ordered custody and visitation terms of your divorce judgement/decree. That relief may take the form of: (1) a contempt of court order against the offending ex-spouse; (2) an actual change in the custody or visitation terms of your divorce; (3) a court-order suspending support payments until visitation is allowed; (4) a court order requiring visitation; or (5) fines and imprisonment for failure to comply with a court order.

Child-snatching is a separate problem which has come under increasing scrutiny of the courts and legislatures. Parental kidnapping by a non-custodial parent is a major problem and has resulted in two powerful pieces of national legislation: The Uniform Child Custody Jurisdiction Act (which has been adopted by all states); and the federal Parental Kidnapping Prevention Act. These laws mandate which single state will have continuing

CHAPTER 13: AFTER YOUR DIVORCE

jurisdiction and control over the custody of a child and are designed to prevent conflicting awards of custody. The court which issued the original custody award generally retains all authority over the case, regardless of where the child is taken.

In addition, in interstate child-snatching situations, the FBI can be brought into the case. For in-state situations, local district attorney or the state attorney general can often intervene. The advice and assistance of a lawyer in such situations is highly recommended.

Domestic Violence

One of the most negative aspects of the modern ease of divorce is the increasing frequency of domestic violence directed against an ex-spouse. Every state now has specific laws which attempt to deal with this problem. Many states have instituted programs for simplified and immediate issuance of restraining orders against domestic violence, whether the abuse us directed against a spouse, ex-spouse, parent, or child. Such protective orders are also being taken much more seriously by local law enforcement agencies who must enforce them.

In most states, there are simplified and standardized forms available from court clerks, social service, or law enforcement agencies which may be filled in without the aid of a lawyer. Courts are, in many cases, required to respond immediately with the issuance of emergency court orders to provide protection to an abused or battered spouse, ex-spouse, or child. The court orders can be very powerful weapons, giving police the authority to immediately arrest a person without a warrant on the basis of violation of a court order. Check with your local police, court clerk, any local domestic violence shelters, or social service agencies for more information.

Modification of Support and Custody Provisions

After your divorce, your life will change to some extent. If you have children, the changes may be extensive. Unanticipated events may also occur in the future which will influence your life and the lives of your children. There are legal provisions in every state for the future modification of child support and custody provisions. The changes may be to provide for an increased or decreased amount of support or to provide for alterations in the amount of custody and visitation. The ex-spouses or parents may mutually consent to the changes without a lengthy court proceeding. In addition, the court that issued the original order always retains jurisdiction to make necessary changes in child support, custody, or visitation provisions of a final divorce decree or judgement.

The legal basis for receiving a modification to a prior support or custody award is, generally, a "significant change in circumstances". The change must be substantial enough to warrant a court proceeding to alter a previous court order. The changes must generally:

(1) not have been considered when the original judgement was entered; (2) be permanent and substantial; (3) affect one's current standard of living.

Various situations can be the basis for an attempt to have a court modify support or custody awards. A substantial increase or decrease in one's income or expenses; remarriage of one of the ex-spouses; a serious illness or injury of an ex-spouse or child; bankruptcy; inheritance; and many other significant changes can be grounds to seek a modification of the terms of a divorce judgement or decree. In all cases, however, a court will not be receptive to making changes in a prior court order unless there is an actual demonstrated need for the modification and a provable substantial change in the circumstances which affect the family.

Any of the court orders in your divorce judgement/decree regarding child custody and visitation are never actually final. They may be altered at any time, if your circumstances have changed substantially. Courts, however, are somewhat reluctant to alter settled custody arrangements unless there is a dramatic change or extraordinary reason. The basis for any modification in custody is the same as it was in the original divorce proceeding: the best interests of the child. Factors which may influence a court are: (1) remarriage; (2) any spouse or child abuse; (3) any drug or alcohol abuse; (4) interference with visitation rights; (5) the child's safety; and (6) any of the factors originally listed in the chapter on **Child Custody and Visitation**.

An attorney may be necessary to assist in dealing with any of these legal difficulties. However, you may be able to handle many of them yourself with the proper guidance. A valuable resource for understanding any of the post-divorce legal problems outlined in this chapter is: "*The Ex-Factor: The Complete Do-it-Yourself Post-Divorce Handbook*", by Bernard Clair and Anthony Daniele. Please refer to the bibliography for further information.

APPENDIX

DIVORCE LAWS OF ALL 50 STATES and WASHINGTON D.C.:

The following Appendix contains a summary of the divorce laws of all states and the District of Columbia. It has been compiled directly from the most recently-available statute books for each state. Every effort has been made to assure that the information contained in this Appendix is accurate and complete. However, laws are subject to constant change. Therefore, those legal points which are particularly important in your situation should be checked directly in the appropriate law book to be certain that the law has not changed since this book was written. After each section of information, the exact name of the law book and the chapter or section number of where the information can be found is noted. Any of these official statute books should be available at any public library. A librarian will be glad to assist you in locating the correct book and in finding the appropriate pages.

The correct terminology for each state is used in these listings. However, some states use certain language interchangeably. In those states, the most commonly-used language is stated. Although it has been simplified to some extent, you will find that the language in the Appendix is somewhat more complicated than the language used in the rest of this book. This is due to the fact that much of the language in the Appendix has been taken directly from the laws and statutes of each state. We apologize for this. We feel, however, that, as a reference, the technical details of the laws should be provided. The following information is listed for each state:

NAME OF COURT IN WHICH TO FILE FOR DIVORCE: The information under this heading shows the name of the correct court in which to file your papers for divorce. It may also show the exact wording necessary for the court name in the caption of your divorce court papers.

DIVORCE YOURSELF

TITLE OF DIVORCE ACTION: The correct language for the title of your request for divorce is listed. This is generally either a Petition for Dissolution of Marriage or a Complaint for Divorce. In some states, the language used to describe the case are also noted. For example: "In the Matter of the Marriage of _____ and _____".

NAME USED TO DESCRIBE SPOUSE FILING FOR DIVORCE: This refers to the person who will officially be the one filing for divorce. Generally, this will either be Plaintiff or Petitioner, although some states allow joint Co-Petitioners.

NAME USED TO DESCRIBE OTHER SPOUSE IN DIVORCE: This refers to the title of the other spouse, technically the one against whom the divorce is filed. Generally, this will be either the Defendant or Respondent, although some states allow joint Co-Petitioners.

TITLE OF FINAL DIVORCE PAPERS: This is the actual title of the document that will declare you divorced. You will prepare this and submit it to the judge for his or her signature.

RESIDENCY REQUIREMENTS AND WHERE TO FILE: The specific time limits that you or your spouse must have lived in your state (and possibly county) are explained. Which particular county (or parish) that you should file for your divorce is also listed. This is technically referred to as the *venue*.

LEGAL GROUNDS FOR DIVORCE: The specific language of the grounds for divorce in each state are listed. Some states have more than one no-fault ground. If this is the case, they are specified by numbering each particular ground Some states have also retained some fault-based divorce grounds. These are referred to as "General" grounds and are only for your information. You will be using a "No-fault" ground.

LEGAL SEPARATION: This information explains the situation in your state relating to legal court-ordered separation. You may live separate and apart under the terms of your Marital Settlement Agreement *without* obtaining a legal court-ordered separation. The grounds and residency requirements for court-ordered separations are included.

SIMPLIFIED OR SPECIAL DIVORCE PROCEDURES: Many states now have instituted procedures which allow for a simplified procedures to be used in obtaining a divorce. In addition, some states have mandatory forms which are required to be used. Other states have specific provisions relating to shortening the divorce process. All of the details of any specific methods to shorten or streamline the divorce process are contained under this heading.

MEDIATION OR COUNSELING REQUIREMENTS: Most states have now instituted voluntary mediation or conciliation services that are available to spouses on request or on the order of the judge. The details regarding this aspect of divorce are listed here.

PROPERTY DISTRIBUTION: A description of which property is subject to division upon divorce and what factors are considered in the distribution are contained in this section. Community, separate, non-marital, and marital property is defined for each state.

ALIMONY/MAINTENANCE/SPOUSAL SUPPORT: The laws and factors for consideration relating to the awarding of alimony are discussed under this heading.

SPOUSE'S NAME: Each state's laws regarding the restoration of a spouse's name are included.

CHILD CUSTODY: The details of how child custody decisions are made are contained under this heading. Each state's particular factors for consideration are explained. Specific state provisions for joint custody are also detailed.

CHILD SUPPORT: The various laws relating to child support are outlined. In recent years, this area has become the most complex aspect of divorce. The availability of specific state child support guidelines and general state requirements to guarantee child support payments are noted.

APPENDIX: DIVORCE LAWS OF ALL 50 STATES

ALABAMA

NAME OF COURT IN WHICH TO FILE FOR DIVORCE: Circuit Court. "In the Circuit Court for _____ County, Alabama". [Code of Alabama; Title 30, Chapter 2-1].

TITLE OF DIVORCE ACTION: Complaint for Divorce. "In Re the Marriage of:_____ and _____".

NAME USED TO DESCRIBE SPOUSE FILING FOR DIVORCE: Plaintiff.

NAME USED TO DESCRIBE OTHER SPOUSE IN DIVORCE: Defendant.

TITLE OF FINAL DIVORCE PAPERS: Judgement of Divorce.

RESIDENCY REQUIREMENTS AND WHERE TO FILE: When one of the spouses is a nonresident of the state, the spouse filing for divorce must have been a resident of the state for at least 6 months before filing for divorce. The divorce may be filed for in any of the following: (1) the county where the defendant resides; (2) the county where the spouses both resided at the time of their separation; or (3) the county where the plaintiff resides if the defendant is a non-resident of Alabama. [Code of Alabama; Title 30, Chapters 2-4 and 2-5].

LEGAL GROUNDS FOR DIVORCE: No-Fault: (1) Irretrievable breakdown of the marriage; (2) complete incompatibility of temperament such that the parties can no longer live together; (3) voluntary separation for over 1 year. [Code of Alabama; Title 30, Chapter 2-1].

General: (1) Adultery; (2) living separate and apart without cohabitation for over 2 years without the husband supporting the wife (divorce must be filed by wife); (3) imprisonment (for over 2 years if the total sentence is over 7 years); (4) unnatural sexual behavior before or after the marriage; (5) alcoholism; (6) drug abuse; (7) confinement for incurable insanity for over 5 years; (8) wife pregnant by another at the time of the marriage without the husband's knowledge; (9) physical abuse or reasonable fear of physical abuse; (10) lack of physical ability to consummate marriage. [Code of Alabama; Title 30, Chapters 2-1 and 2-2].

LEGAL SEPARATION: A divorce "from bed and board" may be granted for cruelty or for any of the same causes for which a standard divorce may be granted if the spouse filing desires that the divorce be limited to a divorce "from bed and board". [Code of Alabama: Title 30, Chapter 2-30].

SIMPLIFIED OR SPECIAL DIVORCE PROCEDURES: The is no legal provision in Alabama for summary divorce. In addition, specific evidence must be presented at a court hearing to support a default judgement in a divorce case. However, acceptance and waiver of service is allowed if signed by the defendant and a credible witness. [Alabama Rules of Civil Procedure; Rules 4 and 55].

MEDIATION OR COUNSELING REQUIREMENTS: There is no legal provision in Alabama for mediation.

PROPERTY DISTRIBUTION: There is no statutory provision in Alabama for property division. Under Alabama case law, Alabama is an "equitable distribution" state and the judge has full discretion to divide the any jointly-owned real estate or personal property, but does not have the authority to award the wife's separate property to the husband (regardless of whether the wife's separate property was obtained before or after the marriage). Gifts and inheritances are considered separate property and are not subject to division unless they have been used for the common benefit of both spouses. The property division need not necessarily be exactly equal, but it must be equitable. Marital fault may be considered in the division of property. (Alabama Case Law).

ALIMONY/MAINTENANCE/SPOUSAL SUPPORT: The judge has full discretion to award an allowance for maintenance to either spouse, if such spouse has insufficient property to provide for his or her own maintenance. This award may be made out of the property belonging to the other spouse, unless it is separate property (acquired by gift or inheritance, or acquired prior to the marriage) and was never used for the common benefit of the marriage. The factors to be considered are: (1) the value of the estate of both spouses; and (2) the condition of the spouse's family. Misconduct of either spouse may be considered in the determination as to whether to award maintenance and may totally bar the right to any maintenance. Any award of maintenance will be terminated if the recipient is living openly with a member of the opposite sex or has remarried. [Code of Alabama: Title 30, Chapters 2-51, 2-52, and 2-55].

SPOUSE'S NAME: An ex-wife may be prevented from using the last name of the ex-husband. Under general common law principles, a wife may be resume the use of her maiden or former name upon divorce. [Code of Alabama: Title 30, Chapter 2-11].

CHILD CUSTODY: Custody of any children of the marriage may be granted to either parent. Factors to be considered are: (1) the age and sex of the child; (2) the safety and well-being of the child; (3) and the moral character of the parents. The wishes of the child are also a factor to be considered. Joint custody may be awarded. However, if the wife abandons the husband and the children are over 7 years old, the husband is granted custody if he is suitable. [Code of Alabama: Title 30, Chapter 3-1 and Alabama Case Law].

CHILD SUPPORT: The court may order either parent to provide child support. However, the father has primary responsibility. There are no specific factors for consideration listed in the statute. [Code of Alabama: Title 30, Chapter 3-1 and Alabama Case Law].

APPENDIX: DIVORCE LAWS OF ALL 50 STATES

ALASKA

NAME OF COURT IN WHICH TO FILE FOR DIVORCE: Superior Court. "Superior Court for the State of Alaska; #_____ Judicial District". [Alaska Rules of Court Procedure and Administration.]

TITLE OF DIVORCE ACTION: Petition for Dissolution of Marriage (if filed on no-fault grounds: See below under "Summary Dissolution of Marriage"); "In the Matter of the Dissolution of the Marriage of _____ and _____". Complaint for Divorce (if filed on fault-based grounds)].

NAME USED TO DESCRIBE SPOUSE FILING FOR DIVORCE/DISSOLUTION OF MARRIAGE: Petitioner (if filed on no-fault grounds); Plaintiff (if filed on fault-based grounds).

NAME USED TO DESCRIBE OTHER SPOUSE IN DIVORCE/DISSOLUTION OF MARRIAGE: Respondent (if filed on no-fault grounds); Defendant (if filed on fault-based grounds).

TITLE OF FINAL DIVORCE/DISSOLUTION OF MARRIAGE PAPERS: Decree of Dissolution of Marriage (if filed on no-fault grounds); Judgement of Divorce\(if filed on fault-based grounds).

DIVORCE/RESIDENCY REQUIREMENTS AND WHERE TO FILE: The spouse filing for a divorce/dissolution of marriage must be a resident. No residency time limit is specified. [Alaska Statutes; Title 25, Chapters 22-10.030 and 24.080].

LEGAL GROUNDS FOR DIVORCE/DISSOLUTION OF MARRIAGE: No-Fault: Incompatibility of temperament which has caused the irremediable breakdown of the marriage. [Alaska Statutes; Title 25, Chapter 24.200].

General: (1) Adultery; (2) incurable mental illness and confinement for 18 months; (3) drug abuse; (4) failure to consummate marriage; (5) conviction of a felony; (6) willful desertion of over 1 year; (7) cruel and/or inhuman treatment; (8) personal indignities; and (9) habitual drunkenness. [Alaska Statutes; Title 25, Chapter 24.050].

LEGAL SEPARATION: There is no specific legal provision in Alaska for legal separation.

SIMPLIFIED OR SPECIAL DISSOLUTION OF MARRIAGE PROCEDURES: The spouses may jointly petition the court for a dissolution of marriage of their marriage on the grounds of incompatibility of temperament which has cause the irremediable breakdown of the marriage, under the following conditions: (1) If there are minor children or the wife is pregnant, the spouses have agreed on the custody, visitation, and support of the child or children. They must also have agreed on whether the child support payments should be made through the state child support enforcement agency, and on the tax consequences of the agreement regarding the child or children; (2) the spouses have agreed to the distribution of all jointly-owned property and the payment of spousal support, if any, and the tax consequences of these payments, if any; (3) the spouses have agreed as to the payment of all unpaid obligations incurred by either or both of them, and to the payment of obligations incurred jointly in the future.

The petition for dissolution of marriage may be made by one spouse individually if: (1) the grounds for the dissolution of marriage is the incompatibility of temperament which has cause the irremediable breakdown of the marriage; (2) the petitioning spouse has been unable to ascertain the other spouse's position regarding the dissolution of marriage of their marriage, the division of their property, and the division of their obligations, custody, support and visitation of any child or children, because the whereabouts of the other spouse is unknown to the petitioning spouse, after reasonable efforts to locate the absent spouse; (3) the other spouse can not be personally served with process inside or outside the state. Filing for a dissolution of marriage does not preclude filing for a divorce.

DIVORCE YOURSELF

Official state forms for obtaining a dissolution of marriage under these provisions may be obtained from the Clerk of any Superior Court, or from the Division of Social Services of the Alaska Department of Health and Social Services. [Alaska Statutes; Title 25, Chapters 24-200 to 24-260].

MEDIATION OR COUNSELING REQUIREMENTS: Either spouse may request mediation of an attempt to reach a settlement. If no request is made, the judge may order the spouses to submit to mediation if it is felt that a more satisfactory settlement may be achieved. The court will appoint a mediator. [Alaska Statutes; Title 25, Chapter 24.060].

PROPERTY DISTRIBUTION: Alaska is an "equitable distribution" state. Both joint and separate property which has been acquired during the marriage will be divided in a "just" manner. Any fault of the spouses shall not be taken into account. If necessary to achieve a fair result in a "fault-based" divorce action, property acquired before the marriage may be divided also. In a "no-fault" dissolution of marriage action, property acquired prior to the marriage will not be divided unless the spouses agree or it is in the best interests of any children to do so. Gifts and inheritances are also subject to division by the court. Non-monetary contributions to the marriage (for example: home-making) are also considered. [Alaska Statutes; Title 25, Chapters 24.160 and 24.230].

ALIMONY/MAINTENANCE/SPOUSAL SUPPORT: Maintenance may be awarded to either spouse for support. The award may be made as a lump-sum or may be ordered paid in installments. Any fault of the spcuses may not be taken into account. Non-monetary contributions to the marriage (for example: home-making) are also considered. [Alaska Statutes; Title 25, Chapter 24.160].

SPOUSE'S NAME: The name of either spouse may be changed in the Judgement for Divorce or in the Decree for Dissolution of Marriage. [Alaska Statutes; Title 25, Chapters 24.160 and 24.230].

CHILD CUSTODY: Custody is determined with the best interests of the child in mind. Factors to be considered are: (1) the capability and desire of each parent to meet the child's needs; (2) the physical, emotional, mental, religious, and social needs of the child; (3) the preference of the child (if the child is of sufficient age and capacity); (4) the love and affection between the child and each parent; (5) the length of time the child has lived in a stable, satisfactory environment and the desirability of maintaining continuity; (6) the desire and ability of each parent to allow an open and loving frequent relationship between the child and the other parent. Neither parent is considered to be entitled to custody. [Alaska Statutes; Title 25, Chapter 24.150].

Joint/shared custody may be awarded, if it is in the best interests of the child. For shared custody to be awarded, the court considers the following factors: (1) the child's needs and education; (2) any special needs of the child that may be better met by one parent; (3) any findings of a neutral mediator; (4) the optimal time for the child to be with each parent; (5) the physical proximity of the parents as it relates to where the child will reside and where the child will attend school; (6) the advantage of keeping the child in the community where he presently resides; (7) whether shared custody will promote more frequent or continuing contact between the child and the parents; (8) the length of time the child has lived in a stable, satisfactory environment and the desirability of maintaining continuity; (9) the fitness and suitability of each of the parents (including any evidence of substance abuse); (10) any history of violence by either parent; (11) the preference of the child (if the child is of sufficient age and capacity); (12) the stability of the home of each parent; and (13) any other relevant factors. [Alaska Statutes; Title 25, Chapter 20.090].

CHILD SUPPORT: Either or both parents may be ordered to provide child support. Factors to be considered are: (1) the child's need for support; (2) the ability of the parents to provide support; (3) the extent to which the parent supported the child prior to the divorce/dissolution of marriage; and (4) the ability of the parents to pay for support after the divorce/dissolution of marriage. Child support payments may be ordered paid to a court-appointed trustee or through the state child support enforcement agency. [Alaska Statutes; Title 25, Chapter 24.160 and Title 47, Chapter 23.060 and Alaska Rules of Civil Procedure; Rule 67].

APPENDIX: DIVORCE LAWS OF ALL 50 STATES

ARIZONA

NAME OF COURT IN WHICH TO FILE FOR DIVORCE: Superior Court. "In the Superior Court in and for the County of _____, Arizona". [Arizona Revised Statutes Annotated; Title 25, Chapter 311].

TITLE OF DIVORCE ACTION: Petition for Dissolution of Marriage. "In Re the Marriage of _____ and _____".

NAME USED TO DESCRIBE SPOUSE FILING FOR DISSOLUTION OF MARRIAGE: Petitioner.

NAME USED TO DESCRIBE OTHER SPOUSE IN DISSOLUTION OF MARRIAGE: Respondent.

TITLE OF FINAL DISSOLUTION OF MARRIAGE PAPERS: Decree of Dissolution of Marriage.

RESIDENCY REQUIREMENTS AND WHERE TO FILE: One of the spouses must have lived in the state at least 90 days before filing for dissolution of marriage. The divorce should be filed in the county in which the petitioner resides at the time of filing. [Arizona Revised Statutes Annotated; Title 12, Chapter 401; and Title 25, Chapter 312].

LEGAL GROUNDS FOR DISSOLUTION OF MARRIAGE: No-Fault: Irretrievable breakdown of the marriage. [Arizona Revised Statutes Annotated; Title 25, Chapter 312].

General: Irretrievable breakdown of the marriage is the only grounds for dissolution of marriage in Arizona. [Arizona Revised Statutes Annotated; Title 25, Chapter 312].

LEGAL SEPARATION: Irretrievable breakdown of the marriage is the only grounds for legal separation in Arizona. One of the spouses must live in the state of Arizona when the action for legal separation is filed. No residency time limit is specified in the statute. [Arizona Revised Statutes Annotated; Titles 25, Chapter 313].

SIMPLIFIED OR SPECIAL DISSOLUTION OF MARRIAGE PROCEDURES: Acceptance and waiver of service is allowed. In addition, Arizona law expressly encourages separation agreements. Also, dissolution of marriage petitions may be heard before a court commissioner if a appearance and waiver is filed. [Arizona Revised Statutes Annotated; Title 25, Chapter 317; and Arizona Rules of Civil Procedure; Rule 5; and Arizona Rules of the Supreme Court; Rule 91].

MEDIATION OR COUNSELING REQUIREMENTS: Prior to filing for dissolution of marriage, either spouse may ask the court to order mediation for the purpose of a reconciliation to save the marriage or to obtain an amicable settlement and avoid further litigation. After a dissolution of marriage has been filed, either spouse may request that the dissolution of marriage proceedings be transferred to the Conciliation Court for mediation. Official forms for requesting this transfer are available from the clerk of any Superior Court. [Arizona Revised Statutes Annotated; Title 25, Chapter 381.09+].

PROPERTY DISTRIBUTION: Arizona is a "community property" state. Separate property is retained by the owner of the property. Community or marital property (property acquired during the marriage) is divided and awarded equitably. Marital misconduct is not considered in the division. The court may consider excessive or abnormal expenditures of community property; and any destruction, concealment, or fraudulent disposition of community property in making the division. [Arizona Revised Statutes Annotated; Title 25, Chapter 318]

ALIMONY/MAINTENANCE/SPOUSAL SUPPORT: Maintenance can be awarded to either spouse, if the spouse seeking maintenance: (1) lacks sufficient property to provide for his or her reasonable needs; or (2) is unable to support him or herself through appropriate employment; or (3) is the custodian of a child whose age and condition is such that the custodian should not be required to seek employment outside the home; or (4) lacks earning ability in the labor market to adequately support him or herself; or (5) contributed to the educational opportunities of the other spouse; or (6) had a marriage of long duration and is of an age which may preclude the possibility of gaining employment adequate to support him or herself.

Marital misconduct is not a factor to be considered. The factors to be considered are: (1) if it is appropriate for the spouse who is custodian of a child to seek outside employment; (2) the time for the spouse to acquire education and training for suitable employment; (3) the spouse's future earning capacity; (4) the spouse's standard of living during the marriage; (5) the duration of the marriage; (6) the ability of the spouse providing maintenance to meet his or her needs while providing the maintenance to the other; (7) the financial resources of the spouse seeking maintenance (including marital property awarded and the spouse's ability to meet his or her needs independently); (8) any destruction, concealment, fraudulent disposition, or excessive expenditures of jointly-held property; (9) the comparative financial resources of the spouses including their comparative earning capacities; (10) the age of the spouses; (11) the physical and emotional condition of the spouses; (12) the usual occupations of the spouses during the marriage; (13) the vocational skills of the spouse seeking maintenance; and (14) any other factors the court may deem just and equitable. Awards of maintenance are to be paid through the court unless the spouses agree otherwise. [Arizona Revised Statutes Annotated; Title 25, Chapters 319 and 322].

SPOUSE'S NAME: A spouse's former or maiden name may be restored upon request. [Arizona Revised Statutes Annotated; Title 25, Chapter 325]

CHILD CUSTODY: In awarding custody, the court considers the best interests of the child and the following factors: (1) the preference of the child; (2) the desire and ability of each parent to allow an open, loving, and frequent relationship between the child and the other parent; (3) the wishes of the parents; (4) the child's adjustment to his or her home, school, and community; (5) the mental and physical health of the child and the parents; (6) the relationship between the child and the parents and any siblings; and (7) any evidence of spouse or child abuse. No preference is to be given to on the basis of the parent's sex.

Although joint or shared custody is not preferred, it may be awarded if the parents submit a written agreement providing for joint or shared custody and it is found to be in the best interests of the child, after a consideration of the general child custody factors (above) and the following additional factors: (1) that neither parent was coerced or influenced by duress into withholding or granting his or her agreement to joint custody; (2) that the parents can sustain an ongoing commitment to the child; and (3) that the joint custody agreement is logistically possible. [Arizona Revised Statutes Annotated; Title 25, Chapter 332 and Arizona Case Law].

CHILD SUPPORT: Either parent may be ordered to pay child support, without regard to marital misconduct, based on the following factors: (1) the financial resources of the child; (2) the standard of living of the child during the marriage; (3) the physical, emotional, and educational needs of the child; (4) the financial resources and obligations of both parents; (5) any destruction, concealment, fraudulent disposition, or excessive expenditure of jointly-held property; (6) the estate and needs of the child; and (7) the duration of child visitation and any related expenses. Awards of child support are to be paid through the court unless the spouses agree otherwise. In addition, there are specific Arizona Supreme Court guidelines for child support payments available from the Clerk of any Superior Court. [Arizona Revised Statutes Annotated; Title 25, Chapters 320 and 322].

APPENDIX: DIVORCE LAWS OF ALL 50 STATES

ARKANSAS

NAME OF COURT IN WHICH TO FILE FOR DIVORCE: Chancery Court. "In the Chancery Court of _____ Arkansas". [Arkansas Code of 1987 Annotated; Title 9, Chapter 12-301].

TITLE OF DIVORCE ACTION: Complaint for Divorce.

NAME USED TO DESCRIBE SPOUSE FILING FOR DIVORCE: Plaintiff.

NAME USED TO DESCRIBE OTHER SPOUSE IN DIVORCE: Defendant.

TITLE OF FINAL DIVORCE PAPERS: Decree of Divorce.

RESIDENCY REQUIREMENTS AND WHERE TO FILE: A spouse must reside in the state for 60 days to file for divorce and for 3 months before a divorce is will be finalized. The divorce should be filed in the county of the plaintiff. However, if the plaintiff is a non-resident of Arkansas, the divorce may be filed for in the county where the defendant resides. The venue requirements may be waived in Arkansas. [Arkansas Code of 1987 Annotated; Title 9, Chapters 12-301 and 12-303].

LEGAL GROUNDS FOR DIVORCE: No-Fault: Voluntarily living separate without cohabitation for 3 years. [Arkansas Code of 1987 Annotated; Title 9, Chapter 12-301].

General: (1) Impotence; (2) adultery; (3) confinement for incurable insanity or separation caused by mental illness for a period of 3 years; (4) conviction of a felony; (5) willful desertion for 1 year; (6) cruel and inhuman treatment which endangers the life of the spouse; (7) personal indignities; (8) habitual intemperance (drunkenness) for 1 year; (9) commission and/or conviction of an infamous crime; and (10) nonsupport whereby the spouse is able to provide support but willfully fails to provide suitable maintenance for the complaining spouse. [Arkansas Code of 1987 Annotated; Title 9, Chapter 12-310].

LEGAL SEPARATION: Legal separation may be granted for the following reasons: (1) impotence; (2) adultery; (3) confinement for incurable insanity or separation caused by mental illness for a period of 3 years; (4) conviction of a felony; (5) willful desertion for 1 year; (6) cruel and inhuman treatment which endangers the life of the spouse; (7) personal indignities; (8) habitual intemperance (drunkenness) for 1 year; (9) commission and/or conviction of an infamous crime; (10) voluntary separation for 3 years; and (11) nonsupport whereby the spouse is able to provide support but willfully fails to provide suitable maintenance for the complaining spouse. [Arkansas Code of 1987 Annotated; Title 9, Chapter 12-301].

SIMPLIFIED OR SPECIAL DIVORCE PROCEDURES: In an uncontested divorce, proof of a spouse's residency, proof of separation, and proof of no cohabitation may be provided by a signed affidavit from a third party. In addition, in an uncontested divorce, proof of the grounds for divorce need not be corroborated by a third party. [Arkansas Code of 1987 Annotated; Title 9, Chapters 12-306, 12-313, and 12-316].

MEDIATION OR COUNSELING REQUIREMENTS: There is no legal provision in Arkansas for mediation.

PROPERTY DISTRIBUTION: Arkansas is an "equitable distribution" state. All of the marital property acquired during the marriage is divided equally between the spouses. However, if the court finds the division to be unfair, it may redistribute the property, after consideration of the following factors: (1) the contribution of each spouse to the acquisition of the marital property, including the contribution of each spouse as homemaker; (2) the length of the marriage; (3) the age and health of the spouses; (4) the occupation of the spouses; (5) the amount and sources of income of the spouses; (6) the vocational skills of the spouses; (7) the employability of the spouses; (8) the estate, liabilities, and needs of each spouse and the opportunity of each for further acquisition of capital assets and income; (9) and the federal income tax consequences of the court's division of the property. Where the grounds for divorce are voluntary separation for 3 years, fault may be considered in dividing the property. The separate property of each spouse, consisting of property acquired prior to the marriage, and any gifts or inheritances, is retained by the spouse owning it, unless the court finds it necessary to divide the separate property in order to achieve an equitable distribution. [Arkansas Code of 1987 Annotated; Title 9, Chapter 12-315].

ALIMONY/MAINTENANCE/SPOUSAL SUPPORT: Alimony may be granted to either spouse in fixed installments for a specific period of time and subject to contingencies such as death of either spouse or remarriage of the receiving spouse. Where the grounds for divorce are voluntary separation for 3 years, fault may be considered in dividing the property. There are no other factors for consideration specified in the statute. Alimony payments may be ordered to be paid through the registry of the court. [Arkansas Code of 1987 Annotated; Title 9, Chapter 12-312].

SPOUSE'S NAME: The court may restore the wife's pre-marriage name. [Arkansas Code of 1987 Annotated; Title 9, Chapter 12-318].

CHILD CUSTODY: Child custody is awarded based on the welfare and best interests of the child, after a consideration of the following factors: (1) the circumstances of the parents and child; and (2) the nature of the case. There are no other specific statutory guidelines for consideration. Although Arkansas has no statutory provision for joint custody, joint or shared custody has been awarded if it is found to be in the best interests of the child. [Arkansas Code of 1987 Annotated; Title 9, Chapter 13-101 and Arkansas Case Law].

CHILD SUPPORT: In awarding a reasonable amount of child support, the court is to consider the following factors: (1) the circumstances of the parents and child; and (2) the nature of the case. Child support payments may be ordered to be paid through the registry of the court. There is an official Arkansas Family Support guidelines chart which is presumed to be correct. This chart should be available from the Clerk of any Chancery Court. [Arkansas Code of 1987 Annotated; Title 9, Chapter 12-312].

APPENDIX: DIVORCE LAWS OF ALL 50 STATES

CALIFORNIA

NAME OF COURT IN WHICH TO FILE FOR DIVORCE: Superior Court. "Superior Court of California, County of _____". [Annotated California Code; Section 4503].

TITLE OF DIVORCE ACTION: Petition for Dissolution of Marriage. "In re the Marriage of _____ and _____". (Official mandatory and optional forms for filing a Dissolution of Marriage are available from the County Clerk of any county). [Annotated California Code; Section 4503 and Judicial Council Forms].

NAME USED TO DESCRIBE SPOUSE FILING FOR DISSOLUTION OF MARRIAGE: Petitioner.

NAME USED TO DESCRIBE OTHER SPOUSE IN DISSOLUTION OF MARRIAGE: Respondent.

TITLE OF FINAL DISSOLUTION OF MARRIAGE PAPERS: Final Judgement of Dissolution of Marriage.

RESIDENCY REQUIREMENTS AND WHERE TO FILE: A spouse filing for dissolution of marriage must have been a resident of the state for 6 months and a resident of the county where the dissolution of marriage is filed for 3 months. [Annotated California Code; Section 4530].

LEGAL GROUNDS FOR DISSOLUTION OF MARRIAGE: No-Fault: Irreconcilable differences which have caused the irremediable breakdown of the marriage. [Annotated California Code; Section 4506].

General: Incurable insanity. [Annotated California Code; Section 4506].

LEGAL SEPARATION: The grounds for obtaining a legal separation in California are: (1) irreconcilable differences; and (2) incurable insanity. A spouse filing for legal separation must have been a resident of the state for 6 months and a resident of the county where the action for legal separation is filed for 3 months. [Annotated California Code; Sections 4506 and 4530].

SIMPLIFIED OR SPECIAL DISSOLUTION OF MARRIAGE PROCEDURES: A marriage of 5 years or less may be dissolved by summary action. A Joint Petition for Summary Dissolution of Marriage may be filed if: (1) either spouse has met the residency requirement for a standard dissolution of marriage; (2) there is an irremediable breakdown of the marriage due to irreconcilable differences; (3) there are no children born of or adopted during the marriage; (4) the wife is not pregnant; (5) neither spouse owns any real estate; (6) there are no unpaid debts exceeding $4,000 incurred during the marriage; (7) the total value of the community property (excluding cars and loans) is less than $12,000; (8) neither spouse has separate property (excluding cars and loans) exceeding $12,000 in value; (9) the spouses have signed an agreement regarding the division of their assets and the assumption of their liabilities and have signed any documents or given proof of any transfers necessary to effectuate the agreement; (10) the spouses waive any rights to spousal support [maintenance]; (11) the spouses waive their right to appeal the dissolution of marriage and their right to a new trial upon entry of the final dissolution of Marriage judgement; (12) the spouses have read and understand the summary dissolution of marriage brochure available from the county clerk; and (13) both spouses desire that the marriage be dissolved.

Official mandatory and optional forms for filing for a Summary Dissolution of Marriage are available from the County Clerk of any county. [Annotated California Code; Sections 4550 and 4551, and Judicial Council Forms].

MEDIATION OR COUNSELING REQUIREMENTS: When spouses seek a no-fault dissolution of marriage (on the grounds of irremediable breakdown of the marriage) and it appears to the court that there is a reasonable possibility of reconciliation, the court will stay the dissolution of marriage proceedings for 30 days. If there is no reconciliation at the end of this 30-day period, either spouse may move for a dissolution of marriage or legal separation. In addition, a confidential counseling statement must be filed in any

DIVORCE YOURSELF

county which has a Conciliation Court. Official forms to this effect are available from the County Clerk of any county which has a Conciliation Court. [Annotated California Code; Section 4508 and California Family Law Court Rule 1224].

PROPERTY DISTRIBUTION: California is a "community property" state. Unless the spouses agree otherwise, all community and quasi-community property is divided equally between the spouses. If economic circumstances warrant, however, the court may award any asset to one spouse on such conditions as it feels proper to provide for a substantially equal distribution of property. In addition, if one of the spouse's has deliberately misappropriated community property, the court may make an unequal division of the community property. Marital contributions to the education and training of the other spouse that substantially increases or enhances the other spouse's earning capacity are reimbursable to the community property. [Annotated California Code; Sections 4800 and 4800.3].

ALIMONY/MAINTENANCE/SPOUSAL SUPPORT: The court may award support to either spouse in any amount and for any period of time that the court deems just and reasonable, based on the standard of living achieved during the marriage. The factors that the court considers are: (1) whether the spouse seeking support is the custodian of a child whose condition or circumstances make it appropriate for that spouse not to seek outside employment; (2) the time necessary to acquire sufficient education and training to enable the spouse to find appropriate employment, and that spouse's future earning capacity; (3) the standard of living established during the marriage; (4) the duration of the marriage; (5) the comparative financial resources of the spouses, including their comparative earning abilities in the labor market; (6) the needs and obligations of each spouse; (7) the contribution of each spouse to the marriage, including services rendered in homemaking, child care, education, and career building of the other spouse; (8) the age and health of the spouses; (9) the physical and emotional conditions of the spouses; (10) the immediate and specific tax consequences to each spouse; (11) the ability of the supporting spouse to pay, taking into account that spouse's earning capacity, earned and unearned income, assets, and standard of living; and (12) any other factor the court deems just and equitable. Marital misconduct is not a factor to be considered in determining the amount of support. [Annotated California Code; Section 4801].

SPOUSE'S NAME: On the wife's request, the court shall restore her former or maiden name, regardless of the fact that a minor child may bear a different name. [Annotated California Code; Section 4457].

CHILD CUSTODY: Joint or sole custody may be awarded based on the best interests of the child. The following factors are considered: (1) the preference of the child, if the child is of sufficient age and capacity; (2) the desire and ability of each parent to allow an open and loving frequent relationship between the child and the other parent; (3) the child's health, safety, and welfare; (4) any history of child abuse; and (5) the nature and amount of contact with both parents. Marital misconduct may also be considered. Custody is awarded in the following order of preference: (1) to both parents jointly; (2) to either parent; (3) to the person in whose home the child has been living; or (4) to any other person deemed by the court suitable to provide adequate and proper care and guidance for the child. However, it is not presumed that joint custody is necessarily the preferred choice, unless there is an agreement between the parents regarding joint custody. No preference in awarding custody is to be given because of parent's sex. [Annotated California Code; Sections 4600, 4600.5, and 4608].

CHILD SUPPORT: Either parent may be ordered to pay an amount necessary for the support, maintenance, and education of the child. The parent required to pay may be required to give reasonable security for the support payments. Child support payments may be awarded on a temporary basis during custody or child support proceeding. There is a mandatory minimum amount of child support which is determined by official forms which are available from the County Clerk of any county. These minimum payment amounts will apply unless there is a reasonable agreement between the parents providing otherwise. [Annotated California Code; Sections 4357, 4720, and 4728, and Judicial Council Forms; and California Rules of Court; Family Law Rule 1285.25].

APPENDIX: DIVORCE LAWS OF ALL 50 STATES

COLORADO

NAME OF COURT IN WHICH TO FILE FOR DIVORCE: District Court. "In the District Court in and for the County of _____ and State of Colorado". [Colorado Revised Statutes; Article 10, Section 14-10-106].

TITLE OF DIVORCE ACTION: Petition for Dissolution of Marriage.

NAME USED TO DESCRIBE SPOUSE FILING FOR DISSOLUTION OF MARRIAGE: Petitioner.

NAME USED TO DESCRIBE OTHER SPOUSE IN DISSOLUTION OF MARRIAGE: Respondent.

TITLE OF FINAL DISSOLUTION OF MARRIAGE PAPERS: Decree of Dissolution of Marriage.

RESIDENCY REQUIREMENTS AND WHERE TO FILE: One spouse must have been a resident of Colorado for 90 days prior to filing for dissolution of marriage. The dissolution of marriage may be filed for in: (1) the county where the respondent resides; or (2) the county in which the petitioner resides if the respondent has been served in the same county or is a non-resident of Colorado. [Colorado Revised Statutes; Article 10, Section 14-10-106; and Colorado Rules of Civil Procedure, Rule 98].

LEGAL GROUNDS FOR DISSOLUTION OF MARRIAGE: No-Fault: Irretrievable breakdown of the marriage. [Colorado Revised Statutes; Article 10, Section 14-10-106].

General: Irretrievable breakdown of the marriage is the only grounds for dissolution of marriage in Colorado. [Colorado Revised Statutes; Article 10, Section 14-10-106],

LEGAL SEPARATION: If there has been an irretrievable breakdown of the marriage, the spouses may file for a legal separation. One spouse must have been a resident of Colorado for 90 days prior to filing for legal separation. [Colorado Revised Statutes; Article 10, Section 14-10-106].

SIMPLIFIED OR SPECIAL DISSOLUTION OF MARRIAGE PROCEDURES: A dissolution of marriage may be obtained by affidavit of either or both of the spouses if: (1) there are no minor children and the wife is not pregnant; or both spouses are represented by counsel and have entered into a separation agreement granting custody and child support; (2) there are no disputes; (3) there is no marital property; or the spouses have agreed on the division of marital property; and (4) the adverse party (non-filing spouse) has been served with the dissolution of marriage papers. A signed affidavit stating the facts in the case must be filed with the petition. [Colorado Revised Statutes; Article 10, Section 14-10-120.3].

MEDIATION OR COUNSELING REQUIREMENTS: At the request of either spouse or their attorney, or at the discretion of the court, the court may appoint a marriage counselor in any dissolution of marriage or legal separation proceeding and delay the proceedings for 30 to 60 days to allow for counseling. [Colorado Revised Statutes; Article 10, Sections 14-12-106 and 14-10-110].

PROPERTY DISTRIBUTION: Colorado is an "equitable distribution" state. The separate property of each spouse which was owned prior to the marriage or obtained by gift or inheritance is retained by that spouse. All other property acquired during the marriage will be divided, without regard to any fault, based on the following: (1) the contribution of each spouse to the acquisition of the marital property, including the contribution of each spouse as homemaker; (2) the value of each spouse's separate property; (3) the economic circumstances of each spouse at the time the division of property is to become effective, including the desirability of awarding the family home or right to live in it to the spouse having custody of any children; (4) and any increase or decrease in the value of the separate property of the spouse during the marriage or the depletion of the separate property for marital purposes. [Colorado Revised Statutes; Article 10, Section 14-10-113].

DIVORCE YOURSELF

ALIMONY/MAINTENANCE/SPOUSAL SUPPORT: Either spouse may be awarded support for a just period of time, without regard to any marital fault, if the spouse seeking maintenance: (1) lacks sufficient property, including his or her share of any marital property, to provide for his or her needs, and (2) is unable to support his or herself through appropriate employment, or has custody of a child and the circumstances are such that the spouse should not be required to seek employment outside the home.

The award of maintenance is based upon a consideration of the following factors: (1) the time necessary to acquire sufficient education and training to enable the spouse to find appropriate employment, and that spouse's future earning capacity; (2) the standard of living established during the marriage; (3) the duration of the marriage; (4) the ability of the spouse from whom support is sought to meet his or her needs while meeting those of the spouse seeking support; (5) the financial resources of the spouse seeking maintenance, including marital property apportioned to such spouse and such spouse's ability to meet his or her needs independently; (6) the age of the spouses; (7) the physical and emotional conditions of the spouses; and (8) any custodial and child support responsibilities. [Colorado Revised Statutes; Article 10, Section 14-10-114].

SPOUSE'S NAME: There is no legal provision in Colorado for restoration of the spouse's name upon divorce. However, there is a general statute which allows for the change of a person's name upon petition to the court. [Colorado Revised Statutes; Section 3-15-101].

CHILD CUSTODY: Joint or sole custody will be determined with regard to the best interests of the child, without regard to the sex of the parent, and after considering the following factors: (1) the preference of the child; (2) the desire and ability of each parent to allow an open and loving frequent relationship between the child and the other parent; (3) the wishes of the parents; (4) the child's adjustment to his or her home, school, and community; (5) the mental and physical health of all individuals involved; (6) the relationship of the child with parents, siblings, and other significant family members; (7) any child abuse or spouse abuse by either parent.

Joint custody may be awarded on the petition of both parents if they submit a reasonable plan for custody. The plan submitted to the court for joint custody should address the following issues: (1) the location of each parent; (2) the periods of time during which each parent will have physical custody of the child; (3) the legal residence of the child; (4) the child's education; (5) the child's religious training, if any; (6) the child's health care; (7) finances to provide for the child's needs; (8) holidays and vacations; and (9) any other factors affecting the physical or emotional health or well-being of the child.

The actual joint custody award is based on all of the factors involved in standard custody decisions and on the following additional factors: (1) the ability of the parents to cooperate and make decisions jointly; (2) the ability of the parents to encourage the sharing of love, affection, and contact between the child and the other parent; (3) whether the past pattern of involvement of the parents with the child reflects a system of values and mutual support which indicates the parent's ability as joint custodians to provide a positive and nourishing relationship with the child; (4) the physical proximity of the parents to each other as this relates to the practical considerations of where the child will reside; (5) the ability of each parent to maintain adequate housing for the child; and (6) whether an award of joint custody will promote more frequent or continuing contact between the child and each of the parents. [Colorado Revised Statutes; Article 10, Sections 14-123 and 14-124].

CHILD SUPPORT: The court may order reasonable and necessary child support to be paid by either or both parents, without regard to marital fault, after considering the following factors: (1) the financial resources of the child; (2) the financial resources of the custodial parents; (3) the standard of living the child would have enjoyed if the marriage had not been dissolved; (4) the physical and emotional conditions and educational needs of the child; and (5) the financial resources, needs, and obligations of both the noncustodial and the custodial parent. Provisions for medical insurance and medical care for any children may be ordered to be provided. There are specific child support guidelines specified in the statute. In addition, standardized child support guideline forms are available from the Clerk of any District Court. Child support payments may be ordered to be paid through the Clerk of the Court. [Colorado Revised Statutes; Article 10, Section 14-10-115].

APPENDIX: DIVORCE LAWS OF ALL 50 STATES

CONNECTICUT

NAME OF COURT IN WHICH TO FILE FOR DIVORCE: Superior Court. [Connecticut General Statutes Annotated; Title 46b, Chapter 42].

TITLE OF DIVORCE ACTION: Complaint for Dissolution of Marriage.

NAME USED TO DESCRIBE SPOUSE FILING FOR DISSOLUTION OF MARRIAGE: Plaintiff.

NAME USED TO DESCRIBE OTHER SPOUSE IN DISSOLUTION OF MARRIAGE: Defendant.

TITLE OF FINAL DISSOLUTION OF MARRIAGE PAPERS: Decree of Dissolution of Marriage.

RESIDENCY REQUIREMENTS AND WHERE TO FILE: The dissolution of marriage may be filed by either spouse if a resident. However, the dissolution of marriage will not be finalized until one spouse has been a resident for one (1) year; unless one of the spouses was a resident of Connecticut at the time of the marriage and returned with the intention of permanent residence; or if the grounds for the dissolution of marriage arose in Connecticut. In cases which involve support, the dissolution of marriage is to be filed in the county in which the plaintiff resides. In all other cases, the dissolution of marriage may be filed in any county which is most convenient to both spouses. [Connecticut General Statutes Annotated; Title 31, Chapter 348; Title 46b, Chapter 44; and Title 51, Chapter 349].

LEGAL GROUNDS FOR DISSOLUTION OF MARRIAGE: No-Fault: (1) Irretrievable breakdown of the marriage; (2) incompatibility and voluntary separation for 18 months with no reasonable prospect for reconciliation. [Connecticut General Statutes Annotated; Title 46b, Chapter 40].

General: (1) Adultery; (2) life imprisonment; (3) confinement for incurable insanity for a total of 5 years; (4) willful desertion and nonsupport for 1 year; (5) 7 years absence; (6) cruel and inhuman treatment; (7) fraud; (8) habitual intemperance (drunkenness); (9) commission and/or conviction of an infamous crime involving a violation of conjugal duty and imprisonment for at least 1 year. [Connecticut General Statutes Annotated; Title 46b, Chapter 40].

LEGAL SEPARATION: A legal separation may be granted on the following grounds: (1) irretrievable breakdown of the marriage; (2) incompatibility and voluntary separation; (3) adultery; (4) life imprisonment; (5) confinement for incurable insanity for a total of 5 years; (6) willful desertion and nonsupport for 1 year; (7) cruel and inhuman treatment; (8) fraud; (9) habitual intemperance (drunkenness); (10) commission and/or conviction of an infamous crime involving a violation of conjugal duty and imprisonment for at least 1 year. There is no residency requirement noted in the statute. [Connecticut General Statutes Annotated; Title 46b, Chapter 40].

SIMPLIFIED OR SPECIAL DISSOLUTION OF MARRIAGE PROCEDURES: Proof of the breakdown of the marriage can be made by: (1) the spouses signing an agreement or statement that their marriage is irretrievably broken; or (2) both spouses stating in court that their marriage is irretrievably broken and submitting an agreement concerning the care, custody, visitation, maintenance or support of their children, if any, and concerning alimony and the disposition of any property. [Connecticut General Statutes Annotated; Title 46b, Chapter 51].

MEDIATION OR COUNSELING REQUIREMENTS: Within 90 days after the dissolution of marriage has been filed, either spouse or the attorney for any minor children may submit a request for conciliation to the clerk of the court. Two mandatory counseling sessions will be ordered. [Connecticut General Statutes Annotated; Title 46b, Chapter 53].

PROPERTY DISTRIBUTION: Connecticut is an "equitable distribution" state. The court may assign to either spouse all or part of the property of the other spouse, including any gifts and inheritances, based on the following factors: (1) the contribution of each spouse to the acquisition of the marital property, including the contribution of each spouse as homemaker; (2) the length of the marriage; (3) the age and health of the spouses; (4) the occupation of the spouses; (5) the amount and sources of income of the spouses; (6) the vocational skills of the spouses; (7) the employability of the spouses; (8) the estate, liabilities, and needs of each spouse and the opportunity of each for further acquisition of capital assets and income; (9) the circumstances that contributed to the estrangement of the spouses; and (10) the causes of the dissolution of marriage. [Connecticut General Statutes Annotated; Title 46b, Chapter 81].

ALIMONY/MAINTENANCE/SPOUSAL SUPPORT: Alimony may be awarded to either spouse, based on the following factors: (1) the causes for the dissolution of marriage, including any marital fault; (2) the distribution of the marital property; (3) whether the spouse seeking support is the custodian of a child whose condition or circumstances make it appropriate for that spouse not to seek outside employment; (4) the duration of the marriage; (5) the age of the spouses; (6) the physical and emotional conditions of the spouses; (7) the usual occupation of the spouses during the marriage; (8) the needs of each spouse; and (9) the vocational skills and employability of the spouse seeking support and alimony. [Connecticut General Statutes Annotated; Title 46b, Chapters 82 and 86].

SPOUSE'S NAME: The wife's former or maiden name shall be restored upon request. [Connecticut General Statutes Annotated; Title 46b, Chapter 63].

CHILD CUSTODY: Joint or sole custody is awarded based upon the best interests of the child and the following factors: (1) the causes for the dissolution of marriage if such causes are relevant to the best interests of the child; and (2) the wishes of the child if the child is of sufficient age and is capable of forming an intelligent choice. There are no other specific state guidelines for consideration. There is a presumption that joint custody is in the best interests of the child if both parents have agreed to joint custody. [Connecticut General Statutes Annotated; Title 46b, Chapters 56, 56a, and 84].

CHILD SUPPORT: Either parent may be ordered to contribute child support, based on the following factors: (1) the financial resources of the child; (2) the age, health, and station of the parents; (3) the occupation of each parent; (4) the earning capacity of each parent; (5) the amount and sources of income of each parent; (6) the vocational skills and employability of each parent; (7) the age and health of the child; (8) the child's occupation; (9) the vocational skills of the child; (10) the employability of the child; (11) the estate and needs of the child; and (12) the relative financial means of the parents. Either parent may be ordered to provide health insurance for the child. [Connecticut General Statutes Annotated; Title 46b, Chapter 84].

APPENDIX: DIVORCE LAWS OF ALL 50 STATES

DELAWARE

NAME OF COURT IN WHICH TO FILE FOR DIVORCE: Family Court. "In the Family Court for the State of Delaware, In and For _____ County". [Delaware Code Annotated; Title 13, Chapters 1504 and 1507].

TITLE OF DIVORCE ACTION: Petition for Divorce. "In Re the Marriage of _____ and _____".

NAME USED TO DESCRIBE SPOUSE FILING FOR DIVORCE: Petitioner.

NAME USED TO DESCRIBE OTHER SPOUSE IN DIVORCE: Respondent.

TITLE OF FINAL DIVORCE PAPERS: Decree of Divorce.

RESIDENCY REQUIREMENTS AND WHERE TO FILE: One spouse must have been a resident for 6 months immediately prior to filing for divorce. The divorce may be filed for in a county where either spouse resides. [Delaware Code Annotated; Title 13, Chapters 1504 and 1507].

LEGAL GROUNDS FOR DIVORCE: No-Fault: (1) Irretrievable breakdown of the marriage and reconciliation is improbable (a marriage is considered "irretrievably broken" when it is characterized by one of the following: (a) voluntary separation; (b) separation caused by the other spouse's misconduct or mental illness; or (c) separation caused by incompatibility; and (2) living apart for 6 months because of incompatibility. [Delaware Code Annotated; Title 13, Chapter 1505].

General: Separation caused by mental illness. [Delaware Code Annotated; Title 13, Chapter 1505].

LEGAL SEPARATION: There is no legal provision in Delaware for legal separation.

SIMPLIFIED OR SPECIAL DIVORCE PROCEDURES: The respondent may file an appearance which will fulfill the requirement of service of process. In addition, a sample Petition for Divorce is contained in Delaware Code Annotated; Title 13, Chapter 1507. [Delaware Code Annotated; Title 13, Chapter 1508].

MEDIATION OR COUNSELING REQUIREMENTS: In a contested divorce, the court may delay the proceedings for 60 days to allow the spouses to seek counseling or order a mediation conference. In addition, there are mediation/arbitration units attached to the Delaware Family Court. [Delaware Code Annotated; Title 13, Chapter 1517].

PROPERTY DISTRIBUTION: Delaware is an "equitable distribution" state. The spouse's separate property obtained prior to the marriage or by inheritance is retained by that spouse. Marital property acquired during the marriage, including any property acquired by gift, is to be divided equitably, without regard to fault, based on the following factors: (1) the contribution of each spouse to the acquisition of the marital property, including the contribution of each spouse as homemaker; (2) the value of each spouse's personal property; (3) the economic circumstances of each spouse at the time the division of property is to become effective; (4) the length of the marriage; (5) the age and health of the spouses; (6) the occupation of the spouses; (7) the amount and sources of income of the spouses; (8) the vocational skills of the spouses; (9) the employability of the spouses; (10) the estate, liabilities, and needs of each spouse and the opportunity of each for further acquisition of capital assets and income; (11) the federal income tax consequences of the court's division of the property; (12) liabilities of the spouses; (13) any prior marriage of each spouse; (14) whether the property award is in stead of or in addition to maintenance; (15) how and by whom the property was acquired; and (16) any custodial provisions for the children. [Delaware Code Annotated; Title 13, Chapter 1513].

ALIMONY/MAINTENANCE/SPOUSAL SUPPORT: Either spouse may be awarded alimony if: (1) he or she is dependent on the other spouse; (2) lacks sufficient property, including any award or marital property, to provide for his or her reasonable needs; and (3) is unable to support him or herself through appropriate employment or is the custodian of a child whose condition or circumstances make it appropriate that he or she not be required to seek employment. Either spouse may be awarded alimony for no longer than a a period of time equal 50% of the length of the marriage. There is, however, no time limit if the marriage lasted for over 20 years.

Marital misconduct is not a factor to be considered in an award or alimony. The factors to be considered are: (1) the time necessary to acquire sufficient education and training to enable the spouse to find appropriate employment, and that spouse's future earning capacity; (2) the standard of living established during the marriage; (3) the duration of the marriage; (4) the ability of the spouse from whom support is sought to meet his or her needs while meeting those of the spouse seeking support; (5) the financial resources of the spouse seeking alimony, including marital property apportioned to such spouse and such spouse's ability to meet his or her needs independently; (6) the tax consequences to each spouse; (7) the age of the spouses; (8) the physical and emotional conditions of the spouses; (9) any custodial and child support responsibilities; (10) whether either spouse has foregone or postponed economic, education or other employment opportunities during the course of the marriage; and (11) any other factor that the court finds just and appropriate. [Delaware Code Annotated; Title 13, Chapter 1512].

SPOUSE'S NAME: Upon request, the wife may resume her former or maiden name. [Delaware Code Annotated; Title 13, Chapter 1514].

CHILD CUSTODY: Joint or sole child custody is awarded based on the best interests of the child and after considering the following factors: (1) preference of the child; (2) the wishes of the parents; (3) the child's adjustment to his or her home, school, and community; (4) the mental and physical health of all individuals involved; and (5) the relationship of the child with parents, siblings, and other significant family members. The conduct of the proposed guardian is to be considered only as it bears on his or her relationship with the child. No is preference to be given because of parent's sex.

In addition, in any case involving minor children, the petitioning parent must submit with the petition an signed affidavit that states that the parent has been advised of or has read the following list of children's rights. The list of rights must be included in the affidavit. The children's rights are: (1) the right to a continuing relationship with both parents; (2) the right to be treated as an important human being, with unique feelings, ideas, and desires; (3) the right to continuing care and guidance from both parents; (4) the right to know and appreciate what is good in each parent without one parent degrading the other; (5) the right to express love, affection, and respect for each parent without having to stifle that love because of disapproval by the other parent; (6) the right to know that the parents' decision to divorce was not the responsibility of the child; (7) the right not to be a source of argument between the parents; (8) the right to honest answers to questions about the changing family relationships; (9) the right to be able to experience regular and consistent contact with both parents and the right to know the reason for any cancellation of time or change of plans; and (10) the right to have a relaxed, secure relationship with both parents without being placed in a position to manipulate one parent against the other. [Delaware Code Annotated; Title 13, Chapters 722 and 1507].

CHILD SUPPORT: Each parent has an equal duty to support any children. The following factors are considered in awards of child support: (1) the financial resources of the child; (2) the standard of living the child would have enjoyed if there had been no divorce; (3) the age and health of the parents; (4) the earning capacity of each parent; (5) the amount and sources of income of each parent; (6) the age, health, or station of the child; (7) the estate and needs of the child; and (8) the relative financial means of the parents. [Delaware Code Annotated; Title 13, Chapters 501, 514, and 701].

APPENDIX: DIVORCE LAWS OF ALL 50 STATES

DISTRICT OF COLUMBIA (WASHINGTON D.C.)

NAME OF COURT IN WHICH TO FILE FOR DIVORCE: Superior Court - Family Division. "In the Superior Court of the District of Columbia - Family Division". [District of Columbia Court Rules; Volume 2, Appendix I].

TITLE OF DIVORCE ACTION: Complaint for Divorce.

NAME USED TO DESCRIBE SPOUSE FILING FOR DIVORCE: Plaintiff.

NAME USED TO DESCRIBE OTHER SPOUSE IN DIVORCE: Defendant.

TITLE OF FINAL DIVORCE PAPERS: Final Decree of Divorce.

RESIDENCY REQUIREMENTS AND WHERE TO FILE: One of the spouses must have been a resident of Washington D.C. for 6 months immediately prior to filing for divorce. Military personnel are considered residents if they have been stationed in Washington D.C. for 6 months. [District of Columbia Code Annotated; Title 16, Chapter 9, Section 902].

LEGAL GROUNDS FOR DIVORCE: No-Fault: (1) Mutual voluntary separation without cohabitation for 6 months; (2) living separate and apart without cohabitation for 1 year. [District of Columbia Code Annotated; Title 16, Chapter 9, Sections 904, 905, and 906].

General: (1) Mutual voluntary separation without cohabitation for 6 months; and (2) living separate and apart without cohabitation for 1 year are the only grounds for divorce in Washington D.C. [District of Columbia Code Annotated; Title 16, Chapter 9, Sections 904, 905, and 906].

LEGAL SEPARATION: Legal separation (from bed and board) may be granted on the following grounds: (1) adultery; (2) cruel and inhuman treatment; (3) voluntary separation; and (4) living separate and apart without cohabitation. One of the spouses must have been a resident for 6 months prior to filing for legal separation. Military personnel are considered residents if they have been stationed in Washington D.C. for 6 months. [District of Columbia Code Annotated; Title 16, Chapter 9, Sections 902 and 904].

SIMPLIFIED OR SPECIAL DIVORCE PROCEDURES: There are no legal provisions in Washington D.C. for simplified divorce.

MEDIATION OR COUNSELING REQUIREMENTS: There is no legal provision in Washington D.C. for mediation.

PROPERTY DISTRIBUTION: Washington D.C. is an "equitable distribution" jurisdiction. If there is no valid property distribution agreement, each spouse retains his or her separate property (acquired before the marriage or acquired during the marriage by gift or inheritance) and any increase in such separate property and any property acquired in exchange for such separate property. All other property, regardless of how title is held, shall be divided equitably and reasonably, based on relevant factors, including: (1) the contribution of each spouse to the acquisition of the marital property, including the contribution of each spouse as homemaker; (2) the length of the marriage; (3) the occupation of the spouses; (4) the vocational skills of the spouses; (5) the employability of the spouses; (6) the estate, liabilities, and needs of each spouse and the opportunity of each for further acquisition of capital assets and income; (7) the assets and debts of the spouses; (8) any prior marriage of each spouse; (9) whether the property award is in stead of or in addition to alimony; (10) any custodial provisions for the children; (11) the age and health of the spouses; and (12) the amount and sources of income of the spouses. The conduct of the spouses during the marriage is not a factor for consideration. [District of Columbia Code Annotated; Title 16, Chapter 9, Section 910].

DIVORCE YOURSELF

ALIMONY/MAINTENANCE/SPOUSAL SUPPORT: Either spouse may be awarded alimony, during the divorce proceeding or after, if it is just or proper. There are no specific factors listed in the statute. However, martial fault may be considered. [District of Columbia Code Annotated; Title 16, Chapter 9, Sections 912 and 913].

SPOUSE'S NAME: Upon request, the birth name or previous name may be restored. [District of Columbia Code Annotated; Title 16, Chapter 9, Section 915].

CHILD CUSTODY: Custody may be granted during and after a divorce proceeding based on the best interests of the child, without regard to spouse's sex or sexual orientation, race, color, national origin, or political affiliations. The following factors shall also be considered: (1) the preference of the child, if the child is of sufficient age and capacity; (2) the wishes of the parents; (3) the child's adjustment to his or her home, school, and community; (4) the mental and physical health of all individuals involved; and (5) the relationship of the child with parents, siblings, and other significant family members. There is no legal provision in Washington D.C. for joint custody. [District of Columbia Code Annotated; Title 16, Chapter 9, Sections 911 and 914].

CHILD SUPPORT: Either parent may be ordered to pay reasonable child support during and after a divorce proceeding. There are no specific factors for consideration set out in the statute, however, detailed specific child support guidelines are contained in The District of Columbia Court Rules (1989); Volume 2, Appendix I. Child support may be ordered to be paid through the Clerk of the Superior Court. [District of Columbia Code Annotated; Title 16, Chapter 9, Section 911].

APPENDIX: DIVORCE LAWS OF ALL 50 STATES

FLORIDA

NAME OF COURT IN WHICH TO FILE FOR DIVORCE: Circuit Court. "In the Circuit Court in and for the County of _____, Florida". [Florida Rules of Civil Procedure].

TITLE OF DIVORCE ACTION: Petition for Dissolution of Marriage. "In Re the Marriage of _____ and _____". [Florida Statutes Annotated; Chapter 61.043].

NAME USED TO DESCRIBE SPOUSE FILING FOR DISSOLUTION OF MARRIAGE: Petitioner.

NAME USED TO DESCRIBE OTHER SPOUSE IN DISSOLUTION OF MARRIAGE: Respondent.

TITLE OF FINAL DISSOLUTION OF MARRIAGE PAPERS: Final Judgement of Dissolution of Marriage.

RESIDENCY REQUIREMENTS AND WHERE TO FILE: One of the spouses must have been a resident for 6 months prior to filing for dissolution of marriage. The dissolution of marriage should be filed in either: (1) the county where the defendant resides; or (2) the county where the spouses last lived together prior to separating. [Florida Statutes Annotated; Chapter 61.021].

LEGAL GROUNDS FOR DISSOLUTION OF MARRIAGE: No-Fault: Irretrievable breakdown of the marriage. [Florida Statutes Annotated; Chapter 61.052].

General: Incurable mental incompetence. [Florida Statutes Annotated; Chapter 61.052].

LEGAL SEPARATION: A spouse may file for separate maintenance and child support. [Florida Statutes Annotated; Chapter 61.09].

SIMPLIFIED OR SPECIAL DISSOLUTION OF MARRIAGE PROCEDURES: Florida has a procedure for a Simplified Dissolution of Marriage. In order to qualify to use this procedure, the spouses must certify that: (1) there are no minor or dependent children of the spouses and the wife is not pregnant; (2) the spouses have made a satisfactory division of their property and have agreed as to payment of their joint obligations; (3) that one of the spouses has been a resident of Florida for 6 months immediately prior to filing for dissolution of marriage; (4) and that their marriage is irretrievably broken. The spouses must appear in court to testify as to these items and file a Certificate of a Corroborating Witness as to the residency requirement. Each must also attach a financial affidavit to the Simplified Dissolution Petition. Specific forms and an instruction brochure are available from the Clerk of any Circuit Court. In addition, sample forms for various aspects of a standard dissolution of marriage are available in the Florida Rules of Civil Procedure. [Florida Rules of Civil Procedure; Rule 1.611 and Forms 1.943(b), 1.943(c), 1.943(d), and 1.943(e)].

MEDIATION OR COUNSELING REQUIREMENTS: If there are minor children involved, or if one of the spouses denies that the marriage is irretrievably broken, the court may delay the proceedings for up to 3 months and order the spouses to seek counseling or may order the spouses to attempt reconciliation. [Florida Statutes Annotated; Chapter 61.052].

PROPERTY DISTRIBUTION: Florida is an "equitable distribution" state. The spouse's non-marital property will be retained by each spouse. Non-marital property is all property acquired prior to the marriage, property acquired by gift or inheritance, and any property considered to be non-marital according to a written agreement between the spouses. All of the spouse's marital property may be divided on an equitable basis, based on the following factors: (1) the contribution of each spouse to the acquisition of the marital property, including the contribution of each spouse as homemaker; (2) the length of the marriage; (3) the age and health of the spouses; (4) the amount and sources of income of the spouses; (5) the estate, liabilities, and needs of each spouse and the opportunity of each for further acquisition of capital assets and income; (6) the standard of living established during the marriage; (7) the time necessary for a spouse to acquire sufficient education to enable the spouse to find appropriate employment; (8) any other factor necessary to do equity and justice between the spouses. Marital misconduct is not specified as a factor in any division of property. [Florida Statutes Annotated: Chapter 61.075].

ALIMONY/MAINTENANCE/SPOUSAL SUPPORT: The court may grant rehabilitative or permanent alimony to either spouse in either lump-sum or periodic payments or both. Adultery is a factor in the award. Other factors which are considered are: (1) the time necessary to acquire sufficient education and training to enable the spouse to find appropriate employment, and that spouse's future earning capacity; (2) the standard of living established during the marriage; (3) the duration of the marriage; (4) the comparative financial resources of the spouses, including their comparative earning abilities in the labor market; (5) the contribution of each spouse to the marriage, including services rendered in homemaking, child care, education, and career building of the other spouse; (6) the age of the spouses; (7) the physical and emotional conditions of the spouses; each spouse's share of marital assets and liabilities; and (9) any other factor the court deems just and equitable. Alimony payments made be ordered to be paid through a state depository. [Florida Statutes Annotated; Chapter 61.08].

SPOUSE'S NAME: There is no legal provision in Florida for restoration of a spouse's name upon divorce. However, there is a general statutory provision that allows for a person to change his or her name by petition filed with the court. [Florida Statutes Annotated; Chapter 68.07].

CHILD CUSTODY: Joint or sole custody may be granted. Joint custody is referred to as "shared parental responsibility". Both parents are given equal consideration in any award of custody. Custody is granted according to the best interests of the child, based on the following factors: (1) the moral character and prudence of the parents; (2) the capability and desire of each parent to meet the child's needs; (3) preference of the child, if the child is of sufficient age and capacity; (4) the love and affection existing between the child and each parent; (5) the length of time the child has lived in a stable, satisfactory environment and the desirability of maintaining continuity; (6) the desire and ability of each parent to allow an open and loving frequent relationship between the child and the other parent; (7) the child's adjustment to his or her home, school, and community; (8) the mental and physical health of all individuals involved; (9) the material needs of the child; (10) the stability of the home environment likely to be offered by each parent; (11) any evidence of spouse abuse; and (12) any other relevant factors. No preference is to be given because of parent's sex. [Florida Statutes Annotated; Chapter 61.13].

CHILD SUPPORT: The court may order either parent to pay child support during and after a dissolution of marriage proceeding in an equitable amount, based on the nature and circumstances of the case. There are no specific factors for consideration in the statute, however, there are specific child support guidelines set out in Florida Statutes Annotated; Chapter 61.30. Health insurance for the child and life insurance covering the life of the parent ordered to pay support may be required by the court. Child support payments made be ordered to be paid through a state depository. [Florida Statutes Annotated; Chapters 61.13 and 61.30].

APPENDIX: DIVORCE LAWS OF ALL 50 STATES

GEORGIA

NAME OF COURT IN WHICH TO FILE FOR DIVORCE: Superior Court. "In the Superior Court of _____ County, Georgia". [Georgia Civil Practice Act and Code of Georgia Annotated; Title 30, Section 107].

TITLE OF DIVORCE ACTION: Petition for Divorce.

NAME USED TO DESCRIBE SPOUSE FILING FOR DIVORCE: Petitioner.

NAME USED TO DESCRIBE OTHER SPOUSE IN DIVORCE: Respondent.

TITLE OF FINAL DIVORCE PAPERS: Final Judgement and Decree of Divorce.

RESIDENCY REQUIREMENTS AND WHERE TO FILE: The spouse filing must have been a resident of Georgia for 6 months and file for divorce in the county of residence. However, a non-resident may file for divorce against a spouse who has been a resident of Georgia for 6 months. In such cases, the divorce must be filed for in the county in which the respondent resides. [Code of Georgia Annotated; Title 30, Section 107].

LEGAL GROUNDS FOR DIVORCE: No-Fault: Irretrievable breakdown of the marriage. [Code of Georgia Annotated; Title 30, Section 102].

General: (1) impotence; (2) adultery; (3) conviction of and imprisonment of over 2 years for an offense involving moral turpitude; (4) alcoholism and/or drug addiction; (5) confinement for incurable insanity; (6) separation caused by mental illness; (7) willful desertion; (8) cruel and inhuman treatment which endangers the life of the spouse; (9) habitual intemperance (drunkenness); (10) consent to marriage was obtained by fraud, duress, or force; (11) spouse lacked mental capacity to consent (including temporary incapacity resulting from drug or alcohol use); (12) the wife was pregnant by another at the time of the marriage unknown to the husband; and (13) incest. [Code of Georgia Annotated; Title 30, Section 102].

LEGAL SEPARATION: There are legal provisions in Georgia for separate maintenance. [Code of Georgia Annotated; Title 30, Section 210].

SIMPLIFIED OR SPECIAL DIVORCE PROCEDURES: There are no legal provisions in Georgia for simplified divorce.

MEDIATION OR COUNSELING REQUIREMENTS: There are no legal provisions in Georgia for divorce mediation.

PROPERTY DISTRIBUTION: Georgia is an "equitable distribution" state. The courts will distribute the marital property, including any gifts and inheritances, equitably. There are no factors to be considered specified in the statute. [Code of Georgia Annotated; Title 30, Section 118 and Georgia Case Law].

ALIMONY//MAINTENANCE/SPOUSAL SUPPORT: Permanent or temporary alimony may be awarded to either spouse, unless the separation was caused by that spouse's desertion or adultery. The following factors are to be considered: (1) the contribution of each spouse to the acquisition of the marital property, including the contribution of each spouse as homemaker, in child care, education and career building of the other spouse; (2) the duration of the marriage; (3) the financial resources of each spouse; (4) the age and physical and emotional condition of both spouses; (5) the value of each spouse's separate property; (6) the earning capacity of each spouse; (7) any fixed liabilities of either spouse; (8) the standard of living established during the marriage; and (9) the time necessary for a spouse to acquire sufficient education to enable the spouse to find appropriate employment. [Code of Georgia Annotated; Title 30, Sections 201 and 209].

DIVORCE YOURSELF

SPOUSE'S NAME: If requested, a spouse's name may be restored. [Code of Georgia Annotated; Title 30, Sections 116 and 121].

CHILD CUSTODY: Custody is granted based upon all circumstances of the case, including the best interests of the child and the health of the parents. A child of 14 may select the parent with whom he or she desires to live. There are no specific factors for consideration set out in the statute. There is no specific provision for joint custody in Georgia. [Code of Georgia Annotated; Title 30, Section 127].

CHILD SUPPORT: Both parents are liable for the support of minor children. The court may award child support from either parent, based on their customary needs and the parents ability to pay. There are no specific factors for consideration set out in the statute. However, there are child support guidelines set out in the statute that are to be followed in all cases in which the parents are not able to reach an agreement. In such cases there are factors which will be followed in special circumstances. The special circumstances include: (1) the age of the children; (2) a child's medical costs or extraordinary needs; (3) educational costs; (4) day care costs; (5) shared physical custody arrangements; (6) a parent's support obligations to another household; (7) hidden income of a parent; (8) the income of the parent with custody; (9) contributions of the parents; (10) extreme economic circumstances; and (11) a parent's own extraordinary needs. [Code of Georgia Annotated; Title 30, Section 207].

APPENDIX: DIVORCE LAWS OF ALL 50 STATES

HAWAII

NAME OF COURT IN WHICH TO FILE FOR DIVORCE: Family Court. [Hawaii Revised Statutes, Title 580, Section 1].

TITLE OF DIVORCE ACTION: Complaint for Divorce.

NAME USED TO DESCRIBE SPOUSE FILING FOR DIVORCE: Plaintiff.

NAME USED TO DESCRIBE OTHER SPOUSE IN DIVORCE: Defendant.

TITLE OF FINAL DIVORCE PAPERS: Decree of Divorce.

RESIDENCY REQUIREMENTS AND WHERE TO FILE: The spouse filing for divorce must have been present in Hawaii for 3 months. However, a final divorce will not be granted unless one spouse has been a resident for 6 months. The divorce should be filed in either: (1) the judicial district where the plaintiff resides; or (2) the judicial district where the spouses last lived together. [Hawaii Revised Statutes; Title 580, Chapter 1].

LEGAL GROUNDS FOR DIVORCE: No-Fault: (1) irretrievable breakdown of the marriage; and (2) living separate and apart without cohabitation for 2 years and it would not be harsh or oppressive to the defendant spouse to grant the divorce. [Hawaii Revised Statutes; Title 580, Chapter 41].

General: Legal separation and there has been no reconciliation. [Hawaii Revised Statutes; Title 580, Chapter 41].

LEGAL SEPARATION: The spouse filing for separation must have been a resident for 3 months. Temporary legal separation may be granted for up to 2 years on the grounds that the marriage is temporarily disrupted. [Hawaii Revised Statutes; Titles 580, Chapter 1, 580, Chapter 71].

SIMPLIFIED OR SPECIAL DIVORCE PROCEDURES: The "irretrievable breakdown of the marriage" may be shown by both spouses stating so in an affidavit. The court, in such cases, may waive a hearing in uncontested divorces. [Hawaii Revised Statutes; Title 580, Section 42].

MEDIATION OR COUNSELING REQUIREMENTS: If one of the spouses denies that there has been an irretrievable breakdown of the marriage, the court may delay the proceedings for 60 days and advise the spouses to seek counseling. [Hawaii Revised Statutes; Title 580, Chapter 42].

PROPERTY DISTRIBUTION: Hawaii is an "equitable distribution" state. The court will distribute all of the spouse's property, including the community, joint, and separate property, in a just and equitable manner, based on the following factors: (1) the burdens imposed upon either spouse for the benefit of the children; (2) the position each spouse will be left in after the divorce; (3) the relative abilities of the spouses; (4) the respective merits of the spouses; and (5) all other circumstances. [Hawaii Revised Statutes; Title 580, Chapter 47].

ALIMONY/MAINTENANCE/SPOUSAL SUPPORT: The court may award either spouse maintenance, for either an indefinite period or a specific period to allow the receiving spouse to become self-supporting. Marital misconduct is not a factor to be considered. The factors to be considered are: (1) the standard of living established during the marriage; (2) the duration of the marriage; (3) the ability of the spouse from whom support is sought to meet his or her needs while meeting those of the spouse seeking support; (4) the ability of the spouse seeking maintenance to meet his or her needs independently; (5) the comparative financial resources of the spouses; (6) the needs and obligations of each spouse; (7) the age of the spouses; (8) the physical and emotional conditions of the spouses; (9) the usual occupation of the spouses during the marriage; (10) the vocational skills and employability of the spouse seeking support and maintenance; (11) the probable duration of the need of the spouse seeking support and maintenance; (12) any custodial and child support responsibilities; and (13) any other factor which measures the financial condition in which the spouses will be left in as a result of any award of maintenance. [Hawaii Revised Statutes; Title 580, Chapter 47].

SPOUSE'S NAME: If requested, the wife may resume the use of her maiden name. [Hawaii Revised Statutes; Title 574, Chapter 5].

CHILD CUSTODY: Joint or sole child custody may be awarded to either or both of the parents based on the best interests of the child and upon the wishes of the child, if the child is of sufficient age and capacity to form an intelligent choice. Joint custody will be allowed if it can be arranged to assure the child of continuing contact with both parents. There are no other specific factors for consideration set out in the statute. [Hawaii Revised Statutes; Title 571, Chapter 46].

CHILD SUPPORT: The court may order either or both parents to provide child support in a just and equitable manner. There are no other specific factors for consideration set out in the statute. [Hawaii Revised Statutes; Title 580, Chapter 47].

APPENDIX: DIVORCE LAWS OF ALL 50 STATES

IDAHO

NAME OF COURT IN WHICH TO FILE FOR DIVORCE: District Court. " In the District Court of the _____ Judicial District for the State of Idaho, In and For the County of _____."

TITLE OF DIVORCE ACTION: Complaint for Divorce.

NAME USED TO DESCRIBE SPOUSE FILING FOR DIVORCE: Plaintiff.

NAME USED TO DESCRIBE OTHER SPOUSE IN DIVORCE: Defendant.

TITLE OF FINAL DIVORCE PAPERS: Decree of Divorce.

RESIDENCY REQUIREMENTS AND WHERE TO FILE: The spouse filing for divorce must have been a resident of Idaho for 6 full weeks immediately prior to filing for divorce. The divorce should be filed in: (1) the county where the defendant resides; or (2) if the defendant is not a resident of Idaho, the county where the plaintiff resides or designates in the complaint. [Idaho Code; Title 5, Chapter 404; and Title 32, Chapter 701].

LEGAL GROUNDS FOR DIVORCE: No-Fault: (1) irreconcilable differences; and (2) living separate and apart without cohabitation for a period of 5 years. [Idaho Code; Title 32, Chapters 603, 610, and 626].

General: (1) adultery; (2) permanent insanity; (3) conviction of a felony; (4) willful desertion for 1 year; (5) cruelty; (6) willful neglect for 1 year; and (7) habitual intemperance (drunkenness). [Idaho Code; Title 32, Chapters 603 to 610].

LEGAL SEPARATION: There is no legal provision in Idaho for legal court-ordered separation. However, the spouses may live separate and apart. [Idaho Code; Title 32, Chapter 610].

SIMPLIFIED OR SPECIAL DIVORCE PROCEDURES: Divorces may be granted upon the default of the defendant. In addition, marital settlement agreements regarding property are specifically authorized. They must be in writing and notarized in the same manner as deeds. If the marital settlement agreement has any provisions which concern real estate, it must be recorded in the county recorder's office. [Idaho Code; Title 32, Chapters 917 and 918].

MEDIATION OR COUNSELING REQUIREMENTS: There is a mandatory 20-day delay in the granting of all divorces, unless there is an agreement by the spouses. During this period, either spouse may request that there be a meeting held to determine if there is any practical chance for reconciliation. If there is determined to be a chance for reconciliation and there are minor children of the marriage, the court may delay the proceedings for up to 90 days for an attempt at reconciliation. [Idaho Code; Title 32, Chapter 716].

PROPERTY DISTRIBUTION: Idaho is a "community property" state. Each spouse's separate property consists of (1) all property acquired prior to the marriage; (2) property acquired by gift either before or during the marriage; and (3) property acquired by individual gift before or during the marriage. The court will divide all other property (the community property) of the spouses in a substantially equal manner, unless there are compelling reasons to provide otherwise. The court will consider the following factors: (1) any marital misconduct, (2) the length of the marriage; (3) the age and health of the spouses; (4) the occupation of the spouses; (5) the amount and sources of income of the spouses; (6) the vocational skills of the spouses; (7) the employability of the spouses; (8) any premarital agreement; (9) the present and potential earning capability of each spouse; (10) any retirement benefits, including social security, civil service, military and railroad retirement benefits; (11) the liabilities of the spouses; (12) the needs of the spouses; and (13) whether the property award is in stead of or in addition to maintenance. [Idaho Code; Title 32, Chapters 712 and 903].

DIVORCE YOURSELF

ALIMONY/MAINTENANCE/SPOUSAL SUPPORT: Marital misconduct is a complete bar to an award of maintenance. The court may award maintenance to the innocent spouse, if that spouse (1) lacks sufficient property to provide for his or her reasonable needs; and (2) is unable to support his or herself through employment. The award of maintenance is based on the following factors: (1) the time necessary to acquire sufficient education and training to enable the spouse to find appropriate employment, and that spouse's future earning capacity; (2) the duration of the marriage; (3) the ability of the spouse from whom support is sought to meet his or her needs while meeting those of the spouse seeking support; (4) the financial resources of the spouse seeking maintenance, including marital property apportioned to such spouse and such spouse's ability to meet his or her needs independently; (5) the tax consequences to each spouse; (6) the age of the spouses; and (7) the physical and emotional conditions of the spouses. [Idaho Code; Title 32, Chapter 705].

SPOUSE'S NAME: There is no legal provision in Idaho for restoration of a spouse's name upon divorce. However, there is a general statutory provision that allows a person to apply for a name change by petition to the court. [Idaho Code; Title 7, Chapter 801-4].

CHILD CUSTODY: Joint or sole child custody may be awarded according to the best interests of the child, and based on the following factors: (1) the preference of the child; (2) the wishes of the parents; (3) the mental and physical health of all individuals involved; (4) the relationship of the child with parents, siblings, and other significant family members; (5) the child's adjustment to his or her home, school, and community; and (6) a need to promote continuity and stability in the life of the child. Joint custody is allowed if it can be arranged to assure the child with frequent and continuing contact with both parents. Unless shown otherwise, it is presumed that joint custody is in the best interests of the child. [Idaho Code; Title 31, Chapter 1101+ and Title 32, Chapters 717 and 717B].

CHILD SUPPORT: The court may order either or both parents to provide child support, without regard to marital misconduct, and based upon the following factors: (1) the financial resources of the child; (2) the standard of living the child would have enjoyed if the marriage had not been dissolved; (3) the physical and emotional conditions and educational needs of the child; (4) the financial resources, needs, and obligations of both the noncustodial and the custodial parent; (5) the availability of reasonable medical insurance coverage for the child; (6) and the actual tax benefits achieved by the parent claiming the federal dependency exemption for income tax purposes. There are provisions in Idaho for child support payments to be paid to the clerk of the court unless otherwise ordered by the court. [Idaho Code; Title 32, Chapters 706 and 710].

APPENDIX: DIVORCE LAWS OF ALL 50 STATES

ILLINOIS

NAME OF COURT IN WHICH TO FILE FOR DIVORCE: Circuit Court. "In the Circuit Court of the _____ Judicial District, _____ County, Illinois." [Illinois Civil Practice Act].

TITLE OF DIVORCE ACTION: Petition for Dissolution of Marriage. "In Re the Marriage of _____ and _____".

NAME USED TO DESCRIBE SPOUSE FILING FOR DISSOLUTION OF MARRIAGE: Petitioner.

NAME USED TO DESCRIBE OTHER SPOUSE IN DISSOLUTION OF MARRIAGE: Respondent.

TITLE OF FINAL DISSOLUTION OF MARRIAGE PAPERS: Judgement for Dissolution of Marriage.

RESIDENCY REQUIREMENTS AND WHERE TO FILE: The spouse filing for dissolution must have been a resident of Illinois for 90 days immediately prior to filing for dissolution of marriage. The dissolution of marriage may be filed in a county where either spouse resides. [Illinois Annotated Statutes; Chapter 40, Paragraphs 104 and 401].

LEGAL GROUNDS FOR DISSOLUTION OF MARRIAGE: No-Fault: Irreconcilable differences has caused the irretrievable breakdown of the marriage *and* reconciliation has failed or further attempts at reconciliation are impractical *and* the spouses have been living separate and apart without cohabitation for 2 years. (If both spouses consent, the time period becomes 6 months). [Illinois Annotated Statutes; Chapter 40, Paragraph 401].

General: (1) impotence; (2) adultery; (3) habitual drunkenness for 2 years and/or drug addiction; (4) conviction of a felony; (5) willful desertion for 1 year; (6) cruel and inhuman treatment; (7) attempted poisoning or otherwise endangering the life of the spouse; (8) infection of the other spouse with a communicable disease; and (9) bigamy. [Illinois Annotated Statutes; Chapter 40, Paragraph 401].

LEGAL SEPARATION: The residency requirement specified in the statute is that an action for legal separation must be brought where the Respondent resides. Any person living separate and apart from his or her spouse, without fault, may obtain a legal separation with provisions for reasonable support and maintenance. [Illinois Annotated Statutes; Chapter 40, Paragraph 402].

SIMPLIFIED OR SPECIAL DISSOLUTION OF MARRIAGE PROCEDURES: Marital settlement agreements are specifically allowed and encouraged. [Illinois Annotated Statutes; Chapter 40, Paragraph 502].

MEDIATION OR COUNSELING REQUIREMENTS: At the request of either spouse, or on the court's own initiative, the court may order a conciliation conference if it is felt that there is a prospect of reconciliation. [Illinois Annotated Statutes; Chapter 40, Paragraph 404].

PROPERTY DISTRIBUTION: Illinois is an "equitable distribution" state. Each spouse retains the non-marital (separate) property that he or she owned prior to the marriage and any property acquired by gift or inheritance during the marriage. The court will distribute all other marital property, without regard to fault, considering the following factors: (1) the contribution of each spouse to the acquisition or dissipation of the marital property, including the contribution of each spouse as homemaker or to the family unit; (2) the value of each spouse's non-marital property; (3) the economic circumstances of each spouse at the time the division of property is to become effective, including the desirability of awarding the family home to the spouse having custody of the children; (4) the length of the marriage; (5) the age and health of the spouses; (6) the occupation of the spouses; (7) the amount and sources of income of the spouses; (8) the vocational skills of the spouses; (9) the employability of the spouses; (10) the estate, liabilities, and needs of each spouse and the opportunity of each for further acquisition of capital assets and income; (11) the federal income tax consequences of the court's division of the property; (12) any premarital agreement;

(13) liabilities of the spouses; (14) whether the property award is in stead of or in addition to maintenance; and (15) any custodial provisions for the children. [Illinois Annotated Statutes; Chapter 40, Paragraph 503].

ALIMONY/MAINTENANCE/SPOUSAL SUPPORT: The court may award maintenance to either spouse for a period of time it considers just, if the court concludes that the spouse seeking maintenance is (1) unable to support him or herself through appropriate employment or is the custodian of a child whose condition or circumstances make it appropriate that he or she not be required to seek employment outside the home; and (2) lacks sufficient resources, including any marital property, to provide for his or her reasonable needs; or (3) is otherwise without sufficient income. Marital fault is not a factor. The factors to be considered are: (1) the time necessary to acquire sufficient education and training to enable the spouse to find appropriate employment; (2) the standard of living established during the marriage; (3) the duration of the marriage; (4) the age of the spouses; (5) the physical and emotional conditions of the spouses (6) the ability of the spouse from whom support is sought to meet his or her needs while meeting those of the spouse seeking support; (7) the financial resources of the spouse seeking maintenance, including marital property apportioned to such spouse and such spouse's ability to meet his or her needs independently; (8) the tax consequences to each spouse; and (9) any custodial and child support responsibilities. [Illinois Annotated Statutes; Chapter 40, Paragraph 504].

SPOUSE'S NAME: Upon the wife's request, her maiden or former name will be restored. [Illinois Annotated Statutes; Chapter 40, Paragraph 413]

CHILD CUSTODY: Sole or joint custody may be awarded, based upon the best interests of the child and upon the following factors: (1) preference of the child; (2) the wishes of the parents; (3) the child's adjustment to his or her home, school, and community; (4) the mental and physical health of all individuals involved; (5) the relationship of the child with parents, siblings, and other significant family members; and (6) any history of violence between the parents. Marital misconduct that does not directly affect the parent's relationship with the child is not to be considered. There is a presumption that the maximum involvement and cooperation of the parent's is in the best interests of the child.

For an award of joint custody, the court will also consider the following factors: (1) the ability of the parents to cooperate effectively and consistently; (2) the residential circumstances of each parent; (3) any agreement between the parents; and (4) any other relevant factor. [Illinois Annotated Statutes; Chapter 40, Paragraphs 602, 602.1, 603.1, and 610].

CHILD SUPPORT: Either or both parents may be ordered to pay reasonable and necessary child support, without regard to marital fault or misconduct. The following factors are considered: (1) the financial resources of the child; (2) the standard of living the child would have enjoyed if the marriage had not been dissolved; (3) the physical and emotional conditions and educational needs of the child; and (4) the financial resources, needs, and obligations of both the noncustodial and the custodial parent. Support payments may be ordered to be paid directly to the clerk of the court. There are guidelines for the amount of support contained in the statute. [Illinois Annotated Statutes; Chapter 40, Paragraphs 505 and 507].

APPENDIX: DIVORCE LAWS OF ALL 50 STATES

INDIANA

NAME OF COURT IN WHICH TO FILE FOR DIVORCE: Superior Court, Circuit Court, or Domestic Relations Court. "_____ Court of _____ County, Indiana." [Annotated Indiana Code; Title 31, Article 1, Chapter 23-10].

TITLE OF DIVORCE ACTION: Petition for Dissolution of Marriage. "In Re the Marriage of _____ and _____."

NAME USED TO DESCRIBE SPOUSE FILING FOR DISSOLUTION OF MARRIAGE: Petitioner.

NAME USED TO DESCRIBE OTHER SPOUSE IN DISSOLUTION OF MARRIAGE: Respondent.

TITLE OF FINAL DISSOLUTION OF MARRIAGE PAPERS: Final Dissolution of Marriage Decree.

RESIDENCY REQUIREMENTS AND WHERE TO FILE: One of the spouses must have been a resident of the state for 6 months and the county in which the petition is filed for 3 months immediately prior to filing for dissolution of marriage. [Annotated Indiana Code; Title 31, Article 1, Chapter 11.5-5.6].

LEGAL GROUNDS FOR DISSOLUTION OF MARRIAGE: No-Fault: Irretrievable breakdown of the marriage. [Annotated Indiana Code; Title 31, Article 1, Chapter 11.5-5.3].

General: (1) impotence; (2) conviction of a felony; and (3) incurable mental illness for 2 years. [Annotated Indiana Code; Title 31, Article 1, Chapter 11.5-5.3].

LEGAL SEPARATION: One of the spouses must have been a resident of the state for 6 months and the county for 3 months immediately prior to filing for legal separation. A legal separation may be granted on the grounds that it is currently intolerable for the spouses to live together. [Annotated Indiana Code; Titles 31, Article 1, Chapters 11.5-5.3 and 11.5-5.6].

SIMPLIFIED OR SPECIAL DISSOLUTION OF MARRIAGE PROCEDURES: The court may enter a summary dissolution decree without holding a court hearing in all cases in which the following requirements have been met: (1) 60 days have elapsed since the filing of a petition for dissolution; (2) the petition was verified and signed by both spouses; (3) the petition contained a written waiver of a final hearing; (4) the petition contained either (a) a statement that there are no contested issues, or (b) that the spouses have made a written agreement in settlement of any contested issues. If there are some remaining contested issues, the court may hold a final hearing on those remaining contested issues. In addition, marital settlement agreements are specifically authorized in Indiana. [Annotated Indiana Code; Title 31, Article 1, Chapters 11.5-8 and 11.5-10].

MEDIATION OR COUNSELING REQUIREMENTS: Upon the request of either spouse or if the court believes that there is a reasonable possibility of reconciliation, the dissolution of marriage proceedings may be delayed for up to 45 days and the spouses may be ordered to seek counseling. [Annotated Indiana Code; Title 31, Article 1, Chapter 11.5-8].

PROPERTY DISTRIBUTION: Indiana is an "equitable distribution" state. The court will divide all of the spouse's property in a just manner, whether jointly or separately owned and whether acquired before or after the marriage, including any gifts or inheritances. There is a presumption that an equal division is just and reasonable. Marital fault is not a factor. The following factors are considered: (1) the contribution of each spouse to the acquisition of the marital property, regardless whether the contribution was income-producing; (2) the economic circumstances of each spouse at the time the division of property is to become effective, including the desirability of awarding the family residence to the spouse having custody of the children; (3) the actual earnings and the present and potential earning capability of each spouse; (4) the extent to which the property was acquired by each spouse prior to marriage or through gift or inheritance; and (5) the conduct of the spouses during the marriage as it relates to the disposition of their property. If there is insufficient marital property, the court may award money to either spouse as reimbursement for the financial contribution by one spouse toward the higher education of the other. [Annotated Indiana Code; Title 31, Article 1, Chapter 11.5-11].

ALIMONY/MAINTENANCE/SPOUSAL SUPPORT: Maintenance will be awarded to a spouse who: (1) is physically or mentally incapacitated to the extent that they are unable to support themselves; or (2) lacks sufficient property to provide support for his or herself and any incapacitated child and must forgo employment to care for the physically or mentally incapacitated child. Marital fault is not a factor. In addition, rehabilitative maintenance may be granted to a spouse for up to 3 years, based on the following factors: (1) the time and expense necessary to acquire sufficient education and training to enable the spouse to find appropriate employment; (2) the educational level of each spouse at the time of the marriage and at the time the action is commenced; (3) whether an interruption in the education, training, or employment of a spouse who is seeking maintenance occurred during the marriage as a result of homemaking or child care responsibilities, or both; (4) the earning capacity of each spouse, including educational background, training, employment skills, work experience, and length of presence or absence from the job market. [Annotated Indiana Code; Title 31, Article 1, Chapter 11.5-11].

SPOUSE'S NAME: Upon request, the wife's former name may be restored. [Annotated Indiana Code; Title 31, Article 1, Chapter 11.5-18].

CHILD CUSTODY: Joint or sole custody is granted based on the best interests of the child, and based upon the following factors: (1) the age and sex of the child; (2) the preference of the child; (3) the wishes of the parents; (4) the child's adjustment to his or her home, school, and community; (5) the mental and physical health of all individuals involved; and (6) the relationship of the child with parents, siblings, and other significant family members.

Joint custody may be awarded if it is in the best interest of the child and based upon the following factors: (1) the physical proximity of the parents to each other as this relates to the practical considerations of where the child will reside; (2) the fitness and suitability of the parents; (3) the nature of the physical and emotional environment in the home of each of the persons awarded joint custody; (4) the willingness and ability of the persons awarded joint custody to communicate and cooperate in advancing the child's welfare; (5) the wishes of the child; and (6) whether the child has established a close and beneficial relationship with both of the persons awarded joint custody. [Annotated Indiana Code; Titles 31, Article 1, Chapter 11.5-21].

CHILD SUPPORT: Either parent may be ordered to pay reasonable child support, without regard to marital fault, based on the following factors: (1) the standard of living the child would have enjoyed if the marriage had not been dissolved; (2) the physical and emotional conditions and educational needs of the child; and (3) the financial resources, needs, and obligations of both the noncustodial and the custodial parent. Support may be ordered to include medical, hospital, dental and educational support. Support payments may be required to be paid through the clerk of the court. Specific Indiana Child Support Guidelines are contained in the Appendix to Title 31, Article 1, Chapter 11.5-12 of the Annotated Indiana Code. These guidelines, however, are not mandatory. [Annotated Indiana Code; Title 31, Article 1, Chapter 11.5-12].

APPENDIX: DIVORCE LAWS OF ALL 50 STATES

IOWA

NAME OF COURT IN WHICH TO FILE FOR DIVORCE: District Court. "In the District Court for the County of _____, Iowa." [Iowa Code Annotated; Section 598.4].

TITLE OF DIVORCE ACTION: Petition for Dissolution of Marriage. "In Re the Marriage of _____ and _____".

NAME USED TO DESCRIBE SPOUSE FILING FOR DISSOLUTION OF MARRIAGE: Petitioner.

NAME USED TO DESCRIBE OTHER SPOUSE IN DISSOLUTION OF MARRIAGE: Respondent.

TITLE OF FINAL DISSOLUTION OF MARRIAGE PAPERS: Decree of Dissolution of Marriage.

RESIDENCY REQUIREMENTS AND WHERE TO FILE: If the defendant spouse is a resident of Iowa and was personally served the dissolution of marriage papers, there is no residency requirement for the spouse filing the dissolution of marriage. Otherwise, there is a 1 year residency requirement. In addition, there is a 90-day waiting period prior to the dissolution of marriage becoming final. The dissolution of marriage may be filed in a county where either spouse resides. [Iowa Code Annotated; Sections 598.2 and 598.6].

LEGAL GROUNDS FOR DISSOLUTION OF MARRIAGE: No-Fault: Breakdown of the marriage relationship to the extent that the legitimate objects of matrimony have been destroyed and there remains no reasonable likelihood that the marriage can be preserved. [Iowa Code Annotated; Sections 598.5 and 598.17].

General: The only grounds for dissolution of marriage in Iowa are that there has been a breakdown of the marriage relationship to the extent that the legitimate objects of matrimony have been destroyed and there remains no reasonable likelihood that the marriage can be preserved. [Iowa Code Annotated; Sections 598.5 and 598.17].

LEGAL SEPARATION: If the defendant spouse is a resident of Iowa and was personally served legal papers, there is no residency requirement for the spouse filing the legal separation. Otherwise, there is a one-year residency requirement. The grounds for legal separation in Iowa are that there has been a breakdown of the marriage relationship to the extent that the legitimate objects of matrimony have been destroyed and there remains no reasonable likelihood that the marriage can be preserved. [Iowa Code Annotated; Sections 598.5, 598.6, 598.17, and 598.28].

SIMPLIFIED OR SPECIAL DISSOLUTION OF MARRIAGE PROCEDURES: There are no legal provisions in Iowa for simplified dissolution of marriage. However, sample petition captions and contents are contained in Iowa Code Annotated; Sections 598.4 and 598.5.

MEDIATION OR COUNSELING REQUIREMENTS: If either spouse requests, or on the court's own initiative, the spouses may be ordered to participate in conciliation procedures for a period of 60 days. [Iowa Code Annotated; Section 598.16].

PROPERTY DISTRIBUTION: Iowa is an "equitable distribution" state. The court will divide all of the spouse's property whether it was acquired before or after the marriage, except any gifts any inheritances received prior to or during the marriage. A portion of the property may be set aside in a fund for the support, maintenance, and education of any minor children. Marital fault is not a factor. The following factors are considered in any division of property: (1) the contribution of each spouse to the acquisition of the marital property, including the contribution of each spouse as homemaker or in child care; (2) the value of any property brought to the marriage; (3) the contribution by one party to the education, training, or increased earning capacity of the other; (4) the length of the marriage; (5) the age and physical and emotional health of the spouses; (6) the vocational skills of the spouses; (7) the employability of the spouses;

DIVORCE YOURSELF

(8) the federal income tax consequences of the court's division of the property; (9) the time and expense necessary for a spouse to acquire sufficient education to enable the spouse to find appropriate employment; (10) any premarital or marital settlement agreement; (11) the present and potential earning capability of each spouse, including educational background, training, employment skills, work experience, and length of absence from the job market; (12) whether the property award is in stead of or in addition to alimony and the amount and duration of any such alimony award; (13) the total economic circumstances of the spouses, including any pension benefits; (14) the desirability of awarding the family home to the spouse with custody of any children; and (15) any custodial provisions for the children. [Iowa Code Annotated; Section 598.21].

ALIMONY/MAINTENANCE/SPOUSAL SUPPORT: Alimony may be granted to either spouse for a limited or indefinite time, based on the following factors: (1) the time necessary to acquire sufficient education and training to enable the spouse to find appropriate employment and become self-supporting; (2) the standard of living established during the marriage; (3) the duration of the marriage; (4) the financial resources of the spouse seeking alimony, including marital property apportioned to such spouse and such spouse's ability to meet his or her needs independently; (5) the tax consequences to each spouse; (6) the age of the spouses; (7) the physical and emotional conditions of the spouses; (8) the work experience and length of absence from the job market of the spouse seeking alimony; (9) the vocational skills and employability of the spouse seeking support and alimony; (10) the probable duration of the need of the spouse seeking support and alimony; (11) custodial and child support responsibilities; (12) the educational level of each spouse at the time of the marriage and at the time the action for support is commenced; (13) any premarital or other agreements; and (14) any other factor the court deems just and equitable. Marital misconduct is not a factor. Alimony payments may be ordered to be paid through the court. [Iowa Code Annotated; Sections 598.21, 598.22, and 598.32].

SPOUSE'S NAME: Upon dissolution of marriage, either spouse may request to change his or her name to a former or maiden name. [Iowa Code Annotated; Section 598.37].

CHILD CUSTODY: Joint or sole custody may be awarded in the best interests of the child and in a manner which will encourage the parents to share the rights and responsibilities of raising the child. Joint custody may be awarded if either parent requests and if it is in the best interests of the child and based on the following factors: (1) the ability of the parents to cooperate and make decisions jointly; (2) the ability of the parents to encourage the sharing of love, affection, and contact between the child and the other parent; (3) the physical proximity of the parents to each other as this relates to the practical considerations of where the child will reside; (4) the fitness and suitability of the parents; (5) the reasonable preference of the child, if the court deems the child to be of sufficient intelligence, understanding, and experience to express a preference; (6) whether both parents have actively cared for the child before and since the separation; (7) whether the psychological and emotional needs and development of the child will suffer because of lack of contact with both parents; (8) whether the safety of the child will be jeopardized by an award of joint custody or unsupervised visitation; and (9) whether one or both parents agree to, or are opposed to, joint custody. [Iowa Code Annotated; Section 598.41].

CHILD SUPPORT: Either or both parents may be ordered to pay a reasonable and necessary amount of child support, based on a consideration of the following factors: (1) the child's need for close contact with both parents; (2) the recognition of joint parental responsibilities for the welfare of the child; (3) the financial resources of the child; (4) the physical and emotional conditions and educational needs of the child; (5) the financial resources, needs, and obligations of both the noncustodial and the custodial parent; (6) the desirability of the parent having either sole custody or physical care of the child remaining in the home as a full-time parent; (7) the cost of day care to the parent having custody or physical care of the child if that parent works outside the home, or the value of the child care services performed by that parent if the parent remains in the home; (8) the tax consequences to each parent; (9) the standard of living the child would have enjoyed if the marriage had not been dissolved; and (10) any other relevant factors. Child support payments may be ordered to be paid directly to the court. Specific Child Support Guidelines for temporary support are contained in the Iowa Rules of the Court. [Iowa Code Annotated; Section 598.21 and Iowa Rules of the Court].

KANSAS

NAME OF COURT IN WHICH TO FILE FOR DIVORCE: District Court. "In the District Court in and for the County of _____, Kansas." [Kansas Statutes Annotated; Chapter 60, Article 16, Subject 1601].

TITLE OF DIVORCE ACTION: Petition for Divorce.

NAME USED TO DESCRIBE SPOUSE FILING FOR DIVORCE: Petitioner.

NAME USED TO DESCRIBE OTHER SPOUSE IN DIVORCE: Respondent.

TITLE OF FINAL DIVORCE PAPERS: Decree of Divorce.

RESIDENCY REQUIREMENTS AND WHERE TO FILE: Either spouse must have been a resident of Kansas for 60 days immediately before filing for divorce. The divorce may be filed for in a county where either spouse resides. [Kansas Statutes Annotated; Chapter 60, Article 16, Subjects 607 and 1603].

LEGAL GROUNDS FOR DIVORCE: No-Fault: Incompatibility. [Kansas Statutes Annotated; Chapter 60, Article 16, Subject 1601].

General: (1) failure to perform a marital duty or obligation; and (2) incompatibility due to mental illness. [Kansas Statutes Annotated; Chapter 60, Article 16, Subject 1601].

LEGAL SEPARATION: Either spouse must have been a resident of Kansas for 60 days immediately before filing for legal separation. The grounds for legal separation are: (1) incompatibility; (2) failure to perform a marital duty or obligation; and (3) incompatibility due to mental illness. [Kansas Statutes Annotated; Chapter 60, Article 16, Subjects 1601 and 1603].

SIMPLIFIED OR SPECIAL DIVORCE PROCEDURES: Only one spouse need testify as to the facts in the divorce. In addition, marital settlement agreements are specifically authorized. [Kansas Statutes Annotated; Chapter 60, Article 16, Subjects 1609 and 1610].

MEDIATION OR COUNSELING REQUIREMENTS: On either spouse's request, or on its own initiative, the court may require that the spouses seek marriage counseling if marriage counseling services are available in the judicial district where the divorce is sought. [Kansas Statutes Annotated; Chapter 60, Article 16, Subjects 1608 and 1617].

PROPERTY DISTRIBUTION: Kansas is an "equitable distribution" state. The court may divide all of the spouse's property, including: (1) any gifts and inheritances, (2) any property owned before the marriage, (3) any property acquired in a spouse's own right during the marriage, and (4) any property acquired by the spouse's joint efforts. Property distribution may include actual division of the property, an award of all or part of the property to one spouse with a just and reasonable payment to the other, or a sale of the property and a division of the proceeds. The court considers the following factors: (1) the value of each spouse's personal property; (2) the length of the marriage; (3) the age and health of the spouses; (4) whether the property award is in stead of or in addition to maintenance; (5) how and by whom the property was acquired; (6) the conduct of the spouses during the marriage as it relates to the disposition of their property; (7) the present and future earning capacity of the spouses; (8) family ties and obligations; and (9) any other factor necessary to do equity and justice between the spouses. [Kansas Statutes Annotated; Chapter 60, Article 16, Subject 1610].

ALIMONY/MAINTENANCE/SPOUSAL SUPPORT: Either spouse may be awarded maintenance for a period of up to 121 months. After 121 months, the recipient may apply for an extension of one more 121-month period. The amount awarded is whatever is judged to be fair, just, and equitable. There are no specific statutory factors for consideration. Marital fault is not a factor to be considered. Payments are to

DIVORCE YOURSELF

be made through the clerk of the court or through the court trustee. [Kansas Statutes Annotated; Chapter 60, Article 16, Subject 1610].

SPOUSE'S NAME: Upon a spouse's request, a wife's maiden name will be restored. [Kansas Statutes Annotated; Chapter 60, Article 16, Subject 1610].

CHILD CUSTODY: If the parents have entered into a written agreement regarding child custody, the court will approve it if it is in the best interests of the child. Where there is no agreement, the court may award joint or sole custody based on the best interests of the child and upon the following factors: (1) the length of time and circumstances under which the child may have been under the care of someone other than a parent; (2) preference of the child; (3) the wishes of the parents; (4) the child's adjustment to his or her home, school, and community; (5) the relationship of the child with parents, siblings, and other significant family members; and (6) the willingness of each parent to respect and appreciate the bond between the child and the other parent. There is to be no preference given based on the sex of the parent. Joint custody may be awarded if the court finds both parents suitable and there has been a joint custody plan submitted by the parents. [Kansas Statutes Annotated; Chapter 60, Article 16, Subject 1610(a)(3)].

CHILD SUPPORT: Either or both parents may be ordered to pay child support, without regard to any marital misconduct, based on the following factors: (1) the financial resources of the child; (2) the physical and emotional conditions and educational needs of the child; and (3) the financial resources, needs, and obligations of both the noncustodial and the custodial parent. Child support payments are to be paid through the clerk of the court or through the court trustee, unless the court orders otherwise. There are specific Supreme Court Child Support Guidelines contained in Kansas Statutes Annotated Chapter 20, Subject 165. [Kansas Statutes Annotated; Chapter 20, Subject 165 and Chapter 60, Article 16, Subject 1610].

APPENDIX: DIVORCE LAWS OF ALL 50 STATES

KENTUCKY

NAME OF COURT IN WHICH TO FILE FOR DIVORCE: Circuit Court. "_____ Circuit Court, Kentucky." [Kentucky Rules of Civil Procedure].

TITLE OF DIVORCE ACTION: Petition for Dissolution of Marriage. "In Re the Marriage of _____ and _____."

NAME USED TO DESCRIBE SPOUSE FILING FOR DISSOLUTION OF MARRIAGE: Petitioner.

NAME USED TO DESCRIBE OTHER SPOUSE IN DISSOLUTION OF MARRIAGE: Respondent.

TITLE OF FINAL DISSOLUTION OF MARRIAGE PAPERS: Decree of Dissolution of Marriage.

RESIDENCY REQUIREMENTS AND WHERE TO FILE: The spouse filing for dissolution of marriage must have been a resident (or a member of the armed services stationed in Kentucky) for 180 days prior to filing. The dissolution of marriage may be filed in a county where either spouse usually resides. [Kentucky Revised Statutes; Title 35, Chapters 403.140 and 452.470].

LEGAL GROUNDS FOR DISSOLUTION OF MARRIAGE: No-Fault: Irretrievable breakdown of the marriage. A final dissolution of marriage will not be granted until the spouses have lived apart for 60 days. ("Living apart" includes living in the same house but not sharing sex). [Kentucky Revised Statutes; Title 35, Chapter 403.140].

General: Irretrievable breakdown of the marriage is the only grounds for dissolution of marriage in Kentucky. [Kentucky Revised Statutes; Title 35, Chapter 403.140].

LEGAL SEPARATION: Irretrievable breakdown of the marriage is the only grounds for legal separation (or divorce from bed and board) in Kentucky. The spouse filing for legal separation must have been a resident (or a member of the armed services stationed in Kentucky) for 180 days prior to filing. [Kentucky Revised Statutes; Title 35, Chapters 403.050 and 403.140].

SIMPLIFIED OR SPECIAL DISSOLUTION OF MARRIAGE PROCEDURES: Marital settlement agreements and separation agreements are specifically authorized. [Kentucky Revised Statutes; Title 35, Chapter 403.180]

MEDIATION OR COUNSELING REQUIREMENTS: If one spouse disagrees that the marriage is irretrievably broken, the court may delay the dissolution of marriage proceeding for 60 days and suggest the spouses seek counseling. In addition, at a spouse's request or on the courts own initiative, a conciliation conference may be ordered by the court. [Kentucky Revised Statutes; Title 35, Chapter 403.170].

PROPERTY DISTRIBUTION: Kentucky is an "equitable distribution" state. The spouses are allowed to keep their separate property (property acquired before the marriage and any gifts or inheritances). All other property (their marital property) is divided, without regard to any marital misconduct, in just proportions, based on the following factors: (1) the contribution of each spouse to the acquisition of the marital property, including the contribution of each spouse as homemaker; (2) the value of each spouse's separate property; (3) the economic circumstances of each spouse at the time the division of property is to become effective, including the desirability of awarding the family home to the spouse awarded custody of any children; (4) the length of the marriage; and (5) any retirement benefits. [Kentucky Revised Statutes; Title 35, Chapter 403.190].

ALIMONY/MAINTENANCE/SPOUSAL SUPPORT: Either spouse may be awarded maintenance if: (1) that spouse lacks the property to provide for his or her own needs; and (2) that spouse is unable to find appropriate employment, or is unable to work because of obligations to care for children or others in his or her custody. Marital fault is not a factor to be considered. The award is then based on the following factors: (1) the time necessary to acquire sufficient education and training to enable the spouse to find appropriate employment, and that spouse's future earning capacity; (2) the standard of living established during the marriage; (3) the duration of the marriage; (4) the ability of the spouse from whom support is sought to meet his or her needs while meeting those of the spouse seeking support; (5) the financial resources of the spouse seeking maintenance, including marital property apportioned to such spouse and such spouse's ability to meet his or her needs independently and any share of a child support award intended for the custodian; and (6) the physical and emotional conditions of the spouses. [Kentucky Revised Statutes; Title 35, Chapter 403.200].

SPOUSE'S NAME: If there are no children, and at the wife's request, the wife's maiden name may be restored. [Kentucky Revised Statutes; Title 35, Chapter 403.230].

CHILD CUSTODY: The court may award sole or joint custody, giving equal consideration to either spouse. Custody is awarded based on the best interests of the child and on the following factors: (1) preference of the child; (2) the wishes of the parents; (3) the child's adjustment to his or her home, school, and community; (4) the mental and physical health of all individuals involved; and (5) the relationship of the child with parents, siblings, and other significant family members. Any conduct of a parent which does not affect the relationship with the child is not to be considered. Abandonment of the family home by a parent is not to be considered if the parent fled due to physical harm or threats of physical harm by the other spouse. [Kentucky Revised Statutes; Title 35, Chapter 403.270].

CHILD SUPPORT: Either or both parents may be ordered to provide a reasonable amount of child support, without regard to any marital misconduct, and based on the following factors: (1) the financial resources of the child; (2) the standard of living the child would have enjoyed if the marriage had not been dissolved; (3) the physical and emotional conditions and educational needs of the child; and (4) the financial resources, needs, and obligations of both the noncustodial and the custodial parent. [Kentucky Revised Statutes; Title 35, Chapter 403.210].

APPENDIX: DIVORCE LAWS OF ALL 50 STATES

LOUISIANA

NAME OF COURT IN WHICH TO FILE FOR DIVORCE: District Court. "_____ Judicial District Court, Parish of _____, Louisiana." [Louisiana Code of Civil Procedure].

TITLE OF DIVORCE ACTION: Petition for Dissolution of Marriage.

NAME USED TO DESCRIBE SPOUSE FILING FOR DISSOLUTION OF MARRIAGE: Petitioner/Plaintiff.

NAME USED TO DESCRIBE OTHER SPOUSE IN DISSOLUTION OF MARRIAGE: Respondent/Defendant.

TITLE OF FINAL DISSOLUTION OF MARRIAGE PAPERS: Judgement of Dissolution of Marriage.

RESIDENCY REQUIREMENTS AND WHERE TO FILE: The spouse filing for dissolution of marriage must have been a resident of Louisiana for 12 months prior to filing for dissolution of marriage. The dissolution of marriage must be filed in the parish of the respondent/defendant. [Louisiana Civil Code Annotated, Article 142; and Louisiana Code of Civil Procedure, Article 42].

LEGAL GROUNDS FOR DISSOLUTION OF MARRIAGE: No-Fault: (1) a legal separation after voluntarily living separate and apart without cohabitation for 6 months without reconciliation; (2) a legal separation after voluntarily living separate and apart without cohabitation for 6 months without reconciliation, if both spouses sign an affidavit that they have lived apart and that there are irreconcilable differences between them to such a degree that living together is insupportable and impossible. For dissolution of marriage actions based on (2), the description on the court papers should read: "In the Matter of _____, Petitioner, and _____, His or Her Spouse".[Louisiana Civil Code Annotated, Articles 138 and 139].

General: (1) adultery; (2) legal separation; and (3) conviction of a felony and a sentence of death or hard labor. [Louisiana Civil Code Annotated, Article 139].

LEGAL SEPARATION: The grounds for legal separation (separation from bed and board) in Louisiana are: (1) adultery; (2) abandonment; (3) conviction of a felony and has fled justice; (4) cruel and inhuman treatment; (5) endangering the life of the spouse; (6) irreconcilable differences and voluntary separation; (7) habitual intemperance (drunkenness); (8) voluntary separation; (9) separation caused by mental illness; (10) sentence to death, imprisonment, or hard labor; (11) public defamation; and (12) nonsupport whereby a spouse is able to provide support but grossly, wantonly, or cruelly refuses or neglects to provide suitable maintenance for the complaining spouse. If the grounds for legal separation have arisen in Louisiana, there is no residency requirement specified in the statute. If the grounds for legal separation arose outside the state, the spouse filing for legal separation must be a resident of Louisiana. [Louisiana Civil Code Annotated, Articles 138 and 142].

SIMPLIFIED OR SPECIAL DISSOLUTION OF MARRIAGE PROCEDURES: Each judicial district in Louisiana may have specific individual rules pertaining to dissolution of marriage actions. Please refer to the Louisiana Rules of Court for the rules in a particular judicial district.

MEDIATION OR COUNSELING REQUIREMENTS: There are no legal provisions in Louisiana for divorce mediation or counseling.

PROPERTY DISTRIBUTION: Louisiana is a "community property" state. A spouse's separate property, consisting of property acquired prior to the marriage and property acquired by gift or inheritance, is awarded to that spouse. The community property is divided equally between the spouses. Personal property necessary for the safety and well-being of the spouse filing for dissolution of marriage and any children in his or her custody (including food, eating utensils, clothing, and any other items necessary for their safety and well-being) will be awarded to the spouse filing. Either spouse may ask the court for use and occupancy of the family residence pending the final division of the community property. The court bases the temporary award of the family residence on the following factors: (1) the value of each spouse's personal property; (2) the economic circumstances of each spouse at the time the division of property is to become effective; and (3) needs of the children. [Louisiana Civil Code Annotated, Article 155].

ALIMONY/MAINTENANCE/SPOUSAL SUPPORT: During the dissolution of marriage proceeding, either spouse may be ordered to pay temporary alimony. Permanent periodic alimony may be granted to the spouse who is without fault and without sufficient means for support. Such alimony shall not exceed one-third of the other spouse's income unless the alimony is to be paid in a lump-sum payment. The factors considered are: (1) whether the spouse seeking support is the custodian of a child whose condition or circumstances make it appropriate for that spouse not to seek outside employment; (2) the time necessary to acquire sufficient education and training to enable the spouse to find appropriate employment, and that spouse's future earning capacity; (3) the financial resources of the spouse seeking alimony, including marital property apportioned to such spouse and such spouse's ability to meet his or her needs independently; (4) the comparative financial resources of the spouses, including their comparative earning abilities in the labor market; (5) the age of the spouses; (6) the physical and emotional conditions of the spouses; (7) the vocational skills and employability of the spouse seeking support and alimony; (8) the financial obligations and assets of the spouses; and (9) any custodial and child support responsibilities. [Louisiana Civil Code Annotated, Articles 141, 148, and 160].

SPOUSE'S NAME: There is no statutory provision in Louisiana for restoration of a spouse's name upon divorce. Case law notes the allowance of resumption of a wife's maiden name. In addtion, a person may generally petition the court for change of name. [Louisiana Statutes Annotated, Article 13-4751; and Louisiana Case Law].

CHILD CUSTODY: Joint or sole custody is awarded based on the best interests of the child. The following order of preference is established: (1) to both parents; (2) to either parent (without regard to race or sex of the parents); (3) to the person or persons with whom the child has been living; or (4) to any other person that the court feels suitable and able to provide an adequate and stable environment for the child. Unless shown otherwise, joint custody is presumed to be in the best interests of the child, and will be awarded based on the following factors: (1) physical, emotional, mental, religious, and social needs of the child; (2) capability and desire of each parent to meet the child's needs; (3) preference of the child, if the child is of sufficient age and capacity; (4) the love and affection existing between the child and each parent; (5) the length of time the child has lived in a stable, satisfactory environment and the desirability of maintaining continuity; (6) the desire and ability of each parent to allow an open and loving frequent relationship between the child and the other parent; (7) the wishes of the parents; (8) the child's adjustment to his or her home, school, and community; (9) the mental and physical health of all individuals involved; (10) the permanence as a family unit of the existing or proposed custodial home; (11) the distance between the potential residences; (12) and the moral fitness of the parents. The conduct of the proposed guardian is to be considered only as it bears on his or her relationship with the child. The parents must submit a plan for joint custody. [Louisiana Civil Code Annotated, Article 146].

CHILD SUPPORT: Both parents are obligated to support any children of a marriage. The factors for consideration listed in the statute are: (1) the needs of the child; and (2) the actual resources of each parent. [Louisiana Civil Code Annotated, Articles 146 and 158].

APPENDIX: DIVORCE LAWS OF ALL 50 STATES

MAINE

NAME OF COURT IN WHICH TO FILE FOR DIVORCE: District Court or Superior Court. "State of Maine, _____ Court, _____ County." [Maine Revised Statutes Annotated: Title 19, Sections 664 and 696].

TITLE OF DIVORCE ACTION: Complaint for Divorce.

NAME USED TO DESCRIBE SPOUSE FILING FOR DIVORCE: Plaintiff.

NAME USED TO DESCRIBE OTHER SPOUSE IN DIVORCE: Defendant.

TITLE OF FINAL DIVORCE PAPERS: Judgement of Divorce.

RESIDENCY REQUIREMENTS AND WHERE TO FILE: Either spouse must be a resident of Maine, or the marriage or the grounds for divorce must have occurred in Maine. Otherwise, a person filing for divorce must be a resident of Maine for 6 months immediately prior to filing. The divorce may be filed for in the District Court in the county where either spouse resides. However, the defendant spouse has the right to have the proceeding moved to Superior Court. [Maine Revised Statutes Annotated: Title 4, Section 155; and Title 19, Section 691].

LEGAL GROUNDS FOR DIVORCE: No-Fault: Irreconcilable marital differences. [Maine Revised Statutes Annotated: Title 19, Section 691(1)].

General: (1) impotence; (2) adultery; (3) alcoholism and/or drug addiction; (4) confinement for incurable insanity for 7 consecutive years; (5) desertion for 3 years; (6) cruelty or abuse; and (7) nonsupport whereby a spouse is able to provide support but grossly, wantonly, or cruelly refuses or neglects to provide suitable maintenance for the complaining spouse. [Maine Revised Statutes Annotated: Title 19, Section 691(1)].

LEGAL SEPARATION: Legal separation will be granted if a spouse has been deserted without just cause or if the spouses are living apart with just cause for at least 60 days. There is no residency requirement specified in the statute. [Maine Revised Statutes Annotated: Title 19, Section 581].

SIMPLIFIED OR SPECIAL DIVORCE PROCEDURES: If the divorce is not contested, testimony of a corroborating witness is not necessary. [Maine Revised Statutes Annotated: Title 19, Section 726].

MEDIATION OR COUNSELING REQUIREMENTS: Mediation is mandatory in Maine if: (1) one of the spouses denies that there are irreconcilable differences; or (2) it is a contested divorce and children are involved. In addition, at any time a court may order mediation. [Maine Revised Statutes Annotated: Title 19, Sections 636, 691 and 752].

PROPERTY DISTRIBUTION: Maine is an "equitable distribution" state. Each spouse retains his or her individual property, including (1) any gifts or inheritances; (2) any property acquired prior to marriage; and (3) any increase in the value of property listed in (1) or (2) or property acquired in exchange for property listed in (1) or (2). The marital property is divided between the spouses after considering the following factors: (1) the contribution of each spouse to the acquisition of the marital property, including the contribution of each spouse as homemaker; (2) the value of each spouse's property; and (3) the economic circumstances of each spouse at the time the division of property is to become effective, including the desirability of awarding the family home to the spouse having custody of any children. Marital fault is not a factor. [Maine Revised Statutes Annotated: Title 19, Section 722-A].

ALIMONY/MAINTENANCE/SPOUSAL SUPPORT: Either spouse may be ordered to pay a reasonable amount of alimony. The court may also order that a spouse's real estate be awarded to the other spouse for life as alimony. The court may also order that a lump-sum be paid to the other spouse as alimony.

DIVORCE YOURSELF

Marital fault is not a factor. The factors for consideration set out in the statute are: (1) the duration of the marriage; (2) the age of the spouses; (3) the standard of living established during the marriage; (4) the ability of each spouse to pay; (5) the employment history and employment potential of each spouse; (6) the income history and income potential of each spouse; (7) the education and training of each spouse; (8) the provisions for retirement and health insurance benefits for each spouse; (9) the tax consequences of the division of marital property, including the tax consequences of the sale of the marital home; (10) the health and disabilities of each spouse; (11) the tax consequences of an alimony award; (12) the contributions of either spouse as homemaker; (13) the contributions of either spouse to the education or earning potential to the other spouse; (14) economic misconduct of either spouse resulting in the diminution of marital property or income; and (15) any other factors the court considers appropriate. [Maine Revised Statutes Annotated: Title 19, Section 721].

SPOUSE'S NAME: During or after a divorce or annulment, and upon request, a wife may have her name changed. [Maine Revised Statutes Annotated: Title 19, Section 752].

CHILD CUSTODY: Based on the best interests of the child, three types of custody may be awarded: (1) Responsibilities for the child's welfare are divided, either exclusively or proportionately. The responsibilities to be divided are: primary physical residence, parent-child contact, support, education, medical and dental care, religious upbringing, travel boundaries and expenses, and any other aspects. A parent awarded responsibility for any aspect may be required to inform the other parent of any major changes. (2) Parental responsibilities are shared. Most or all of the responsibilities are made on the basis of joint decisions and the parents retain equal parental rights and responsibilities. (3) One parent is granted full and exclusive rights and responsibility for the child's welfare, except for the responsibility of child support.

The factors to be considered are: (1) the age of the child; (2) the capability and desire of each parent to meet the child's needs; (3) the preference of the child, if the child is of sufficient age and capacity; (4) the length of time the child has lived in a stable, satisfactory environment and the desirability of maintaining continuity; (5) the desire and ability of each parent to allow an open and loving frequent relationship between the child and the other parent; (6) the child's adjustment to his or her home, school, and community; (7) the relationship of the child with parents, siblings, and other significant family members; (8) the stability of the home environment likely to be offered by each parent; (9) a need to promote continuity and stability in the life of the child; (10) the parent's capacity and willingness to cooperate; (11) methods for dispute resolution; (12) the effect on the child of one parent having sole authority over his or her upbringing; and (13) any other factors having a reasonable bearing on the child's upbringing. No preference is to be given because of parent's sex. [Maine Revised Statutes Annotated: Title 19, Section 752].

CHILD SUPPORT: Either or both parents may be ordered to pay child support, regardless of any marital fault. An order for support may require that a parent be responsible for payment of or obtain an insurance policy covering the child's medical, hospital, and other health care expenses. There are no factors for consideration set out in the statute. [Maine Revised Statutes Annotated: Title 19, Section 752(10).

APPENDIX: DIVORCE LAWS OF ALL 50 STATES

MARYLAND

NAME OF COURT IN WHICH TO FILE FOR DIVORCE: Circuit Court. "In the Circuit Court for _____, Maryland."

TITLE OF DIVORCE ACTION: Bill for Divorce. [Maryland Rules, Rule S-72].

NAME USED TO DESCRIBE SPOUSE FILING FOR DIVORCE: Plaintiff.

NAME USED TO DESCRIBE OTHER SPOUSE IN DIVORCE: Defendant.

TITLE OF FINAL DIVORCE PAPERS: Decree of Divorce.

RESIDENCY REQUIREMENTS AND WHERE TO FILE: If the grounds for divorce occurred outside of Maryland, one of the spouses must have lived in Maryland for at least 1 year prior to filing for divorce. Otherwise, either spouse may file for divorce in Maryland. If insanity is the grounds for divorce, the residency requirement is increased to 2 years. The divorce may be filed for in a county where either spouse resides. [Annotated Code of Maryland; Family Law, Title 7, Section 7-103; and Maryland Rules, Rule S-70].

LEGAL GROUNDS FOR (ABSOLUTE) DIVORCE: No-Fault: (1) the spouses have voluntarily lived separate and apart for 1 year without interruption or cohabitation and there is no reasonable expectation of reconciliation; or (2) the spouses have lived separate and apart without interruption for 2 years. [Annotated Code of Maryland; Family Law, Title 7, Section 7-103].

General: (1) adultery; (2) deliberate desertion for 12 months with no chance for reconciliation; (3) confinement for incurable insanity of at least 3 years; and (4) conviction of a felony or a misdemeanor with at least a 3-year sentence and after 1 year having been served. [Annotated Code of Maryland; Family Law, Title 7, Section 7-103].

LEGAL SEPARATION: The grounds for a legal separation (limited divorce) are: (1) willful desertion; (2) cruel and inhuman treatment; (3) voluntary separation and living separate and apart without cohabitation. The legal separation may be temporary or permanent. The spouses must make a good-faith effort to reconcile their difference. [Annotated Code of Maryland; Family Law, Title 7, Section 7-102].

SIMPLIFIED OR SPECIAL DIVORCE PROCEDURES: Summary divorces are not permitted in Maryland. However, marital settlement agreements are specifically authorized by statute and may be used for full corroboration of a plaintiff's testimony that a separation was voluntary if (1) the agreement states that the spouses voluntarily agreed to separate and (2) the agreement was signed under oath before the application for divorce was filed. [Annotated Code of Maryland; Courts and Judicial Procedure, Section 3-409; Maryland Rule S-77; and Title 8, Section 8-104].

MEDIATION OR COUNSELING REQUIREMENTS: In cases where the custody of a child is in dispute, the court may order the parents to attempt to mediate that issue. However, both parents must be represented by an attorney and there must not be any evidence of child abuse. [Maryland Rules, Rule S-73A]

PROPERTY DISTRIBUTION: Maryland is an "equitable distribution" state. The spouses retain their separate property, including (1) any gifts and inheritances; (2) property acquired prior to the marriage; and (3) property which is directly traceable to property listed in (1) or (2). Marital property, including retirement benefits and military pensions, is then divided on an equitable basis. The court may order a division of the property, a sale of the property and a division of the proceeds, or a money award as an adjustment of the values. The court may award the family home to either party. The following factors area considered: (1) the monetary and non-monetary contributions of each spouse to the acquisition of the marital property, including the contribution of each spouse as homemaker; (2) the value of each spouse's property; (3) the economic circumstances of each spouse at the time the division of property is to become effective; (4)

the length of the marriage; (5) whether the property award is in stead of or in addition to alimony; (6) how and by whom the property was acquired, including any retirement, profit-sharing, or deferred compensation plans; (7) the circumstances that contributed to the estrangement of the spouses; (8) the age, physical and mental condition of the spouses; and (9) any other factor necessary to do equity and justice between the spouses. [Annotated Code of Maryland; Family Law, Title 7, Sections 8-202, 8-203, and 8-205].

ALIMONY/MAINTENANCE/SPOUSAL SUPPORT: Either spouse may be awarded alimony, without regard to marital fault, and based on the following factors: (1) the time necessary to acquire sufficient education and training to enable the spouse to find appropriate employment, and that spouse's future earning capacity; (2) the standard of living established during the marriage; (3) the duration of the marriage; (3) the ability of the spouse from whom support is sought to meet his or her needs while meeting those of the spouse seeking support; (4) the financial resources of the spouse seeking alimony, including marital property apportioned to such spouse and such spouse's ability to meet his or her needs independently; (5) the comparative financial resources of the spouses, including their comparative earning abilities in the labor market; (6) the contribution of each spouse to the marriage, including services rendered in homemaking, child care, education, and career building of the other spouse; (7) the age of the spouses; (8) the physical and emotional conditions of the spouses; (9) any mutual agreement between the spouses concerning financial or service contributions by one spouse with the expectation of future reciprocation or compensation by the other; and (10) any other factor the court deems just and equitable. [Annotated Code of Maryland; Family Law, Title 7, Section 11-106].

SPOUSE'S NAME: Either spouse's former or birth name may be restored if the purpose is not illegal, fraudulent, or immoral. [Annotated Code of Maryland; Family Law, Title 7, Section 7-105].

CHILD CUSTODY: Joint or sole custody may be awarded to either or both parents, based on the best interests of the child. Custody may be denied if the child has been abused by the parent seeking custody. There are no other factors for consideration set out in the statute. The court shall attempt to allow the child to live in the environment and community that are familiar to the child and will generally allow the use and possession of the family home by the person with custody of the child(ren). [Annotated Code of Maryland; Family Law, Title 7, Sections 5-203, 8-207, 8-208, and 9-101; and Maryland Case Law].

CHILD SUPPORT: Child support may be awarded. There are specific child support guidelines and charts supplied in the statute. However, there are no factors for consideration set out in the statute. The family home may be awarded to the parent who has custody of a child to enable the child to continue to live in the environment and community that are familiar to the child. [Annotated Code of Maryland; Family Law, Title 7, Sections 12-101, 12-201, 12-202, 12-203, 12-204 and 8-206].

APPENDIX: DIVORCE LAWS OF ALL 50 STATES

MASSACHUSETTS

NAME OF COURT IN WHICH TO FILE FOR DIVORCE: Superior Court or Probate Court for the Commonwealth of Massachusetts. "Commonwealth of Massachusetts, The Trial Court, The Probate and Family Court Department, _____ Division." [Massachusetts General Laws Annotated; Chapter 208, Section 6B].

TITLE OF DIVORCE ACTION: For fault-based divorce: Complaint for Divorce; For no-fault divorce with or without a separation agreement: Petition for Divorce [See below under **Simplified Or Special Divorce Procedures**].

NAME USED TO DESCRIBE SPOUSE FILING FOR DIVORCE: For fault-based divorce: Plaintiff; For no-fault divorce without a separation agreement: Petitioner; For no-fault divorce with a separation agreement: Co-Petitioner.

NAME USED TO DESCRIBE OTHER SPOUSE IN DIVORCE: For fault-based divorce: Defendant; For no-fault divorce without a separation agreement: Respondent; For no-fault divorce with a separation agreement: Co-Petitioner.

TITLE OF FINAL DIVORCE PAPERS: Judgement of Divorce.

RESIDENCY REQUIREMENTS AND WHERE TO FILE: If the grounds for divorce occurred in Massachusetts, one spouse must be a resident. If the grounds occurred outside of the state, the spouse filing must have been a resident for 1 year. The divorce should be filed for in the county in which the spouses last lived together. If neither spouse currently lives in that county then the divorce may be filed for in a county where either spouse currently resides. [Massachusetts General Laws Annotated; Chapter 208, Sections 4, 5, and 6].

LEGAL GROUNDS FOR DIVORCE: No-Fault: Irretrievable breakdown of the marriage (May be filed for either with or without a separation agreement. For no-fault divorce filed in conjunction with a separation agreement, see below under **Simplified Or Special Divorce Procedures**.) [Massachusetts General Laws Annotated; Chapter 208, Sections 1, 1A, and 1B].

General: (1) impotence; (2) imprisonment for over 5 years; (3) adultery; (4) alcoholism and/or drug addiction; (5) desertion without support of spouse for 1 year before the filing for divorce; (6) cruel and inhuman treatment; and (7) nonsupport whereby a spouse is able to provide support but grossly, wantonly, or cruelly refuses or neglects to provide suitable maintenance for the complaining spouse. [Massachusetts General Laws Annotated; Chapter 208, Sections 1, 1A, 1B and 2].

LEGAL SEPARATION: The grounds for legal separation are: (1) a spouse fails without cause to provide support; (2) desertion; or (3) gives the other spouse justifiable cause to live apart. The court may award support to the spouse and children living apart. If the grounds for legal separation occurred in Massachusetts, one spouse must be a resident. If the grounds occurred outside of the state, the spouse filing must have been a resident for 1 year. [Massachusetts General Laws Annotated; Chapter 208, Section 20].

SIMPLIFIED OR SPECIAL DIVORCE PROCEDURES: An action for divorce on the grounds of irretrievable breakdown of the marriage may be instituted by filing: (1) a petition signed by both spouses; and (2) a sworn affidavit that an irretrievable breakdown of the marriage exists; and (3) a notarized separation agreement signed by both spouses. A marital settlement agreement is an acceptable substitute for a separation agreement. No summons will be required. Such petitions are to be given a speedy hearing. Marital fault is not to be considered in any decision of the court on property division or maintenance. In addition, there are sample divorce forms for use in fault-based divorces set out in the Massachusetts Rules of Court Appendix of Forms. [Massachusetts General Laws Annotated; Chapter 208, Sections 1A and Massachusetts Rules of Court].

MEDIATION OR COUNSELING REQUIREMENTS: In cases where "irreconcilable differences" are used as the grounds for divorce, the court may refer the spouses and children for marriage and family counseling. [Massachusetts General Laws Annotated; Chapter 208, Sections 1A and Massachusetts Rules of Court].

PROPERTY DISTRIBUTION: Massachusetts is an "equitable distribution" state. The court may divide all of the spouse's property, including any gifts and inheritances, based on the following factors: (1) the contribution of each spouse to the acquisition, preservation, or appreciation in value of the property, including the contribution of each spouse as homemaker; (2) the length of the marriage; (3) the age and health of the spouses; (4) the occupation of the spouses; (5) the amount and sources of income of the spouses; (6) the vocational skills of the spouses; (7) the employability of the spouses; (8) the liabilities and needs of each spouse and the opportunity of each for further acquisition of capital assets and income; (9) the conduct of the parties during the marriage (if the grounds for divorce are fault-based); and (10) any health insurance coverage. Fault is not a factor if the grounds for the divorce are irretrievable breakdown of the marriage filed in conjunction with a separation/settlement agreement. [Massachusetts General Laws Annotated; Chapter 208, Sections 1A and 34].

ALIMONY/MAINTENANCE/SPOUSAL SUPPORT: Either spouse may be ordered to pay maintenance to the other. The factors to be considered are: (1) the contribution of each spouse to the acquisition, preservation, or appreciation in value of any property, including the contribution of each spouse as homemaker; (2) the length of the marriage; (3) the age and health of the spouses; (4) the occupation of the spouses; (5) the amount and sources of income of the spouses; (6) the vocational skills of the spouses; (7) the employability of the spouses; (8) the liabilities and needs of each spouse and the opportunity of each for further acquisition of capital assets and income; (9) the conduct of the parties during the marriage (if the grounds for divorce are fault-based); and (10) any health insurance coverage. Fault is not a factor if the grounds for the divorce are irretrievable breakdown of the marriage filed in conjunction with a separation/settlement agreement. Health insurance coverage may be ordered to be provided as part of the maintenance award. [Massachusetts General Laws Annotated; Chapter 208, Sections 1A, and 34].

SPOUSE'S NAME: The wife may be restored to the use of her former or maiden name. [Massachusetts General Laws Annotated; Chapter 208, Section 23].

CHILD CUSTODY: Custody may be awarded to either or both parents or to a third party. Joint custody may be awarded if both parents agree and unless the court finds that joint custody is not in the best interests of the child. There are no factors for consideration specified in the statute. [Massachusetts General Laws Annotated; Chapter 208, Section 28].

CHILD SUPPORT: The court may order either parent to provide maintenance, support (including insurance), and education for any minor child. There are no factors for consideration specified in the statute. [Massachusetts General Laws Annotated; Chapter 208, Section 28].

APPENDIX: DIVORCE LAWS OF ALL 50 STATES

MICHIGAN

NAME OF COURT IN WHICH TO FILE FOR DIVORCE: Circuit Court. "State of Michigan, _____ Judicial Circuit, _____ County". [Michigan Compiled Laws Annotated; Section 552.6].

TITLE OF DIVORCE ACTION: Complaint for Divorce.

NAME USED TO DESCRIBE SPOUSE FILING FOR DIVORCE: Plaintiff.

NAME USED TO DESCRIBE OTHER SPOUSE IN DIVORCE: Defendant.

TITLE OF FINAL DIVORCE PAPERS: Judgement of Divorce.

RESIDENCY REQUIREMENTS AND WHERE TO FILE: Immediately prior to filing for divorce, both spouses must have been residents of Michigan for 180 days and residents of the county where the divorce is filed for 10 days. The residency requirement is 1 year if the cause of the divorce arose outside of Michigan. [Michigan Compiled Laws Annotated; Section 552.9].

LEGAL GROUNDS FOR DIVORCE: No-Fault: A breakdown of the marriage relationship to the extent that the objects of matrimony have been destroyed and there remains no reasonable likelihood that the marriage can be preserved. [Michigan Compiled Laws Annotated; Section 552.6]

General: A breakdown of the marriage relationship to the extent that the objects of matrimony have been destroyed and there remains no reasonable likelihood that the marriage can be preserved is the only grounds for divorce in Michigan. [Michigan Compiled Laws Annotated; Section 552.6].

LEGAL SEPARATION: The only grounds for legal separation (separate maintenance) in Michigan is a breakdown of the marriage relationship to the extent that the objects of matrimony have been destroyed and there remains no reasonable likelihood that the marriage can be preserved. There is no residency requirement specified in the statute. [Michigan Compiled Laws Annotated; Section 552.7].

SIMPLIFIED OR SPECIAL DIVORCE PROCEDURES: There are mandatory official approved and simplified (fill-in-the-blank) forms available for all phases of the divorce process. These forms are contained in the official Michigan Supreme Court Administrative Office Forms Book and should be available from the clerk of the Circuit Court in any Michigan county. [Michigan Court Rules 3.204].

MEDIATION OR COUNSELING REQUIREMENTS: Voluntary mediation services are available in all situations involving custody and visitation of children. [Michigan Compiled Laws Annotated; Section 552.513].

PROPERTY DISTRIBUTION: Michigan is an "equitable distribution" state. The court may divide the all of the spouse's property, including any gifts or inheritances, in a just and reasonable manner, if it appears that the spouse contributed to the acquisition, improvement, or accumulation of the property. The factors to be considered are: (1) the contribution of each spouse to the acquisition of the marital property, including the contribution of each spouse as homemaker; (2) the length of the marriage; (3) any retirement benefits, including social security, civil service, military and railroad retirement benefits; (4) any prior marriage of each spouse; (5) the circumstances that contributed to the estrangement of the spouses; (6) the source of the property; (7) the cause of the divorce; and (8) each spouse's financial circumstances and rights to any insurance policies. [Michigan Compiled Laws Annotated; Sections 552.19, 552.101, and 552.401 and Michigan Case Law].

ALIMONY/MAINTENANCE/SPOUSAL SUPPORT: Either spouse may be ordered to pay alimony. The alimony may be awarded if the property awarded to a spouse is insufficient to allow that spouse suitable support and maintenance. Factors for consideration specified in the statute are: (1) the ability of either spouse to pay; (2) the character and situation of the spouses; and (3) all other circumstances of the case. [Michigan Compiled Laws Annotated; Sections 552.13 and 552.23].

SPOUSE'S NAME: At the wife's request, the court may restore the birth or former name, if there is no fraudulent intent. [Michigan Compiled Laws Annotated; Section 552.391].

CHILD CUSTODY: Sole or joint custody is awarded based on the best interests of the child and on the following factors: (1) moral character and prudence of the parents; (2) physical, emotional, mental, religious, and social needs of the child; (3) capability and desire of each parent to meet the child's emotional, educational, and other needs; (4) preference of the child, if the child is of sufficient age and capacity; (5) the love and affection and other emotional ties existing between the child and each parent; (6) the length of time the child has lived in a stable, satisfactory environment and the desirability of maintaining continuity; (7) the desire and ability of each parent to allow an open and loving frequent relationship between the child and the other parent; (8) the child's adjustment to his or her home, school, and community; (9) the mental and physical health of all individuals involved; (10) the permanence as a family unit of the proposed custodial home or homes; and (11) any other factors.

If joint custody is an issue, the court will consider all of the above factors and the following additional factors: (1) whether the parents will be able to cooperate and generally agree concerning important decisions affecting the welfare of the child; and (2) if the parents agree on joint custody. [Michigan Compiled Laws Annotated; Sections 552.16, 722.23 and 722.26a]

CHILD SUPPORT: Either parent may be ordered to provide a just and proper amount of child support. There are no factors for consideration specified in the statute. There is, however, a child support formula to be used as a guideline. This formula is contained in Michigan Compiled Laws Annotated, Section 552.519. The court may require the parent providing support to file a bond guaranteeing the support payments. Support may include health care, dental care, child care, and education of the child. The Judgement of Divorce must include a provision that requires one or both of the parents to provide health care coverage, if such coverage is available at a reasonable cost as a benefit of employment. [Michigan Compiled Laws Annotated; Sections 552.16, 552.452, and 552.519].

APPENDIX: DIVORCE LAWS OF ALL 50 STATES

MINNESOTA

NAME OF COURT IN WHICH TO FILE FOR DIVORCE: County Court or District Court. "State of Minnesota, District Court, County of _____, _____ Judicial District".

TITLE OF DIVORCE ACTION: Petition for Dissolution of Marriage. "In Re: The Marriage of _____ and _____".

NAME USED TO DESCRIBE SPOUSE FILING FOR DISSOLUTION OF MARRIAGE: Petitioner [or Co-Petitioner if the petition is filed jointly. See below under **Simplified Or Special Dissolution Of Marriage Procedures**].

NAME USED TO DESCRIBE OTHER SPOUSE IN DISSOLUTION OF MARRIAGE: Respondent [or Co-Petitioner if the petition is filed jointly. See below under **Simplified Or Special Dissolution Of Marriage Procedures**].

TITLE OF FINAL DISSOLUTION OF MARRIAGE PAPERS: Decree of Dissolution of Marriage.

RESIDENCY REQUIREMENTS AND WHERE TO FILE: One of the spouses must have been a resident of Minnesota for at least 180 days immediately before the petition for dissolution of marriage is filed. The dissolution of marriage may be filed for in a county where either spouse resides. [Minnesota Statutes Annotated; Chapters 518.07 and 518.09].

LEGAL GROUNDS FOR DISSOLUTION OF MARRIAGE: No-Fault: Irrevocable breakdown of the marriage shown by (1) living separate and apart for 180 days; or (2) serious marital discord adversely affecting the attitude of one or both of the spouses toward the marriage. [Minnesota Statutes Annotated; Chapters 518.06 and 518.13].

General: Irrevocable breakdown of the marriage is the only grounds for dissolution of marriage in Minnesota. [Minnesota Statutes Annotated; Chapter 518.06].

LEGAL SEPARATION: The grounds for a legal separation in Minnesota are that it will be granted if the court finds that the spouses need a legal separation. One of the spouses must have been a resident of Minnesota for at least 6 months before the petition for legal separation is filed. [Minnesota Statutes Annotated; Chapter 518.06 and 518.07].

SIMPLIFIED OR SPECIAL DISSOLUTION OF MARRIAGE PROCEDURES: The petition may be brought by both spouses jointly as Co-Petitioners. This eliminates the need for service of process or the use of a summons. [Minnesota Statutes Annotated; Chapters 518.09 and 518.11].

MEDIATION OR COUNSELING REQUIREMENTS: Mediation may be ordered in cases in which the custody of children is contested. [Minnesota Statutes Annotated; Chapter 518.619].

PROPERTY DISTRIBUTION: Minnesota is an "equitable distribution" state. Each spouse retains his or her non-marital (separate) property, consisting of: (1) property acquired prior to the marriage; (2) any gifts or inheritances; or (3) property exchanged for or an increase in value of such non-marital property. All other marital property, including any pension and retirement plans, is divided, without regard to fault, after a consideration of the following factors: (1) the contribution of each spouse to the acquisition of the marital property, including the contribution of each spouse as homemaker; (2) the economic circumstances of each spouse at the time the division of property is to become effective; (3) the length of the marriage; (4) the age and health of the spouses; (5) the occupation of the spouses; (6) the amount and sources of income of the spouses; (7) the vocational skills of the spouses; (8) the employability of the spouses; (9) the liabilities and needs of each spouse and the opportunity of each for further acquisition of capital assets and income; (10) any prior marriage of each spouse; and (11) any other factor necessary to do equity and justice between the spouses. [Minnesota Statutes Annotated; Chapter 518.58].

ALIMONY/MAINTENANCE/SPOUSAL SUPPORT: Either spouse may be awarded maintenance, without regard to marital fault, if the spouse seeking maintenance: (1) lacks sufficient property to provide for reasonable needs considering the standard of living attained during the marriage; or (2) is unable to provide adequate self-support, considering the standard of living attained during the marriage, through appropriate employment; or (3) is the custodian of a child whose condition or circumstances make it appropriate that the custodian not be required to seek employment outside the home. The award of maintenance is based on a consideration of the following factors: (1) the sacrifices the homemaker has made in terms of earnings, employment, experience, and opportunities; (2) the time necessary to acquire sufficient education and training to enable the spouse to find appropriate employment, and that spouse's future earning capacity and the probability of completing education and training and becoming fully or partially self-supporting; (3) the standard of living established during the marriage; (4) the duration of the marriage and, in the case of a homemaker, the length of absence from employment and the extent to which any education, skills, or experience have become outmoded and earning capacity has become permanently diminished; (5) the ability of the spouse from whom support is sought to meet his or her needs while meeting those of the spouse seeking support; (6) the financial resources of the spouse seeking maintenance, including marital property apportioned to such spouse and such spouse's ability to meet his or her needs independently; (7) the contribution of each spouse to the marriage, including services rendered in homemaking, child care, education, and career building of the other spouse; (8) the age of the spouses; (9) the physical and emotional conditions of the spouses; (10) any loss of earnings, seniority, retirement benefits or other employment opportunities foregone by the spouse seeking maintenance; and (11) any other factor the court deems just and equitable. [Minnesota Statutes Annotated; Chapter 518.552].

SPOUSE'S NAME: Upon request, either spouse may change his or her name, unless there is intent to mislead or defraud. [Minnesota Statutes Annotated; Chapter 518.27].

CHILD CUSTODY: Joint or sole custody may be awarded. If sole custody is sought, it will be awarded based on the best interests of the child and upon the following factors: (1) the child's cultural background; (2) physical, emotional, mental, religious, and social needs of the child; (3) capability and desire of each parent to meet the child's needs; (4) preference of the child, if the child is of sufficient age and capacity; (5) the length of time the child has lived in a stable, satisfactory environment and the desirability of maintaining continuity; (6) the wishes of the parents; (7) the child's adjustment to his or her home, school, and community; (8) the mental and physical health of all individuals involved; (9) the relationship of the child with parents, siblings, and other significant family members; (10) the conduct of the proposed guardian only as it bears on his or her relationship with the child; (11) the stability of the home environment likely to be offered by each parent; (12) a need to promote continuity and stability in the life of the child; and (13) any other factors.

If joint custody is sought, the award will be based on a consideration of the above factors and a consideration of the following: (1) dispute resolution methods; (2) the effect of one parent having custody; and (3) the ability of the parents to cooperate and make decisions jointly. If both parents seek custody of a child who is too young to express a preference, the "primary caretaker" is to be awarded custody. [Minnesota Statutes Annotated; Chapter 518.17 and Minnesota Case Law].

CHILD SUPPORT: In determining the amount of child support to award, the following factors are considered: (1) the financial resources of the child; (2) the financial resources of the custodial parents; (3) the standard of living the child would have enjoyed if the marriage had not been dissolved; (4) the physical and emotional conditions and educational needs of the child; (5) the amount of public aid received by the child; and (6) any income tax consequences of the payment of support. If the parent to receive the support payments is receiving or has applied for public aid, the support payments must be made to the public agency responsible for child support enforcement in Minnesota. There are official child support guidelines contained in Minnesota Statutes Annotated; Chapter 518.551 [Minnesota Statutes Annotated; Chapters 518.551 and 518.552].

APPENDIX: DIVORCE LAWS OF ALL 50 STATES

MISSISSIPPI

NAME OF COURT IN WHICH TO FILE FOR DIVORCE: Chancery Court. "Chancery Court of _____ County, State of Mississippi". [Mississippi Code Annotated; Section 11, Chapter 5-67].

TITLE OF DIVORCE ACTION: Bill of Complaint for Divorce.

NAME USED TO DESCRIBE SPOUSE FILING FOR DIVORCE: Complainant.

NAME USED TO DESCRIBE OTHER SPOUSE IN DIVORCE: Defendant.

TITLE OF FINAL DIVORCE PAPERS: Decree of Divorce.

RESIDENCY REQUIREMENTS AND WHERE TO FILE: The spouse filing for divorce must have been a resident for at least 6 months, and not have secured residency for the purpose of obtaining a divorce. A member of the armed services and his or her spouse are considered residents if stationed in Mississippi. A divorce on the grounds of irreconcilable differences should be filed for in: (1) the county where either spouse resides, if both spouses are residents of Mississippi; or (2) the county where one spouse resides if the other spouse is a non-resident of Mississippi. A divorce sought on fault-based grounds should be filed for in: (1) the county where the defendant resides if he or she is a resident of Mississippi; or (2) the county where the plaintiff resides if the defendant is a non-resident of Mississippi; or (3) the county where the spouses last lived prior to separating, if the defendant is still a resident of Mississippi. [Mississippi Code Annotated; Section 93, Chapters 5-5 and 5-11].

LEGAL GROUNDS FOR DIVORCE: No-Fault: Irreconcilable differences. However, no divorce on these grounds will be granted unless: (1) the divorce is not contested or the irreconcilable differences are not denied by the other spouse; and (2) adequate child custody, maintenance, and property distribution arrangements have been made by the spouses by a written agreement. In addition, an affidavit must be filed stating that there is no collusion between the spouses. (See also below under Summary Divorce). [Mississippi Code Annotated; Section 93, Chapters 5-1, 5-2, and 5-7].

General: (1) impotence; (2) adultery; (3) imprisonment; (4) alcoholism and/or drug addiction; (5) confinement for incurable insanity for at least 3 years before the divorce is filed; (6) wife is pregnant by another at the time of marriage without husband's knowledge; (7) willful desertion for at least 1 year; (8) cruel and inhuman treatment; (9) spouse lacked mental capacity to consent (including temporary incapacity resulting from drug or alcohol use); and (10) incest. In addition, an affidavit must be filed stating that there is no collusion between the spouses. [Mississippi Code Annotated; Section 93, Chapters 5-1 and 5-7].

LEGAL SEPARATION: There are provisions in Mississippi for separate maintenance. [Mississippi Code Annotated; Section 93, Chapter 5-23].

SIMPLIFIED OR SPECIAL DIVORCE PROCEDURES: A no-fault divorce on the grounds of irreconcilable differences will be granted if: (1) a joint bill of complaint for divorce is filed by both the husband and wife; or (2) a bill of complaint has been filed and (a) the defendant has entered an appearance by written waiver of process; or (b) has been personally served with the divorce papers. In addition, there must be a written agreement between the spouses for the care and custody of any children and for the division of all property. The agreement may be incorporated into the decree. There is a 60 day waiting period after filing before a hearing may be scheduled. A bill filed meeting these qualifications will be taken as confessed and no testimony or proof will be required at the hearing. [Mississippi Code Annotated; Section 93, Chapter 5-2].

MEDIATION OR COUNSELING REQUIREMENTS: There is no legal provision in Mississippi for mediation

DIVORCE YOURSELF

PROPERTY DISTRIBUTION: Mississippi is a "title" state. Each spouse retains his or her property for which they have title. There are no statutory provisions in Mississippi for considerations regarding property division. Mississippi is the only state remaining that has not enacted either the equitable division or community property systems of property division. Mississippi law is based on former English common law principles that hold that the owner of property is the spouse whose name is on the title. This system has had harsh results in the past by denying the wife in a marriage a fair share of the property accumulated during a marriage, even if it was substantially the wife's efforts that provided the largest contribution. Recently, however, Mississippi judges have softened the strict application of this property division system by allowing for ample lump-sum alimony awards to take the place of an equitable distribution of property. A recent court decision (1988) has allowed for a wife's contributions to the acquisition of assets to provide the court with authority to divide any jointly accumulated assets on an "equitable" basis. [Mississippi Case Law].

ALIMONY/MAINTENANCE/SPOUSAL SUPPORT: Either spouse may be awarded maintenance if it is equitable and just. Marital fault is not considered. There are no other factors for consideration specified in the statute. [Mississippi Code Annotated; Section 93, Chapter 5-23].

SPOUSE'S NAME: Either spouse may petition the court for a name change. [Mississippi Code Annotated; Section 93, Chapter 17-1].

CHILD CUSTODY: Joint or sole child custody is awarded based on the best interests of the child. There are no specific factors for consideration in the statute. The court may award: (1) joint physical and legal custody to one or both parents; (2) physical custody to both parents and legal custody to one parent; (3) legal custody to both parents and physical custody to one parent; or (4) custody to a third party if the parents have abandoned the child or are unfit. If irreconcilable differences are the grounds for divorce, both parents must apply for joint custody. Otherwise, either parent may apply for joint custody. If both parents are fit and the child is 12 or older, the child may choose the parent he or she wishes to live with. [Mississippi Code Annotated; Section 93, Chapters 3-23, 5-24, and 11-65].

CHILD SUPPORT: Child support may be ordered as the court finds just and equitable. There are no factors for consideration specified in the statute. However, where both parents have income or estates, each parent may be ordered to provide support in proportion to his or her relative financial ability. A parent may be required to provide health insurance coverage for the child, if such insurance coverage is available at a reasonable cost through an employer or organization. Bond or sureties may be required to guarantee payments. [Mississippi Code Annotated; Section 93, Chapters 5-23, 11-64, and 11-65].

APPENDIX: DIVORCE LAWS OF ALL 50 STATES

MISSOURI

NAME OF COURT IN WHICH TO FILE FOR DIVORCE: Circuit Court. "In the Circuit Court of _____ County, Missouri".

TITLE OF DIVORCE ACTION: Petition for Dissolution of Marriage. "In Re the Marriage of _____ and _____". [Annotated Missouri Statutes; Title 30, Chapter 452, Section 300].

NAME USED TO DESCRIBE SPOUSE FILING FOR DISSOLUTION OF MARRIAGE: Petitioner [or Co-Petitioner if the petition is filed jointly. See below under **Simplified Or Special Dissolution Of Marriage Procedures**].

NAME USED TO DESCRIBE OTHER SPOUSE IN DISSOLUTION OF MARRIAGE: Respondent [or Co-Petitioner if the petition is filed jointly. See below under **Simplified Or Special Dissolution Of Marriage Procedures**].

TITLE OF FINAL DISSOLUTION OF MARRIAGE PAPERS: Decree of Dissolution of Marriage.

RESIDENCY REQUIREMENTS AND WHERE TO FILE: One of the spouses must be a resident of Missouri for 90 days before filing for dissolution of marriage. The dissolution of marriage should be filed in the county where the Petitioner resides. In addition, there is a 30-day waiting period after filing before a dissolution of marriage will be granted. [Annotated Missouri Statutes; Title 30, Chapter 452, Sections 300.1 and 305].

LEGAL GROUNDS FOR DISSOLUTION OF MARRIAGE: No-Fault: Irretrievable breakdown of the marriage and no reasonable likelihood that the marriage can be preserved. [Annotated Missouri Statutes; Title 30, Chapter 452, Section 305].

General: Irretrievable breakdown of the marriage with no reasonable likelihood that the marriage can be preserved is the only grounds for dissolution of marriage in Missouri. [Annotated Missouri Statutes; Title 30, Chapter 452, Section 305].

LEGAL SEPARATION: The grounds for legal separation in Missouri are an irretrievable breakdown of the marriage, which may include the following factors: (1) adultery; (2) abandonment; and (3) separation caused by misconduct. One of the spouses must be a resident of Missouri for 90 days before filing for legal separation. [Annotated Missouri Statutes; Title 30, Chapter 452, Sections 305 and 320].

SIMPLIFIED OR SPECIAL DISSOLUTION OF MARRIAGE PROCEDURES: Missouri allows for a joint petition by both spouses to be filed. In such cases, each spouse should be titled as a "Co-Petitioner". Settlement agreements are expressly authorized by statute in Missouri. In addition, some counties have approved pre-printed forms for filing for dissolution of marriage which are available upon request from the court clerk. [Annotated Missouri Statutes; Title 30, Chapter 452, Sections 320 and 325].

MEDIATION OR COUNSELING REQUIREMENTS: The court can delay a divorce proceeding for 30-180 days and suggest that the spouses seek counseling. [Annotated Missouri Statutes; Title 30, Chapter 452, Section 320].

PROPERTY DISTRIBUTION: Missouri is an "equitable distribution" state. Each spouse retains his or her separate property obtained prior to the marriage, including any gifts or inheritances. In addition, any property exchanged for separate property or interest obtained from holding separate property remains as separate. Marital property (all property acquired after the marriage, whether held individually or jointly) is divided after a consideration of the following factors: (1) the contribution of each spouse to the acquisition of the marital property, including the contribution of each spouse as homemaker; (2) the value of each spouse's property; (3) the economic circumstances of each spouse at the time the division of property is to become effective; (4) the conduct of the spouses during the marriage generally and as it relates to the disposition of their property; (5) the desirability of awarding the family home to the spouse having custody of the children; and (6) any custodial arrangements for children. [Annotated Missouri Statutes; Title 30, Chapter 452, Section 330].

ALIMONY/MAINTENANCE/SPOUSAL SUPPORT: Either spouse may be awarded maintenance if that spouse can show: (1) an inability to support his or herself; and (2) a lack of sufficient property (including his or her share of any marital property) to provide for his or her own needs; or (3) that the spouse seeking support is the custodian of a child whose condition or circumstances make it appropriate for that spouse not to seek outside employment. The following factors are considered: (1) the time necessary to acquire sufficient education and training to enable the spouse to find appropriate employment, and that spouse's future earning capacity; (2) the standard of living established during the marriage; (3) the duration of the marriage; (4) the ability of the spouse from whom support is sought to meet his or her needs while meeting those of the spouse seeking support; (5) the financial resources of the spouse seeking maintenance, including marital property apportioned to such spouse and such spouse's ability to meet his or her needs independently; (6) the age of the spouses; (7) the physical and emotional conditions of the spouses; (8) the obligations, assets, and separate property of the spouses; (9) the comparative earning capacities of each spouse; and (10) the conduct of the spouses during the marriage. [Annotated Missouri Statutes; Title 30, Chapter 452, Section 335].

SPOUSE'S NAME: A spouse may petition the court for a change of name. A public notice of any name change should be published in a local newspaper in the county where the person resides. [Annotated Missouri Statutes; Chapter 527, Sections 270 and 290].

CHILD CUSTODY: Joint or sole custody is awarded based on the best interests of the child and upon consideration of the following factors: (1) the preference of the child; (2) the wishes of the parents; (3) the child's adjustment to his or her home, school, and community; (4) the mental and physical health of all individuals involved; (5) any history of child or spouse abuse; (6) the child's need for a continuing relationship with both parents; (7) both parents willingness and ability to perform parental obligations; (8) the intention of either parent to relocate his or her residence outside Missouri; (9) which parent is more likely to allow the child frequent and meaningful contact with the other parent; and (10) the relationship of the child with parents, siblings, and other significant family members. No preference is to be given because of parent's sex. There is now a legislative encouragement of joint custody. [Annotated Missouri Statutes; Title 30, Chapter 452, Section 375].

CHILD SUPPORT: Although the father has the primary responsibility for the support of the child, either or both parents may be ordered to provide child support. The following factors are considered: (1) the financial resources and needs of the child; (2) the standard of living the child would have enjoyed if the marriage had not been dissolved; (3) the physical and emotional conditions and educational needs of the child; and (4) the financial resources, needs, and obligations of both the noncustodial and the custodial parent. A parent may be required to provide health insurance coverage for any children if such coverage is available at a reasonable cost from an employer, union, or other organization. [Annotated Missouri Statutes; Title 30, Chapter 452, Sections 340 and 353].

APPENDIX: DIVORCE LAWS OF ALL 50 STATES

MONTANA

NAME OF COURT IN WHICH TO FILE FOR DIVORCE: District Court. "District Court for the State of Montana and for the County of _____." [Montana Code Annotated; Section 40, Titles 1-104 and 1-105].

TITLE OF DIVORCE ACTION: Petition for Dissolution of Marriage. "In re the Marriage of _____ and _____."

NAME USED TO DESCRIBE SPOUSE FILING FOR DISSOLUTION OF MARRIAGE: Petitioner [or Co-Petitioner if the petition is filed jointly. See below under **Simplified Or Special Dissolution Of Marriage Procedures**].

NAME USED TO DESCRIBE OTHER SPOUSE IN DISSOLUTION OF MARRIAGE: Respondent [or Co-Petitioner if the petition is filed jointly. See below under **Simplified Or Special Dissolution Of Marriage Procedures**].

TITLE OF FINAL DISSOLUTION OF MARRIAGE PAPERS: Decree of Dissolution of Marriage.

RESIDENCY REQUIREMENTS AND WHERE TO FILE: One of the spouses must be a resident of Montana for 90 days immediately prior to filing. The dissolution of marriage should be filed for in the county where the petitioner has been a resident for the previous 90 days. [Montana Code Annotated; Section 25, Title 2-118; and Section 40, Title 1-104].

LEGAL GROUNDS FOR DISSOLUTION OF MARRIAGE: No-Fault: Irretrievable breakdown of the marriage and serious marital discord which adversely affects the attitude of both spouses towards the marriage and no reasonable prospect of reconciliation and living separate and apart for 180 days prior to filing. All three of these factors must be met to satisfy the grounds for dissolution of marriage. [Montana Code Annotated; Section 40, Title 1-104].

General: Irretrievable breakdown of the marriage and living separate and apart for 180 days prior to filing are the only grounds for dissolution of marriage in Montana. [Montana Code Annotated; Section 40, Title 1-104].

LEGAL SEPARATION: Irretrievable breakdown of the marriage is the only grounds for legal separation in Montana. One of the spouses must be a resident of Montana for 90 days immediately prior to filing for legal separation. [Montana Code Annotated; Section 40, Title 1-104].

SIMPLIFIED OR SPECIAL DISSOLUTION OF MARRIAGE PROCEDURES: Joint petitions for dissolution of marriage are allowed. In such cases, both spouses should be titled as "Co-Petitioners" on the petition. In addition, separation or settlement agreements are specifically authorized by law. [Montana Code Annotated; Section 40, Titles 1-107 and 1-201].

MEDIATION OR COUNSELING REQUIREMENTS: If there are minor children or one spouse denies that the marriage is irretrievably broken, the court may delay the proceedings for 30 to 60 days and refer the spouses to one of the following: (1) a psychiatrist, (2) a physician, (3) an attorney, (4) a social worker, (5) a pastor or director of any religious denomination to which the spouses belong, or (6) any other person who is competent and qualified in personal counseling. [Montana Code Annotated; Section 40, Titles 3-111, 3-724, and 4-107].

PROPERTY DISTRIBUTION: Montana is an "equitable distribution" state. All of the spouse's property, including any held prior to the marriage and any gifts and inheritances, is divided by the court, without regard to marital misconduct, based on consideration of the following factors: (1) the contribution of each spouse to the acquisition of the marital property, including the contribution of each spouse as homemaker; (2) the length of the marriage; (3) the age and health of the spouses; (4) the occupation of the spouses; (5)

the amount and sources of income of the spouses; (6) the vocational skills of the spouses; (7) the employability of the spouses; (8) the liabilities and needs of each spouse and the opportunity of each for further acquisition of capital assets and income; (9) the time necessary for a spouse to acquire sufficient education to enable the spouse to find appropriate employment; (10) any premarital agreement; (11) any prior marriage of each spouse; (12) whether the property award is instead of or in addition to maintenance; and (13) any custodial provisions for the children. [Montana Code Annotated; Section 40, Title 4-202].

ALIMONY/MAINTENANCE/SPOUSAL SUPPORT: Either spouse may be awarded maintenance if that spouse can show: (1) an inability to support his or herself; and (2) a lack of sufficient property (including his or her share of any marital property) to provide for his or her own needs; or (3) that the spouse seeking support is the custodian of a child whose condition or circumstances make it appropriate for that spouse not to seek outside employment. The award is made without regard to marital fault, based on the following factors: (1) the time necessary to acquire sufficient education and training to enable the spouse to find appropriate employment, and that spouse's future earning capacity; (2) the standard of living established during the marriage; (3) the duration of the marriage; (4) the ability of the spouse from whom support is sought to meet his or her needs while meeting those of the spouse seeking support; (5) the financial resources of the spouse seeking maintenance, including marital property apportioned to such spouse and any child support and such spouse's ability to meet his or her needs independently; (6) the age of the spouses; and (7) the physical and emotional conditions of the spouses. [Montana Code Annotated; Section 40, Title 4-203].

SPOUSE'S NAME: Upon the wife's request, her former or maiden name will be restored. [Montana Code Annotated; Section 40, Title 4-108].

CHILD CUSTODY: Sole or joint custody is awarded based on the best interests of the child and upon a consideration of the following factors: (1) the preference of the child; (2) the wishes of the parents; (3) the child's adjustment to his or her home, school, and community; (4) the mental and physical health of all individuals involved; (5) any history of child or spouse abuse; (6) any chemical dependency or abuse by a parent; (7) the relationship of the child with parents, siblings, and other significant family members; and (8) which parent is more likely to allow frequent and continuing contact with the non-custodial parent. A parent's sex is not to be considered. [Montana Code Annotated; Section 40, Titles 4-212, 4-223, and 4-224].

CHILD SUPPORT: Either or both parents may be ordered to pay child support, based on a consideration of the following factors: (1) the financial resources of the child; (2) the standard of living the child would have enjoyed if the marriage had not been dissolved; (3) the physical and emotional conditions and educational needs of the child; (4) the financial resources, needs, and obligations of both the noncustodial and the custodial parent; (5) the age of the child; (6) the cost of any day care; (7) the custody arrangements for the child; (8) the needs of any other person that a parent is obligated to support; and (9) the amount, if any, received by the child under the Aid to Families with Dependent Children. A portion of the parent's property may be set aside in a trust fund for the support of the children. A parent may be ordered to provide health insurance coverage for a child if such coverage is available at a reasonable cost. There are uniform child support guidelines adopted by the Montana Department of Social and Rehabilitative Services that are to be considered by the court. [Montana Code Annotated; Section 40, Title 4-204].

NEBRASKA

NAME OF COURT IN WHICH TO FILE FOR DIVORCE: District Court. "In the District Court for _____ County, Nebraska". [Revised Statutes of Nebraska; Chapter 42, Section 353].

TITLE OF DIVORCE ACTION: Petition for Dissolution of Marriage.

NAME USED TO DESCRIBE SPOUSE FILING FOR DISSOLUTION OF MARRIAGE: Petitioner [or Co-Petitioner if the petition is filed jointly. See below under **Simplified Or Special Dissolution Of Marriage Procedures**].

NAME USED TO DESCRIBE OTHER SPOUSE IN DISSOLUTION OF MARRIAGE: Respondent [or Co-Petitioner if the petition is filed jointly. See below under **Simplified Or Special Dissolution Of Marriage Procedures**].

TITLE OF FINAL DISSOLUTION OF MARRIAGE PAPERS: Decree of Dissolution of Marriage.

RESIDENCY REQUIREMENTS AND WHERE TO FILE: (1) one of the spouses must have been a resident of Nebraska for at least 1 year; or (2) the marriage was performed in Nebraska and one of the spouses has lived in Nebraska for the entire marriage. The dissolution of marriage may be filed for in a county where either spouse resides. [Revised Statutes of Nebraska; Chapter 42, Section 348].

LEGAL GROUNDS FOR DISSOLUTION OF MARRIAGE: No-Fault: Irretrievable breakdown of the marriage. [Revised Statutes of Nebraska; Chapter 42, Section 361].

General: Spouse lacked mental capacity to consent (including temporary incapacity resulting from drug or alcohol use). [Revised Statutes of Nebraska; Chapter 42, Section 362].

LEGAL SEPARATION: Irretrievable breakdown of the marriage is the only grounds for a legal separation in Nebraska. There are no residency requirements specified in the statute. If the residency requirements for dissolution of marriage are met after the petition for legal separation has been filed, the spouse filing may change the proceeding to a proceeding for dissolution of marriage. [Revised Statutes of Nebraska; Chapter 42, Section 350].

SIMPLIFIED OR SPECIAL DISSOLUTION OF MARRIAGE PROCEDURES: Joint petitions for dissolution of marriage may be filed by both spouses. In such cases, the spouses should be referred to as "Co-Petitioners" on the court documents. In addition, marital settlement agreements are specifically authorized by law. [Revised Statutes of Nebraska; Chapter 42, Sections 361 and 366].

MEDIATION OR COUNSELING REQUIREMENTS: A dissolution of marriage will not be granted until every reasonable effort for a reconciliation has been made. If it appears to the court that there is some reasonable possibility of reconciliation, dissolution of marriage actions may be transferred to a conciliation court or the spouses may be referred to a qualified marriage counselor, family service agency, or other agency which provides conciliation services. Official conciliation counselors are available in counties of over 250,000 persons. [Revised Statutes of Nebraska; Chapter 42, Sections 360 and 808].

PROPERTY DISTRIBUTION: Nebraska is an "equitable distribution" jurisdiction. The spouses retain their separate property acquired prior to the marriage. All of the spouse's marital property, including any gifts and inheritances acquired during the marriage, may be divided, based on a consideration of the following factors: (1) the contribution of each spouse to the acquisition of the marital property, including the contribution of each spouse as homemaker; (2) the economic circumstances of each spouse at the time the division of property is to become effective; (3) the length of the marriage; and (4) any custodial provisions for the children. [Revised Statutes of Nebraska; Chapter 42, Section 365].

ALIMONY/MAINTENANCE/SPOUSAL SUPPORT: Either spouse may be ordered to pay reasonable alimony, without regard to marital fault, based on a consideration of the following factors: (1) the circumstances of both spouses; (2) the duration of the marriage; (3) the contribution of each spouse to the marriage, including services rendered in homemaking, child care, education, and career building of the other spouse; (4) any interruption of personal careers or education; and (5) the ability of the supported spouse to engage in gainful employment without interfering with the interests of any minor children in his or her custody. Reasonable security for the payments may be required. [Revised Statutes of Nebraska; Chapter 42, Section 365].

SPOUSE'S NAME: Either spouse may include a request to restore his or her former name in the petition for dissolution of marriage. [Revised Statutes of Nebraska; Chapter 42, Section 380].

CHILD CUSTODY: Joint or sole custody of children is determined according to the best interests of the child and based on a consideration of the following factors: (1) the physical, emotional, mental, and social needs of the child; (2) the preference of the child, if the child is of sufficient age and capacity; (3) the child's relationship with each parent prior to the filing for dissolution of marriage; and (4) the relationship of the child with parents, siblings, and other significant family members. No preference is to be given because of parent's sex. Joint custody may be awarded if both parents agree. [Revised Statutes of Nebraska; Chapter 42, Section 364].

CHILD SUPPORT: The amount of child support is determined based on a consideration of the earning capacity of each parent. There are official Supreme Court child support guidelines which should be available from the clerk of the court. [Revised Statutes of Nebraska; Chapter 42, Section 364].

NEVADA

NAME OF COURT IN WHICH TO FILE FOR DIVORCE: District Court. "In the District Court for _____ County, Nevada".

TITLE OF DIVORCE ACTION: Complaint for Divorce.

NAME USED TO DESCRIBE SPOUSE FILING FOR DIVORCE: Plaintiff.

NAME USED TO DESCRIBE OTHER SPOUSE IN DIVORCE: Defendant.

TITLE OF FINAL DIVORCE PAPERS: Decree of Divorce.

RESIDENCY REQUIREMENTS AND WHERE TO FILE: One of the spouses must have been a resident of Nevada for 6 weeks immediately prior to filing for divorce. The divorce may be filed in: (1) the county where either spouse resides; or (2) the county where the spouses last lived together. [Nevada Revised Statutes; Chapter 125; Section 020].

LEGAL GROUNDS FOR DIVORCE: No-Fault: (1) incompatibility; or (2) living separate and apart without cohabitation for 1 year. [Nevada Revised Statutes; Chapter 125; Section 010].

General: Insanity which existed for at least 2 years before filing for the divorce. [Nevada Revised Statutes; Chapter 125; Section 010].

LEGAL SEPARATION: If a spouse has any of the grounds for divorce or if he or she has been deserted for over 90 days, a suit for separate maintenance of his or herself and any children may be filed. In addition, the spouses may agree to an immediate separation and make appropriate provisions for spousal and child support. There is no residency requirement specified in the statute. [Nevada Revised Statutes; Chapter 125; Sections 080 and 190].

SIMPLIFIED OR SPECIAL DIVORCE PROCEDURES: There are two provisions for summary divorce in Nevada. First, a summary divorce may be granted if the following conditions are met: (1) either spouse is a resident of the state for at least 6 weeks; (2) the spouses are incompatible or have lived separate and apart without cohabitation for 1 year; (3) there are no minor children (born or adopted) and the wife is not pregnant; (4) the spouses have signed an agreement regarding the division of their property and the assumption of their liabilities; (5) both spouses waive their rights to spousal support (maintenance); (6) both spouses waive (a) their rights to notice of entry of the final decree of divorce, (b) their rights to appeal the divorce, (c) their rights to request findings of fact and conclusions of law in the divorce proceeding, and (d) their rights to a new trial; (7) both spouses want the court to enter the decree of divorce.

In addition, a spouse may apply for a decree of divorce by default by affidavit. In such situations, oral testimony will not normally be required. If there is a marital settlement agreement, it should be identified in the affidavit and attached to it when filed. The affidavit should state that: (1) the residency requirements have been met; (2) all of the information in the petition is correct and true on the personal knowledge of the person signing the affidavit; (3) that the affidavit contains only facts that would be admissible into evidence; (4) give factual support for each allegation in the application; and (5) establish that the person signing the affidavit is competent to testify. [Nevada Revised Statutes; Chapter 125; Sections 123 and 181].

MEDIATION OR COUNSELING REQUIREMENTS: There are no legal provisions in Nevada for divorce mediation.

PROPERTY DISTRIBUTION: Nevada is a "community property" state. The spouses retain all of their separate property, acquired prior to the marriage or by gift or inheritance. The court will divide all of the spouse's community property and all of the property held jointly by the spouses on or after July 1, 1979, including any military retirement benefits. The following factors are considered: (1) the economic circumstances of each spouse at the time the division of property is to become effective; (2) how and by whom the property was acquired; (3) the merits of each spouse; and (4) the burdens imposed upon either spouse for the benefit of the children. Marital fault is not mentioned as a factor. Either spouse's property is also then subject to distribution for spousal or child support. [Nevada Revised Statutes; Chapter 125; Section 150].

ALIMONY/MAINTENANCE/SPOUSAL SUPPORT: Either spouse may be awarded maintenance, without regard to marital fault. There are no factors for consideration specified in the statute. [Nevada Revised Statutes; Chapter 125; Section 150].

SPOUSE'S NAME: For a reasonable cause, the court will restore the wife's former name. [Nevada Revised Statutes; Chapter 125; Section 130].

CHILD CUSTODY: Joint or sole custody is awarded based on the best interests of the child and upon the following factors: (1) the preference of the child, if the child is of sufficient age and capacity; (2) which parent is more likely to allow frequent associations and continuing relationships with the non-custodial parent; and (3) the wishes of the parents. No preference is to be given because of parent's sex. [Nevada Revised Statutes; Chapter 125; Section 480].

CHILD SUPPORT: Temporary (during the divorce proceeding) and permanent child support may be granted. There are no factors for consideration specified in the statute. [Nevada Revised Statutes; Chapter 125; Section 230].

APPENDIX: DIVORCE LAWS OF ALL 50 STATES

NEW HAMPSHIRE

NAME OF COURT IN WHICH TO FILE FOR DIVORCE: Superior Court. "The State of New Hampshire, Superior Court in and for _____."

TITLE OF DIVORCE ACTION: Petition for Divorce.

NAME USED TO DESCRIBE SPOUSE FILING FOR DIVORCE: Petitioner.

NAME USED TO DESCRIBE OTHER SPOUSE IN DIVORCE: Respondent.

TITLE OF FINAL DIVORCE PAPERS: Decree of Divorce.

RESIDENCY REQUIREMENTS AND WHERE TO FILE: (1) Both spouses must be residents of the state when the divorce is filed for; or (2) the spouse filing for divorce must have been a resident of New Hampshire for 1 year immediately prior to filing for divorce; or (3) the cause of divorce must have arisen in New Hampshire and one of the spouses must be living in New Hampshire when the divorce is filed for. The divorce may be filed for in a county where either spouse resides. [New Hampshire Revised Statutes Annotated; Chapters 458:5, 458:6, and 458.9].

LEGAL GROUNDS FOR DIVORCE: No-Fault: Irreconcilable differences which have caused the irremediable breakdown of the marriage. [New Hampshire Revised Statutes Annotated; Chapter 458:7]

General: (1) impotence; (2) adultery; (3) abandonment and not been heard of for 2 years; (4) imprisonment with a sentence of more than 1 year served; (5) physical abuse or reasonable apprehension of physical abuse; (6) desertion without support of spouse by husband for 2 years; (7) cruel and inhuman treatment; (8) habitual intemperance (drunkenness) for 2 years; (9) living separate and apart without cohabitation (wife left without husband's consent for 2 years); (10) mental abuse; (11) when either spouse has joined a religious society which professes that the relationship of the husband and wife is unlawful and refuses to cohabit with the other for 6 consecutive months; (12) when the wife of any citizen of New Hampshire leaves the state without her husband's consent and lives elsewhere for 10 consecutive years without returning to claim her marriage rights; and (13) when the wife lives in New Hampshire and her husband becomes the citizen of a foreign country without supporting the wife. [New Hampshire Revised Statutes Annotated; Chapter 458:7, 458:7a, and 458:26].

LEGAL SEPARATION: The grounds for legal separation in New Hampshire are the same as for divorce. The spouse filing for legal separation must have been a resident of New Hampshire for 1 year; or the cause of legal separation must have arisen in New Hampshire and one of the spouses must be living in New Hampshire when the action for legal separation is filed for. [New Hampshire Revised Statutes Annotated; Chapters 458:5, 458:6, 458:7, 458:7a, and 458:26].

SIMPLIFIED OR SPECIAL DIVORCE PROCEDURES: There are no legal provisions in New Hampshire for simplified divorce procedures.

MEDIATION OR COUNSELING REQUIREMENTS: At either spouse's request or if the court feels that there is a reasonable chance at reconciliation, it may delay the divorce proceedings and order the spouses to submit to marriage counseling. There are also provisions for voluntary marital mediation of issues involved in the divorce. [New Hampshire Revised Statutes Annotated; Chapters 458:6, 458:7B, and 458:15].

PROPERTY DISTRIBUTION: New Hampshire is an "equitable distribution" state. The court will divide all of the spouse's property, including (1) gifts; (2) inheritances; (3) property acquired prior to the marriage; and (4) any retirement or pension benefits, as is equitable and just. An equal division is presumed to be equitable. The factors for consideration specified in the statute are: (1) the length of the marriage; (2) the age and health of the spouses; (3) the occupation of the spouses; (4) the vocational skills of the spouses; (5) the employability of the spouses; (6) the value of each spouse's property; (7) the amount and sources of income of the spouses; (8) the liabilities and needs of each spouse; (9) the opportunity of each for further acquisition of capital assets and income; (10) the ability of the custodial parent to engage in gainful employment without interfering with the interests of any minor children in custody; (11) the need of the custodial parent to occupy or own the marital residence and any household furnishings; (12) the actions of either spouse during the marriage which contributed to the increase or decrease in value of any property; (13) the contribution of each spouse to the acquisition of the marital property, including the contribution of each spouse as homemaker; (14) any retirement or pension benefits; (15) the federal income tax consequences of the court's division of the property; (16) any marital fault if such fault caused pain and suffering or economic loss; (17) the value of any property acquired prior to marriage; (18) the value of any gifts or inheritances; (19) any contribution to the education or career development of the other spouse; and (20) any interruption in education or career opportunities to benefit the other's career, the marriage, or any children. [New Hampshire Revised Statutes Annotated; Chapter 458:19 and New Hampshire Case Law].

ALIMONY/MAINTENANCE/SPOUSAL SUPPORT: Either spouse may be ordered to pay support to the other if: (1) the spouse in need lacks sufficient income or property to provide for reasonable needs, taking into account the standard of living during the marriage; and (2) the spouse to pay is able to meet his or her reasonable needs, taking into account the standard of living during the marriage; and (3) the spouse in need is unable to support him or herself at a reasonable standard of living or is the custodian of a child whose condition or circumstances make it appropriate that the custodian not seek employment outside the home. The factors for consideration are: (1) the duration of the marriage; (2) the age of the spouses; (3) the physical and emotional conditions of the spouses; (4) the vocational skills and employability of the spouse seeking support; (5) the tax consequences to each spouse; (6) the amount and sources of income of the spouses; (7) the occupation of the spouses; (8) the value of each spouse's property; (9) the liabilities and needs of each spouse; (10) the opportunity of each for further acquisition of capital assets and income; (11) the fault of either spouse; and (12) the contribution of each spouse to the acquisition of the marital property, including the contribution of each spouse as homemaker. [New Hampshire Revised Statutes Annotated; Chapter 458:19].

SPOUSE'S NAME: The wife's former or maiden name may be restored in a divorce. [New Hampshire Revised Statutes Annotated; Chapter 458:24].

CHILD CUSTODY: Joint legal custody (joint responsibility for all parental rights and decisions, except physical custody) is presumed to be in the best interests of the child unless there has been child abuse by one of the parents. Custody is awarded based on a consideration of the following factors: (1) preference of the child; (2) the education of the child; (3) any findings or recommendations of a neutral mediator; and (4) any other factors. No preference is given to either parent based on the parent's sex. [New Hampshire Revised Statutes Annotated; Chapters 458:17 and 458:17a].

CHILD SUPPORT: The court may order reasonable provisions for the support and education of a child. There are specific child support guidelines set out in the statute. The factors for consideration specified in the statute are: (1) any extraordinary medical, dental, or educational expenses of the child; (2) a significantly higher or lower income of either parent; (3) the economic consequences of the presence of any stepparents or stepchildren; (4) any extraordinary costs associated with physical custody; (5) the economic consequences to either parent of the disposition of the marital home; (6) any state or federal tax consequences; (7) any split or shared custody arrangements; and (8) any other significant factor. The court may order health insurance coverage as a method of support. There are also provisions for wage assignments and wage withholding to secure the payment of any child support. [New Hampshire Revised Statutes Annotated; Chapters 458:17, 458:18, 458-C:1-5].

NEW JERSEY

NAME OF COURT IN WHICH TO FILE FOR DIVORCE: Superior Court. "Superior Court of New Jersey, Chancery Division, Family Part, _____ County".

TITLE OF DIVORCE ACTION: Complaint for Divorce.

NAME USED TO DESCRIBE SPOUSE FILING FOR DIVORCE: Plaintiff.

NAME USED TO DESCRIBE OTHER SPOUSE IN DIVORCE: Defendant.

TITLE OF FINAL DIVORCE PAPERS: Judgement of Divorce.

RESIDENCY REQUIREMENTS AND WHERE TO FILE: (1) One of the spouses must be a resident of New Jersey for at least 1 year prior to filing for divorce; or (2) when the cause for divorce is adultery and took place in New Jersey, one of the spouses must have been a resident (no time limit). The divorce may be filed for in any county in New Jersey. [New Jersey Statutes Annotated; Title 2A, Chapters 34-8 and 34-10].

LEGAL GROUNDS FOR DIVORCE: No-Fault: Living separate and apart for 18 months and no reasonable prospect of reconciliation. [New Jersey Statutes Annotated; Title 2A, Chapter 34-2].

General: (1) adultery; (2) imprisonment for 18 months; (3) unnatural sexual behavior before or after marriage; (4) alcoholism and/or drug addiction; (5) confinement for incurable insanity; (6) willful desertion for 1 year; (7) cruel and inhuman treatment; and (8) separation for 2 years caused by confinement for mental illness. [New Jersey Statutes Annotated; Title 2A, Chapter 34-2].

LEGAL SEPARATION: The grounds for legal separation (or a divorce from bed and board) are the same as for divorce. One of the spouses must be a resident of New Jersey for at least 1 year prior to filing for legal separation or when the cause for legal separation is adultery and took place in New Jersey, one of the spouses must have been a resident (no time limit). [New Jersey Statutes Annotated; Title 2A, Chapter 24-3].

SIMPLIFIED OR SPECIAL DIVORCE PROCEDURES: The filing of an acknowledgement of service of process or appearance is specifically authorized. Also, there is a required Case Information Statement which must be filed as shown in New Jersey Civil Practice Rules, Appendix V. [New Jersey Statutes Annotated; Title 2A, Chapter 34-11].

MEDIATION OR COUNSELING REQUIREMENTS: There are no legal provisions in New Jersey for divorce mediation.

PROPERTY DISTRIBUTION: New Jersey is an "equitable distribution" state. A spouse's separate property acquired before a marriage is retained by that spouse. All of the spouse's other property (except that acquired by gift and inheritance) is divided equitably, based on the following factors: (1) the value of each spouse's marital property; (2) the value of the separate property of the spouses; (3) the length of the marriage; (4) the age and health of the spouses; (5) the amount and sources of income of the spouses; (6) the liabilities and needs of each spouse and the opportunity of each for further acquisition of capital assets and income; (7) the standard of living established during the marriage; (8) how and by whom the property was acquired; (9) the tax consequences to each spouse; (10) the contribution of each spouse to the acquisition of the marital property, including the contribution of each spouse as homemaker; (11) the economic circumstances of each spouse at the time the division of property is to become effective; (12) any written agreement between the spouses; (13) the income and earning capacity of the spouses; (14) the educational background, training, employment skills of the spouses; (15) any custodial responsibilities; (16) the length of absence from the job market; (17) the time and expense necessary to enable the spouse to acquire sufficient education or training to enable the spouse to become self-supporting at a standard of living reasonably comparable to that enjoyed during the marriage; (18) the need for the parent with custody of any children to own or occupy the marital residence; (19) the need to create a trust fund for the future medical or educational needs of a spouse or children; and (20) any other factor necessary to do equity and justice between the spouses. [New Jersey Statutes Annotated; Title 2A, Chapter 34-23.1].

ALIMONY/MAINTENANCE/SPOUSAL SUPPORT: Either spouse may be ordered to pay alimony, without regard to marital fault, based on the following factors: (1) the duration of the marriage; (2) the actual needs, obligations, and ability to pay of each spouse; (3) the standard of living established during the marriage; (4) the time necessary to acquire sufficient education and training to enable the spouse to find appropriate employment, and that spouse's future earning capacity; (5) the age of the spouses; (6) the physical and emotional conditions of the spouses; (7) the earning capacities, educational levels, vocational skills, and employability of the spouses; (8) the length of absence from the job market; (9) any child custodial responsibilities of the spouse seeking alimony; (10) the availability of training and employment; (11) the opportunity for the future acquisition of capital and income; (12) the contribution of each spouse to the acquisition of the marital property, including the contribution of each spouse to the care and custody of children and interruption of personal careers or educational opportunities; (13) and any other factor the court deems just and equitable. [New Jersey Statutes Annotated; Title 2A, Chapter 34-23].

SPOUSE'S NAME: The court may allow either spouse to use his or her former name. [New Jersey Statutes Annotated; Title 2A, Chapter 34-21].

CHILD CUSTODY: Sole or joint custody may be awarded based on the following factors: (1) the physical, emotional, mental, religious, and social needs of the child; and (2) the preference of the child, if the child is of sufficient age and capacity. No preference is to be given because of parent's sex. A father may not forcibly take a minor child from a mother's actual physical custody. [New Jersey Statutes Annotated; Titles 2A, Chapter 34-23, 9:2-4 and New Jersey Case Law].

CHILD SUPPORT: The court may award child support for the care, maintenance, and education of a child. The factors for consideration specified in the statute are: (1) the needs of the child; (2) the standard of living and economic circumstances of both parents; (3) the financial resources, needs, and obligations of both the noncustodial and the custodial parent; (4) the earning ability of each parent, including educational background, training, employment skills, work experience, custodial responsibility for the children, cost of child care, and the length and cost of education and training to obtain employment; (5) the need and capacity of the child for education, including higher education; (6) the age and health station of the child and the parents; (7) the income, assets, and earning ability of the child; (8) the responsibility of the parents for the support of others; (9) any other relevant factors. There are specific New Jersey Supreme Court child support guidelines contained in New Jersey Civil Practice Rules, Appendix IX. [New Jersey Statutes Annotated; Title 2A, Chapter 34-23].

NEW MEXICO

NAME OF COURT IN WHICH TO FILE FOR DIVORCE: District Court. "State of New Mexico, In the District Court, _____ County."

TITLE OF DIVORCE ACTION: Petition for Dissolution of Marriage.

NAME USED TO DESCRIBE SPOUSE FILING FOR DISSOLUTION OF MARRIAGE: Petitioner.

NAME USED TO DESCRIBE OTHER SPOUSE IN DISSOLUTION OF MARRIAGE: Respondent.

TITLE OF FINAL DISSOLUTION OF MARRIAGE PAPERS: Decree of Dissolution of Marriage.

RESIDENCY REQUIREMENTS AND WHERE TO FILE: One of the spouses must have been a resident of New Mexico for at least 6 months immediately preceding the filing for dissolution of marriage and have a home in New Mexico. The dissolution of marriage may be filed in any county where either spouse resides. [New Mexico Statutes Annotated; Article 4, Section 40-4-5].

LEGAL GROUNDS FOR DISSOLUTION OF MARRIAGE: No-Fault: Incompatibility because of discord and conflicts of personalities such that the legitimate ends of the marriage relationship have been destroyed preventing any reasonable expectation of reconciliation. [New Mexico Statutes Annotated; Article 4, Sections 40-4-1 and 40-4-2].

General: (1) adultery; (2) abandonment; and (3) cruel and inhuman treatment. [New Mexico Statutes Annotated; Article 4, Section 40-4-1].

LEGAL SEPARATION: If the spouses have permanently separated and do not live together or cohabit, either spouse may begin proceedings for property division, child custody and support, and maintenance, without asking for a dissolution of marriage. One of the spouses must have been a resident of New Mexico for at least 6 months immediately preceding the filing for legal separation and have a home in New Mexico. [New Mexico Statutes Annotated; Article 4, Section 40-4-3].

SIMPLIFIED OR SPECIAL DISSOLUTION OF MARRIAGE PROCEDURES: Marital settlement agreements are specifically authorized by law. Any marital settlement agreements should be recorded in the county where the spouses reside. [New Mexico Statutes Annotated; Article 4, Sections 40-2-4 and 40-2-5].

MEDIATION OR COUNSELING REQUIREMENTS: There provisions in New Mexico for the establishment of domestic relations mediation programs. If such programs have been established in the county where the dissolution of marriage is filed for, parents may request the use of such programs, or the court may order the parents to enter the program. [New Mexico Statutes Annotated; Article 4, Section 40-12-5].

PROPERTY DISTRIBUTION: New Mexico is a "community property" state. Each spouse retains his or her separate property acquired prior to the marriage and any gifts or inheritances. The spouse's community property is to be divided equally between the spouses. Marital fault is not considered. There are no factors for consideration set out in the statute. [New Mexico Statutes Annotated; Article 4, Section 40-4-7].

ALIMONY/MAINTENANCE/SPOUSAL SUPPORT: Either spouse may be awarded a just and proper amount of maintenance, without regard to marital fault. The factors that the court will consider are: (1) the duration of the marriage; (2) the ability of the spouse from whom support is sought to meet his or her needs while meeting those of the spouse seeking support; (3) the financial resources of the spouse seeking maintenance, including any community property apportioned to such spouse and such spouse's ability to meet his or her needs independently; (4) the needs and obligations of each spouse; (5) the age of the spouses; (6) the amount of property that each spouse owns; and (7) the physical and emotional conditions of the spouses. [New Mexico Statutes Annotated; Article 4, Section 40-4-7 and New Mexico Case Law].

SPOUSE'S NAME: The court may order the restoration of a spouse's former name. [New Mexico Statutes Annotated; Article 4, Section 40-8-1].

CHILD CUSTODY: Joint or sole child custody is to be determined according to the best interests of the child. There is a presumption that joint custody is in the best interests of the child, unless shown otherwise. The factors for consideration in all custody situations are: (1) the wishes of the child; (2) the wishes of the parents; (3) the relationship of the child with parents, siblings, and other significant family members; (4) the child's adjustment to his or her home, school, and community; and (5) the mental and physical health of all individuals involved. If a minor is 14 years old or older, the court may consider the wishes of the minor.

In addition, the factors that are considered in determining joint custody are as follows: (1) the ability of the parents to cooperate and make decisions jointly; (2) the physical proximity of the parents to each other as this relates to the practical considerations of where the child will reside; (3) whether an award of joint custody will promote more frequent or continuing contact between the child and each of the parents; (4) the love, affection, and other emotional ties existing between the parents and the child; (5) the capacity and disposition of the parents to provide the child with food, clothing, medical care, and other material needs; (6) whether each parent is willing to accept all the responsibilities of parenting, including a willingness to accept or relinquish care at specified times; (7) whether each parent is able to allow the other to provide care without intrusion; and (8) the suitability of a parenting plan for the implementation of joint custody. [New Mexico Statutes Annotated; Article 4, Section 40-4-9].

CHILD SUPPORT: Either parent may be ordered to provide child support, based on a consideration of the financial resources of that parent. No other factors for consideration are set out in the statute. However, specific child support guidelines and worksheets are provided. The assignment and withholding of wages to secure the payment of child support payments may be ordered. [New Mexico Statutes Annotated; Article 4, Sections 40-4-7 and 40-4-11]

APPENDIX: DIVORCE LAWS OF ALL 50 STATES

NEW YORK

NAME OF COURT IN WHICH TO FILE FOR DIVORCE: Supreme Court. "Supreme Court of the State of New York, _____ County."

TITLE OF DIVORCE ACTION: Complaint for Divorce.

NAME USED TO DESCRIBE SPOUSE FILING FOR DIVORCE: Plaintiff.

NAME USED TO DESCRIBE OTHER SPOUSE IN DIVORCE: Defendant.

TITLE OF FINAL DIVORCE PAPERS: Judgement of Divorce.

RESIDENCY REQUIREMENTS AND WHERE TO FILE: If only one spouse resides in New York at the time of filing the divorce, the residency requirement is 2 years. However, the requirement is reduced to 1 year if: (1) the spouses were married in New York and either spouse is still a resident; or (2) they once resided in New York and either spouse is still a resident; or (3) the grounds for divorce arose in New York. In addition, there is no residency time limit requirement if both of the spouses were residents of New York at the time of filing the divorce and the grounds for divorce arose in New York. The divorce may be filed for in a county where either spouse resides. [Consolidated Laws of New York Annotated; Domestic Relations Law, Sections 230 and 231; and New York Civil Practice Laws and Rules, Rule 503].

LEGAL GROUNDS FOR DIVORCE: No-Fault: (1) living separate and apart for 1 year under the terms of a separation agreement which is in writing and signed and notarized. (Proof of compliance with the terms of the settlement agreement must be submitted when the divorce is filed. In addition, a copy of the agreement or a brief memorandum of the agreement must be filed in the office of the clerk of the county; or (2) living separate and apart for 1 year under the terms of a judicial separation decree. [Consolidated Laws of New York Annotated; Domestic Relations Law, Section 170].

General: (1) adultery; (2) abandonment for 1 year; (3) imprisonment for 3 or more consecutive years; (4) cruel and inhuman treatment; and (5) abandonment and absence for 5 years. [Consolidated Laws of New York Annotated; Domestic Relations Law, Section 170].

LEGAL SEPARATION: The grounds for legal separation (separation from bed and board) in New York are: (1) adultery; (2) abandonment; (3) imprisonment for 3 or more consecutive years; (4) neglect of and failure to provide support for a wife; and (5) cruel and inhuman treatment. If only one spouse resides in New York at the time of filing the legal separation, the residency requirement is 2 years. However, the requirement is reduced to 1 year if: (1) the spouses were married in New York and either spouse is still a resident; or (2) they once resided in New York and either spouse is still a resident; or (3) the grounds for legal separation arose in New York. In addition, there is no residency time limit requirement if both of the spouses were residents of New York at the time of filing the legal separation and the grounds for legal separation arose in New York. [Consolidated Laws of New York Annotated; Domestic Relations Law, Sections 200, 230, and 231].

SIMPLIFIED OR SPECIAL DIVORCE PROCEDURES: A summary divorce may be granted in New York if: (1) the spouses lived apart for 1 year according to the terms of a separation decree or a separation agreement; and (2) satisfactory proof is submitted to the court that the spouse seeking the divorce has substantially performed all the terms and conditions of the separation decree or separation agreement. There are sample divorce forms contained in the statute, including the language necessary to state specific grounds and residency requirements. [Consolidated Laws of New York Annotated; Domestic Relations Law, Section 170].

MEDIATION OR COUNSELING REQUIREMENTS: There are no legal provisions in New York for divorce mediation.

PROPERTY DISTRIBUTION: New York is an "equitable distribution" state. Separate property, including property acquired before a marriage and any gifts or inheritances whenever acquired, is to remain with the spouse who owns it. Separate property also includes any increase in value or property acquired in exchange for separate property. Marital property acquired during the marriage will be equitably divided between the spouses, based on the following factors: (1) the contribution of each spouse to the acquisition of the marital property, including the contribution of each spouse as homemaker; (2) the value of each spouse's property at the time of the marriage and at the time of filing for divorce; (3) the economic circumstances of each spouse at the time the division of property is to become effective; (4) the length of the marriage; (5) the age and health of the spouses; (6) the amount and sources of income of the spouses; (7) the present and potential earning capability of each spouse; (8) any retirement benefits, including social security, civil service, military and railroad retirement benefits; (9) whether the property award is instead of or in addition to maintenance; (10) custodial provisions for the children and the need for a custodial parent to occupy the marital home; (11) the type of marital property in question (whether it is liquid or non-liquid); (12) the impossibility or difficulty of evaluating an interest in an asset such as a business, profession, or corporation and the desirability of keeping such an asset intact and free from interference by the other spouse; (13) the tax consequences to each party; (14) the wasteful dissipation of assets; (15) any transfer made in anticipation of divorce; and (16) any other factor necessary to do equity and justice between the spouses. Marital fault may be considered. Financial disclosure of assets and income are mandatory. [Consolidated Laws of New York Annotated; Domestic Relations Law, Section 236, Part B].

ALIMONY/MAINTENANCE/SPOUSAL SUPPORT: Either spouse may be awarded maintenance, without regard to marital fault, based on a consideration of the following factors: (1) the income and property of the spouses; (2) the time necessary to acquire sufficient education and training to enable the spouse to find appropriate employment, and that spouse's future earning capacity; (3) the duration of the marriage; (4) the wasteful dissipation of marital property; (5) the contribution of each spouse to the marriage and the career of the other spouse, including services rendered in homemaking, child care, education, and career building of the other spouse; (6) the tax consequences to each spouse; the age of the spouses; (7) the physical and emotional conditions of the spouses; (8) any custodial and child support responsibilities; (9) the ability of the spouse seeking support to become self-supporting and the time and training necessary; (10) any reduced lifetime earning capacity as the result of having foregone or delayed education, training, employment, or career opportunities during the marriage; and (11) any other factor the court deems just and equitable. [Consolidated Laws of New York Annotated; Domestic Relations Law, Section 236, Part B].

SPOUSE'S NAME: At the wife's request, upon divorce the court may restore her maiden or other former name. [Consolidated Laws of New York Annotated; Domestic Relations Law, Section 240a].

CHILD CUSTODY: Joint or sole child custody is to be determined according to the best interests of the child. Neither parent is entitled to a preference. There are no factors for consideration specified in the statute. [Consolidated Laws of New York Annotated; Domestic Relations Law, Section 240 and New York Case Law,].

CHILD SUPPORT: Either or both parents may be ordered to pay child support necessary for the support, maintenance, and education of the child. Health insurance coverage may be ordered to be provided. The factors to be considered are: (1) the financial resources of the child; (2) the standard of living the child would have enjoyed if the marriage had not been dissolved; (3) the physical and emotional conditions and educational needs of the child; (4) the financial resources, needs, and obligations of both the noncustodial and the custodial parent; (5) the tax consequences to each parent; (6) the non-monetary contributions that the parents will make towards the care and well-being of the child; (7) the educational needs of either parent; (8) whether one parent's income is substantially less than the other parent's; and (8) any other relevant factors. Security may be required for the payments. [Consolidated Laws of New York Annotated; Domestic Relations Law, Sections 32, 33, 236-Part B, and 243].

APPENDIX: DIVORCE LAWS OF ALL 50 STATES

NORTH CAROLINA

NAME OF COURT IN WHICH TO FILE FOR DIVORCE: Superior Court or District Court. "In the General Court of Justice, _____ Division, North Carolina, _____ County".

TITLE OF DIVORCE ACTION: Complaint for Divorce.

NAME USED TO DESCRIBE SPOUSE FILING FOR DIVORCE: Plaintiff.

NAME USED TO DESCRIBE OTHER SPOUSE IN DIVORCE: Defendant.

TITLE OF FINAL DIVORCE PAPERS: Decree of Divorce.

RESIDENCY REQUIREMENTS AND WHERE TO FILE: Either spouse must have been a resident of North Carolina for at least 6 months prior to filing for divorce. Divorce may be filed for in the county of residence of either spouse. [General Statutes of North Carolina; Chapter 50, Section 50-8].

LEGAL GROUNDS FOR DIVORCE: No-Fault: Living separate and apart without cohabitation for 1 year. [General Statutes of North Carolina; Chapter 50, Section 50-5.6]

General: (1) confinement for incurable insanity for 3 years; or (2) incurable mental illness based on examinations for 3 years. [General Statutes of North Carolina; Chapter 50, Sections 50-5.1].

LEGAL SEPARATION: The grounds for legal separation (divorce from bed and board) are as follows: (1) abandonment; (2) adultery; (3) alcoholism and/or drug addiction; (4) cruel and inhuman treatment endangering the life of the spouse; (5) personal indignities; and (6) turning a spouse out-of-doors. Either spouse must have been a resident of North Carolina for at least 6 months prior to filing for divorce from bed and board. [General Statutes of North Carolina; Chapter 50, Sections 50-7 and 50-8].

SIMPLIFIED OR SPECIAL DIVORCE PROCEDURES: There are no legal provisions in North Carolina for simplified divorce procedures.

MEDIATION OR COUNSELING REQUIREMENTS: If child custody is a contested issue, the court may order the parents to submit to mandatory mediation of that issue. [General Statutes of North Carolina; Chapter 50, Section 50-13.1].

PROPERTY DISTRIBUTION: North Carolina is an "equitable distribution" state. Separate property, including (1) any property acquired before the marriage; (2) any gifts and inheritances acquired during the marriage; (3) any property acquired in exchange for separate property; and (4) any increase in the value of separate property, will be retained by the spouse who owns it. Marital property (property acquired by either or both spouses during the marriage and before the separation, including any pension or retirement fund benefits) will be divided equally unless the court finds that an equal division is not fair. The division is based on the following factors: (1) any direct or indirect contributions to the career or education of the other spouse; (2) any depletion or waste of property; (3) the net value of the property; (4) the liquid or non-liquid character of the property; (5) the difficulty of evaluating any component asset or interest in a business or profession and the desirability of returning such asset free from any claim by the other spouse; (6) the contribution of each spouse to the acquisition of the marital property, including the contribution of each spouse as homemaker; (7) the economic circumstances of each spouse at the time the division of property is to become effective; (8) any increase or decrease in the value of the separate property of the spouse during the marriage or the depletion of the separate property for marital purposes; (9) the length of the marriage; (10) the age and health of the spouses; (11) the federal income tax consequences of the court's division of the property; (11) liabilities of the spouses; (12) any retirement benefits, including social security, civil service, military and railroad retirement benefits; (13) any prior marriage of each spouse; (14) any custodial provisions for the children, including the desirability of the spouse with custody of any children occupying the marital residence; and (15) any other factor necessary to do equity and justice between the spouses. [General Statutes of North Carolina; Chapter 50, Section 50-20].

ALIMONY/MAINTENANCE/SPOUSAL SUPPORT: Either spouse may be awarded alimony. The factors for consideration are: (1) the standard of living established during the marriage; (2) the comparative financial resources of the spouses, including their comparative earning abilities in the labor market and their incomes; (3) the physical and emotional conditions of the spouses; and (4) any other factor the court deems just and equitable. The court may require bond for security for the alimony payments. [General Statutes of North Carolina; Chapter 50, Sections 50-16.2, 50-16.5, 50-16.6, and 50-16.7].

SPOUSE'S NAME: Upon request, the court may allow a woman may resume the use of her former or maiden name. A woman may also make application to the clerk of the court for resumption of the use of her maiden or former name. [General Statutes of North Carolina; Chapter 50, Section 50-12].

CHILD CUSTODY: Joint or sole child custody is determined according to the interests and welfare of the child. There is no presumption that either parent is better suited to have custody. No other factors for consideration are specified in the statute. [General Statutes of North Carolina; Chapter 50, Section 50-13.2].

CHILD SUPPORT: Both parents are primarily responsible for the support of a minor child and either parent may be ordered to pay child support. The factors to be considered are: (1) the needs of the child; (2) the earnings, conditions, and accustomed standard of living of the child; (3) the child care and homemaker contributions of each parent; (4) any joint or shared custody arrangements; and (5) the parents ability to pay. There are official child support guidelines which are effective as of July 1, 1990. Child support payments may be required to be paid through the clerk of the court. Income withholding may be used if child support payments become delinquent. [General Statutes of North Carolina; Chapter 50, Section 50-13.4].

NORTH DAKOTA

NAME OF COURT IN WHICH TO FILE FOR DIVORCE: District Court. " State of North Dakota, County of _____, In the District Court, _____ Judicial District".

TITLE OF DIVORCE ACTION: Complaint for Divorce.

NAME USED TO DESCRIBE SPOUSE FILING FOR DIVORCE: Plaintiff.

NAME USED TO DESCRIBE OTHER SPOUSE IN DIVORCE: Defendant.

TITLE OF FINAL DIVORCE PAPERS: Decree of Divorce.

RESIDENCY REQUIREMENTS AND WHERE TO FILE: The spouse filing for divorce must be a resident of North Dakota for at least 6 months prior to the entry of the final divorce. If the defendant is a resident of North Dakota, the divorce must be filed in the county where the defendant resides. If the defendant is not a resident, the divorce may be filed for in any county that the plaintiff designates in the complaint. [North Dakota Century Code; Volume 3A, Chapters 14-05-17 and 28-04-05].

LEGAL GROUNDS FOR DIVORCE: No-Fault: Irreconcilable differences. [North Dakota Century Code; Volume 3A, Chapter 14-05-03].

General: (1) adultery; (2) confinement for incurable insanity for a period of 5 years; (3) conviction of a felony; (4) willful desertion; (5) cruel and inhuman treatment; (6) willful neglect; and (7) habitual intemperance (drunkenness). [North Dakota Century Code; Volume 3A, Chapter 14-06-01].

LEGAL SEPARATION: The grounds for legal separation (separation from bed and board) in North Dakota are: (1) irreconcilable differences; (2) adultery; (3) confinement for incurable insanity for a period of 5 years; (4) conviction of a felony; (5) willful desertion; (6) cruel and inhuman treatment; (7) willful neglect; and (8) habitual intemperance (drunkenness). The spouse filing for legal separation must be a resident of North Dakota for at least 6 months prior to the entry of the legal separation. [North Dakota Century Code; Volume 3A, Chapters 14-05-03, 14-06-01, and 14-06-06].

SIMPLIFIED OR SPECIAL DIVORCE PROCEDURES: Separation agreements are specifically authorized by statute. [North Dakota Century Code; Volume 3A, Chapter 14-07-07].

MEDIATION OR COUNSELING REQUIREMENTS: In an action for divorce or legal separation where child support or child custody is an issue, the court may order the parents to submit to mediation. [North Dakota Century Code; Volume 3A, Chapter 14-09.1-02].

PROPERTY DISTRIBUTION: North Dakota is an "equitable distribution" state. All of the spouse's property, including gifts, inheritances, and any acquired prior to the marriage, will be equitably distributed as the court feels is just and proper. There are no factors for consideration specified in the statute. [North Dakota Century Code; Volume 3A, Chapter 14-05-24].

ALIMONY/MAINTENANCE/SPOUSAL SUPPORT: Either spouse may be required to make allowances for the support of the other spouse for his or her entire life or a shorter period. All of the circumstances of the situation, including any marital fault, may be considered. There are no other specific factors for consideration set out in the statute. Support payments may be required to be made through the clerk of the court. [North Dakota Century Code; Volume 3A, Chapter 14-05-24].

SPOUSE'S NAME: Upon request, a wife's former or maiden name may be restored. [North Dakota Case Law].

CHILD CUSTODY: Child custody is awarded according to the best interests and welfare of the child, and based on the following factors: (1) moral character and prudence of the parents; (2) capability and desire of each parent to meet the child's needs; (3) preference of the child, if the child is of sufficient age and capacity; (4) the love and affection existing between the child and each parent; (5) the length of time the child has lived in a stable, satisfactory environment and the desirability of maintaining continuity; (6) the child's adjustment to his or her home, school, and community; (7) the mental and physical health of all individuals involved; (8) the stability of the home environment likely to be offered by each parent; (9) the child's interaction with anyone who resides with a parent; (10) any spouse or child abuse; and (11) any other factors. Both parents are considered to be equally entitled to custody of a child. [North Dakota Century Code; Volume 3A, Chapters 14-05-22, 14-09-06, 14-09-06.1 and 14-09-06.2].

CHILD SUPPORT: Either parent may be ordered to pay child support. The amount awarded will be based on a consideration of the following factors: (1) the net income of the parents; (2) the other resources available to the parents; and (3) any circumstances that might be considered in reducing the amount of support on the basis of hardship. There are specific child support guidelines that the court will consider which have been prepared by the North Dakota Department of Human Services. Child support payments may be required to be paid through the clerk of the court. The court can order child support payments be guaranteed by wage assignments and wage withholding orders. [North Dakota Century Code; Volume 3A, Chapters 14-05-24, 14-08-07, 14-09-08, 14-09-09.1, 14-09-09.2, and 14-09-09.7]

OHIO

NAME OF COURT IN WHICH TO FILE FOR DIVORCE: Court of Common Pleas. "In the Court of Common Pleas of _____ County, Ohio."

TITLE OF DIVORCE ACTION: Petition for Dissolution of Marriage (See below under Summary Divorce); or Complaint for Divorce. [See below under **Simplified Or Special Dissolution Of Marriage Procedures**].

NAME USED TO DESCRIBE SPOUSE FILING FOR DIVORCE: Petitioner if in Petition for Dissolution of Marriage; or Plaintiff if in Complaint for Divorce. [See below under **Simplified Or Special Dissolution Of Marriage Procedures**].

NAME USED TO DESCRIBE OTHER SPOUSE IN DIVORCE: Co-Petitioner if in Petition for Dissolution of Marriage; or Defendant in Complaint for Divorce. [See below under **Simplified Or Special Dissolution Of Marriage Procedures**].

TITLE OF FINAL DIVORCE PAPERS: Decree of Dissolution of Marriage; or Decree of Divorce. [See below under **Simplified Or Special Dissolution Of Marriage Procedures**].

RESIDENCY REQUIREMENTS AND WHERE TO FILE: The spouse filing for divorce or dissolution of marriage must have been a resident of Ohio for at least 6 months and a resident of the county for at least 90 days immediately prior to filing. [Ohio Revised Code Annotated; Section 3105.03 and Ohio Rules of Civil Procedure, Rule 3].

LEGAL GROUNDS FOR DIVORCE: No-Fault: (1) incompatibility; or (2) living separate and apart without cohabitation and without interruption for 1 year. [Ohio Revised Code Annotated; Section 3105.01].

General: (1) adultery; (2) imprisonment; (3) confinement for incurable insanity for 4 years; (4) willful desertion for 1 year; (5) cruel and inhuman treatment; (6) bigamy; (7) habitual intemperance (drunkenness); (8) when a final divorce decree has been obtained outside of the state of Ohio that does not release the other spouse from the obligations of the marriage inside the state of Ohio; (9) fraud; and (10) neglect. [Ohio Revised Code Annotated; Section 3105.01].

LEGAL SEPARATION: A suit for alimony only (not coupled with divorce) may be brought when the spouses have been living separate and apart. Maintenance will be granted based a finding of ill treatment and upon consideration of the following factors: (1) adultery; (2) abandonment; (3) imprisonment; (4) habitual intemperance (drunkenness); and (5) neglect. [Ohio Revised Code Annotated; Sections 3105.03 and 3105.17].

SIMPLIFIED OR SPECIAL DIVORCE PROCEDURES: Both spouses may jointly file a petition for dissolution of marriage. The petition must: (1) be signed by both spouses; (2) have attached to it a separation agreement which provides for (a) division of property, (b) alimony (including the authorization of the court to modify any alimony terms), and (c) custody, visitation, and child support, if there are any minor children. Between 30 and 90 days after filing such a petition, both spouses must appear in court and state under oath that he or she: (1) voluntarily signed the agreement; (2) is satisfied with the agreement; and (3) seeks dissolution of the marriage. In addition, settlement agreements are also authorized by statute and may be used in a divorce proceeding. A sample divorce complaint form is contained in Ohio Rules of Civil Procedure, Appendix of Forms, Form #20. Finally, there may be local court rules which apply to divorce proceedings in Ohio. [Ohio Revised Code Annotated; Sections 3105.03, 3105.10, 3105.61-65].

MEDIATION OR COUNSELING REQUIREMENTS: At the request of either spouse or on the court's own initiative, the court may order the spouses to undergo conciliation procedures for up to 90 days. The court will set forth the procedures and name the conciliator. [Ohio Revised Code Annotated; Sections 3105.091 and 3117.01+].

DIVORCE YOURSELF

PROPERTY DISTRIBUTION: An equitable division of all of the spouse's property, including gifts, inheritances, and property acquired prior to the marriage, is allowed in conjunction with an award of maintenance, based on the following factors: (1) whether the spouse seeking support is the custodian of a child whose condition or circumstances make it appropriate for that spouse not to seek outside employment; (2) the earning ability of both spouses; (3) the financial resources of both spouses, including each spouse's ability to meet his or her needs independently; (4) the needs and obligations of each spouse; (5) the contribution of each spouse to the marriage, including services rendered in homemaking, child care, education, and career building of the other spouse; (6) the age of the spouses; (7) the physical and emotional conditions of the spouses; (8) any custodial and child support responsibilities; (9) the educational level of each spouse at the time of the marriage and at the time the action for divorce or is commenced; (10) any inheritances of either spouse; (11) any pension or retirement benefits of either spouse; (12) the duration of the marriage; and (13) what property was brought to the marriage by each spouse. Marital fault is not a consideration. [Ohio Revised Code Annotated; Sections 3105.17 and 3105.18].

ALIMONY/MAINTENANCE/SPOUSAL SUPPORT: Either spouse may be awarded reasonable alimony, in lump sum or in periodic payments, based on a consideration of the following factors: (1) whether the spouse seeking support is the custodian of a child whose condition or circumstances make it appropriate for that spouse not to seek outside employment; (2) the earning ability of both spouses; (3) the financial resources of both spouses, including marital property apportioned to each spouse and each spouse's ability to meet his or her needs independently; (4) the needs and obligations of each spouse; (5) the contribution of each spouse to the marriage, including services rendered in homemaking, child care, education, and career building of the other spouse; (6) the age of the spouses; (7) the physical and emotional conditions of the spouses; (8) custodial and child support responsibilities; (9) the educational level of each spouse at the time of the marriage and at the time the action for support is commenced; (10) any inheritances of either spouse; (11) any pension or retirement benefits of either spouse; (12) the duration of the marriage; and (13) what property was brought to the marriage by each spouse. Marital fault is not a consideration. [Ohio Revised Code Annotated; Sections 3105.17 and 3105.18].

SPOUSE'S NAME: Upon request, the court will restore a person's former or maiden name. [Ohio Revised Code Annotated; Sections 3105.16 and 3105.34].

CHILD CUSTODY: Joint or sole child custody may be awarded according to the best interests of the child. Factors to be considered are: (1) the preference of the child, if the child is of sufficient age and capacity; (2) the wishes of the parents; (3) the child's adjustment to his or her home, school, and community; (4) the mental and physical health of all individuals involved; (5) the relationship of the child with parents, siblings, and other significant family members; and (6) any findings or recommendations of a neutral mediator. Both parents are considered to have equal rights to custody. A child of 12 or older will be allowed to choose his or her custodian, unless it appears that the parent is unfit or may endanger the child. In addition, for joint custody to be awarded, both parents must request it and submit a plan for joint custody. [Ohio Revised Code Annotated; Sections 3109.03 and 3109.04].

CHILD SUPPORT: Either or both parents may be ordered to pay child support. Marital misconduct is not to be considered in this award. The factors that will be considered are: (1) the financial resources of the child; (2) the standard of living the child would have enjoyed if the marriage had not been dissolved; (3) the physical and emotional conditions of the child; (4) the medical and educational needs of the child; and (5) the financial resources, needs, and obligations of both the noncustodial and the custodial parent. Health care insurance may be ordered to be provided for the child. Child support payments may be ordered to be paid through the state child support agency. [Ohio Revised Code Annotated; Section 3105.05].

APPENDIX: DIVORCE LAWS OF ALL 50 STATES

OKLAHOMA

NAME OF COURT IN WHICH TO FILE FOR DIVORCE: District Court. "State of Oklahoma, In the District Court, _____ County."

TITLE OF DIVORCE ACTION: Petition for Divorce.

NAME USED TO DESCRIBE SPOUSE FILING FOR DIVORCE: Plaintiff.

NAME USED TO DESCRIBE OTHER SPOUSE IN DIVORCE: Defendant.

TITLE OF FINAL DIVORCE PAPERS: Decree of Divorce.

RESIDENCY REQUIREMENTS AND WHERE TO FILE: Either spouse must have been a resident of Oklahoma for 6 months immediately prior to filing for divorce. The divorce may be filed for in the county in which the plaintiff has been a resident for 30 days or in the county where the defendant resides. [Oklahoma Statutes Annotated; Title 43, Sections 102 and 103].

LEGAL GROUNDS FOR DIVORCE: No-Fault: Incompatibility. [Oklahoma Statutes Annotated; Title 43, Section 101].

General: (1) impotence; (2) adultery; (3) abandonment for 1 year; (4) imprisonment; (5) confinement for incurable insanity for 5 years; (6) cruel and inhuman treatment; (7) fraud; (8) habitual intemperance (drunkenness); (9) the wife pregnant by another at the time of the marriage; and (10) gross neglect. [Oklahoma Statutes Annotated; Title 43, Section 101].

LEGAL SEPARATION: A spouse may sue the other spouse for alimony without filing for divorce. The grounds for requesting non-divorce-based alimony are: (1) impotence; (2) adultery; (3) abandonment for 1 year; (4) imprisonment; (5) confinement for incurable insanity for 5 years; (6) cruel and inhuman treatment; (7) fraud; (8) habitual intemperance (drunkenness); (9) the wife pregnant by another at the time of the marriage; (10) gross neglect; and (11) incompatibility. [Oklahoma Statutes Annotated; Title 43, Section 129].

SIMPLIFIED OR SPECIAL DIVORCE PROCEDURES: Separation agreements are specifically authorized by statute. [Oklahoma Statutes Annotated; Title 43, Section 205].

MEDIATION OR COUNSELING REQUIREMENTS: The court may appoint an arbitrator for joint custody disputes which take place after a divorce. [Oklahoma Statutes Annotated; Title 43, Section 109].

PROPERTY DISTRIBUTION: Oklahoma is an "equitable distribution" state. Each spouse is entitled to keep: (1) the property owned by him or her before the marriage; and (2) any gifts or inheritances acquired during the marriage. All property held or acquired jointly during the marriage will be divided between the spouses in a just and reasonable manner. A portion of the jointly-held property may be set aside to one spouse for the support of any children who may live with that spouse. The only factors for consideration set out in the statute are: (1) the way in which the property in question was held; and (2) the time and manner of the acquisition of the property. Marital fault is not a factor. [Oklahoma Statutes Annotated; Title 43, Section 121].

ALIMONY/MAINTENANCE/SPOUSAL SUPPORT: Alimony may be awarded to either spouse. The award may be in money or property, in lump sum or installments, having regard for the value of the property at the time of the award. Marital fault is not a consideration. There are no other factors for consideration set out in the statute. Alimony payments may be required to be paid through the clerk of the court. [Oklahoma Statutes Annotated; Title 43, Sections 121 and 136].

SPOUSE'S NAME: Upon request, a wife may have her former or maiden name restored upon divorce. [Oklahoma Statutes Annotated; Title 43, Section 121].

CHILD CUSTODY: Joint or sole child custody may be awarded based on the best interests of the physical, mental, and moral welfare of the child, and upon a consideration of the preference of the child. No other factors for consideration are specified in the statute. The court may require that the parents submit a joint custody plan to the court if joint custody is desired. [Oklahoma Statutes Annotated; Title 43, Section 109].

CHILD SUPPORT: The parent awarded custody of the child must provide for the education and support of the child to the best of his or her ability. If such support is inadequate, the non-custodial parent must assist in the support to the best of his or her ability. A portion of the non-custodial parents property may be set aside for the custodial parent's use in supporting the child. The only factors for consideration set out in the statute are: (1) the income and means of the parents; and (2) the property and assets of the parents. There are official child support guidelines and forms provided by the Oklahoma Department of Human Services. Child support payments may be required to be paid through the clerk of the court. Security or bond may be required for the payments and income withholding may be used to guarantee the payments. [Oklahoma Statutes Annotated; Title 43, Sections 110, 112, 118, and 136; and Title 56, Sections 235+].

APPENDIX: DIVORCE LAWS OF ALL 50 STATES

OREGON

NAME OF COURT IN WHICH TO FILE FOR DIVORCE: Circuit Court. "In the Circuit Court for the State of Oregon for the County of _____."

TITLE OF DIVORCE ACTION: Petition for Dissolution of Marriage. "In the Matter of the Marriage of _____ and _____."

NAME USED TO DESCRIBE SPOUSE FILING FOR DISSOLUTION OF MARRIAGE: Petitioner [or Co-Petitioner if the petition is filed jointly. See below under **Simplified Or Special Dissolution Of Marriage Procedures**].

NAME USED TO DESCRIBE OTHER SPOUSE IN DISSOLUTION OF MARRIAGE: Respondent [or Co-Petitioner if the petition is filed jointly. See below under **Simplified Or Special Dissolution Of Marriage Procedures**].

TITLE OF FINAL DISSOLUTION OF MARRIAGE PAPERS: Decree of Dissolution of Marriage.

RESIDENCY REQUIREMENTS AND WHERE TO FILE: If the marriage was not performed in Oregon, one of the spouses must have been a resident of Oregon for 6 months immediately prior to filing. If the marriage was performed in Oregon and either of the spouses is a resident at the time of filing, there is no durational residency requirement. The dissolution of marriage may be filed in a county where either spouse resides. There is a 90-day waiting period before a hearing will be scheduled which begins after the respondent has been served with papers or has filed an Appearance. [Oregon Revised Statutes; Volume 2, Sections 14.070, 107.065, and 107.075].

LEGAL GROUNDS FOR DISSOLUTION OF MARRIAGE: No-Fault: Irreconcilable differences between the spouses which have caused the irretrievable breakdown of the marriage. Misconduct of the spouses will only be considered when child custody is an issue or if necessary to prove irreconcilable differences. [Oregon Revised Statutes; Volume 2, Section 107.025].

General: (1) consent to marriage was obtained by fraud, duress, or force; (2) minor married without lawful consent; (3) spouse lacked mental capacity to consent (including temporary incapacity resulting from drug or alcohol use). Misconduct of the spouses will only be considered when child custody is an issue. [Oregon Revised Statutes; Volume 2, Section 107.015]

LEGAL SEPARATION: The grounds for legal separation (separation from bed and board) in Oregon are irreconcilable differences between the spouses which have caused the irretrievable breakdown of the marriage. The spouses may enter a separation agreement to live apart for at least 1 year. At least one of the spouses must be a resident of Oregon when the action for legal separation is filed. The legal separation may be filed for in a county where either spouse lives. [Oregon Revised Statutes; Volume 2, Sections 14.070, 107.025, 107.075, 107.455, 107.565, and 107.475].

SIMPLIFIED OR SPECIAL DISSOLUTION OF MARRIAGE PROCEDURES: The spouses may qualify for a summary dissolution of marriage procedure if the following qualifications are met: (1) the residency requirements are fulfilled; (2) There are no minor children and the wife is not pregnant; (3) the marriage is not over 10 years in length; (4) neither spouse owns any real estate; (5) there are no unpaid debts in excess of $15,000 incurred by either or both spouses during the marriage; (6) the total value of all of the spouse's personal property is less than $30,000, excluding any unpaid balances on loans; (7) the petitioner waives the right to spousal support (alimony); (8) the petitioner waives the right to any pendente lite orders, except for the prevention of spouse abuse (temporary court orders pending the final divorce); (9) the petitioner knows of no other pending domestic relations suit in Oregon or any other state. There are specific mandatory forms for filing for summary dissolution of marriage that are available from the clerk of the court in each circuit.   Separation agreements are also expressly authorized. In addition, in all other cases, the spouses can jointly file for a dissolution of marriage. [Oregon Revised Statutes; Volume 2, Sections 107.065, 107.085, 107.105, 107.485+].

MEDIATION OR COUNSELING REQUIREMENTS: Certain Oregon courts offer conciliation services. If a court does offer such services, either spouse or the court may delay the dissolution of marriage proceedings for 45 days while a reconciliation or settlement is attempted. In addition, if child custody or child support issues are contested, the court will refer the parents to mediation for up to 90 days. [Oregon Revised Statutes; Volume 2, Sections 107.179, 107.540, 107.550, 107.755+].

PROPERTY DISTRIBUTION: Oregon is an "equitable distribution" state. All of the spouses property is subject to division by the court, including any gifts, inheritances, and property acquired prior to the marriage. Regardless of whether the property is held jointly or individually, there is a presumption that the spouses contributed equally to the acquisition of any property, unless shown otherwise. All property will be divided, without regard to any fault of the spouses, based on the following factors: (1) the cost of any sale of assets; (2) the amount of taxes and liens on the property; (3) the contribution of each spouse to the acquisition of the marital property, including the contribution of each spouse as homemaker; (4) any retirement benefits, including social security, civil service, military and railroad retirement benefits; (5) any life insurance coverage; and (6) whether the property award is instead of or in addition to spousal support. [Oregon Revised Statutes; Volume 2, Sections 107.036 and 107.105].

ALIMONY/MAINTENANCE/SPOUSAL SUPPORT: Either spouse may be ordered to pay spousal support to the other spouse, without regard to marital fault. The factors for consideration are: (1) the need for and the time necessary to acquire sufficient education and training to enable the spouse to find appropriate employment to become self-supporting, and that spouse's future earning capacity; (2) the standard of living during the marriage; (3) the duration of the marriage; (4) the comparative financial resources of the spouses, including their comparative earning abilities in the labor market; (5) the tax consequences to each spouse; (6) the age of the spouses; (7) the physical and emotional conditions of the spouses; (8) the usual occupation of the spouses during the marriage; (9) the vocational skills and employability of the spouse seeking support; (10) any custodial and child support responsibilities; (11) the educational level of each spouse at the time of the marriage and at the time the divorce is filed for; (12) any life insurance; (13) the costs of health care; (14) the extent that a spouse's earning capacity is impaired due to absence from the job market to be homemaker and the extent that job opportunities are unavailable considering the age of the spouse and the anticipated length of time for appropriate training; and (15) the contribution of each spouse to the marriage, including services rendered in homemaking, child care, education, and career building of the other spouse; (16) any other factor the court deems just and equitable. If a spouse has been out of the job market for a long time while acting as homemaker and the other spouse has an economically advantageous position due to joint efforts of both spouses, spousal support will be awarded as compensation. The spouse receiving spousal support must make a reasonable effort to become self-supporting within 10 years or the support may be terminated. The court may order the spouse to pay the support to carry life insurance with the other spouse as beneficiary. In addition, a spouse may have a right to continued health insurance coverage under the other spouse's policy. [Oregon Revised Statutes; Volume 2, Sections 107.036, 107.105, 107.412, and 743.600].

SPOUSE'S NAME: The spouses may resume the use of their prior names after a dissolution of marriage. [Oregon Revised Statutes; Volume 2, Section 107.105].

CHILD CUSTODY: Joint custody, joint responsibility for the child, and extensive contact between the child and both parents is encouraged. Joint or sole custody is determined based on the best interests of the child and the following factors: (1) the love and affection existing between the child and each parent; (2) the attitude of the child: (3) the length of time the child has lived in a stable, satisfactory environment and the desirability of maintaining continuity; (4) any spouse abuse; (5) the relationship of the child with parents, siblings, and other significant family members; and (6) the parent's interests and attitudes towards the child. The conduct, income, social environment, and life style of the proposed guardian is to be considered only if it is shown to cause emotional or physical damage to the child. No preference is to be given because of parent's sex. The court will not order joint custody unless both parents agree to the terms of the custody. [Oregon Revised Statutes; Volume 2, Sections 107.105, 107.137, 107.169].

CHILD SUPPORT: Either parent may be ordered to pay child support, based on the following factors: (1) the economic needs of the child; (2) the parent's ability to pay support; (3) the standard of living the child would have enjoyed if the marriage had not been dissolved; (4) the physical and emotional conditions and educational needs of the child; (5) the relative financial means of the parents, including their income, resources, and property; (6) the potential earnings of the parents; (7) the needs of any other dependents of a parent; (8) the desirability of the parent having either sole custody or physical care of the child remaining in the home as a full-time parent; (9) the cost of day care to the parent having custody or physical care of the child if that parent works outside the home, or the value of the child care services performed by that parent if the parent remains in the home; (10) the tax consequences to each parent; and (11) any other relevant factors. There are official child support scales and formulas available. The child support payments may be required to be paid through the clerk of the court. There may be court orders issued to withhold wages to pay for the child support and the court may also order the parent required to pay support to maintain life insurance coverage with the child as beneficiary. [Oregon Revised Statutes; Volume 2, Sections 25.275, 107.105, and 107.820].

DIVORCE YOURSELF

PENNSYLVANIA

NAME OF COURT IN WHICH TO FILE FOR DIVORCE: Court of Common Pleas. "Court of Common Pleas, _____ County, Pennsylvania."

TITLE OF DIVORCE ACTION: Complaint for Divorce.

NAME USED TO DESCRIBE SPOUSE FILING FOR DIVORCE: Plaintiff.

NAME USED TO DESCRIBE OTHER SPOUSE IN DIVORCE: Defendant.

TITLE OF FINAL DIVORCE PAPERS: Decree of Divorce.

RESIDENCY REQUIREMENTS AND WHERE TO FILE: Either spouse must have been a resident of Pennsylvania for at least 6 months before filing. The divorce may be filed for in a county where either spouse lives or a county that both spouses have agreed upon. [Pennsylvania Statutes Annotated, Title 23, Sections 301 and 302].

LEGAL GROUNDS FOR DIVORCE: No-Fault: (1) irretrievable breakdown of the marriage with the spouses living separate and apart without cohabitation for 2 years; or (2) irretrievable breakdown of the marriage and the spouses have both filed affidavits that they consent to the divorce. In the case of no-fault ground #(2), 90 days must elapse after the filing for divorce before the court will grant a divorce. [Pennsylvania Statutes Annotated, Title 23, Section 201].

General: (1) adultery; (2) bigamy; (3) imprisonment for 2 or more years; (4) confinement for incurable insanity for 18 months; (5) willful desertion for 1 year; (6) cruel and inhuman treatment endangering the life of the spouse; and (7) personal indignities. [Pennsylvania Statutes Annotated, Title 23, Section 201].

LEGAL SEPARATION: The spouses may enter into a binding separation agreement if it is made on reasonable terms. There is no residency requirement specified by statute. [Pennsylvania Statutes Annotated, Title 23, Section 401].

SIMPLIFIED OR SPECIAL DIVORCE PROCEDURES: The spouses may file for divorce on the grounds of irretrievable breakdown of the marriage and if both spouses consent to the divorce, it will be handled in an expedited manner. There are official sample forms for filing a complaint for divorce on the grounds of irretrievable breakdown of the marriage. There are also official forms available for filing the required affidavit of consent. There are also other sample divorce proceeding forms available in Pennsylvania Rules of Civil Procedure, Actions of Divorce of Annulment Section, Rule 1920.01+. In addition, separation agreements are expressly authorized. [Pennsylvania Statutes Annotated, Title 23, Section 201; and Pennsylvania Rules of Civil Procedure, Rules 1920.01+].

MEDIATION OR COUNSELING REQUIREMENTS: If the court determines that there is a reasonable prospect for reconciliation, it may order the spouses to seek counseling for a period of between 90 and 120 days. Upon the request of one of the spouses, three counseling sessions may be required. If no reconciliation is reached, and one of the spouses states that the marriage is irretrievably broken, a divorce may be granted. Counseling sessions may also be ordered by the court in conjunction with child custody. [Pennsylvania Statutes Annotated, Title 23, Sections 201 and 202].

PROPERTY DISTRIBUTION: Pennsylvania is an "equitable distribution" state. Separate property that is (1) acquired prior to the marriage; (2) acquired in exchange for any separate property; and (3) any gifts and inheritances will be retained by the spouse owning it. All other marital property will be divided equitably, without regard to any marital misconduct, based on the following factors: (1) the contribution of each spouse to the acquisition of the marital property, including the contribution of each spouse as homemaker; (2) the age and health of the spouses; (3) the sources of income of the spouses; (4) the value of each spouse's property; (5) the economic circumstances of each spouse at the time the division of property is to become effective; (6) the length of the marriage; (7) the tax consequences to each spouse; (8) the occupation of the spouses; (9) the amount and sources of income of the spouses, including retirement and any other benefits; (10) the vocational skills of the spouses; (11) the employability of the spouses; (12) the liabilities and needs of each spouse and the opportunity of each for further acquisition of capital assets and income; (13) the standard of living established during the marriage; (14) any premarital agreement; (15) any retirement benefits, including social security, civil service, military and railroad retirement benefits; (16) any prior marriage of each spouse; (17) the conduct of the spouses during the marriage as it relates to the disposition of their property; (18) any contributions toward the education, training, or increased earning power of the other spouse; and (19) any other factor necessary to do equity and justice between the spouses. [Pennsylvania Statutes Annotated, Title 23, Section 401].

ALIMONY/MAINTENANCE/SPOUSAL SUPPORT: Alimony may be awarded to either spouse if necessary. In determining the alimony award, the following factors are considered: (1) whether the spouse seeking alimony lacks sufficient property to provide for his or her own needs; (2) whether the spouse is unable to be self-supporting through appropriate employment; (3) whether the spouse seeking alimony is the custodian of a child; (4) the time necessary to acquire sufficient education and training to enable the spouse to find appropriate employment, and that spouse's future earning capacity; (5) any tax consequences; (6) the standard of living established during the marriage; (7) the duration of the marriage; (8) the financial resources of the spouse seeking alimony, including marital property apportioned to such spouse and such spouse's ability to meet his or her needs independently; (9) the comparative financial resources of the spouses, including their comparative earning abilities in the labor market; (10) the needs and obligations of each spouse; (11) the contribution of each spouse to the marriage, including services rendered in homemaking, child care, education, and career building of the other spouse; (12) the age of the spouses; (13) the physical and emotional conditions of the spouses; (14) the probable duration of the need of the spouse seeking support and alimony; (15) the educational level of each spouse at the time of the marriage and at the time the action for alimony is commenced; (16) the conduct of the spouses during the marriage; (17) the spouse's sources of income, including retirement benefits, inheritances, assets and liabilities, and any property brought into the marriage by either spouse; and (18) any other factor the court deems just and equitable. The courts are authorized to use spousal support guidelines. Alimony payments may be ordered to be paid through the Domestic Relations Section of the court. [Pennsylvania Statutes Annotated, Title 23, Sections 501 and 504].

SPOUSE'S NAME: Any woman may resume the use of her former or maiden name upon divorce. A written notice to that effect must be filed in the office of the prothonotary of the court where the divorce was entered. [Pennsylvania Statutes Annotated, Title 23, Section 702].

CHILD CUSTODY: Joint (shared) or sole custody may be awarded based on the best interests of the child, and upon a consideration of the following factor: which parent is more likely to encourage, permit, and allow frequent and continuing contact, including physical access between the other parent and the child. Both parents may be required to attend counseling sessions regarding child custody. The recommendations of the counselor may be used in determining child custody. In shared custody situations, the court may also require the parents to submit a written plan for child custody to the court. [Pennsylvania Statutes Annotated, Title 23, Sections 5303, 5304, and 5305].

CHILD SUPPORT: Either or both parents may be ordered to provide child support according to their ability to pay. The factors for consideration set out by statute are: (1) the net income of the parents; (2) the earning capacity of the parents; (3) the assets of the parents; (4) any unusual needs of the child or the parents; and (5) any extraordinary expenses. Child support payments may be ordered to be paid through the Domestic Relations Section of the court. There are official child support guidelines available. The court may require that health insurance coverage be provided for any child is it is available at a reasonable cost. [Pennsylvania Statutes Annotated, Title 23, Section 4322].

DIVORCE YOURSELF

RHODE ISLAND

NAME OF COURT IN WHICH TO FILE FOR DIVORCE: Family Court. "State of Rhode Island, Family Court, _____ Division."

TITLE OF DIVORCE ACTION: Complaint for Divorce. [Rhode Island Rules of Procedure for Domestic Relations, Rule 7].

NAME USED TO DESCRIBE SPOUSE FILING FOR DIVORCE: Plaintiff.

NAME USED TO DESCRIBE OTHER SPOUSE IN DIVORCE: Defendant.

TITLE OF FINAL DIVORCE PAPERS: Final Judgement of Divorce.

RESIDENCY REQUIREMENTS AND WHERE TO FILE: Either spouse must have been a resident of Rhode Island for 1 year prior to filing for divorce. The divorce may be filed for in the county of residence of the plaintiff, unless the 1-year residency requirement has been satisfied by the defendant's residence. In such case, the divorce must be filed for in the county of the defendants residence. [General Laws of Rhode Island; Title 15, Chapter 15-5-12].

LEGAL GROUNDS FOR DIVORCE: No-Fault: (1) irreconcilable differences which have caused the irremediable breakdown of the marriage; or (2) living separate and apart without cohabitation for 3 years. [General Laws of Rhode Island; Title 15, Chapters 15-5-1, 15-5-3, and 15-5-5].

General: (1) impotence; (2) adultery; (3) abandonment and presumed dead; (4) alcoholism and/or drug addiction; (5) confinement for incurable insanity; (6) failure to consummate marriage; (7) willful desertion for 5 years (or less within the discretion of the court); (8) cruel and inhuman treatment; (9) bigamy; (10) life imprisonment; (11) spouse is of unsound mind; (12) incest; and (13) gross neglect. [General Laws of Rhode Island; Title 15, Chapters 15-5-1 and 15-5-2].

LEGAL SEPARATION: Legal separation (or divorce from bed and board) may be granted for the following reasons: (1) impotence; (2) adultery; (3) abandonment and presumed dead; (4) alcoholism and/or drug addiction; (5) confinement for incurable insanity; (6) failure to consummate marriage; (7) willful desertion for 5 years (or less within the discretion of the court); (8) cruel and inhuman treatment; (9) bigamy; (10) life imprisonment; (11) spouse is of unsound mind; (12) incest; (13) gross neglect; (14) irreconcilable differences which have caused the irremediable breakdown of the marriage; and (15) living separate and apart without cohabitation for 3 years. The spouse seeking legal separation must have been a resident for a period of time that the court deems proper. [General Laws of Rhode Island; Title 15, Chapters 15-5-1, 15-5-2, 15-5-3, 15-5-5, and 15-5-9].

SIMPLIFIED OR SPECIAL DIVORCE PROCEDURES: A court hearing will be required in all divorce cases. However, official sample forms are available for use in preparing the Complaint for Divorce and other documents. These forms are found in: Rhode Island Court Rules Annotated, Rules of Procedure for Domestic Relations, Appendix of Forms.

MEDIATION OR COUNSELING REQUIREMENTS: In cases which involve child custody or visitation, the court may direct the parents to participate in mediation in an effort to resolve any differences. There is an official Family Court counseling form which must be filed with the Complaint for Divorce. [General Laws of Rhode Island; Title 15, Chapter 15-5-29].

PROPERTY DISTRIBUTION: Rhode Island is an "equitable distribution" state. Separate property which a spouse owned prior to the marriage and any property which a spouse receives by gift or inherits (either before, during, or after a marriage) is not subject to division. Any other property (including any income from separate property that was earned during the marriage) may be divided by the court. In determining the nature and value of the property, the following factors are considered: (1) the contribution of each

APPENDIX: DIVORCE LAWS OF ALL 50 STATES

spouse to the acquisition of the marital property, including the contribution of each spouse as homemaker; (2) the length of the marriage; and (3) the conduct of the spouses during the marriage. [General Laws of Rhode Island; Title 15, Chapter 15-5-16.1].

ALIMONY/MAINTENANCE/SPOUSAL SUPPORT: Either spouse may be awarded alimony after a divorce or legal separation. In determining the amount of alimony, the following factors are to be considered: (1) the duration of the marriage; (2) the amount of property awarded each spouse; (3) the conduct of the spouses; (4) the comparative financial resources of the spouses, including their comparative earning abilities in the labor market; (5) the needs and obligations of each spouse; (6) the age of the spouses; (7) the physical and emotional conditions of the spouses; (8) the usual occupation of the spouses during the marriage; and (9) the vocational skills and employability of the spouse seeking alimony. [General Laws of Rhode Island; Title 15, Chapters 15-5-16 and 15-5-16.1].

SPOUSE'S NAME: Any woman may request that her name be changed, even if there were children born during the prior marriage. [General Laws of Rhode Island; Title 15, Chapter 15-5-17].

CHILD CUSTODY: Child custody is determined according to the best interests of the child. Reasonable visitation should be granted to the non-custodial parent, unless it would be harmful to the child. There are no factors for consideration set out by statute. There is no specific provision for joint custody in Rhode Island. [General Laws of Rhode Island; Title 15, Chapter 15-5-16].

CHILD SUPPORT: Either parent may be ordered to provide child support, after a consideration of the following factors: (1) the financial resources of the child; (2) the standard of living the child would have enjoyed if the marriage had not been dissolved; (3) the physical and emotional conditions and educational needs of the child; (4) the earning potential of the parents; (5) any other dependents of the parents; (6) the financial resources, needs, and obligations of both the noncustodial and the custodial parent; and (7) any other factors. Family Court child support guidelines have been adopted. In order to guarantee child support payments, the court may require: (1) income or property assignments; (2) posting of bond; or (3) wage withholding. [General Laws of Rhode Island; Title 15, Chapters 15-5-16.1, 15-5-16.2, 15-5-16.6, 15-5-22, and 15-9-1].

DIVORCE YOURSELF

SOUTH CAROLINA

NAME OF COURT IN WHICH TO FILE FOR DIVORCE: Circuit Court or Family Court (if requested). "State of South Carolina, The _____ Court of the _____ Judicial Circuit."

TITLE OF DIVORCE ACTION: Complaint for Divorce.

NAME USED TO DESCRIBE SPOUSE FILING FOR DIVORCE: Plaintiff.

NAME USED TO DESCRIBE OTHER SPOUSE IN DIVORCE: Defendant.

TITLE OF FINAL DIVORCE PAPERS: Decree of Divorce.

RESIDENCY REQUIREMENTS AND WHERE TO FILE: The spouse filing for divorce must have been a resident of South Carolina for at least 1 year, unless both spouses are residents, in which case the spouse filing must only have been a resident for 3 months. There is a required 90-day delay from the time of filing to the time of the final decree of divorce. The divorce may be filed for in: (1) the county where the defendant resides; (2) the county where the plaintiff resides if the defendant does not live in South Carolina; or (3) the county where the spouses last lived together if both still live in South Carolina. [Code of Laws of South Carolina; Chapter 3, Sections 20-3-30, 20-3-60, and 20-3-80].

LEGAL GROUNDS FOR DIVORCE: No-Fault: Living separate and apart without cohabitation for 1 year. [Code of Laws of South Carolina; Chapter 3, Section 20-3-10].

General: (1) adultery; (2) alcoholism and/or drug addiction; (3) physical abuse or reasonable apprehension of physical abuse; and (4) willful desertion for 1 year. [Code of Laws of South Carolina; Chapter 3, Section 20-3-10].

LEGAL SEPARATION: South Carolina authorizes legal separation (separate maintenance). [Code of Laws of South Carolina; Chapter 3, Section 20-3-140].

SIMPLIFIED OR SPECIAL DIVORCE PROCEDURES: The court is authorized to develop and make available sample or mandatory forms for use in divorce matters. These may be available locally from the clerk of the court. [South Carolina Rules of Family Court, Rule 3].

MEDIATION OR COUNSELING REQUIREMENTS: The court may refer the spouses to a referee, who must make an honest effort to bring about a reconciliation between the spouses. In such cases, no divorce may be granted unless certified by the judge or the referee that the reconciliation efforts were unsuccessful. [Code of Laws of South Carolina; Chapter 3, Sections 20-3-90 and 7-8-50].

PROPERTY DISTRIBUTION: South Carolina is an "equitable distribution" state. Each spouse is entitled to keep his or her non-marital property, consisting of property: (1) which was acquired prior to the marriage; (2) acquired by gift or inheritance; (3) acquired in exchange for non-marital property; or (4) was acquired due to an increase in the value of any non-marital property. All other property acquired during the marriage is subject to division, based on a consideration of the following factors: (1) the duration of the marriage; (2) the age of the spouses; (3) any marital misconduct; (4) any economic misconduct; (5) the value of the marital property; (6) the contribution of each spouse to the acquisition of the marital property, including the contribution of each spouse as homemaker; (7) the income of each spouse; (8) the earning potential of each spouse and the opportunity for the future acquisition of capital assets; (9) the physical and emotional health of each spouse; (10) the needs of each spouse for additional training or education in order to achieve their earning potential; (11) the non-marital property of each spouse; (12) any retirement benefits; (13) whether alimony has been awarded; (14) the desirability of awarding the family home to the spouse having custody of any children; (15) the tax consequences; (16) any other support obligations of either spouse; (17) any marital debts of the spouses; (18) any child custody arrangements; and (19) any other relevant factors. [Code of Laws of South Carolina; Chapter 3, Sections 20-7-472 and 20-7-473].

ALIMONY/MAINTENANCE/SPOUSAL SUPPORT: Either spouse may be awarded alimony. There are no factors for consideration specified in the statute. [Code of Laws of South Carolina; Chapter 3, Section 20-3-120].

SPOUSE'S NAME: Upon request, the court may allow a woman to resume the use of her former or maiden name. [Code of Laws of South Carolina; Chapter 3, Section 20-3-180].

CHILD CUSTODY: In awarding child custody, the factors for consideration are as follows: (1) the circumstances of the spouses; (2) the nature of the case; (3) the religious faith of the parents and child; (4) the welfare of the child; and (5) the best spiritual and other interests of the child. The parents both have equal rights regarding any award of custody of children. [Code of Laws of South Carolina; Chapter 3, Sections 20-3-160, 20-7-100 and 20-7-1520].

CHILD SUPPORT: Both parents have joint responsibility for child support. In awarding child support, the factors for consideration are as follows: (1) the circumstances of the spouses; (2) the nature of the case; and (3) the best spiritual and other interests of the child. The court may require income withholding for the guarantee of child support payments. [Code of Laws of South Carolina; Chapter 3, Sections 20-3-160, 20-7-40, 20-7-100, and 20-7-1315].

SOUTH DAKOTA

NAME OF COURT IN WHICH TO FILE FOR DIVORCE: Circuit Court. "State of South Dakota, County of _____, In the Circuit Court, _____ Judicial District."

TITLE OF DIVORCE ACTION: Complaint for Divorce.

NAME USED TO DESCRIBE SPOUSE FILING FOR DIVORCE: Plaintiff.

NAME USED TO DESCRIBE OTHER SPOUSE IN DIVORCE: Defendant.

TITLE OF FINAL DIVORCE PAPERS: Decree of Divorce.

RESIDENCY REQUIREMENTS AND WHERE TO FILE: The spouse filing for divorce must be a resident of South Dakota or a member of the Armed Forces stationed in South Dakota at the time of the filing and must remain a resident until the divorce is final. There is no durational residency requirement. The divorce may be filed for in the county where either spouse resides, but the defendant has the right to have it transferred to his or her county of residence if desired. In addition, there is a 60-day waiting period after filing before a hearing will be held or the divorce will be granted. [South Dakota Codified Laws; Title 25, Chapters 25-4-30, 25-4-30.1, and 25-4-34].

LEGAL GROUNDS FOR DIVORCE: No-Fault: Irreconcilable differences which have caused the irretrievable breakdown of the marriage. [South Dakota Codified Laws; Title 25, Chapters 25-4-2, 25-4-17.2, and 25-4-18].

General: (1) adultery; (2) confinement for incurable insanity for 5 years; (3) conviction of a felony; (4) willful desertion; (5) cruel and inhuman treatment; (6) willful neglect; (7) habitual intemperance (drunkenness); and (8) separation caused by misconduct. [South Dakota Codified Laws; Title 25, Chapters 25-4-2 and 25-4-18].

LEGAL SEPARATION: The grounds for legal separation (separate maintenance) in South Dakota are: (1) adultery; (2) confinement for incurable insanity for 5 years; (3) conviction of a felony; (4) willful desertion; (5) cruel and inhuman treatment; (6) willful neglect; (7) habitual intemperance (drunkenness); and (8) irreconcilable differences which have caused the irretrievable breakdown of the marriage. The spouse filing for legal separation must be a resident of South Dakota or a member of the Armed Forces stationed in South Dakota at the time of the filing and must remain a resident until the legal separation is final. [South Dakota Codified Laws; Title 25, Chapters 25-4-17.2 and 25-4-40].

SIMPLIFIED OR SPECIAL DIVORCE PROCEDURES: If both spouses consent to the use of "irreconcilable differences" as the grounds for divorce, the court may grant the divorce based entirely on affidavits of the spouses which establish the required residency and grounds for the divorce. In such cases, a personal appearance in court by either of the spouses will not generally be required. [South Dakota Codified Laws; Title 25, Chapters 25-4-17.3].

MEDIATION OR COUNSELING REQUIREMENTS: If the court determines that there is a reasonable possibility for reconciliation between the spouses, the divorce proceedings can be delayed for up to 30 days while the spouses seek counseling. [South Dakota Codified Laws; Title 25, Chapters 25-4-17.2].

PROPERTY DISTRIBUTION: South Dakota is an "equitable distribution" state. All of the spouse's property is equitably divided by the court. Marital fault is not to be considered unless it is relevant to the acquisition of property during the marriage. The only factor specified in the statute is a consideration of the circumstances of the spouses. South Dakota courts have interpreted this to include the following factors for consideration: (1) the contribution of each spouse to the acquisition of the marital property, including the contribution of each spouse as homemaker; (2) the value of each spouse's property; (3) the length of the marriage; (4) the age and health of the spouses; (5) the present and potential earning capability of each spouse; (6) the value of the property; and (7) the income-producing capacity of the spouse's assets. [South Dakota Codified Laws; Title 25, Chapters 25-4-44 and 25-4-45.1; and South Dakota Case Law].

ALIMONY/MAINTENANCE/SPOUSAL SUPPORT: Either spouse may be awarded maintenance for life or a shorter period. The only factor specified in the statute is a consideration of the circumstances of the spouses. South Dakota courts have interpreted this to include the following factors for consideration: (1) the duration of the marriage; (2) the ability of the spouse from whom support is sought to meet his or her needs while meeting those of the spouse seeking support; (3) the financial resources of the spouse seeking maintenance, including marital property apportioned to such spouse and such spouse's ability to meet his or her needs independently; (4) the comparative financial resources of the spouses, including their comparative earning abilities in the labor market; (5) the age of the spouses; (6) the physical and emotional conditions of the spouses; (7) the fault of the spouses during the marriage. Reasonable security may be required to guarantee the payment of maintenance. [South Dakota Codified Laws; Title 25, Chapters 25-4-42, 25-4-44, 25-4-45.1, 25-7A-20; and South Dakota Case Law].

SPOUSE'S NAME: Upon request or on the court's own initiative, a wife's former or maiden name may be restored. [South Dakota Codified Laws; Title 25, Chapter 25-4-47].

CHILD CUSTODY: Sole or joint child custody is to be awarded based on the discretion of the court and the best interests of the child. Fault is not to be considered unless it is relevant to the fitness of a parent to have custody. Neither parent is considered the preferred parent based on the parent's sex. The preference of the child may be considered. In joint custody decisions, the court may consider the expressed desires of the parents and the best interests of the child. No other specific factors are specified. [South Dakota Codified Laws; Title 25, Chapters 25-3-11, 25-4-25, 25-4-45.1, and 25.5-7.1-7.3; and South Dakota Case Law].

CHILD SUPPORT: Either or both parents may be ordered to provide child support. There is an official child support obligation schedule set forth in the statute. Deviation from the official schedule may be based on a consideration of the following factors: (1) the financial condition of either parent that would make application of the schedule inequitable; (2) income tax consequences; (3) any special needs of the child; (4) income from other persons; (5) the effect of custody and visitation provisions; (6) child care expenses necessary to obtain employment, education, or training; (7) agreements between the parents which provide other forms of support for the direct benefit of the child; (8) a voluntary reduction in the income of either parent; (9) any other support obligations of a parent. The support payments may be ordered to be paid through the court clerk. Wage withholding orders may also be ordered. [South Dakota Codified Laws; Title 25, Chapters 25-3-11, 25-4-38, 25-4-45, and 25-7A-9.]

DIVORCE YOURSELF

TENNESSEE

NAME OF COURT IN WHICH TO FILE FOR DIVORCE: Circuit Court or Chancery Court. "In the _____ Court of _____ County, Tennessee."

TITLE OF DIVORCE ACTION: Petition for Divorce.

NAME USED TO DESCRIBE SPOUSE FILING FOR DIVORCE: Petitioner.

NAME USED TO DESCRIBE OTHER SPOUSE IN DIVORCE: Respondent.

TITLE OF FINAL DIVORCE PAPERS: Final Decree of Divorce.

RESIDENCY REQUIREMENTS AND WHERE TO FILE: The spouse seeking divorce must have been a resident of Tennessee when the grounds for divorce arose. If the grounds for divorce arose outside of Tennessee and the petitioner resided outside of Tennessee, either spouse must have been a resident for 6 months prior to filing. The divorce may be filed for in any of the following counties: (1) the county in which both spouses lived at the time of their separation; (2) the county in which the respondent lives if he or she is a resident of Tennessee; or (3) the county in which the petitioner lives if the respondent is a non-resident of Tennessee. [Tennessee Code Annotated; Volume 6A, Title 36, Sections 36-4-104 and 36-4-105].

LEGAL GROUNDS FOR DIVORCE: No-Fault: (1) irreconcilable differences; or (2) living separate and apart without cohabitation for 3 years when there are no minor children. [Tennessee Code Annotated; Volume 6A, Title 36, Section 36-4-101]

General: (1) impotence; (2) adultery; (3) conviction of a felony and imprisonment; (4) alcoholism and/or drug addiction; (5) wife is pregnant by another at the time of marriage without husband's knowledge; (6) willful desertion for 1 year; (7) bigamy; (8) endangering the life of the spouse; (9) commission and/or conviction of an infamous crime; and (10) refusing to move to Tennessee with a spouse and willfully absenting oneself from a new residence for 2 years. [Tennessee Code Annotated; Volume 6A, Title 36, Section 36-4-101].

LEGAL SEPARATION: The grounds for legal separation (divorce from bed and board) are as follows: (1) such cruel and inhuman conduct that cohabitation is unsafe or improper; (2) that the husband made the wife's condition intolerable with personal indignities; (3) that the husband has abandoned the wife; and (4) that the husband has forced the wife to leave the marital home without providing for her. There is no residency requirement specified in the statute. [Tennessee Code Annotated; Volume 6A, Title 36, Sections 36-4-102, and 36-4-119].

SIMPLIFIED OR SPECIAL DIVORCE PROCEDURES: If the divorce is based on irreconcilable differences, the spouses may enter into a notarized marital settlement agreement. The agreement must: (1) make specific reference to a pending divorce by the name of the court and the docket number; or (2) state that the respondent is aware that a divorce will be filed for in the state of Tennessee and that the respondent waives service of process and waives filing an answer. The waiver of service will be valid for 120 days after the respondent signs the agreement and will constitute a general appearance by the respondent and give the court personal jurisdiction over the respondent. The petition for divorce must have been on file for over 60 days before a hearing will be held if the spouses have no minor children and 90 days if they have any minor children. A final decree may be entered without any corroborating proof or testimony. Some counties may require the respondent to sign any appearance and waiver form before the court clerk for it to be valid. In addition, in any petition for divorce, the wife's maiden name must be stated and the race and color of each spouse must be stated. Financial affidavits may also be required. [Tennessee Code Annotated; Volume 6A, Title 36, Sections 36-4-103 and 35-4-116; and Tennessee Rules of Court].

MEDIATION OR COUNSELING REQUIREMENTS: Upon the request of either spouse, the court may delay a divorce proceeding to allow an attempt at reconciliation. [Tennessee Code Annotated; Volume 6A, Title 36, Section 36-4-126].

PROPERTY DISTRIBUTION: Tennessee is an "equitable distribution" state. The separate property of each spouse which was: (1) acquired prior to marriage; (2) by gift or inheritance; or (3) in exchange for any separate property, is retained by that spouse. The marital property, including: (1) any property acquired during the marriage by either spouse; (2) any increase in value of any property; and (3) any retirement benefits, is divided by the court, without regard to any marital fault, and after a consideration of the following factors: (1) the contribution of each spouse to the acquisition of the marital property, including the contribution of each spouse as homemaker, wage-earner, or parent; (2) the value of each spouse's property; (3) the economic circumstances of each spouse at the time the division of property is to become effective; (4) any increase or decrease in the value of the separate property of the spouse during the marriage or the depletion of the separate property for marital purposes; (5) the length of the marriage; (6) the age and health of the spouses; (7) the vocational skills of the spouses; (8) the employability of the spouses; (9) the liabilities and needs of each spouse and the opportunity of each for further acquisition of capital assets and income; (10) the federal income tax consequences of the court's division of the property; (11) the present and potential earning capability of each spouse; (12) the tangible and intangible contributions made by one spouse to the education, training, or increased earning power of the other spouse; and (13) any other factor necessary to do equity and justice between the spouses. [Tennessee Code Annotated; Volume 6A, Title 36, Section 36-4-121].

ALIMONY/MAINTENANCE/SPOUSAL SUPPORT: Alimony may be awarded to either spouse, based on a consideration of the following: (1) the value of any separate property and the value of the spouses share of any marital property; (2) whether the spouse seeking alimony is the custodian of a child whose condition or circumstances make it appropriate for that spouse not to seek outside employment; (3) the need for and the time necessary to acquire sufficient education and training to enable the spouse to find appropriate employment, and that spouse's future earning capacity; (4) the standard of living established during the marriage; (5) the duration of the marriage; (6) the comparative financial resources of the spouses, including their comparative earning abilities in the labor market and any retirement benefits; (7) the needs and obligations of each spouse; (8) the contribution of each spouse to the marriage, including services rendered in homemaking, child care, education, and career building of the other spouse; (9) the relative education and training of the spouses; (10) the age of the spouses; (11) the physical and mental condition of the spouse; (12) the tax consequences to each spouse; (13) the usual occupation of the spouses during the marriage; (14) the vocational skills and employability of the spouse seeking alimony; (15) the conduct of the spouses during the marriage; and (16) any other factor the court deems just and equitable. The court may require that alimony payments be made through the clerk of the court. [Tennessee Code Annotated; Volume 6A, Title 36, Section 36-5-101].

SPOUSE'S NAME: There is no statutory provision in Tennessee for the restoration of a wife's name upon divorce. However, Tennessee Case law provide that a wife may resume the use of her former or maiden name [Tennessee Case Law].

CHILD CUSTODY: Joint or sole custody is awarded according to the best interests of the child and considering the child's preference. There is no presumption that either parent is more suited to obtain custody. However, if the child is of tender years, the sex of the parent seeking custody is a factor which may be taken into consideration. No other factors are listed in the statute. [Tennessee Code Annotated; Volume 6A, Title 36, Sections 36-6-101 and 36-6-102].

CHILD SUPPORT: Either or both of the parents may be ordered to provide child support. However, if the father is awarded custody, the mother can not be ordered to provide support. The factors for consideration are as follows: (1) the financial resources of the child; (2) the standard of living the child would have enjoyed if the marriage had not been dissolved; (3) the physical and emotional conditions and educational needs of the child; (4) the financial resources, needs, and obligations of the parents; (5) the earning capacity of each parent; (6) the age and health of the child; (7) the monetary and non-monetary contributions of each parent to the well-being of the child; (8) any pension or retirement benefits of the parents;

(9) whether the non-custodial parent's visitation is over 110 days per year or under 55 days per year; and (10) any other relevant factors. The court may require that health insurance coverage be provided for the child or that the spouse to who is to pay the support maintain a life insurance policy for the benefit of the child. The court can require that the child support payments be paid through the clerk of the court. The posting of bond, wage assignments, and wage withholding may also be ordered. Effective July 1, 1990, there will be official Tennessee Supreme Court child support guidelines. Standardized forms for determining child support are also to be available. [Tennessee Code Annotated; Volume 6A, Title 36, Sections 36-5-101, 36-5-501, 36-5-604; and Tennessee Court Rules Annotated, Supreme Court Rules].

APPENDIX: DIVORCE LAWS OF ALL 50 STATES

TEXAS

NAME OF COURT IN WHICH TO FILE FOR DIVORCE: District Court. "In the District Court of _____ County, Texas, _____ Judicial District."

TITLE OF DIVORCE ACTION: Petition for Divorce. "In the Matter of the Marriage of _____ and _____." [Texas Codes Annotated; Family Code, Chapter 3.51].

NAME USED TO DESCRIBE SPOUSE FILING FOR DIVORCE: Petitioner.

NAME USED TO DESCRIBE OTHER SPOUSE IN DIVORCE: Respondent.

TITLE OF FINAL DIVORCE PAPERS: Decree of Divorce.

RESIDENCY REQUIREMENTS AND WHERE TO FILE: One of the spouses must have resided in Texas for 6 months prior to filing and in the county where the divorce is filed for 90 days prior to filing. In addition, there is a 60-day waiting period after filing before a divorce will be granted. [Texas Codes Annotated; Family Code, Chapters 3.21 and 3.60].

LEGAL GROUNDS FOR DIVORCE: No-Fault: (1) the marriage has become insupportable because of discord or conflict of personalities that has destroyed the legitimate ends of the marriage relationship and prevents any reasonable expectation of reconciliation; or (2) living separate and apart without cohabitation for 3 years. [Texas Codes Annotated; Family Code, Chapters 3.01 and 3.06].

General: (1) adultery; (2) abandonment; (3) confinement for incurable insanity for 3 years; (4) conviction of a felony; and (5) cruel and inhuman treatment. [Texas Codes Annotated; Family Code, Chapters 3.02, 3.03, 3.04, 3.05, 3.06, and 3.07].

LEGAL SEPARATION: Separation agreements are expressly authorized by statute. [Texas Codes Annotated; Family Code, Chapters 3.631, 5.52, 5.53, and 5.54].

SIMPLIFIED OR SPECIAL DIVORCE PROCEDURES: Separation agreements and property settlements are expressly authorized. [Texas Codes Annotated; Family Code, Chapters 3.631, 5.52, 5.53, and 5.54].

MEDIATION OR COUNSELING REQUIREMENTS: Upon request, the court can order both spouses to consult a marriage counselor. If the counselor's report indicates a reasonable expectation of reconciliation, the court can order further counseling for up to 60 additional days. Upon every filing for divorce, the court clerk is required to furnish a statement to the person filing regarding the availability of marital counseling services. In addition, if there has been a history of conflict and difficulties in resolving questions of access to any children, the court may order either parent to participate in counseling. [Texas Codes Annotated; Family Code, Chapters 3.54 and 14.03].

PROPERTY DISTRIBUTION: Texas is a "community property" state. The spouse's separate property, consisting of (1) any property owned prior to the marriage; (2) any property acquired during the marriage by gift or inheritance; and (3) any recovery for personal injuries which occurred during the marriage, will be retained by the spouse who owns it. The marital property, consisting of any other property acquired by either spouse during the marriage, will be divided equally, unless the court finds that equal division would be unjust. The only factors for consideration specified in the statute are a due regard for the rights of each party and any children. A court can determine the rights of the spouses in any pension or retirement plan. [Texas Codes Annotated; Family Code, Chapters 3.63, 3.633, and 5.01].

ALIMONY/MAINTENANCE/SPOUSAL SUPPORT: The statutes and public policy of Texas do not sanction alimony or maintenance for the wife after divorce. However, alimony can be awarded for the time

DIVORCE YOURSELF

period between the filing for divorce and the granting of a final divorce (including any time for appeals). [Texas Case Law].

SPOUSE'S NAME: Upon request, the name of either spouse may be changed. [Texas Codes Annotated; Family Code, Chapter 3.64].

CHILD CUSTODY: Joint or sole managing conservatorship (custody) is determined according to the best interests of the child. The sex of the parents is not a factor for consideration. The wishes of the child may be considered. The factors to be considered in determining the terms and conditions for possession of a child by the possessory conservator (parent with visitation) are as follows: (1) the age, circumstances, needs, and best interests of the child; (2) the circumstances of the parents; (3) evidence of any spouse or child abuse; and (4) any other relevant factor. The factors specified in the statute for consideration in decisions regarding joint managing conservatorship are: (1) whether the physical, psychological, or emotional needs and development of the child will benefit; (2) the ability of the parents to give first priority to the welfare of the child and reach shared decisions in the child's best interests; (3) whether each parent can encourage and accept a positive relationship between the child and the other parent; (4) whether both parents participated in child rearing before the filing of the suit; (5) the geographical proximity of the homes of the parents; and (6) if the child is 14 years old or older, the preference of the child. Parents may file a written agreement with the court regarding joint managing conservatorship. In addition, there are standard terms for a court's order on a child's conservatorship set out in the statute that are presumed to be the minimum allowable time that the parent who is not awarded the primary physical residence of the child is to have the child. (This is, essentially, a statutory "visitation" schedule). [Texas Codes Annotated; Family Code, Chapters 3.55, 14.01, 14.03, 14.021, 14.032, 14.033, 14.034, and 36.02].

CHILD SUPPORT: Either or both parents may be ordered to make periodic, lump-sum, or both type of child support payments. There are official child support guidelines set out in the statute and these are presumed to be reasonable. The factors for consideration are: (1) the age and needs of the child; (2) the ability of the parents to contribute to the support of the child; (3) any financial resources available for the support of the child; (4) the amount of possession and access to the child; (5) the net resources of the parent to pay support; (6) any child care expenses necessary for the employment of either parent; (7) whether a parent has custody of another child; (8) the amount of alimony; (9) provisions for health care; (10) any special educational or health care needs of the child; (11) any debts or obligations of a parent; (12) the cost of traveling to visit the child; and (13) any other relevant factor. The court may order health insurance coverage to be provided for the child. In addition, the court may order income withholding to secure the payment of child support. [Texas Codes Annotated; Family Code, Chapters 14.05, 14.051-14.058, and 14.061].

APPENDIX: DIVORCE LAWS OF ALL 50 STATES

UTAH

NAME OF COURT IN WHICH TO FILE FOR DIVORCE: District Court (may be Family Court Division of District Court). "In the District Court of the _____ Judicial District, In and for _____ County, State of Utah."

TITLE OF DIVORCE ACTION: Complaint for Divorce.

NAME USED TO DESCRIBE SPOUSE FILING FOR DIVORCE: Plaintiff.

NAME USED TO DESCRIBE OTHER SPOUSE IN DIVORCE: Defendant.

TITLE OF FINAL DIVORCE PAPERS: Decree of Divorce.

RESIDENCY REQUIREMENTS AND WHERE TO FILE: The spouse filing for divorce must have been resident of Utah (or a member of the Armed Forces stationed in Utah) and a resident of the county where the divorce is filed for more than 3 months immediately prior to filing. In addition, there is a 90-day waiting period after filing before a divorce will be granted. [Utah Code Annotated; Sections 30-3-1 and 30-3-18].

LEGAL GROUNDS FOR DIVORCE: No-Fault: (1) irreconcilable differences of the marriage; or (2) living separate and apart without cohabitation for 3 years under a judicial decree of separation. [Utah Code Annotated; Section 30-3-1].

General: (1) impotence; (2) adultery; (3) conviction of a felony; (4) willful desertion for 1 year; (5) cruel and inhuman treatment; (6) willful neglect; (7) incurable insanity; and (8) habitual intemperance (drunkenness). [Utah Code Annotated; Section 30-3-1].

LEGAL SEPARATION: The grounds for legal separation are: (1) willful desertion; (2) living separate and apart without cohabitation; and (3) gross neglect. The deserting spouse must be a resident of Utah, or own property in the state which the deserted spouse lives in. [Utah Code Annotated; Section 30-4-1].

SIMPLIFIED OR SPECIAL DIVORCE PROCEDURES: Uncontested divorce hearings may be held before a court commissioner. In addition, a sample Complaint for Divorce is contained in Utah Rules of Civil Procedure, Appendix of Forms, Form #18. [Utah Code Annotated; Section 30-3-4.2].

MEDIATION OR COUNSELING REQUIREMENTS: Upon the request of either or both of the spouses (shown by filing a Petition for Conciliation with the court), the court may refer both of the spouses to a domestic relations counselor. [Utah Code Annotated; Sections 30-3-15.2 and 30-3-16.2

PROPERTY DISTRIBUTION: Utah is an "equitable distribution" state. All of the spouse's property, including gifts, inheritances, and any property acquired prior to or during the marriage, will be divided equitably by the court. There are no factors for consideration specified in the statute. [Utah Code Annotated; Sections 30-3-5 and 30-3-12].

ALIMONY/MAINTENANCE/SPOUSAL SUPPORT: Either spouse may be ordered to pay an equitable amount of alimony to the other. There are no factors for consideration specified in the statute. Marital fault is not specified as a factor. [Utah Code Annotated; Sections 30-3-3 and 30-3-5].

SPOUSE'S NAME: There is no statutory provision in Utah for restoration of a wife's maiden name upon divorce. However, there is a general statutory provision for changing a name upon petition to the court. [Utah Code Annotated; Sections 42-1-1].

CHILD CUSTODY: Joint or sole child custody is determined according to the best interests of the child, and after a consideration of the following factors: (1) the past conduct and moral standards of the parents; (2) the welfare of the child; (3) the child's preference; (4) which parent is likely to act in the best interests of the child; and (5) which parent is likely to allow frequent and continuing contact with the other parent. There is a presumption that a spouse who has been abandoned by the other spouse is entitled to custody of the children.

Joint custody may be ordered if both parents agree and based upon a consideration of the following factors: (1) whether the physical, psychological, or emotional needs and development of the child will benefit; (2) the ability of the parents to give first priority to the welfare of the child and reach shared decisions in the child's best interests; (3) whether each parent can encourage and accept a positive relationship between the child and the other parent; (4) whether both parents participated in child rearing before the filing of the divorce; (5) the geographical proximity of the homes of the parents; and (6) if the child is 12 years old or older, the preference of the child. [Utah Code Annotated; Sections 30-2-10, 30-3-5, 30-3-10.1, 30-3-10.2, and 30-3-10.3].

CHILD SUPPORT: Either or both parents may be ordered to provide child support, including medical and dental expenses and health insurance. The court may also order the non-custodial parent to provide day care and child care expenses while the custodial parent is at work or undergoing training. Income withholding may be ordered by a court to guarantee any child support payments. [Utah Code Annotated; Sections 30-3-5 and 30-3-5.1].

APPENDIX: DIVORCE LAWS OF ALL 50 STATES

VERMONT

NAME OF COURT IN WHICH TO FILE FOR DIVORCE: Superior Court. "State of Vermont, Superior Court, _____ County."

TITLE OF DIVORCE ACTION: Complaint for Divorce.

NAME USED TO DESCRIBE SPOUSE FILING FOR DIVORCE: Plaintiff.

NAME USED TO DESCRIBE OTHER SPOUSE IN DIVORCE: Defendant.

TITLE OF FINAL DIVORCE PAPERS: Decree of Divorce.

RESIDENCY REQUIREMENTS AND WHERE TO FILE: Either spouse must have been a resident of Vermont for at least 6 months before the divorce is filed. Additionally, either spouse must have been a resident for 1 year before the divorce is made final. There is a 6 month waiting period after the defendant has been served with the divorce papers before a hearing will be held. The divorce may be filed for in any county where either or both of the spouses reside. [Vermont Statutes Annotated; Title 15, Sections 592 and 593; Vermont Rules of Civil Procedure, Rule 80].

LEGAL GROUNDS FOR DIVORCE: No-Fault: Living separate and apart without cohabitation for 6 consecutive months and the resumption of marital relations is not reasonably probable. [Vermont Statutes Annotated; Title 15, Section 555].

General: (1) adultery; (2) imprisonment for 3 years or more or for life; (3) willful desertion for 7 years; (4) cruel and inhuman treatment of intolerable severity; (5) incurable mental illness; and (6) gross neglect. [Vermont Statutes Annotated; Title 15, Section 551].

LEGAL SEPARATION: The grounds for legal separation (divorce from bed and board) are: (1) living separate and apart without cohabitation for 6 months; (2) adultery; (3) imprisonment for 3 years or more or for life; (4) willful desertion for 7 years; (5) cruel and inhuman treatment of intolerable severity; (6) incurable mental illness; and (7) gross neglect. Either spouse must be a resident of Vermont for 6 months before filing for legal separation. [Vermont Statutes Annotated; Title 15, Sections 551, 555, and 592].

SIMPLIFIED OR SPECIAL DIVORCE PROCEDURES: There are no legal provision in Vermont for simplified divorce procedures. In all divorce cases in Vermont, a hearing as required. An official statistical data sheet must also be filed with the Complaint. [Vermont Rules of Civil Procedure; Rule 80].

MEDIATION OR COUNSELING REQUIREMENTS: If one of the spouses denies under oath that they have lived apart for the required period, the court may delay the proceedings for 30 to 60 days and suggest that the spouses seek counseling. [Vermont Statutes Annotated; Title 15, Section 552].

PROPERTY DISTRIBUTION: Vermont is an "equitable distribution" state. All of the spouses property is subject to being divided on an equitable basis, regardless of when it was acquired or how the title is held, including any gifts and inheritances. The factors to be considered are: (1) the contribution of each spouse to the acquisition of the property, including the contribution of each spouse as homemaker; (2) the value of each spouse's property; (3) the length of the marriage; (4) the age and health of the spouses; (5) the occupation of the spouses; (6) the amount and sources of income of the spouses; (7) the vocational skills of the spouses; (8) the employability of the spouses; (9) the liabilities and needs of each spouse and the opportunity of each for further acquisition of capital assets and income; (10) whether the property award is instead of or in addition to maintenance; (11) how and by whom the property was acquired; (12) the merits of each spouse; (13) the burdens imposed upon either spouse for the benefit of the children; (14) any custodial provisions for the children, including the desirability of awarding the family home to the parent with custody of any children; (15) the conduct of the spouses during the marriage; and (16) the contribution by one spouse to the education, training, or increased earning power of the other. [Vermont Statutes Annotated; Title 15, Section 751].

ALIMONY/MAINTENANCE/SPOUSAL SUPPORT: Either spouse may be ordered to pay maintenance to the other, without regard to marital fault. The maintenance may be rehabilitative (temporary) or permanent and will be awarded if the court finds that the spouse seeking maintenance: (1) lacks sufficient income or property to provide for his or her reasonable needs; and (2) is unable to support him or herself through appropriate employment at the standard of living established during the marriage or is the custodian of any children. The factors to be considered are: (1) the time necessary to acquire sufficient education and training to enable the spouse to find appropriate employment, and that spouse's future earning capacity; (2) the standard of living established during the marriage; (3) the duration of the marriage; (4) the ability of the spouse from whom support is sought to meet his or her needs while meeting those of the spouse seeking support; (5) the financial resources of the spouse seeking maintenance, including property apportioned to such spouse and such spouse's ability to meet his or her needs independently; (6) the age of the spouses; (7) the physical and emotional conditions of the spouses; (8) the effects of inflation on the cost of living; and (9) the lack of sufficient income or property, including property obtained from the property division. The court may require security for any maintenance payments. [Vermont Statutes Annotated; Title 15, Sections 752 and 757].

SPOUSE'S NAME: A wife may resume the use of her former or maiden name upon divorce, unless a good cause is shown why she should not. [Vermont Statutes Annotated; Title 15, Section 558].

CHILD CUSTODY: Joint or sole child custody may be awarded based on the best interests of the child, and upon a consideration of all relevant factors, including the following: (1) the wishes of the parents; (2) the child's adjustment to his or her home, school, and community; (3) the relationship of the child with parents, siblings, and other significant family members; (4) the ability and disposition of each parent to provide love, affection, and guidance; (5) the ability of each parent to provide food, clothing, medical care, other material needs, and a safe environment; (6) the ability of each parent to meet the child's present and future developmental needs; (7) the ability and disposition of each parent to foster a positive relationship and frequent and continuing contact with the other parent, including physical contact unless it will result in harm to the child or parent; (8) the quality of the child's relationship with the primary care provider, given the child's age and development; and (9) the ability and disposition of the parents to communicate, cooperate with each other, and make joint decisions concerning the children where parental rights and responsibilities are to be shared. Neither parent is assumed to have a superior right to have custody. No preference to be given because of parent's sex. [Vermont Statutes Annotated; Title 15, Section 652].

CHILD SUPPORT: Either or both of the parents may be required to pay child support, based on a consideration of the following factors: (1) the financial resources of the child; (2) the standard of living the child would have enjoyed if the marriage had not been dissolved; (3) the physical and emotional conditions and educational needs of the child; (4) the financial resources, needs, and obligations of both the noncustodial and the custodial parent; (5) inflation with relation to the cost of living; and (6) any other relevant factors. Health insurance coverage for the child may be ordered to be provided. The court may require security or wage withholding. Every order of child support must be made subject to a wage assignment in the event of delinquency. There are official child support guidelines available from the Vermont Department of Human Services. [Vermont Statutes Annotated; Title 15, Sections 651, 654-669, 757, and 781-783; and Vermont Rules of Civil Procedure, Rule 80].

APPENDIX: DIVORCE LAWS OF ALL 50 STATES

VIRGINIA

NAME OF COURT IN WHICH TO FILE FOR DIVORCE: Circuit Court or Juvenile and Domestic Relations Court or Experimental Family Court (as of January 1, 1990). "Virginia: In the _____ Court of _____."

TITLE OF DIVORCE ACTION: Complaint for Divorce.

NAME USED TO DESCRIBE SPOUSE FILING FOR DIVORCE: Plaintiff.

NAME USED TO DESCRIBE OTHER SPOUSE IN DIVORCE: Defendant.

TITLE OF FINAL DIVORCE PAPERS: Decree of Divorce.

RESIDENCY REQUIREMENTS AND WHERE TO FILE: One of the spouses must have been a resident of Virginia for at least 6 months prior to filing for divorce. The divorce may be filed for in: (1) the county in which the spouses last lived together; or (2) the county where the defendant resides; or (3) if the defendant is a non-resident of Virginia, the county where the plaintiff resides. [Code of Virginia; Title 8, Section 8.01-261; and Title 20, Sections 20-96 and 20-97].

LEGAL GROUNDS FOR DIVORCE: No-Fault: (1) living separate and apart without cohabitation for 1 year; or (2) living separate and apart without cohabitation for 6 months if there are no minor children and the spouses have entered into a separation agreement. [Code of Virginia; Title 20, Section 20-91].

General: (1) adultery (including homosexual acts); (2) abandonment; (3) conviction of a felony and imprisonment for 1 year; (4) cruelty; and (5) willful desertion. [Code of Virginia; Title 20, Section 20-91].

LEGAL SEPARATION: The grounds for legal separation are: (1) cruelty; (2) willful desertion; (3) abandonment; and (4) reasonable apprehension of bodily injury. One of the spouses must have been a resident of Virginia for at least 6 months prior to filing for legal separation. [Code of Virginia; Title 20, Sections 20-95 and 20-97].

SIMPLIFIED OR SPECIAL DIVORCE PROCEDURES: Separation agreements are specifically authorized by statute and will reduce the time required for living apart by 6 months. In addition, a spouse may waive service of process, but the waiver of service of process form must be signed in front of the clerk of the court. The testimony of either spouse must also, generally, be corroborated by a witness. [Code of Virginia; Title 20, Sections 20-99, 20-99.1:1, and 20-109.1].

MEDIATION OR COUNSELING REQUIREMENTS: There are no legal provisions in Virginia for divorce mediation.

PROPERTY DISTRIBUTION: Virginia is an "equitable distribution" state. The separate property of each spouse, consisting of property (1) acquired prior to the marriage; (2) any gifts and inheritances; (3) any increase in the value of separate property; and (4) any property acquired in exchange for separate property, will be retained by the spouse who owns it. The marital property, consisting of all other property acquired during the marriage, will be divided equitably by the court. The court may also order a payment from one spouse's retirement or profit-sharing benefits to the other spouse. The factors for consideration are: (1) the contribution of each spouse to the acquisition of the marital property, including the contribution of each spouse as homemaker; (2) the liquid or non-liquid character of the property; (3) the length of the marriage; (4) the age and health of the spouses; (5) the federal income tax consequences; (6) any liabilities of the spouses; (7) any retirement benefits, including social security, civil service, military and railroad retirement benefits; (8) how and by whom the property was acquired; (9) the circumstances that contributed to the divorce; (10) the character of all marital property; (11) the contribution of each spouse to the well-being of the family; and (12) any other factor necessary to do equity and justice between the spouses. [Code of Virginia; Title 20, Section 20-107.3].

ALIMONY/MAINTENANCE/SPOUSAL SUPPORT: Either spouse may be awarded maintenance, to be paid in either a lump sum, periodic payments, or both. The factors for consideration are: (1) the ability and time necessary to acquire sufficient education and training to enable the spouse to find appropriate employment, and that spouse's future earning capacity; (2) the standard of living established during the marriage; (3) the duration of the marriage; (4) the financial resources of the spouse seeking maintenance, including marital property apportioned to such spouse and such spouse's ability to meet his or her needs independently; (5) the comparative financial resources of the spouses, including their comparative earning abilities in the labor market and any pension or retirement funds; (6) the needs and obligations of each spouse; (7) the contribution of each spouse to the marriage, including services rendered in homemaking, child care, education, and career building of the other spouse; (8) the tax consequences to each spouse; (9) the age of the spouses; (10) the physical and emotional conditions of the spouses; (11) the educational level of each spouse at the time of the marriage and at the time the action for support is commenced; (12) the property of the spouses; (13) the circumstances which contributed to the divorce; and (14) any other factor the court deems just and equitable. However, permanent maintenance will not be awarded to a spouse who was at fault in a divorce granted on the grounds of adultery, unless such a denial of support would be unjust. [Code of Virginia; Title 20, Sections 20-95 and 20-107.1].

SPOUSE'S NAME: Upon request, a spouse may have his or her former name restored. [Code of Virginia; Title 20, Section 20-121.4].

CHILD CUSTODY: Joint or sole child custody will be awarded based on the welfare of the child, and upon a consideration of the following factors: (1) the age of the child; (2) the child's preference; (3) the needs of the child; (4) the love and affection existing between the child and each parent; (5) the mental and physical health of all individuals involved; (6) the material needs of the child; and (7) the role each parent has played in the care of the child. No preference is to be given to either parent. [Code of Virginia; Title 20, Section 20-107.2].

CHILD SUPPORT: Child support may be ordered to be paid by either parent, and is based on a consideration of the following factors: (1) the financial resources of the child; (2) the standard of living the child would have enjoyed if the marriage had not been dissolved; (3) the physical and emotional conditions and educational needs of the child; (4) the earning capacity of each parent; (5) the age and health of the child; (6) the division of marital property; (7) the monetary or non-monetary contributions of the parents to the family's well-being; (8) the education of the parents; (9) the ability of the parents to secure education and training; (10) the income tax consequences of child support; (11) any special medical, dental, or child care expenses; (12) the obligations, needs, and financial resources of the parents; and (13) any other relevant factors. Official child support guidelines are provided in the statute. [Code of Virginia; Title 20, Sections 20-107.2, 20-108.1, and 20-108.2].

APPENDIX: DIVORCE LAWS OF ALL 50 STATES

WASHINGTON

NAME OF COURT IN WHICH TO FILE FOR DIVORCE: Superior Court; or Family Court (on request). "In the _____ Court of the State of Washington, In and For the County of _____."

TITLE OF DIVORCE ACTION: Petition for Dissolution of Marriage. "In re the Marriage of _____ and _____."

NAME USED TO DESCRIBE SPOUSE FILING FOR DISSOLUTION OF MARRIAGE: Petitioner.

NAME USED TO DESCRIBE OTHER SPOUSE IN DISSOLUTION OF MARRIAGE: Respondent.

TITLE OF FINAL DISSOLUTION OF MARRIAGE PAPERS: Decree of Dissolution of Marriage.

RESIDENCY REQUIREMENTS AND WHERE TO FILE: The spouse filing for dissolution of marriage must be a resident of Washington or a member of the Armed Forces stationed in Washington. The dissolution of marriage may be filed for in any county where either the petitioner or respondent resides. In addition, the court will not act on the petition until 90 days has elapsed from the filing and the service of summons on the respondent. [Revised Code of Washington Annotated; Title 26, Chapter 26.09.030].

LEGAL GROUNDS FOR DISSOLUTION OF MARRIAGE: No-Fault: Irretrievable breakdown of the marriage. [Revised Code of Washington Annotated; Title 26, Chapter 26.09.030].

General: Irretrievable breakdown of the marriage is the only grounds for dissolution of marriage in Washington. [Revised Code of Washington Annotated; Title 26, Chapter 26.09.030].

LEGAL SEPARATION: The only grounds for legal separation in Washington is the irretrievable breakdown of the marriage. The spouse filing for legal separation must be a resident of Washington or a member of the Armed Forces stationed in Washington. The court will not act on the petition until 90 days has elapsed from the filing and the service of summons on the respondent. [Revised Code of Washington Annotated; Title 26, Chapter 26.09.030].

SIMPLIFIED OR SPECIAL DISSOLUTION OF MARRIAGE PROCEDURES: Separation agreements are specifically authorized by law and, if fair, all portions of the agreements are binding on the court, except those relating to parental rights and responsibilities. The spouses must file a Washington Department of Health and Human Services Certificate with the petition. There are also certain local court rules which apply to dissolutions of marriage. These are found in Washington Local Court Rules, Rule 94.04. [Revised Code of Washington Annotated; Title 26, Chapters 26.09.020 and 26.09.080].

MEDIATION OR COUNSELING REQUIREMENTS: Upon the request of either of the spouses, or on the court's own initiative, the spouses may be referred to a counseling service of their choice. A report must be requested from the counseling service within 60 days of the referral. Contested issues relating to custody or visitation will be referred to mediation. There may also be mandatory settlement conferences if there are contested issues. [Revised Code of Washington Annotated; Title 26, Chapters 26.09.015, 26.09.030, and 26.09.181].

PROPERTY DISTRIBUTION: Washington is a "community property" state. Each spouse retains his or her separate property, consisting of: (1) all property acquired prior to marriage; (2) any gifts or inheritances; and (3) any increase in value of the separate property. The court will divide the community property of the spouses, consisting of all other property acquired during the marriage, equally or equitably, after a consideration of the following: (1) the nature and extent of each spouse's separate property; (2) the economic circumstances of each spouse at the time the division of property is to become effective; (3) the length of the marriage; (4) any custodial provisions for the children; (5) the nature and extent of community property; and (6) the desirability of awarding the family home and the right of occupancy for reasonable periods to the custodial parent if there are minor children. Marital misconduct is not to be considered. [Revised Code of Washington Annotated; Title 26, Chapters 26.09.080, 26.16.010, 26.16.020, 26.16.030, and 26.16.220].

ALIMONY/MAINTENANCE/SPOUSAL SUPPORT: Either spouse may be ordered to pay maintenance to the other spouse. Marital misconduct is not to be considered. The factors for consideration are: (1) the time necessary to acquire sufficient education and training to enable the spouse to find appropriate employment, and that spouse's future earning capacity; (2) the standard of living established during the marriage; (3) the duration of the marriage; (4) the ability of the spouse from whom support is sought to meet his or her needs while meeting those of the spouse seeking support; (5) the financial resources of the spouse seeking maintenance, including separate or community property apportioned to such spouse and such spouse's ability to meet his or her needs independently; (6) the needs and obligations of each spouse; (7) the age of the spouses; (8) the physical and emotional conditions of the spouses; and (9) any custodial and child support responsibilities. Maintenance payments may be required to be paid through the clerk of the court. [Revised Code of Washington Annotated; Title 26, Chapters 26.09.050, 26.09.090, and 26.09.120].

SPOUSE'S NAME: Upon request and for a just and reasonable cause, the wife's former or maiden name may be restored. [Revised Code of Washington Annotated; Title 26, Chapter 26.09.150].

CHILD CUSTODY: Joint or sole child custody will be determined according to the best interests of the child. Every petition for dissolution of marriage in which a minor child is involved must include a proposed parenting plan. The parents may make an agreement regarding a parenting plan. The objectives of the parenting plan are to: (1) provide for the child's physical care; (2) maintain the child's emotional stability; (3) provide for the child's changing needs, as the child grows and matures, in a way that minimizes the need for future modifications; (4) set out the authority and responsibility of each parent; (5) minimize the child's exposure to harmful parental conflict; and (6) encourage the parents to reach agreements rather than go to court. The factors which are considered in determining custody are: (1) the strength, nature, and stability of the child's relationship with each parent, including the parent's performance of daily parental functions; (2) any spouse or child abuse or neglect; (3) the history of participation of each parent in decision-making and child-rearing; (4) whether the parents have an ability and desire to cooperate; (5) whether the parent's can agree on joint custody; (6) the emotional needs of the child; (7) the wishes of the parents; (8) the wishes of the child, if of sufficient age and maturity to express an opinion; (9) the child's relationship with siblings and other significant family members; and (10) the child's involvement with home, community, or school. Factor (1) is to be given the most weight. [Revised Code of Washington Annotated; Title 26, Chapters 26.09.050, and 26.09.181- 26.09.210].

CHILD SUPPORT: Either parent may be ordered to pay child support. Marital misconduct is not a factor to be considered. All relevant factors may be considered. Official child support guidelines and worksheets are available from the Washington Department of Social and Health Services. Mandatory wage assignments may be required if the child support payments are over 15 days past due. Child support payments may be required to be paid through the clerk of the court or through the Washington Department of Social and Health Services. [Revised Code of Washington Annotated; Title 26, Chapters 26.09.050, 26.09.100, 26.09.120, 26.18.070, 26.19.040, 26.23.050, and 26.23.135].

APPENDIX: DIVORCE LAWS OF ALL 50 STATES

WEST VIRGINIA

NAME OF COURT IN WHICH TO FILE FOR DIVORCE: Circuit Court. "Circuit Court of _____ County, West Virginia."

TITLE OF DIVORCE ACTION: Complaint for Divorce.

NAME USED TO DESCRIBE SPOUSE FILING FOR DIVORCE: Plaintiff.

NAME USED TO DESCRIBE OTHER SPOUSE IN DIVORCE: Defendant.

TITLE OF FINAL DIVORCE PAPERS: Decree of Divorce.

RESIDENCY REQUIREMENTS AND WHERE TO FILE: One of the spouses must have been a resident of West Virginia for at least 1 year immediately prior to filing. However, if the marriage was performed in West Virginia and one spouse is a resident when filing, there is no durational time limit. The divorce should be filed for in: (1) county in which the spouses last lived together; or (2) the county where the defendant lives if a resident; or (3) the county where the plaintiff lives, if the defendant is a non-resident. [West Virginia Code; Sections 48-2-6, 48-2-7, and 48-2-8].

LEGAL GROUNDS FOR DIVORCE: No-Fault: (1) irreconcilable differences have arisen between the spouses; or (2) living separate and apart without cohabitation and without interruption for 1 year. [West Virginia Code; Section 48-2-4].

General: (1) adultery; (2) abandonment for 6 months; (3) alcoholism and/or drug addiction; (4) confinement for incurable insanity for 3 years; (5) physical abuse or reasonable apprehension of physical abuse of a spouse or of a child; (6) conviction of a felony; (7) cruel and inhuman treatment, including false accusations of adultery or homosexuality; (8) willful neglect of a spouse or a child; and (9) habitual intemperance (drunkenness). [West Virginia Code; Section 48-2-4].

LEGAL SEPARATION: The grounds for legal separation (separate maintenance) are the same as for divorce. One of the spouses must have been a resident of West Virginia for at least 1 year prior to filing for legal separation. [West Virginia Code; Sections 48-2-7 and 48-2-28].

SIMPLIFIED OR SPECIAL DIVORCE PROCEDURES: If one spouse files a verified complaint for divorce on the grounds of "irreconcilable differences", the other spouse may file a verified "answer" admitting the "irreconcilable differences" and a divorce will be granted. Circuit clerks are required to have supplies of an official "answer" form on hand, free of charge. No witnesses will be necessary for any proof for a divorce on the grounds of "irreconcilable differences". In other cases, witnesses will be required. The court may approve or reject a marital settlement agreement of the spouses. Standard financial disclosure forms may be required to be filed. [West Virginia Code; Sections 48-2-4, 48-2-16, and 48-2-33; and West Virginia Rules of Civil Procedure-Rule 80].

MEDIATION OR COUNSELING REQUIREMENTS: There are no legal provisions in West Virginia for divorce mediation or counseling.

PROPERTY DISTRIBUTION: West Virginia is an "equitable distribution" state. Each spouse may retain his or her separate property: (1) acquired prior to the marriage; (2) acquired by gift or inheritance during the marriage; (3) any increase in value of the separate property; and (4) any property acquired in exchange for any separate property. Marital property, consisting of all other property acquired during the marriage, is to be divided equally and without regard to any marital misconduct. However, this equal division may be altered based on a consideration of the following factors: (1) the contribution of each spouse to the acquisition of the marital property, including the contribution of each spouse as homemaker and in child-care; (2) the value of each spouse's separate property; (3) the amount and sources of income of the spouses; (4) the conduct of the spouses during the marriage only as it relates to the disposition of their property; (5) the value of the labor performed in a family business or in the actual maintenance or improvement of tangible marital property; (6) the contribution of one spouse toward the education or training of the other which has increased the income-earning ability of the other spouse; (7) the foregoing by either spouse of employment or other income-earning activity through an understanding of the spouses or at the insistence of the other spouse; and (8) any other factor necessary to do equity and justice between the spouses. [West Virginia Code; Sections 48-2-21 and 48-2-32].

ALIMONY/MAINTENANCE/SPOUSAL SUPPORT: Either spouse may be ordered to provide the other spouse with alimony. The factors to be considered are: (1) whether the spouse seeking alimony is the custodian of a child whose condition or circumstances make it appropriate for that spouse not to seek outside employment; (2) the time and expense necessary to acquire sufficient education and training to enable the spouse to find appropriate employment, and that spouse's future earning capacity; (3) the duration of the marriage; (4) the comparative financial resources of the spouses, including their comparative earning abilities in the labor market; (5) the needs and obligations of each spouse; (6) the tax consequences to each spouse; (7) the age of the spouses; (8) the physical and emotional conditions of the spouses; (9) the vocational skills and employability of the spouse seeking alimony; (10) any custodial and child support responsibilities; (11) the educational level of each spouse at the time of the marriage and at the time the action for divorce is commenced; (12) the cost of education of minor children and of health care for each spouse and the minor children; (13) the distribution of marital property; (14) any legal obligations of the spouses to support themselves or others; and (15) any other factor the court deems just and equitable. The marital misconduct of the spouses will be considered and compared. Alimony will not be awarded to any spouse who: (1) was adulterous; (2) has been convicted of a felony during the marriage; or (3) deserted or abandoned his or her spouse for 6 months. The court may require health and/or hospitalization insurance coverage as alimony. [West Virginia Code; Sections 48-2-13, 48-2-15, and 48-2-17].

SPOUSE'S NAME: Upon request, either spouse may resume the use of his or her former name. [West Virginia Code; Section 48-2-23].

CHILD CUSTODY: Either parent may be awarded custody. There is a presumption in favor of the parent who has been the primary caretaker of the child. There are no other factors for consideration specified in the statute. There is no specific statutory provision in West Virginia for joint custody. [West Virginia Code; Section 48-2-15].

CHILD SUPPORT: Either parent may be required to provide periodic child support payments, including health insurance coverage. The factors for consideration specified in the statute are: (1) whether the spouse seeking support is the custodian of a child whose condition or circumstances make it appropriate for that spouse not to seek outside employment; (2) the time and expense necessary to acquire sufficient education and training to enable the spouse to find appropriate employment, and that spouse's future earning capacity; (3) the duration of the marriage and the actual period of cohabitation as husband and wife; (4) the comparative financial resources of the spouses, including their comparative earning abilities in the labor market; (5) the needs and obligations of each spouse; (6) the tax consequences to each spouse; (7) the age of the spouses; (8) the physical and emotional conditions of the spouses; (9) the vocational skills and employability of the spouse seeking support and maintenance; (10) any custodial responsibilities; (11) the educational level of each spouse at the time of the marriage and at the time the action for divorce is commenced; (12) the cost of education of minor children and of health care for each spouse and the minor children; (13) the distribution of marital property; (14) any legal obligations of the spouses to support themselves or others; and (15) any other factor the court deems just and equitable. One of the parents may also be granted exclusive use of the family home, and all of the goods and furniture necessary to help in the rearing of the children. This use may be temporary or on a long-term basis. The court may require a parent to make payments for rent, utilities, mortgage loan payments, taxes, home-owners insurance, or other necessary household expenses. The court may require health and hospitalization insurance coverage as child support. Income withholding may be ordered to guarantee the support payments. Child support guidelines are available from the West Virginia Child Advocate Office. [West Virginia Code; Sections 48-2-13, 48-2-15, 48-2-15a, 48-2-16, and 48A-2-8].

APPENDIX: DIVORCE LAWS OF ALL 50 STATES

WISCONSIN

NAME OF COURT IN WHICH TO FILE FOR DIVORCE: Circuit Court/Family Court. "State of Wisconsin: Circuit Court, _____ County."

TITLE OF DIVORCE ACTION: Petition for Divorce. "In re the marriage of _____ and _____."

NAME USED TO DESCRIBE SPOUSE FILING FOR DIVORCE: Petitioner [or Co-Petitioner if the petition is filed jointly. See below under **Simplified Or Special Dissolution Of Marriage Procedures**].

NAME USED TO DESCRIBE OTHER SPOUSE IN DIVORCE: Respondent [or Co-Petitioner if the petition is filed jointly].

TITLE OF FINAL DIVORCE PAPERS: Decree of Divorce.

RESIDENCY REQUIREMENTS AND WHERE TO FILE: One of the spouses must have been a resident of Wisconsin for 6 months and of the county where the divorce is filed for 30 days immediately prior to filing. No hearing on the divorce will be scheduled until 120 days after the defendant is served the summons or after the filing of a joint petition. [Wisconsin Statutes Annotated; Sections 767.05 and 767.083].

LEGAL GROUNDS FOR DIVORCE: No-Fault: Irretrievable breakdown of the marriage. The irretrievable breakdown of the marriage may be shown by : (1) a joint petition by both spouse's requesting a divorce on these grounds; or (2) living separate and apart for 12 months immediately prior to filing; or (3) if the court finds an irretrievable breakdown of the marriage with no possible chance at reconciliation. [Wisconsin Statutes Annotated; Section 767.07].

General: Irretrievable breakdown of the marriage is the only grounds for divorce in Wisconsin. [Wisconsin Statutes Annotated; Section 767.07].

LEGAL SEPARATION: Irretrievable breakdown of the marriage is the only grounds for legal separation in Wisconsin. The residency requirements are the same as for divorce. [Wisconsin Statutes Annotated; Sections 767.05 and 767.07].

SIMPLIFIED OR SPECIAL DIVORCE PROCEDURES: The spouses may file a joint petition for divorce in which they both consent to personal jurisdiction of the court and waive service of process. A copy of a guide to Wisconsin Court procedures for obtaining a divorce is to be provided to the spouses upon filing for divorce. Also, if children are involved an official child support form (which is available from the court clerk) must be filed with the petition. In addition, separation agreements are specifically authorized by law. [Wisconsin Statutes Annotated; Sections 767.081, 767.085 and 767.10].

MEDIATION OR COUNSELING REQUIREMENTS: The court must inform the spouses of the availability of counseling services. Upon request or on the court's own initiative, the court may order counseling and delay the divorce proceedings for up to 90 days. If custody of a child is a contested issue, mediation is required. If joint custody is requested, mediation may be required. [Wisconsin Statutes Annotated; Sections 767.081, 767.082, 767.083, and 767.11].

PROPERTY DISTRIBUTION: Wisconsin is now a "community property" state. There is a presumption that all marital property should be divided equally. Marital property is all of the spouse's property except separate property consisting of: (1) property inherited by either spouse; (2) property received as a gift by either spouse; or (3) property paid for by funds acquired by inheritance or gift. The equal distribution may be altered by the court, without regard to marital misconduct, based on the following factors: (1) the contribution of each spouse to the acquisition of the marital property, including the contribution of each spouse as homemaker; (2) the value of each spouse's separate property; (3) the length of the marriage; (4) the age and health of the spouses; (5) the occupation of the spouses; (6) the amount and sources of

299

income of the spouses; (7) the vocational skills of the spouses; (8) the employability and earning capacity of the spouses; (9) the federal income tax consequences of the court's division of the property; (10) the standard of living established during the marriage; (11) the time necessary for a spouse to acquire sufficient education to enable the spouse to find appropriate employment; (12) any premarital or marital settlement agreements; (13) any retirement benefits; (14) whether the property award is instead of or in addition to maintenance; (15) any custodial provisions for the children; and (16) any other relevant factor. The court may also divide any of the spouse's separate property in order to prevent a hardship on a spouse or on the children of the marriage. [Wisconsin Statutes Annotated; Sections 766.01 to 766.97 and 767.255].

ALIMONY/MAINTENANCE/SPOUSAL SUPPORT: Either spouse may be ordered to pay maintenance to the other spouse, without regard to marital misconduct. The factors for consideration are as follows: (1) the time necessary to acquire sufficient education and training to enable the spouse to find appropriate employment, and that spouse's future earning capacity; (2) the duration of the marriage; (3) the financial resources of the spouse seeking maintenance, including marital property apportioned to such spouse and such spouse's ability to meet his or her needs independently; (4) the comparative financial resources of the spouses, including their comparative earning abilities; (5) the contribution of each spouse to the marriage, including services rendered in homemaking, child care, education, and career building of the other spouse; (6) the tax consequences to each spouse; (7) the age of the spouses; (8) the physical and emotional conditions of the spouses; (9) the vocational skills and employability of the spouse seeking maintenance; (10) the length of absence from the job market; (11) the probable duration of the need of the spouse seeking maintenance; (12) any custodial and child support responsibilities; (13) the educational level of each spouse at the time of the marriage and at the time the divorce is filed for; (14) any mutual agreement between the spouses; and (15) any other relevant factor. The court may combine maintenance and child support payments into a single family support payment. The maintenance payments may be required to be paid through the clerk of the court. [Wisconsin Statutes Annotated; Sections 767.26, 767.261, and 767.29]

SPOUSE'S NAME: Upon request, either spouse's former name may be restored. [Wisconsin Statutes Annotated; Section 767.20].

CHILD CUSTODY: Joint or sole child custody (referred to as "legal custody and physical placement") may be awarded based on the best interests of the child, and the following factors: (1) preference of the child; (2) the wishes of the parents; (3) the child's adjustment to his or her home, school, and community; (4) the mental and physical health of all individuals involved; (5) the relationship of the child with parents, siblings, and other significant family members; (6) any findings or recommendations of a neutral mediator; (7) the availability of child care; (8) any spouse or child abuse; (9) any significant drug or alcohol abuse; (10) whether one parent is likely to unreasonably interfere with the child's continuing relationship with the other parent; and (11) any other factors. The sex and race of the parent is not to be considered. [Wisconsin Statutes Annotated; Section 767.24].

CHILD SUPPORT: Either or both parents may be ordered to pay child support and health care expenses. The factors to be considered are: (1) the financial resources of the child; (2) the standard of living the child would have enjoyed if the marriage had not been dissolved; (3) the physical and emotional conditions and educational needs of the child; (4) the financial resources, needs, and obligations of the parents; (5) the age and health of the child; (6) the desirability of the parent having custody remaining in the home as a full-time parent; (7) the cost of day care to the parent having custody if that parent works outside the home, or the value of the child care services performed by that parent; (8) the tax consequences to each parent; (9) the award of substantial periods of physical placement to both parents (joint custody); (10) any extraordinary travel expenses incurred in exercising the right to periods of physical placement; and (11) any other relevant factors. The court may combine maintenance and child support payments into a single family support payment. There are official guidelines and percentage standards for child support are available from the Wisconsin Department of Health and Social Services. The court may require that child support payments be guaranteed by an assignment of income. The court may also require that the payments be made through the clerk of the court. In addition, the court may require health insurance coverage for the children. [Wisconsin Statutes Annotated; Sections 767.10, 767.25, 767.261, 767.265, 767.27, and 767.29]

APPENDIX: DIVORCE LAWS OF ALL 50 STATES

WYOMING

NAME OF COURT IN WHICH TO FILE FOR DIVORCE: District Court. "In the District Court In and For _____ County, Wyoming."

TITLE OF DIVORCE ACTION: Complaint for Divorce.

NAME USED TO DESCRIBE SPOUSE FILING FOR DIVORCE: Plaintiff.

NAME USED TO DESCRIBE OTHER SPOUSE IN DIVORCE: Defendant.

TITLE OF FINAL DIVORCE PAPERS: Decree of Divorce.

RESIDENCY REQUIREMENTS AND WHERE TO FILE: (1) the spouse filing for divorce must have been a resident of Wyoming for 60 days immediately prior to filing; or (2) the marriage must have been performed in Wyoming and the spouse filing must have resided in Wyoming from the time of the marriage until the time of the filing. The divorce may be filed for in the county where either spouse lives. There is a waiting period of 20 days after filing before a divorce will be granted. [Wyoming Statutes Annotated; Title 20, Chapters 20-2-104, 20-2-107, and 20-2-108].

LEGAL GROUNDS FOR DIVORCE: No-Fault: Irreconcilable differences. [Wyoming Statutes Annotated; Title 20, Chapter 20-2-104].

General: Confinement for incurable insanity for 2 years. [Wyoming Statutes Annotated; Title 20, Chapter 20-2-105].

LEGAL SEPARATION: The grounds for legal separation are; (1) irreconcilable differences; and (2) confinement for incurable insanity for 2 years. The spouse filing for legal separation must have been a resident of Wyoming for 60 days immediately prior to filing or the marriage must have been performed in Wyoming and the spouse filing must have resided in Wyoming from the time of the marriage until the time of the filing. The legal separation may be filed for in the county where either spouse lives. [Wyoming Statutes Annotated; Title 20, Chapters 20-2-102, 20-2-104, 20-2-106, and 20-2-107].

SIMPLIFIED OR SPECIAL DIVORCE PROCEDURES: A sample Complaint for Divorce form is contained in Wyoming Rules of Civil Procedure, Appendix of Forms, Form #15.

MEDIATION OR COUNSELING REQUIREMENTS: There are no legal provisions in Wyoming for divorce mediation.

PROPERTY DISTRIBUTION: Wyoming is an "equitable distribution" state. All of the spouse's property will be divided in an equitable manner, including property acquired prior to the marriage, and gifts and inheritances, based on a consideration of the following factors: (1) the economic circumstances of each spouse at the time the division of property is to become effective; (2) how and by whom the property was acquired; (3) the merits of each spouse; (4) the burdens imposed upon either spouse for the benefit of the children; (5) the conduct of the spouses; and (6) any other factor necessary to do equity and justice between the spouses. [Wyoming Statutes Annotated; Title 20, Chapter 20-2-114].

ALIMONY/MAINTENANCE/SPOUSAL SUPPORT: Either spouse may be awarded alimony in the form of a specific sum or property after consideration of the other's ability to pay. Real estate or profits from real estate may be ordered transferred to the other spouse for alimony for life. Marital fault is not a factor. No other factors are specified in the statute. [Wyoming Statutes Annotated; Title 20, Chapter 20-2-114].

SPOUSE'S NAME: There is no statutory provision in Wyoming for the restoration of a wife's name upon divorce. However, there is a general statutory provision for name change upon petitioning the court. [Wyoming Statutes Annotated; Title 1, Chapter 1-25-101].

CHILD CUSTODY: Child custody will be awarded according to the best interests of the child. The sex of the parent is not to be considered. The child's wishes may be considered. The relative competency of both parents is the only other factor specified to be considered. There are no specific provisions for joint custody in Wyoming. [Wyoming Statutes Annotated; Title 20, Chapter 20-2-113].

CHILD SUPPORT: Either parent may be ordered to pay child support. No factors for consideration are specified. A trustee may be appointed to invest the support payments and apply the income to the support of the children. Child support payments may be ordered to be paid through the clerk of the court. A court may order income withholding to guarantee any child support payments. [Wyoming Statutes Annotated; Title 20, Chapters 20-2-112, 20-2-113, and 20-6-221].

GLOSSARY OF LEGAL TERMS

ACTION: A lawsuit or proceeding in a court of law.

AFFIDAVIT: A written statement of facts which is made under oath and which is signed before a notary public or court official.

AGREEMENT: A verbal or written resolution of disputed issues.

ALLEGATIONS: The claims or charges against the other person which are made in a lawsuit.

ALIMONY: A payment of support for one spouse provided by the other spouse. May be paid in periodic payments, in one lump-sum payment, or a combination of both. May be paid temporarily or on a permanent basis. (Same as *spousal support* or *maintenance*.)

ANNULMENT: A legal action which has the result of treating a marriage as if it had never occurred.

ANSWER: A formal written response to the charges or allegations in a complaint. The answer is filed by a defendant in a lawsuit. (Same as a *response*.)

ANTENUPTIAL AGREEMENT: A legal contract signed by two people before they get married. Such an agreement generally limits a spouse's rights to property, support, or inheritance upon divorce. (Same as a *prenuptial agreement*.)

APPEAL: A legal proceeding in which the losing party in a lawsuit requests that a higher court review the decision.

APPEARANCE: The formal submission by a defendant in a lawsuit to the jurisdiction of the court. The appearance may be made in person or by filing a formal document (an answer, response, or appearance and waiver) with the court.

ASSIGNMENT: The transfer of a right or interest in property from one person to another.

AWARD: A decision by a court in a lawsuit to compensate a person in some fashion.

BILL OF PARTICULARS: The formal title for a document in a lawsuit which adds information to the facts contained in a complaint or petition.

CAUSE OF ACTION: The legal theories or basis upon which a lawsuit is based.

CIVIL COURT: A court which presides over non-criminal matters.

CLAIM: A charge by one person against another.

COHABITATION: Living together. Generally, if sex is shared.

COMMON-LAW MARRIAGE: A marriage in which there has been no formal ceremony or marriage license. Not recognized as valid in all states.

COMMUNITY PROPERTY: Generally, all income and property which is acquired by either or both spouses during the course of a marriage, except property acquired by individual gift or inheritance. Community property does not include property that was acquired prior to a marriage. In most community property states, both spouses are considered to own an equal share of all of the community property. (See *separate property*.)

COMPLAINT: The title given to the first document filed in a lawsuit for divorce or dissolution of marriage. The complaint sets out the facts of the case and the allegations against the other spouse and requests that the court grant the divorce or dissolution. (See *petition*.)

CONTESTED DIVORCE: A divorce where at least one issue has not been settled prior to court. A court must decide any issues that have not been agreed upon in a contested case.

COUNT: A statement of facts in a complaint or petition which outlines the case.

COUNTER-CLAIM: A complaint (or *petition*) filed by a defendant (or *respondent*) which states claims against the plaintiff (or *petitioner*.)

CUSTODIAL PARENT: The parent with whom a child normally lives.

DECREE: The title of the final ruling in a case, as in Final Decree of Divorce. (See *judgement*.)

DEFAULT ORDER/JUDGEMENT: An order or judgement of a court based only on the plaintiff's (or *petitioner's*) case. The defendant (or *respondent*) has not answered the allegations or made an appearance in the case.

DEFENDANT: The person who defends against a lawsuit brought against him or her by another. (See *respondent*.)

GLOSSARY OF LEGAL TERMS

DIVORCE: A legal judgement that severs the marriage of two people and restores them to the status of single persons. (Same as *dissolution of marriage*.)

DISSOLUTION OF MARRIAGE: A legal judgement that severs the marriage of two people and restores them to the status of single persons. (Same as *divorce*.)

DOMICILE: The place where a person lives, and intends to return if he or she is temporarily absent.

EQUITABLE DIVISION: A method of property division in a divorce (or *dissolution of marriage*) which is generally based on a variety of factors in an attempt to allocate a fair and just amount of property to each spouse.

FAULT-BASED DIVORCE: A type of divorce which may only be granted on a showing that one of the spouses was guilty of some form of marital misconduct.

GROUNDS: The legal basis for the divorce (or *dissolution of marriage*). The grounds may be no-fault or fault-based.

HEARING: Any proceeding before a court where testimony is given or arguments heard.

HOLD-HARMLESS: A phrase used to describe an agreement by which one person agrees to assume full liability for an obligation and protect another from any loss or expense based on that obligation.

JOINT LEGAL CUSTODY: A form of custody of minor children in which the parents share the responsibilities and major decision making relating to the child. Generally, one parent is awarded actual physical custody of the child and the other parent is awarded liberal visitation rights. (See *joint physical custody*, *sole custody*, and *split custody*.)

JOINT PHYSICAL CUSTODY: A form of custody of minor children in which the parents share the actual physical custody of the child. Generally, an alternating method of custody is used. (See *joint legal custody*, *sole custody*, and *split custody*.)

JOINT PROPERTY: Property which is held or titled in the name of more than one person. (See *joint tenancy, community property,* and *marital property*.)

JOINT TENANCY: A form of joint ownership of property by which each joint owner has an equal share in the property. Generally, a joint tenancy is used in connection with a right of survivorship. (See *right of survivorship*.)

JUDGEMENT: A ruling or order of a court. (See *decree*.)

JURISDICTION: The power or authority of a court to rule in a particular case. A court must have jurisdiction over both the subject matter of the case and the people involved in the dispute in order to have the authority to hear a case and make binding decisions.

LEGAL SEPARATION: A legal lawsuit for support while the spouses are living separate and apart. A legal separation may deal with the same issues as in a divorce, but does not dissolve the marriage. (See *separate maintenance*.)

LUMP-SUM ALIMONY: Spousal support that is made in a single payment or is a fixed amount, but paid in specific installments.

MAINTENANCE: Support for a spouse provided by the other spouse. May be paid in periodic payments, in one lump-sum payment, or a combination of both. May be paid temporarily or on a permanent basis. Same as *alimony* or *spousal support*.

MARITAL PROPERTY: Term used to describe the property which is subject to division by a court upon divorce or dissolution. Generally, all property which was acquired during a marriage by either or both spouses, except individual gifts and inheritances. Marital property does not generally include property that was acquired by either spouse prior to the marriage. (See *community property, joint property, separate property, non-marital property*.)

MARITAL SETTLEMENT AGREEMENT: A written agreement entered into by divorcing spouses that spells out their rights and agreements regarding property, support, and children. (Same as a *separation agreement*.)

MOTION: A written or oral request to a court for some type of action, such as a motion to continue a trial to a later date.

NO-FAULT DIVORCE: A type of divorce which may be granted without the necessity of showing that either spouse was guilty of some form of marital misconduct.

NON-MARITAL PROPERTY: Term used to describe separate property in some states which provide for the equitable distribution of property. Generally, non-marital property consists of property acquired prior to a marriage and property acquired by individual gift or inheritance either before or during a marriage. (See *marital property, community property,* and *separate property*.)

ORDER: A court's official ruling on some matter before it. Generally, a court order will be in writing and signed by the judge.

PALIMONY: The payment of support by one lover to another when the persons were never married.

PARTY: A person directly involved in a lawsuit; either a plaintiff/petitioner or a defendant/respondent.

PERSONAL JURISDICTION: The power or authority of a court to make orders regarding a certain person and have those orders legally enforced.

PETITION: The title given to the first document filed in an action for divorce or dissolution of marriage. The petition sets out the facts of the case and the allegations against the other spouse and requests that the court grant the divorce or dissolution. (See *complaint*)

PETITIONER: The person who initiates a lawsuit by filing a petition with the court. (Same as *plaintiff*.)

GLOSSARY OF LEGAL TERMS

PLAINTIFF: The person who initiates a lawsuit by filing a complaint with the court. (Same as *petitioner*.)

PLEADING: Any formal written document filed with a court which requests action by the court. Includes complaints, petitions, answers to the complaint, responses to a petition, motions, etc.

PRAYER: That portion of a complaint or petition which contains the action that the person is requesting of the court. Also referred to as a prayer for relief.

PRENUPTIAL AGREEMENT: A legal contract signed by two people before they get married. Such an agreement generally limits a spouse's rights to property, support, or inheritance upon divorce. (Same as a *antenuptial agreement*.)

PRIMARY CARETAKER: The parent who provides the majority of the day-to-day care for a minor child.

RESIDENCE: The place where a person lives. (Generally, same as *domicile*.)

RESPONSE: The formal document filed by a respondent in answer to the allegations in a petition. (Same as an *answer*.)

RIGHT OF SURVIVORSHIP: The right of joint owners of a piece of property to automatically be given the other's share of the property upon the death of the other owner. This right must, generally, be specifically stated on any documents of title for it to apply. For example: a joint tenancy with the right of survivorship.

SEPARATE MAINTENANCE: A lawsuit for support in a situation where the spouses live separate and apart but are not presently pursuing a divorce or dissolution. (Same as a *legal separation*.)

SEPARATE PROPERTY: Property considered to be owned individually by one spouse and not subject to division upon divorce in most states. Separate property generally consists of property acquired prior to a marriage and property acquired by individual gift or inheritance either before or during a marriage. (See *marital property, community property,* and *non-marital property*.)

SEPARATION AGREEMENT: A written agreement entered into by divorcing spouses that spells out their rights and agreements regarding property, support, and children. (Same as a *marital settlement agreement*.)

SERVICE OF PROCESS: The actual act of presenting the defendant or respondent in a lawsuit with a summons notifying him or her of the lawsuit. Also generally includes providing the defendant or respondent with a copy of the actual complaint or petition in the lawsuit.

SETTLEMENT: An agreement that resolves certain disputed issues.

SETTLEMENT AGREEMENT: The written version of a settlement which resolves certain issues. It is generally a valid contract.

DIVORCE YOURSELF

SOLE CUSTODY: A form of child custody in which one parent is given both physical custody of the child and the right to make all of the major decisions regarding the child's upbringing. Generally, the other parent is awarded reasonable visitation rights. (See *joint custody* and *split custody*.)

SPLIT CUSTODY: A form of child custody in which the actual time of physical custody is split between the parents, with both retaining the rights to participate in decisions regarding the child. (See *joint custody* and *sole custody*.)

SPOUSAL SUPPORT: Support for a spouse provided by the other spouse. May be paid in periodic payments, in one lump-sum payment, or a combination of both. May be paid temporarily or on a permanent basis. (Same as *alimony* or *maintenance*.)

STIPULATION: An agreement between persons in a lawsuit or their lawyers, usually relating to court procedure.

SUBJECT-MATTER JURISDICTION: The power or authority of a court to decide issues relating to certain subjects. For example: a Family Court may decide issues relating to the affairs of families; divorces, annulments, separations, custody, etc.

SUBPOENA: A document which is served upon (delivered to) a person who is not directly involved in a lawsuit, requesting that he or she appear in court to give testimony.

SUMMONS: A document which is served upon (delivered to) a person who is named as a defendant or respondent in a lawsuit. The summons notifies the person that the lawsuit has been filed against him or her and tells them that they have a certain time limit in which to file an answer or response in reply.

TENANCY-BY-THE-ENTIREITIES: A form of joint ownership in which two married persons hold title to a piece of property in equal shares and each has an automatic right to the other's share upon death.

TENANCY-IN-COMMON: A form of joint ownership in which two or more persons own particular shares of a piece of property. The shares need not be equal and the persons have no legal right to any shares of another upon death.

TRIAL: A formal court hearing to decide disputed issues raised by a complaint and answer or by a petition and response.

UNCONTESTED DIVORCE: A divorce proceeding in which their is no dispute as to any of the legal issues involved. The lack of dispute may be because the other spouse is missing, refuses to participate in the proceeding, or agrees with the other spouse on all issues.

VISITATION: The right of a parent who does not have physical custody to visit a child or have a child visit him or her.

VERIFIED/VERIFICATION: A written statement that is signed under oath.

WAIVER: A written document that relinquishes a person's rights.

BIBLIOGRAPHY OF DIVORCE-RELATED BOOKS

Belli, Melvin and Krantzler, Mel: *Divorcing*, St. Martin's Press, New York, 1988.

Briles, Judith: *The Dollars & Sense of Divorce: A Financial Guide for Women*, Master Media Ltd., 1988.

Clair, Bernard and Daniele, Anthony: *The Ex-Factor - The Complete Do-It-Yourself Post Divorce Handbook*, Donald I. Fine Inc., New York, 1987.

Blades, Joan: *Mediate Your Divorce: A Guide to Cooperative Custody, Property, and Support Agreements*, Prentice-Hall, Englewood Cliffs, NJ, 1985.

Friedman, James: *The Divorce Handbook*, Random House, New York, 1984.

Galper, Miriam: *Joint Custody and Co-Parenting Handbook*, Running Press, Philadelphia, 1980.

Green, Samuel: *Marriage and Family Agreements*, Shephard's/McGraw-Hill, Colorado Springs CO, 1985.

Jacob, Herbert: *The Silent Revolution*, University of Chicago Press, Chicago, 1988.

Kaslow, Florence: *The Dynamics of Divorce*, Bruner/Mazel Publishers, New York, 1987.

Krauskopf, Joan: *Marital and Non-Marital Contracts*, American Bar Association, Chicago, 1983.

Lindley, Alexander: *Separation Agreements and Antenuptial Contracts*, Matthew Bender & Co., New York, 1989.

Mitchelson, Marvin: *Living Together*, Simon and Schuster, New York, 1980.

Neumann, Diane: *Divorce Mediation: How to Cut the Cost and Stress of Divorce*, H. Holt, New York, 1989.

Plesent, Stanley: *Preparing Matrimonial Agreements*, Practising Law Institute, New York, 1989.

Rogers, Mary: *Women, Divorce, and Money*, McGraw-Hill, New York, 1981.

Sack, Steven: *The Complete Legal Guide to Marriage, Divorce, Custody & Living Together*, Fisher Books, 1987.

Saunders, Melanie: *Divorce: Citizen's Legal Manual*, HALT, Washington DC, 1984.

Schneider, Karan and Myles: *Divorce Mediation: The Constructive New Way to End a Marriage Without Big Legal Bills*, Acropolis Books, Washington DC, 1984.

Schnell, Barry: *The Child Support Survivor's Guide*, The Consumer Awareness Learning Laboratory, Salem NJ, 1984.

Sherman, Charles: *Practical Divorce Solutions: A Guidebook*, Nolo Press, Occidental CA, 1988.

Ware, Ciji: *Sharing Parenthood After Divorce*, Viking Press, New York, 1982.

Weitzman, Lenore: *The Divorce Revolution*, Free Press, New York, 1985.

Woolley, Persia: *The Custody Handbook*, Summit Books, New York, 1979,

Available Self-Help Divorce Books:

The following is a listing of all of the known books on the subject of self-help divorce which are relatively readily available. Some, however, may be difficult to find. The quality of these guides varies widely from very poor to excellent. The information contained in some of them may also be considerably (and possibly dangerously) out-of-date. They should be used with caution. They may, however, be useful for information on the use of local forms or local court rules. This list is for reference only, and a listing here does not imply that any of these books are recommended.

ARIZONA: Robinson, Sue: *First Steps: A Divorce Information Guidebook, Arizona Edition*, Sue Robinson, 1986.

CALIFORNIA: Sherman, Charles: *How To Do Your Own Divorce In California*, Nolo Press, Occidental CA, 1989.

COLORADO: Whicher, Susan: *Guide to Colorado Dissolution of Marriage Forms*, Bradford Publishing Co., 1988.

CONNECTICUT: Avery, Michael: *Do Your Own Divorce in Connecticut*, Pro-Se Divorce Group/Cobblesmith, 1981.

FLORIDA: Maloy, Richard: *Your Questions Answered About Florida Divorce Law*, Windward Publishers, 1984.

FLORIDA: Keane, Gerald, and Breslau, Jill: *Florida Divorce Handbook*, Pineapple Press, 1989.

HAWAII: Herman, Peter: *A Practical Guide to Divorce in Hawaii*, University of Hawaii Press, 1986.

BIBLIOGRAPHY OF DIVORCE-RELATED BOOKS

ILLINOIS: Andrews, Jill: *Pro-Se Litigant's Manual: Dissolution of Marriage*, Jill Andrews, 1988.

ILLINOIS: Block, Winston: *The In's and Out's of Illinois Divorce Law in Plain English*, Tanler Publishers, 1988.

ILLINOIS: Albert, Nancy: *Insider's Guide to Divorce in Illinois: The Practical Consumer Divorce Manual*, N. Albert, 1984.

ILLINOIS: Gerhard, Fred: *The Illinois Do-it-Yourself Divorce Kit*, Contemporary Books, Chicago, 1984.

ILLINOIS: LawLab: *Filing Your Own Uncontested Divorce*, LawLab, Chicago, 1985.

LOUISIANA: Eddy, R. Lee: *What You Should Know About Marriage, Divorce, Annulment, Separation, & Community Property In Louisiana*, Exposition-Phoenix, 1974.

LOUISIANA: Lowe, Robert: *Louisiana Divorce*, Lawyers-Cooperative Publishing Co., 1984.

MAINE: Divorce Reform Inc.: *Do Your Own Divorce In Maine*, Divorce Reform Inc., Cobblesmith, 1978.

MARYLAND: Kalenik, Sandra: *How to Get A Divorce: A Practical Guide for Residents of the District of Columbia, Maryland & Virginia Who Are Contemplating Divorce*, Washington Book Trading Co., 1984.

MASSACHUSETTS: Sibbison, Wendy: *Massachusetts Divorce: A Consumer Guide*, Mansir/Holden Printing Company, 1987.

MASSACHUSETTS: Triantafillou, Katherine: *Do Your Own No-Fault Divorce: (Massachusetts)*, Portia Press, 1979.

MICHIGAN: Maran, Michael: *The Michigan Divorce Book: A Guide to Doing an Uncontested Divorce Without an Attorney*, Grand River, 1986.

MICHIGAN: Easen, David, and Suo, Sidney: *Michigan Divorce*, The Lawyers-Cooperative Publishing Co., 1984.

MISSISSIPPI: Goldner, Jesse: *Mississippi Divorce, Alimony, and Child Custody - With Forms*, Harrison Co., 1987.

NEVADA: Grumet, Robert: *How To Do Your Own Divorce In Nevada*, Utopia Press. 1982.

NEW YORK: Bernard, Clyne: *New York Divorce Book: Step-by-Step Guide With Forms*, Moyer Bell Ltd., 1988.

NEW YORK: Gitlitz, James: *New York Uncontested Divorce and Annulments*, Gould, 1989.

NEW YORK: Anosike, Benji: *How to Do Your Own Divorce Without a Lawyer (New York)*, Do-It-Yourself Legal Publishers, 1981.

NORTH CAROLINA: Kelso, Lloyd: *North Carolina Divorce, Alimony, and Child Custody - With Forms*, Harrison Co., 1989.

NORTH CAROLINA: McGee, Michael: *Separation and Divorce in North Carolina: How to Do it with or Without a Lawyer*, Globe Pequot, 1984.

OHIO: Gilchrist, John: *Divorce in Ohio: A People's Guide to Marriage, Divorce, Dissolution, Alimony, Custody, Child Support, & Visitation*, Pro Se Publishers, 1988.

OREGON: Baldwin, Richard: *Divorce Guide for Oregon*, International Self Counsel Press, Seattle, 1984.

OREGON: English, Katherine and McFarlane, Julie: *Parting - A Handbook for Self-Help Divorce in Oregon*, Parting Inc., 1979.

PENNSYLVANIA: Frankel, Mark and Gates, Samuel: *No-Fault Divorce in Pennsylvania: What Everyone Should Know About Divorce,* G. Shumway Pub., 1983.

TEXAS: Sherman, Charles and Simon, Jim: *How to Do Your Own Divorce In Texas*, Nolo Press, Occidental CA, 1988.

TEXAS: Gilstrap, Frank: *How To Do Your Own Texas Divorce for under Fifteen Dollars*, How-To Press, 1983.

VIRGINIA: Kalenik, Sandra: *How to Get A Divorce: A Practical Guide for Residents of the District of Columbia, Maryland & Virginia Who Are Contemplating Divorce*, Washington Book Trading Co., 1984.

WASHINGTON, D.C.: Kalenik, Sandra: *How to Get A Divorce: A Practical Guide for Residents of the District of Columbia, Maryland & Virginia Who Are Contemplating Divorce*, Washington Book Trading Co., 1984.

WASHINGTON: Giboney, Daniel: *So You Want A Divorce: How To Do It Yourself in the State of Washington,* Giboney, 1986.

WASHINGTON: Patersen, M.: *Divorce Guide for Washington: Step-by-Step Guide for Obtaining Your Own Divorce*, International Self-Counsel Press, Seattle, 1989.

WASHINGTON: Evergreen Legal Services: *Getting Your Own Divorce in Washington*, Evergreen Legal Services, 1988.

WASHINGTON: Washington Legal Blanks: *Do Your Own Divorce: A Complete Marriage Dissolution Kit*, Washington Legal Blanks, Issaquah, WA, 1984.

INDEX

additional child support clause 116
adultery 10, 49
Alabama 199
Alaska 201
alimony 11, 71-80
alimony modification 78, 195
alimony payable in lump-sum payment clause 79
alimony payable in monthly payments clause 78
alimony questionnaire 72
alternating custody 88
American Arbitration Association 19
appearance, consent, and waiver 152, 172, 179
Arizona 203
Arkansas 205
attachment 193

bank accounts 34, 49, 190
bankruptcy 193
basic monthly child support clause 114
bills 31, 45, 48, 190
bonds 35
business assets 37

California 207
caption 143, 197
cars 36, 56, 190
certificate of divorce 163, 190
certificates of deposit 35
change in circumstances 195
child abuse 15, 195
child custody 11, 81-102
child custody and visitation clauses 97, 99, 100
child custody and visitation worksheet 95
child custody arrangements 87
child custody jurisdiction 94

child custody jurisdiction form 155
child custody questionnaire 82
child support 12, 103-118
child support chart 112
child support guidelines 107
child support worksheet 110
child's bill of rights 93
children identification clause 28
citation 144
Colorado 209
community property 44-46, 120
complaint 147
Connecticut 211
contempt 193
contested divorce 13
continuance 183
court appearance rules 180
court clerk 145
court hearing 179
court testimony guide 182
criminal prosecution 193

debts 45, 48
deeds 53
defendant 147
Delaware 213
District of Columbia 215
divided custody 88
division of bills clause (bills listed) 63
division of property clause (by sale) 63
divorce by agreement 14
divorce papers 141
document checklist 24
domestic violence 195
domicile 25

economic misconduct 49
educational degrees 56
Employee Stock Option Plans (ESOP's) 54
enforcement of alimony 194
enforcement of child support 107, 192
enforcement of custody and visitation 194
equitable distribution states 46
equitable division 57

family home 32, 51, 63
Family Services of America 19
Family Support Act of 1988 104
federal pensions and benefits 55
filing documents 164
final decree 159
final divorce checklist 190
final judgement 159
financial statement 64
Florida 217

garnishment of wages 193
general agreement clause 30
Georgia 219
gifts 44, 47
grounds for divorce 26
guardian ad litem 90

Hawaii 221
"head of household" tax return 123
hold harmless 63
HR-10 Retirement Plans (KEOGH's) 54

Idaho 223
Illinois 225
income assignment 193
income tax 36
income tax exemption 122
incompatibility 27
indemnification 63
Indiana 227
Individual Retirement Accounts (IRA's) 38, 54
inheritance 44, 47
insurance clause 80
Iowa 229
irreconcilable differences 27
irretrievable breakdown of the marriage 27
IRS 401(K) Retirement Plans 54

joint bank accounts 49, 190
joint credit accounts 190
joint custody 88
joint loans 190
joint tax return 123
joint tenancy 53
judgement of divorce (sample) 177

jurisdiction 26
Kansas 231
Kentucky 233
KEOGH's 54

legal custody 88
legal separation 21
liens 193
life and health insurance clauses 115
life insurance clause 80
living separate and apart 27
Louisiana 235

Maine 237
maintenance 11, 71-80
mandatory clause 124
marital fault 9, 49
marital property 10, 47
marital settlement agreement clauses
    additional child support 116
    alimony payable in lump-sum payment 79
    alimony payable in monthly payments 78
    child custody and visitation clauses 97, 99, 100
    children identification 28
    division of bills (bills listed) 63
    division of property (by sale) 63
    general agreement 30
    insurance clause 80
    life and health insurance clauses 115
    life insurance clause 80
    mandatory clause 124
    name change clause 123
    no alimony to either spouse 77
    preliminary explanation 29
    property division clauses 61, 62
    signature and notary clause 125
    taxation clause 122
marriage license 25
Maryland 239
Massachusetts 241
master 179
mediation 18
Michigan 243
military pensions and disability benefits 55
military service 15
Minnesota 245
Mississippi 49, 247
Missouri 249
modification of child support 107, 195
modification of custody and visitation 90, 195
money market accounts 35
Montana 251
mortgages 32, 53

INDEX

name change clause 123
Nebraska 253
necessary documents 144
Nevada 255
New Hampshire 257
New Jersey 259
New Mexico 261
New York 263
no alimony to either spouse clause 77
no-fault divorce 10
no-fault grounds 27
non-marital property 47
North Carolina 265
North Dakota 267
notary public 128

Ohio 269
Oklahoma 271
Oregon 273
Organization for the Enforcement of Child Support 194

Parental Kidnapping Prevention Act 194
payroll deduction 193
Pennsylvania 276
pension plans 53
personal property 34
petition 147, 168
petitioner 147
physical custody 87
plaintiff 147
post-divorce legal problems 192
pregnancy 28
preliminary explanation clause 29
preliminary questionnaire 23
primary care-giver 89
profit-sharing plans 55
property division 31-69
property division clause (list included) 62
property division clause (property not listed) 61
property division worksheet 56
property document checklist 42
property questionnaire 32

real estate 32
release 190
residency 25
respondent 147
restraining orders 195
retirement plans 53
Rhode Island 280

sample divorce papers 167-178
Self-Employed Person's Individual Retirement Account (SEP-IRA's) 54
separate property 40, 44

separate tax return 123
separation clause 30
shared custody 88
signature and notary clause 125
signing documents 164
social security benefits 55
sole custody 87, 97
South Carolina 282
South Dakota 282
split custody 88
spousal support 71-80
spouse abuse 15, 195
stock-option plans 55
stocks 35
summons 144

tax consequences 119
    alimony 121
    child support and custody 122
    property transfers 120
tax refund intercept 193
tax sheltered annuities (TSA's) 54
taxation clause 122
tenancy by the entireities 53
"tender years" doctrine 86
Tennessee 284
terminology 19
testimony worksheet 183
Texas 287
title and introductory clause 28

uncontested divorce 13
Uniform Child Custody Jurisdiction Act 94, 155, 174, 194
Uniform Reciprocal Enforcement of Support Act 107, 192
Utah 289

vehicles 56
venue 26
Vermont 291
Virginia 293
visitation 81, 89

wage deduction 193
wage withholding orders 193
Washington 295
Washington D.C. 215
West Virginia 297
wills 191
Wisconsin 299
Wyoming 301